Environment and the Law
A Dictionary

CONTEMPORARY
LEGAL 🏛 ISSUES

Environment
and the Law
A Dictionary

Vicki R. Patton-Hulce

ABC-CLIO

Santa Barbara, California
Denver, Colorado
Oxford, England

Library of Congress Cataloging-in-Publication Data

Patton-Hulce, Vicki R.
     Environment and the law : a dictionary / Vicki R. Patton-Hulce.
        p.   cm.
     Includes bibliographical references and index.
        1.   Environmental law—United States—Dictionaries.
     2.   Environmental protection—Dictionaries.   3.   Pollutants—
     Dictionaries.   I.   Title.
     KF3775.A68P38   1995   344.73'046'03—dc20   [347.3044603]   95-46013

ISBN 0-87436-749-2 (alk. paper)

01 00 99 98 97 96 95   10 9 8 7 6 5 4 3 2 1 (cloth)

ABC-CLIO, Inc.
130 Cremona Drive, P.O. Box 1911
Santa Barbara, California 93116-1911

This book is printed on acid-free paper ∞.
Manufactured in the United States of America

Contents

Preface

Environmental awareness exploded onto the scene in the late 1960s. Before then, average citizens in the United States did not worry much about air, water, soil, and groundwater pollution. States either regulated or did not regulate, balancing the demands of the voters with competition for industrial development. The federal government stayed discretely in the background.

That is not to say that natural resource stewardship was ignored until the environmental explosion. A succession of vocal and insistent conservationists has carried the banner for protecting national forests and parks, as well as wildlife, for at least a century. But the concerns of Teddy Roosevelt's day focused on aesthetics and love for nature; later generations dealt with survival and quality of life issues.

The focus shifted because of dramatic events that demonstrated the fragility of ecological balance. When rivers burned, smokestacks coughed enough soot to impact breathing, pesticides damaged the food chain, factories spewed chemicals into communities, and buried hazardous wastes oozed into playgrounds, drinking water, and basements, voters—and Congress—registered their alarm. In the 1970s, environmental statutes poured out of Congress and state legislatures. The government created new organizations to implement the laws, and in the quarter century that followed, environmental law became a distinct field of law with its own language and quirks.

Environmental law is not only for lawyers. It influences how we live: what we drive and what fuel we use, what we eat and how our food is grown, where we put our garbage, how clean our water and air are, and the cost of many products. Since we are impacted by environmental laws and regulations, it is important to understand them and how they come into being. Only then can we hope to direct future emphasis. This reference book is a source of that information.

The book opens with an overview that explains basic environmental principles, how pollution is regulated, and who the players are. No prior experience or knowledge is assumed, so anyone with an interest can immediately benefit from the book. That approach carries into the individual entries as well, where an encyclopedia of the terms that are fundamental in environmental law is presented.

The book is written for high school, college, and postgraduate students as well as researchers and people interested in environmental studies. Entries are comprehensive to reduce the number of cross-references needed to understand the topic, but they also refer to additional entries that may aid the reader, and terms that have their own entries in the book are in boldfaced type the first time they appear in another entry. Cases are generally woven into the text. A table of cases is provided so that the reader can locate cases mentioned in the book. This approach emphasizes the true value of cases, for they are usually only slivers of the total picture surrounding the law. Tables of statutes and regulations are also included, along with a bibliography and a general subject index.

This reference book will not make an expert out of the reader. But it will give the reader a solid, commonsense explanation of the fundamental principles of environmental law.

Environment and the Law

All organisms generate waste. That is the nature of life. But the waste disposal and environmental pollution problems we now face are not natural, in the biological sense of the word. They have grown monumentally due to two human factors—the unprecedented increase in the human population and mega-scale worldwide industrial activity. These two factors, in turn, have led to many other problems—ozone depletion, acid rain, polluted air and water, and extinction of many wildlife species. Though the threats to wildlife are among the most serious we face, I will touch only briefly on conservation laws here. Instead, I will focus on pollution as it impacts the air, water, and earth.

It is easy to blame our pollution problems on someone else—our neighbor down the street or some nameless industry. But we cannot afford to forget, as we address these challenges in the decades to come, that many of our favorite conveniences, such as the automobile, and many of the technological advances we value most—in medicine, agriculture, industry—have come at a price: pollution. In the past, when we have not known how to address waste disposal issues, we simply deferred them to the future. We can no longer afford that solution. Our challenge now and in the decades to come is finding ways to live responsibly—to keep our environment (and thus, ourselves) healthy and still maintain our way of life. This issue is one of the central concerns behind environmental law.

Environmental law encompasses statutes and regulations that deal with pollution control, prevention of pollution, cleanup of hazardous waste sites, management of waste, restoration of resources, and compensation for resources destroyed. In addition, old, well-established tort theories, such as negligence or trespass, may be used to address environmental damage, even though they are not found in statutes and regulations. Most of the applicable statutes were passed in the 1970s and early 1980s. They aimed

1

largely for control of pollutants and cleanup of existing messes. Recently enacted environmental laws, however, have moved to another arena: minimizing the amount of waste generated. In other words, we have shifted our focus from "What do we do with this waste?" to "How can we avoid or minimize the creation of waste?"

We have learned some costly lessons about pollution in the last fifty years, and we are still learning. A comprehensive list of environmental issues that will become or remain concerns in the next decade would be impossible to compile, but some of the larger issues can be predicted. Our struggle for basic needs—uncontaminated air, water, and land—will continue. More controversial issues—depletion of the ozone layer, reducing the amount of waste generated, keeping the global warming trend in check, and cooperating with other nations to handle difficult matters—will prove even more challenging.

Through environmental law, we have attempted to patch the dike and prevent our past practices from flooding through and threatening our present. The person with responsibility for putting the concepts of environmental law into practice is the environmental attorney.

Modern environmental statutes generally address one type of pollution control—water, air, or solid waste—at a time. As a result, a large body of law has grown up around each of the media (as the Environmental Protection Agency refers to these categories), making it nearly impossible for one attorney to be an expert in all subfields. Thus, attorneys who practice environmental law often specialize in a part of the field.

Beneath the general media in the specialization hierarchy, another level of subspecialists exists. For example, large law firms may have an attorney who only does water permitting, one who handles all the asbestos cases the firm receives, or one who specializes in corrective action for permitted waste facilities. Lawyers who specialize in older theories of law, such as negligence or trespass, may be environmental attorneys as well, but they are just as likely to be personal injury attorneys.

Keeping up with the changes in federal environmental law challenges all environmental lawyers. The statutes go through regular revisions, the regulations respond to those changes, and the courts interpret what they mean in a particular situation. To add to the difficulty, the federal government is not the only entity making environmental law. State and even local government, too, often enact environmental laws or administer federal law through delegation.

Changes in environmental statutes occur more frequently than in other areas because provisions in the laws themselves require periodic reauthorization of the statute. During the reauthorization process, the statute is dissected and pasted together until both legislative houses can pass it.

Each time a major environmental statute has undergone revision, it emerges from the process more complex, lengthier, and more remote to the general population.

Ideas for making environmental law more manageable are always on the table. A more integrated legislative approach to environmental regulation would be particularly helpful to practitioners. However, the system of dividing environmental law into pieces, like air and water, shows no sign of changing. Indeed, if all of the statutes were melded in some way, the length of the statute would be appalling.

THE GREENING OF INDUSTRY

Although environmental compliance can be expensive, sloppy environmental practices can be even more costly: they can bankrupt a company. Millions of dollars pour into Superfund sites (hazardous waste disposal sites so dangerous they have been placed on the National Priority List for cleanup), and that money comes, for the most part, from businesses that sent waste to a site for disposal. Because of the disastrous effect the costs of a Superfund cleanup or other environmental costs can have on businesses, the Securities and Exchange Commission now requires all companies that sell securities publicly to disclose potential expenditures involving the environment in all public filings to apprise investors of possible impacts on the company's earnings.

Handling waste and dealing with the environment responsibly are good public interest gestures. Companies that are active partners in the effort to take care of the environment gain a positive public image, which can increase revenues and interest investors. Businesses also benefit financially by reducing their wastes, especially if hazardous wastes are generated. Disposal of hazardous waste is costly, and unless it is destroyed or neutralized in some fashion, it remains a potential liability. If the hazardous waste site becomes a Superfund site in twenty or thirty years, the parties who sent the waste there will have to clean it up, even if the facility was properly permitted at the time.

As people become aware of the importance of regulating what goes into the environment, they also become more amenable to paying for a cleaner place to live. Changes in advertising to include environmental claims indicate the degree of importance businesses believe the public places on the environment. Packaging now often includes recycling messages, statements about environmental impacts of the product, and concentrated products have reduced the sizes of containers. Many dispensers can be used more than once, lessening the volume of waste. Clearly, the consumers have demanded the modifications and are ready to purchase products that are less taxing for the environment. One of the problems the consumer must face is determining whether the assertions are accurate or not. More regulation should be anticipated concerning the substantiation of environmental declarations.

ATMOSPHERIC CONTAMINATION

Although ozone depletion, global warming, and acid deposition are separate topics, the causes leading to all these problems are the same: air emissions. The propellants and refrigerants used in products, fossil fuel burning, and population growth have combined to disturb the balance of our ecosystem.

Ozone Depletion

At ground level, ozone is harmful, impacting breathing and lung efficiency. It is one of the major components of smog and is regulated indirectly by controlling volatile organic compounds, emissions commonly associated with fossil fuel combustion. High above the earth in the stratosphere, though, a layer of ozone protects life on earth by serving as a screen to filter out some of the sun's more harmful ultraviolet rays. So in 1985, scientists were alarmed to discover a hole developing in that layer above Antarctica that is constantly growing bigger.

The main culprit in ozone depletion is a group of chemicals called chlorofluorocarbons (CFCs). Like so many chemicals that have turned into Frankenstein's monsters, CFCs were originally hailed as a scientific breakthrough. Very stable compounds, they are used as propellants, refrigerants, fire-fighting agents, air conditioning fluids. They are not immediately harmful to humans, except in extreme overexposure.

The complication: CFCs break apart in the stratosphere when they come in contact with ultraviolet radiation. Then they form chlorine ions, which react with and destroy the ozone molecules.

Global Warming

Global warming is a controversial theory. Depending on whom you ask, global warming is definitely established, only contested by a few mavericks, totally unproven, or a hoax. There is no reliable way to verify the effects of the gases in our upper atmosphere, short of measuring them over a long period. So, given the controversial nature of the evidence, a nonbinding agreement among a few nations to reduce the amount of carbon dioxide they emit is the most stringent anti–global warming measure enacted so far.

The issue keeps surfacing, though. Because of the dire implications of a global temperature increase, it is, and will likely remain, one of the most important environmental issues in the next decade and longer, while scientists gather more information.

Though many question the validity of the global warming theory, no one doubts the existence of the greenhouse effect. It is caused by carbon dioxide combined with water vapor, which traps some of the heat from the sun in the upper atmosphere so that it doesn't all return to its source. It is an essential part of earth's systems, serving to keep the world warm and habitable—under the right conditions, that is. The problem associated with the greenhouse effect, as perceived by many scientists, is both in the increase of carbon dioxide in the atmosphere and the addition of other gases. The carbon dioxide levels in the upper atmosphere have increased by 25 percent since the beginning of the Industrial Revolution. As more and more heat is trapped, the temperatures on earth may begin to rise. Up until the last decade or so, carbon dioxide was almost the sole constituent of the greenhouse gases.

The culprits that could bring about projected intensification of the greenhouse effect are CFCs, methane, nitrous oxide, carbon dioxide, and other trace gases that have increased in the upper atmosphere. The carbon dioxide and nitrous oxide comes from the same primary activities: fossil fuel burning, deforestation, and soil cultivation. Methane is generated by landfills, cattle, rice paddies, and some other agricultural activities. Molecule for molecule, methane and nitrous oxide are the biggest part of the problem.

The controversial aspect of global warming turns on the difficulty of isolating the relative effects of various natural phenomena on weather patterns. Many events influence the atmosphere. A volcano discharges enough debris to lower temperatures over periods lasting up to a year or more. Erosion and dust storms have a similar effect. Population growth and the need for food and other basic comforts influence human activity, which increases greenhouse gases or conditions that cause them. With all of these factors to account for, it is difficult to establish the effect of a single factor. But one fact remains: we have altered the mixture of gases in the upper atmosphere, setting the stage for changing normal weather cycles.

Acid Deposition

Acid deposition, usually referred to as acid rain, is another newly created problem when viewed from the perspective of the earth's history. It results from the burning of fossil fuels, primarily coal. Industrial activity, power generation, and transportation—primarily automobiles—have caused most of these emissions. The combustion process releases sulfur dioxide and nitrous oxides, which combine with water vapor to form acidic clouds. Acid clouds move along air currents, then release their moisture in the form of acid rain, snow, or other precipitation.

Acid deposition damages forests and other vegetation, lakes and streams, aquatic life, and even etches buildings. Canada has been disturbed by the acid deposition it has received as the immediate neighbor of the heavily industrialized northeastern United States. Because Europe, too, is heavily industrialized, it has also grappled with the difficulties caused by its industries.

INTERNATIONAL COOPERATION

Environmental issues are global. Air pollution from the United States affects the rain and snow in Canada; air and water pollution in Mexico impacts the quality of life in the United States; chemicals that harm the ozone layer endanger the fragile protection for all countries, regardless of where they originate. Thus, treaties between nations are often the starting point for addressing international issues. The Montreal Protocol, for example, initiated a critical effort to protect the ozone layer. In the United States, the provisions of the Montreal Protocol are being implemented through the Clean Air Act Amendments. Most of the signatories to the treaty have stepped up their efforts to phase out CFCs.

Exporting hazardous waste is prohibited by U.S. law, and ocean dumping is strictly limited. The United States was one of the first countries to realize the dangers posed by pollution and enact laws to control it. Now environmental law is maturing in the United States, but other countries are catching up or even passing more stringent controls on pollution. Environmental attorneys in the United States are focusing their attention on the evolving and innovative environmental laws of the European Community.

Business competition, too, presents an international environmental problem. When it is cheaper to establish and carry on industry in countries with little environmental awareness, businesses will move toward those locations. Technologically adanced countries have learned the hard way about the impact of pollution, but developing countries may not want to address environmental needs immediately when other needs are so pressing, or they may not be able to. It is not surprising, then, that at the 1992 United Nations Conference on Environment and Development (UNCED), nicknamed the Earth Summit, a sharp division between developed and developing countries was apparent. But cooperation is essential. International involvement in environmental protection is a matter of survival for all nations.

WASTE MINIMIZATION

Although reducing and controlling the discharge of pollution has been the method of regulation adopted in the major environmental laws, another option is more attractive: waste minimization.

After waste products are treated at the end of the manufacturing process, they must be disposed of. Environmental statutes and regulations specify the ways waste may be disposed. But by streamlining processes, businesses may be able to reduce the amount of resulting waste. This reduction benefits not only the environment, but also the business, which has less waste to manage. If the waste is hazardous, the price of disposal will be greatly reduced, because all costs for hazardous waste handling, transportation and disposal are high, and future liability for cleanup will remain as long as the generator of the waste exists.

Waste can be minimized in several ways: reducing the amount of raw products introduced in the system, selecting more efficient technology, using fewer toxic or hazardous components in the system, increasing the amount of recycled goods used in manufactured products, recycling waste, and treating spent materials so they can be reused within the system in which they were created. The end result, a reduction in the amount of waste produced, is good for all of us.

Recycling is an effective way to reduce waste. In many jurisdictions, it is not optional. Particularly in states and cities where land is hard to find, new landfills simply cannot be built after the old landfills close. When a state runs out of room for waste, it turns to other states for assistance, but the citizens in the receiving states usually do not appreciate being a dumping ground.

Thus disposal of waste has become a difficult political and social issue. No one wants a landfill in his or her community. In fact, the citizens' rallying cry "Not in my backyard!" has become so common it has earned an acronym: NIMBY. Proposed incineration sites have been strongly opposed by communities in the past few years, and industrial and hazardous waste sites are extremely unpopular.

Even if the discussion is limited to nontoxic domestic waste, we clearly have no room to continue disposing at the rate we have in the past. One answer is reducing waste at the source. For the average consumer, this means selecting products with less packaging, rejecting products if the products themselves or their packaging are not earth-friendly, recycling, and buying recycled goods.

Recycling has become a popular solution. But for recycling to work, a complete loop must be created. The goods have to be made of recyclable products, people must deliver the recyclable component, a recycler must process the product, then it must be incorporated into new goods. Finally, the consumer must select recycled goods in sufficient amounts to establish and sustain a market.

The direct advantages of recycling include keeping the product from becoming a waste and reducing the volume of virgin resources needed. However, the indirect effect is also important. If fewer new products have to be manufactured from raw materials, production wastes should shrink.

To encourage reduction in packaging, Germany requires producers of products to accept packaging it creates. The consumer simply brings the packaging back to the seller. This procedure encourages manufacturers to reduce volume of waste and returns the packaging to those most able to reuse it.

ADDRESSING ENVIRONMENTAL POLLUTION WITH OLD THEORIES

Even though no statute expressly gives a person a specific right, it does not follow that the right does not exist. English law established the idea that each person had a bundle of rights associated with living. These rights are called *protected interests,* because courts have recognized them and awarded damages to people whose interests were invaded. These rights were cherished by the emigrants and became a part of the legal tradition in the colonies. Since that time, they have also changed considerably.

Torts

An injury caused by an interference with an individual's protected interest is a *tort.* The same act may also be prohibited by the government because it disturbs the public peace. If that is the case, the act is also a crime. Torts come in many shapes. Some are intentional, some are negligent, and some are simply unavoidable. The right to sue someone for a tort belongs to a particular person or class of persons—the individual or individuals whose protected interest was violated.

Tort law, which developed through cases rather than statutes, is important to our legal system. This type of law—common law—reflects society's values at the time of the decision. It changes very slowly, in contrast to statutory laws, which can be abruptly altered by new statutes. The edifice of common law is built brick by brick as judges determine what issues will be pivotal in deciding liability. Once a principle is established in a case, it remains in the background to be used as a rule for similar cases in that court or in lesser courts. One case may expand the earlier rule, another may clarify it or draw a distinction between the rule and the current case. Still, legal principles require that it be followed unless the court overrules it. This element of law lends predictability to the outcome of cases.

Other types of laws include constitutions, treaties, executive orders, and regulations. All of these categories play a role in dealing with environmental pollution.

In environmental matters, a number of torts are important, particularly trespass, conversion, nuisance, negligence, and strict liability. They are significant not only as theories for lawsuits but also because the concepts are woven into many of the statutes. Two basic principles underlie the torts to be examined: (1) an individual has the right to prevent someone else from invading his or her body's integrity; and (2) an individual has the right to peaceful and undisturbed possession of property—real or personal—that he or she owns or has a right to possess.

Trespass has long been recognized as a wrong. A trespass to realty occurs if a person enters property belonging to another and that person does not have permission to be there. Property is either real or personal. Real property is associated with land, including the land itself, attachments to the land, and fixtures. Personalty, or personal property, is any item that can be possessed physically and is not real property.

Trespass to personal property occurs when someone touches or otherwises uses personal property without the permission of the owner; a trespass to a person involves a nonprivileged touching of that person. *Conversion* is more intrusive; it occurs when a person who is not the owner or rightful user of property takes possession of the property to the exclusion of the rightful owner. *Nuisance* is an interference with the use and peaceful enjoyment of property.

The tort of *negligence* underlies the majority of personal injury lawsuits. As its name implies, intent is not a factor, but a number of elements must be proven for the courts to find liability. First, a duty of some sort must be owed to the injured party (plaintiff) by the one who caused the injury (defendant); second, the duty must be breached through an act or omission by the defendant; third, an injury must in fact occur, and the breach of the duty must be the proximate cause of the injury.

Proximate cause is a method of terminating liability. Only if the breach of duty is the proximate cause of the injury, and all the other elements are present, can the defendant be responsible. A direct connection must exist between what a person did and the injury that occurred. The plaintiff must be within the class of people who would be protected by performance of the duty, and the injury has to be foreseeable by a reasonable person who contemplated the consequences of breaching the duty. The exact person injured and extent of injury, however, need not be foreseeable.

The proximate cause concept is not simply causation. It is confusing even to law students who spend weeks or even months trying to grasp the idea. Basically, the body of law behind the concept limits recovery for injuries to the person who did the original act. Sometimes the focus is on who the duty was owed to. However, the end result is to draw a line to determine what injuries a particular defendant should be responsible for and who must be compensated.

In a simple case of negligence, such as the following, the connection is easy to see. Driver A drives recklessly, runs a stoplight, and hits Driver B. Driver B suffers physical injuries and property damage to the car. Passenger C is also injured. The injuries to Driver B and Passenger C and the property damage to Driver B's car are the result of Driver A's negligence. Driver A owed a duty to the public at large—the government—and to other drivers to obey the law and drive carefully. The foreseeable victims of a breach of that duty include other drivers and their passengers. Driver B's breach of the duty is also the proximate cause of the injuries. Their respective lawyers would, of course, examine the degree of injuries to determine whether all or some of the injuries complained of did stem from the wreck.

Moving on to a situation that is less clear, but a classic case in tort law, here is a fact situation involving an unforeseeable plaintiff. The case is *Palsgraf v. Long Island Rail Co.* (1928). A passenger was running to catch a train. When he got to the door, one of the defendant's employees tried to help him board it. He dislodged a package that contained fireworks, which then fell on the rails and exploded. Many feet away, some scales were overturned by the blast; they landed on the plaintiff and injured her.

The *Palsgraf* case stands for the principle that a defendant is not responsible for the unforeseeable plaintiff. The duty of the railroad was to the public and its passengers. By jostling the man who was boarding, some harm could have been expected to him or nearby pedestrians, or to the package itself, but stretching that action of negligence to cover the plaintiff was too far. Therefore, no proximate cause existed.

Legal experts grapple with the proximate cause concept, and it is impossible to explain all its nuances in the context of this book. One of the leading scholars of tort law, Professor William J. Prosser, sums up the purpose of proximate cause in a relatively clear manner in the *Law of Torts* [1971: 236–237]:

> As a practical matter, legal responsibility must be limited to those causes which are so closely connected with the result and of such

significance that the law is justified in imposing liability. Some bound-
ary must be set to liability for the consequences of any act, upon the
basis of some social idea of policy or justice.

As English society became industrialized, new products were introduced
and activities surrounding their creation generated problems of their own.
Negligence, still a useful theory of liability, was joined by *strict (or absolute) liability*. As the term suggests, strict liability does not depend on fault.
Some activities are inherently dangerous, regardless of the amount of care
the participant exercises. The classic example of such an activity is dynamiting. Likewise, some products, such as automobiles or electric saws,
are capable of great injury if they are improperly designed or manufactured. Although society values the activities or the products, the principle
behind strict liability is that the person who introduces the danger should
bear the cost if an innocent party is harmed as a result.

Applying Traditional Tort Theories to Environmental Law

Before statutes gave individuals explicit rights involving environmental
pollution, the only means of addressing pollution was through a tort-based
lawsuit. The torts mentioned above are still available to an injured party.
For example, migration of contamination into water from a source that is
not on the owner's property may be a conversion, trespass, or nuisance,
depending on the specific facts. If the plaintiff sustained a personal injury
as a result of the discharge, a trespass occurred.

Negligence is well suited for both cases involving personal injury and
injury to property caused by environmental pollution. In addition, if toxic
or hazardous pollutants are involved in causing personal injury, strict liability is a good alternative to negligence.

A new class of new torts has arisen—*toxic torts*. The class includes the
theories discussed above: trespass, nuisance, conversion, negligence and
strict liability. But toxic torts also require the plaintiff to show that some
type of toxic agent, such as a chemical pollutant or a drug, was involved.
Toxic tort suits frequently allege a violation of a statute or regulation, and
proof of the violation goes a long way toward proving the case. These tort
theories can be applied to personal injury as well as real property damage.

EVOLUTION OF AN ENVIRONMENTAL SYSTEM

Prior to the late 1960s and early 1970s, statutes dealing with environmental pollution were both rare and toothless. The primary environmental
law in the United States, the Refuse Act, dated back to 1899. It made the

Corps of Engineers the protectors of the waterways and prohibited discharges without a permit. But proof of violation under the Refuse Act was difficult. No method had been established to measure pollutants, and the states had been ineffective in setting standards for water quality. Pesticides were subject to the Insecticide Act of 1910, which regulated nothing but labeling. In 1947, the Federal Insecticide, Fungicide, and Rodenticide Act (FIFRA) was passed; it required registration and labeling, but it did not deal with safety.

Regulating pollution was also thwarted by the way responsibility for controlling it was sliced into pieces. The Department of Interior (DOI) received the water piece, and the Federal Water Quality Administration worked under the DOI umbrella. Pesticide studies were also concentrated in that department. The Department of Health, Education, and Welfare (HEW) took the air part along with solid waste and some of the pesticides issues. Programs were managed by a number of different agencies within HEW: the National Air Pollution Control Administration, the Bureau of Solid Waste Management, the Bureau of Water Hygiene, the Bureau of Radiological Health of the Environmental Control Administration, and the Food and Drug Administration. Pesticide registration and related activities vested in the Department of Agriculture. Radiation criteria and standards fell within the Atomic Energy Commission and the Federal Radiation Council. Another agency, the Council on Environmental Quality (CEQ), was responsible for studies relating to ecological systems.

Creation of the Environmental Protection Agency

Law that existed when Richard Nixon was president allowed him to issue an order for reorganization of departments and other agencies. So in 1970, Nixon issued an executive order for reorganization, Reorganization Plan No. 3, which created the Environmental Protection Agency and moved the environmental duties of the other agencies to the EPA. In his transmittal, he indicated that it was time to bring the functions of environmental protection into one agency. That was only the beginning of the work for the EPA, for soon Congress enacted numerous statutes that took advantage of the new system and greatly enlarged the EPA's authority.

EPA headquarters is in Washington, D.C., but it also has ten regional offices. The headquarters, which houses the administrator (appointed by the president), deputy administrator, and assistant administrators, funnels information to the regional offices, reviews regional operations for consistency, establishes policy for the agency, and makes the final decision on many issues. Each regional office has a regional administrator (RA).

All RAs are political appointees, and all have the authority to represent the EPA within their regions. Their authority is not uncontrolled, however, for many of the RA's decisions are reviewed by headquarters.

As a regulatory agency, the EPA performs all three duties of government: legislating, executing, and judging. The EPA establishes standards with its legislative function, and procedural precautions make certain the public knows about the rulemaking.

By the time the EPA was created, people had begun to feel some of the effects of pollution and react to them. Smog choked the industrial corridors; water became so polluted it burst into flames; and Rachel Carson, in *Silent Spring*, focused the nation's attention on the toxic by-products of civilization. By the middle of the 1970s, the first comprehensive laws regulating water pollution, air pollution, environmental policy, and drinking water had been passed. By the beginning of the next decade, laws were in place to govern toxic substances, hazardous waste sites, hazardous materials and substances. These laws have not been forgotten like the old Refuse Act was for so many years. Instead, most of the federal environmental statutes have been extensively revised, reflecting the changes that have occurred in the American approach to environmental pollution.

Administrative Agencies

A number of complex statutes deal with many aspects of environmental law. Even so, they do not in themselves contain all of the legal guidance for environmental compliance. Regulations written by government agencies make up the bulk of the rules.

Administrative agencies have been a part of American government since the early 1900s, when the Interstate Commerce Commission and the Federal Trade Commission were established. They burgeoned, however, in the 1930s, as the country was struggling to recover from the Great Depression. Part of Franklin D. Roosevelt's New Deal involved the creation of many agencies. They can be advisory, with no real power to force anyone to do more than listen, or they can be regulatory, with authority to make law, enforce it, and judge whether it has been violated. The EPA is a regulatory agency.

At first, statutes that delegated authority to agencies were very detailed. For example, cattle were to be destroyed if the cattle inspector found they had hoof-and-mouth disease. Under such a law, the inspector was told exactly what to do and exactly when to do it. Later the authority was amplified, allowing the cattle inspector to act if he found the cattle had a contagious disease. The inspector had to determine what cattle diseases were contagious and what type of action to take.

Today, the administrative agency may be given a broad responsibility, such as the EPA's mandate to protect human health and the environment. But Congress hasn't given sweeping control to the Environmental Protection Agency and then let it go off to decide what to do. Many current environmental statutes require the EPA to deal with specific issues. Also, given the agency's history of missing deadlines for regulations, Congress not only sets the deadlines, but includes default provisions that take effect if the EPA fails to act. These are called hammer provisions.

The administrator of an agency may be one person, as it is within the EPA, or a group of people. The name for this position varies: commissioner, secretary, board, trustee, or administrator. When a statute names an agency to handle particular issues, the power it grants goes to the administrator, who then may delegate it to others within the agency.

Unless one's activity is regulated by an administrative agency, one may not notice what it does or question its right to govern. Indeed, in our system today, agencies are so commonplace that they are taken for granted. Examples of agencies with muscle are the Internal Revenue Service, the National Labor Relations Board, the Food and Drug Administration, the Federal Communications Commission, the Security and Exchange Commission, and the Environmental Protection Agency.

Boards or bureaus, other types of administrative agencies, determine licensing requirements for many professions, issue the licenses, hear complaints, and have the power to revoke the licenses. Agencies determine a citizen's right to Social Security payments, welfare, and other forms of governmental benefits. They may be authorized to disburse money in the form of grants or loans. All regulatory agencies get their power from a statute.

One of the main reasons for the creation of an agency is the need for expertise in particular areas. Legislators, as a general rule, come into public office with a background in politics, and the experience they bring spans many fields and interests. But the average legislator would not be qualified to determine whether a drug is safe and effective, a chemical compound should be used as a pesticide, or an airplane is air-worthy.

The answer to this dilemma is delegation. Legislators and executives in government found they could accomplish more if they wrote only the general principles into a statute and then created specialized organizations or agencies to flesh out the details through regulations. The agencies would operate within defined areas of expertise, and their employees would themselves be experts in the types of issues that arise within the purview of the agency.

Although agencies are likely to be the interface between citizens and government today, they are oddities. The power they have defies our idea of separation of powers, and they are not mentioned in the Constitution, where the founders specified the roles of the branches.

Americans elect legislators and executives, not agencies, so a number of constitutional challenges arose in the early days of agency law. Perhaps the most critical question was whether Congress could delegate its legislative function. Courts determined that Congress was not prohibited from all delegations. Administrative agencies can indeed issue enforceable rules, but certain guidelines apply. First, Congress must define what types of rules the agency can create and state the parameters in the enabling legislation. Second, the regulations must fall within the scope of the statute. Today, attacks on agencies often focus on whether the agency stepped outside the bounds Congress set.

In addition to the limitations written into the enabling statutes, agencies' powers are also limited in other ways. In 1946, Congress enacted the Administrative Procedure Act (APA), a statute that fills in the gaps for federal agencies when the enabling law isn't clear about procedures. U.S. citizens have a right to due process under the Constitution, and the APA builds in safeguards to ensure that due process extends to agency action. Unbridled agency action is also limited by the Freedom of Information Act, a statute that requires federal agencies to supply citizens with information upon request, provided the information does not fall within an exception. Many states have similar laws.

Legislative Powers

Before a federal regulation can become law, it must be published in the *Federal Register,* a daily publication that prints all proposed and final regulations generated by federal administrative agencies. After it is published, the public may provide comments to the agency and in some cases, a hearing is held. The agency must consider the comments it receives. When the final regulation is published, the agency will also provide a summary of the comments and its response to them. A final regulation may be challenged by interested parties after it is promulgated. But in most situations, it must be disputed within a short period of time, and the suit can only be brought in a specified court.

Examples of regulations the EPA has established demonstrate the breadth of its power to legislate. Toxic air and water pollutants and hazardous substances have been listed, procedures have been set for obtaining permits, testing criteria have been established, cleanup criteria for hazardous waste sites have been detailed, air quality districts have been outlined, targeted industries have been given directives, and hazardous waste sites have been ranked in order of priority for cleanup.

Just as statutes are presumed valid, so are rules created by the EPA or other administrative agency. Statutes can only be contested on the basis of their constitutionality; a regulation may be disputed on both constitutional and statutory grounds. The rule must be consistent with congressional intent, authorized by the enabling statute, and cannot be arbitrary and capricious. The arbitrary and capricious standard is the one used by courts to determine whether an agency acted in good faith, basing its decision on the record. It is difficult to prove that an action was arbitrary and capricious, though. The expertise of the agency receives great deference.

Executive Power

In its executive role, the EPA maintains records, issues permits, investigates allegations of unlawful activity, responds in emergencies, and enforces the law. When a permit is granted, the permittee is subject to a number of reporting activities. Since the agency collects and reviews the reports, the permittee is in the uncomfortable position of providing the enforcer with evidence of its permit violations. Filing a false report, however, is a crime.

The administrator or regional administrator of the EPA has discretion to act or not act in most situations involving a violation of a law. This common principle is called prosecutorial discretion and is carried over from criminal law. If action is determined necessary, the administrator has many options, ranging from merely investigating the situation to bringing a criminal lawsuit against the regulated person. Because enforcement authority is such an extensive topic, it is discussed more fully later in this introduction.

Judicial Power

The EPA has the power to judge whether a law has been violated. The judicial function is exercised both formally and informally. The EPA may arrange for the regulated person to meet informally with an agency employee to respond to a letter or proposed order. At such a meeting, the person has the opportunity to explain or otherwise contest the finding of violation. The regional administrator determines later what action should be taken based on the internal record and the regulated person's evidence.

A more formal way to reach a decision is through a hearing. There are two types of hearings for enforcement proceedings: APA hearings and non-APA hearings. APA hearings are formal and must follow the guidelines in the APA. Non-APA hearings are subject to the EPA's own rules, which are called the Consolidated Rules of Practice. In either case, the person who acts as judge is an employee of the EPA, and the final decision is made by the administrator. The informal hearing judge is a hearing officer, generally appointed by the regional administrator out of the Office of Regional Counsel. After the hearing, recommendations are made to the RA, who decides the outcome. In an APA hearing, an administrative law judge (ALJ) decides the case. ALJs are not quartered in the regional offices. They receive cases according to docket assignment, listen to the evidence and review the record, then reach a decision. The administrator may, however, reject the ALJ's judgment.

In 1992, the EPA established an Environmental Appeals Board. The Board comprises three members, and at least two of them must meet and agree on a decision or the administrator must break the tie. One of the main reasons the board was created was the increase in administrative actions. Due to amendments of major statutes, the EPA now has greater authority to impose penalties through administrative actions than it had in its infancy. Not only are penalty actions growing as a result, but the regulated person may face many other types of regulatory decisions that could greatly impact it, such as permit decisions or cancellation of registration of a pesticide. Those appeals may also be taken to the Environmental Appeals Board.

Standing in the wings, watching over administrative agency decisions, is the branch of government one would expect: the federal judiciary. After a person has gone through the administrative process, an appeal of the final agency decision may be taken to a district court. The court will still use the arbitrary and capricious standard for judgment calls, but constitutional challenges or a challenge based on the statutory guidance may be successful.

SHARING RESPONSIBILITY FOR POLLUTION CONTROL

The EPA is the best known of the agencies charged with protecting the environment, but it is by no means the only one. Even after the EPA assumed centralized responsibility for environmental laws, other federal agencies have some input into what the EPA does, and a few have exclusive authority in identified areas. Thus, the Coast Guard deals with coastal pollution and ocean dumping; the Corps of Engineers is tasked with initially issuing permits for dredge and fill operations in wetlands; the Fish and Wildlife Service designates endangered and threatened species; the Occupational Safety and Health Administration governs the work environment; and the Department of Transportation deals with hazardous materials during transportation. These are only a few federal agencies that have environmental responsibilities.

With the increasing use of computers, many agencies, including the EPA, can and do make their databases available to other agencies. The data sharing arrangement is usually formalized under some type of agreement called a memorandum of agreement (MOA) or memorandum of understanding (MOU). Such agreements are difficult to finalize, but a formal agreement is not the only way to get the procedure under way. Cross-training for inspectors is also common, particularly in the OSHA- and EPA-dominated spheres. An OSHA inspector may spot an environmental violation and notify the EPA, and the EPA inspector reciprocates.

Defining the scope of an agency's power involves the concept of jurisdiction, which simply means the power to govern. No governmental body can create its own jurisdiction; it must come either from a statute or from the Constitution. Agencies have no authority beyond that given to them in statutes. One agency may share responsibilities with another or have exclusive responsibility. An agency may have the right to a voice in another agency's decision, or it may be able to determine the outcome.

The closer the government is to the polluted area, the greater its interest in the welfare of the people affected and the protection of the natural resources. So even though state and local governments have no jurisdiction beyond the limits of their physical territories, they, too have an interest in the environment. Often they have a stronger interest than the federal government.

State law is very important in dealing with environmental pollution. The reason is simple: a state cannot negate federal law by passing less demanding environmental laws, but it can and often does pass tougher laws. It may also choose to regulate activities that are not regulated by the federal government. The only restrictions on states' power in this regard are the U.S. Constitution, federal laws, and the state's own statutes and constitution. When Ronald Reagan was president, he pushed for localized control over environmental pollution. In response, legislators began to incorporate into the statutes provisions for the transfer of some federal environmental programs to states.

But federal law is the supreme law of the land; its position of primacy is determined by the Constitution. Congress has exclusive jurisdiction over national issues, such as interstate commerce. Furthermore, if it is in the interest of the United States, Congress may pass a law that essentially takes away the states' right to regulate. Such a move is called preemption.

When it comes to the environment, many issues must be determined at the federal level for several reasons. First, even though land lies completely within the borders of a state, surface water, groundwater, and air do not, and the EPA has been given broad authority to regulate issues that impact the United States as a whole. Also, competition among states for business

and industry often presents problems that make federal control preferable to state control. If one state can attract businesses because its environmental requirements are less burdensome than those in another state, the
environment may suffer. Hazardous wastes present related problems. Siting a hazardous waste facility in a particular state or bringing in hazardous waste from another state may generate terrific political pressure. Yet
hazardous waste is generated, and it must go somewhere until we know
how to destroy it or render it harmless. For that reason, state laws prohib-
iting importing hazardous waste have been declared unconstitutional as
a burden on interstate commerce.

Congress, therefore, established the groundrules of jurisdiction in statutes and gave the EPA many specific assignments with the general goal of
protecting the environment. When it acts, the EPA sets the bottom limit
for conduct relating to the environment within the United States and the
Territories. States cannot circumvent the impact of the regulation or statute by enacting laws that do not have the same bite, because federal law
applies within the state.

Often, though, states prefer to handle their own enforcement of environmental violations. Two methods make it possible for the state to be the
primary regulator of pollution. The first is for the state to develop laws
that are more stringent than the federal ones. If the laws do not invade an
area reserved to the federal government and are not unconstitutional under the state's constitution, they are valid and can be enforced by the state.
The second method, delegation, is made possible by federal provision and
is commonly used today. To get the EPA to delegate its authority to the
state, the state must design a regulatory program, write regulations that
are consistent with the federal ones, and then ask the EPA to give it authority to assume the program. The Clean Air Act was the first law to
incorporate a delegation scheme, but other statutes now have comparable
provisions.

When a program is delegated, the state becomes the primary or lead
environmental agency. It issues permits, receives the reports and notices
required by the law, holds hearings and enforces. The EPA takes a backseat
in the areas that are delegated but stays involved by monitoring the state's
actions and periodically reexamining the state program. If it chooses, it
can step in and enforce. If the state regulations are identical to the federal
ones, as is often the case, it doesn't matter which regulations are the basis
for the enforcement action. But if the state standards are more difficult to
meet and the program has been delegated, the EPA can enforce the state
regulations if it chooses to do so.

The major problem for the regulated community occurs when states
opt for stricter standards in federally covered programs. If the business or

regulated person has an interstate business, different requirements may apply in different states, and keeping up with the variations is an intensive endeavor.

CONSTITUTIONAL GUARANTEES AND ADMINISTRATIVE AGENCY LAW

Common law rights that existed before the Constitution was ratified were incorporated into it. Since administrative agencies were not a part of the legal system at that time, no common law principles concerning them were developed. For that reason, the applicability of some constitutional rights to administrative agency action is murky.

If agencies are not mentioned but are entitled to bring lawsuits or even determine the rights of the parties, how does the right to a trial by jury apply? If a hearing is held instead of a trial, is the due process guaranteed by the Constitution being ignored? Can an agency deprive citizens of the use of their own property without compensation? Can an agency deny to one citizen a right that it grants to another without giving the citizen a chance to speak? Is it constitutional for an agency to require that evidence be submitted without a subpoena? What if the evidence is incriminating?

Some of these questions have been answered by the courts, and some have been resolved through statutes. Both the legislature and judiciary, conscious of the sensitivities of Americans, have shaped administrative law so that rights are not taken away by the whim of an agency.

Due Process

Due process is a complicated legal idea, but the Bill of Rights, in the Fifth Amendment, prohibits taking life, liberty, or property without "due process of law." How it applies to agency actions has presented some particularly interesting questions for the Environmental Protection Agency.

In the executive mode, the EPA may deny a permit, either shutting down a business or mandating control measures for the activity. In its judicial role, the EPA may order the payment of a penalty, cleanup of contaminated property, or upgrades to equipment. Acting as a legislator, the EPA can change the rules or add new rules that will require new equipment, processes, or perhaps prohibit a business from operating as it has in the past. In all of these cases, the expectation of due process seems clear. To act constitutionally, the agency must allow the regulated party the opportunity to be heard.

Even though U.S. citizens, familiar with the concepts of lawsuits and public meetings, may expect the Fifth Amendment to protect their rights to a public hearing when an agency acts, courts have disagreed, even when a property right is at issue. The question, then, is what type of process is necessary before the agency action can go forward constitutionally?

Courts have allowed administrative agencies to fashion their own procedures for balancing the citizen's rights with the agency's need to fulfill its function. Often, that means dealing with a large number of regulated persons and handling most of the regulatory functions with limited resources. The legislature may define in the statutes the hearing process the agencies are charged to implement. This is often the case in environmental law. But to get a hearing, one must usually request it; and the hearing may be extremely informal, such as the submission of information or a casual meeting with a few representatives of the agency. If the enabling law does not specify the type of hearing to be held, the Administrative Procedure Act (APA) applies, and the agency must follow APA rules. Also, if the EPA has reached a decision impacting the rights of a citizen and that person has exhausted all the means of dealing with the complaint within the agency, courts usually have jurisdiction to hear appeals.

When an agency acts in a legislative capacity, the protection of due process is different. Again, the APA fills the void with its specifications for rulemaking procedures, notification requirements, and time limits for proper publication. However, it is important to note that the APA is a default system, providing guidelines when the enabling law does not. On the other hand, a specific statute can require a hearing or notice even if the APA would not. In most cases, regulated or interested parties may submit comments to the agency, and the agency must consider them.

Compensation for Private Property

The Bill of Rights, again in the Fifth Amendment, guarantees compensation when the government takes private property in the interest of the public or for its own use. In the environmental arena, this right has been construed in different ways, but a pattern seems to be emerging.

Regulators have traditionally restricted uses of property, usually through zoning and permitting. Zoning allows particular uses of real estate within a given area; permitting allows the permit holder to engage in a certain activity. Sometimes zoning takes away a beneficial use of the property, particularly when its current use is prohibited in rezoning. Similarly, if a person obtains property to put it to a certain use and cannot get a permit to do it, the property's value to that owner has decreased.

The government has the right of eminent domain—the right to take private property for the good of the government, but it does not have the right to take property without just compensation. Yet early cases involving environmental restrictions did not usually find that a taking of the property had occurred. The right of the government was upheld simply because the regulation was in the interest of the public, and the property owner did not get compensated for his or her loss.

Wetlands cases have been turning this practice around. To fill a wetlands, a person needs a permit. If the use envisoned by the owner requires conversion of the land to dry land and the permit is not granted, alternatives to development may not exist, and the owner's property value might decline significantly. In a recent case, a circuit court decided that the property had been taken from the owner and compensation had to be made. This case is not the only one with such a holding. When Ronald Reagan was president, he issued an executive order requiring agencies to calculate the amount that might be owed to a property owner because of the government's action. However, calculating the current value of property is a difficult issue that may have to be resolved by the courts.

Self-Incrimination

The Bill of Rights grants a person the right not to incriminate himself or herself. Unfortunately, a regulated person subject to an administrative agency may not be able to rely on this Fifth Amendment right.

The term regulated person includes businesses. However, the right to refuse to incriminate oneself does not apply to businesses, because they are not natural persons. The right against self-incrimination has been interpreted to mean that a person cannot be compelled to testify. However, it does not cover the common situation where a business or other person created documents and submitted them to an agency, since the evidence was not compelled at the time it was created. Another restriction on the right is the context. If a criminal proceeding is not anticipated when the information is requested, the right does not apply. Or if the person is not actually in custody or under order of the court to speak, the privilege is not available.

These principles sound simple, but they are not, because business information can easily incriminate a human being. A corporation may be required to submit information that is incriminating to a natural person within the corporation, such as an officer or director. But the Fifth Amendment will not protect the information, so the person cannot hide behind the shield.

Since agencies exist to provide expertise in specialized areas of regulation, requirements for recordkeeping and report submission are common in administrative law. They have been viewed by courts as necessary oversight of the regulated community. Engaging in a particular business, such as selling firearms or liquor, or manufacturing something that creates pol-luted water or air, is not considered an unlimited right. If the government regulates the activity, the government will establish the conditions under which the business can operate.

The EPA issues permits, and the permit conditions include submis-sion of reports, notification of upset conditions, and periodic testing. Environmental laws mandate registration of certain types of equipment as well as monitoring and reporting of releases of contaminants to the environ-ment. Also, upon the request of the EPA, the regulated person must furnish information about processes, events, and other issues so the administrator can determine if a violation of a law occurred. Though this sort of required recordkeeping sounds like forced self-incrimina-tion, it has not been declared unconstitutional for the reasons cited above. Not only must the records be kept and submitted, but it is a crime to falsify information.

Searches and Seizures

The Fourth Amendment right against unreasonable searches and seizures (and the provision requiring a warrant in most cases) does apply to ad-ministrative agencies. However, administrative searches are usually treated differently under the law than a search for evidence of a crime.

Along with their broad powers in asking for information, agencies are often given statutory authority to inspect regulated businesses. The EPA has this type of power under the major environmental laws. Regulated businesses are expected to cooperate with the government; the refusal to allow an inspection is a separate violation. However, a business has a right to refuse entry to an inspector without a search warrant. Refusing entry may not be prudent, though, for the inspector will most likely obtain a warrant with ease and be upset for the inconvenience.

Administrative search cases have established two different standards. The first is the traditional one: the Fourth Amendment says "no warrant shall issue without probable cause." This guarantee is used in connection with criminal investigations. Probable cause is a legal standard under which the person requesting the warrant demonstrates that a crime has most likely been or is about to be committed, and the person who is the subject of the investigation more likely than not is involved, and the place to be searched is likely to contain evidence concerning the crime. The seeker of the warrant must go to a judge to get the warrant.

The second type of administrative search warrant is much different than the first. Although the investigator must still go to a court for the warrant, the rules are relaxed. The investigator must simply show that the target of the investigation is a regulated party and that the search is part of routine neutral or random inspection of the regulated parties. Most administrative searches are this type. Although the EPA does have criminal cases to investigate, its primary goal in inspections is to keep a visible presence in the regulated community to emphasize compliance.

The Toxic Substances Control Act (TSCA) grants a sweeping power to the EPA to issue administrative subpoenas. Those documents can require appearance and testimony, and like other subpoenas, order the person to bring records to the hearings. If the subpoena is not obeyed, the EPA can ask the district court to enforce it. Since TSCA covers numerous chemicals and mixtures of chemicals, the EPA does not simply use the subpoena power when gathering information about potential TSCA violations; it uses the tool whenever it deems it appropriate, regardless of the statute it is enforcing, as long as a chemical is involved.

Jury Trial Rights

When an environmental case becomes a criminal one, the defendant is entitled to a jury trial; the Sixth Amendment to the Constitution guarantees it. Whenever a person is charged with a crime, the personal impact of the allegation is assumed to be greater than when a civil lawsuit is brought. Freedom is perhaps the most prized of our rights, and conviction could result in losing some or all of it.

Jury trials may also be important in civil cases, however. The person seeking a jury trial may be either the plaintiff or the defendant—either of the parties may think a jury would be more favorable to his or her point of view. The Seventh Amendment of the Constitution assures parties to a civil case of the right to a jury in certain situations. But for a while, the right to a jury in civil cases involving environmental statutes was in doubt.

The Seventh Amendment specifies when a jury trial may be demanded for a civil case: "In suits at common law, where the value in controversy shall exceed twenty dollars, the right of trial by jury shall be preserved." But environmental lawsuits were not part of the common law when the Constitution came into being, and lawyers argued about what type of common law case the environmental enforcement most resembled. The controversy centered around two discrete categories of lawsuits, equity cases and legal cases. In English jurisprudence, the cases were taken to separate courts.

Equity cases were brought when money damages alone could not address the wrong the defendant committed. An example would be an action to force a seller of real estate to perform a contract if the seller changed his or her mind and didn't want to sell. Real estate has traditionally been treated differently than other goods because each property is unique. Legal cases, on the other hand, asked for a remedy involving money damages. They often went beyond simply making the plaintiff whole; they punished the wrongdoer.

Public nuisance cases belonged in the equity court. In these cases, the government would be asking the court to order the defendant to stop doing whatever was creating the nuisance. Also, if restitution was desired instead of punishment, the plaintiff would file the case in a court of equity. But if the government had a right to sue someone for civil penalties, the penalty was considered a legal issue, and that case would be subject to the court of law. One of the primary distinctions between the courts was the right to a jury trial. Either party to a legal suit could demand a jury. Equity cases were tried only before a judge.

When the American legal system was born, the two types of courts merged into a single court that could hear both equity and legal cases. But juries can still decide only cases brought in law, not in equity.

In the early days of environmental enforcement, the government often successfully argued that the defendants in environmental lawsuits were not entitled to a jury. The Supreme Court finally ruled on the issue in 1987 in a case involving the Clean Water Act. In cases involving penalties over the $25 limit, the parties have a right to a jury trial, but juries can only decide whether the defendant is liable. Unless the statutes change, the judge is the only person who can determine the amount of the penalty. The Supreme Court did not have constitutional objections to denying the defendant a jury on the penalty determination.

ENFORCEMENT

Advisory agencies, unlike regulatory agencies, have no power to enforce the law; they simply give advice. Regulatory agencies get their power from the statutes they implement. If enforcement is not specifically mentioned within the law, the agency does not have the power to enforce. The specific types of relief, penalties, cases, and actions within the administrator's authority are usually spelled out in a discrete section of the statute, with reference to the section numbers that explain what is regulated.

The Clean Water Act, for example, begins with a general prohibition against discharges into waters of the United States without a permit. It goes on to describe the permitting process and gives the administrator the power to permit, set conditions in the permit, and promulgate regulations about permits. The statute then explains the penalties for not obeying the law and grants the EPA administrator the power to apply those sanctions. In the Clean Water Act, a special section says that if a person violates the statute, the permit conditions, reporting requirements, or the regulations, the administrator of the EPA has a number of enforcement options, including assessing penalties, issuing orders for compliance, and bringing a civil or criminal lawsuit for penalties and injunctive relief. Under other statutes, the EPA has additional powers, especially when a violation of the law is causing an imminent threat to health or the environment.

Administrative Orders

One by one, environmental statutes have granted the EPA more power to deal with violations through the administrative process rather than the courts. This saves the agency time and money and allows it to address the problems more quickly.

Before it issues an order for compliance, the agency often issues some type of notice to the regulated party. The name of the notice varies, depending on the statute underlying the violation. It may be a notice of noncompliance, a notice of violation, a show cause order, or a letter requesting information. The purpose of this step is to allow the person to meet with the agency before the order is issued.

The compliance order may be issued first as a proposed compliance order, which corrects the problem but does not collect fines. It puts the violator on notice, but it also creates another standard that the regulated person must meet. In fact, violating an administrative order is yet another offense the regulated party must face if a case is brought later, and penalties may be written into the order for failure to meet the deadlines.

A compliance order does not replace the permit, but it sometimes gives relief to the person having difficulty meeting the terms of a permit. Generally compliance orders are issued after discussion of the problems and a technical evaluation of the solution. They may be consent orders, in which the regulated person agrees to the specifications in the order. Deadlines are set for reaching interim goals and for final compliance. The orders carefully preserve the right of the government to ignore the order and require compliance with the terms of the permit, but in reality, the government generally respects the order as long as the regulated party is complying with it.

The EPA administrator can issue penalty orders under a number of statutes. The process will vary based upon the amount of the proposed penalty, and a cap has been placed on the total amount of the penalty that may be assessed through a penalty order.

Until the Clean Water Act was amended in 1987, the administrative penalty order process was used most frequently with the Toxic Substances Control Act (TSCA). The procedure involves issuing a complaint, which is filed with the administrative law judge, and proceeding through the hearing before a penalty is assessed. Penalties under TSCA must be assessed by the administrator before a civil suit can be brought. If the violator refuses to pay or chooses to appeal, the case is brought before a federal court. TSCA cases go immediately to court only for imminent hazards.

The Clean Water Act establishes two classes of penalties: Class I and Class II. Class I penalties are limited to a total of $25,000, with a limit of $10,000 per day on individual violations. Class II penalties cannot exceed $125,000 total, with the same daily violation penalty. For comparison, consider the statute's maximum: for a violation of the Clean Water Act, the penalty may go as high as $25,000 per day per violation. If a person has a permit, violates it for one day, but three of the limits were exceeded, the potential penalty is $75,000 for that day. But if the agency wants to obtain that amount, it cannot assess a penalty under an order; it must go to court.

Since the punishment increases significantly when the penalty goes from Class I to Class II, the administrative procedures change, too. A person who received a proposed order for a Class I penalty is entitled to an informal hearing before the penalty is assessed. But a person who is subject to a Class II penalty gets more protection: he is allowed a formal Administrative Procedures Act hearing before an administrative law judge.

In addition to the EPA, two other agencies have penalty power under the Clean Water Act: the Coast Guard and the Corps of Engineers. However, they have specific duties in relation to the act and can only enforce certain violations.

In 1990, the Clean Air Act Amendments added administrative penalties to the EPA's arsenal for violations of that law. The EPA may assess higher penalties than those allowed under the Clean Water Act—up to $200,000. In addition to those types of penalties, the EPA can now issue field citations during inspections and assess up to $5,000 per day in that manner. Field citations are subject to an informal hearing.

Emergency Orders

Like other agencies that handle problems that could be life-threatening, the EPA has the right to act quickly if the need arises. Because emergency orders are not subject to review before they are issued, the standard for the EPA is stringent: an imminent threat to health or the environment must be present.

The EPA can issue emergency orders for seizure of toxic substances. The most common emergency actions, however, deal with hazardous substances under the Comprehensive Environmental Response, Compensation, and Liability Act (CERCLA), releases of petroleum under the Clean Water Act and the Oil Pollution Act, or other spills of hazardous or toxic substances governed by the Emergency Planning and Community Right-To-Know Act. They center around removal of the threat or neutralizing the danger.

Civil Law Suits

Administrative actions may be quick and easy, but they also have disadvantages. The penalties that can be assessed under administrative actions are limited by statute. Also, under the Clean Air Act, the administrator has to address a violation more quickly than is necessary if a lawsuit is brought. Therefore, taking a case to court is sometimes preferable to handling it administratively.

The EPA does not act as its own lawyer if a case is to be brought through the judicial system. Even though the agency hires attorneys, once the case becomes a civil action, it is required by statute to refer the case to the Department of Justice (DOJ). The EPA does not have the authority to file a lawsuit directly unless the DOJ refuses to handle it and the region, with the agreement of the Office of General Counsel, notifies the DOJ that it will proceed on its own.

If it chooses to proceed, the regional office pursuing the lawsuit prepares a referral package, which includes a description of the facility, the laws alleged to have been violated, the history of the violations, previous attempts to bring the facility into compliance, summaries of the applicable penalty provisions, a discussion of the strengths and weaknesses of the case, and a recommendation that the Department of Justice file a lawsuit. Penalty calculations are based on the EPA's computer model for penalty assessment.

The regional administrator forwards the case to the Office of General Counsel (OGC) of the EPA in Washington, D.C. The Department of Justice may receive a courtesy copy of the referral from the region, but it does not act on the information unless OGC concurs with the region. Once the referral is rolling toward the DOJ, the regional office can begin negotiations with the defendant. Whether it does so or not depends on the likelihood of settlement, which the Office of Regional Counsel will determine. It is not unusual for the consent decree to be filed at the same time as the complaint.

Another office involved in the civil lawsuit is the U.S. Attorney's Office in the district where the lawsuit is filed. Participation of that office will vary from jurisdiction to jurisdiction. Sometimes the DOJ will act as lead counsel throughout the case, but some Attorney General's offices are more involved and may be primary counsel.

Under most of the major environmental provisions, the penalty for non-compliance is up to $25,000 per day per violation. When the government files a lawsuit, it requests the maximum penalty allowed by law. Environmental statutes now specify guidelines for assessing the penalties. They are commonsense considerations: how severe was the violation, how long did it continue, what is the defendant's history of compliance, did the defendant cooperate in correcting the problem, and what was the economic benefit of not complying with the law? If an economic benefit has been realized, it must be part of the penalty; however, even the determination of economic benefit is subjective to some extent. The reason is simple: deferring expenses for compliance may be greatly beneficial economically. The purpose of the economic benefit segment of the penalty is to make sure the violator does not gain an advantage over law-abiding citizens.These factors are programmed into the computer model the EPA uses when it prepares a settlement figure for the referral package. The EPA also addresses one other issue: the likelihood that the lawsuit will succeed.

Much of the EPA's enforcement, both civil and administrative, ends in a consent agreement, which means that the defendant has already agreed to pay a stipulated penalty if it fails to comply with the agreement. If the EPA has made a demand for payment and the demand is not honored, the DOJ gets the case. It handles the collection cases. It also handles Superfund and Resource Conservation and Recovery Act lawsuits for the EPA.

Superfund is an unusual statute. It has been around since 1980, and its main purpose is to get hazardous waste sites cleaned up. To accomplish that purpose, it identifies certain persons as potentially responsible parties (PRPs), that is, persons who may be held separately and jointly responsible for all of the costs of cleanup. That designation is not based on fault or an allegation of a violation but depends on the party's relationship to a hazardous waste site. If the EPA has already done some work at the hazardous waste site, it will also sue for cost recovery. Superfund lawsuits may involve hundreds of PRPs and their attorneys, a battery of attorneys from the DOJ and at least two from the EPA. The PRPs often form a committee, called a Steering Committee, that speaks for the majority on common issues. Though the cleanup costs are not penalties, they are likely to be much higher than penalties.

When Congress addressed the problems associated with hazardous waste sites in the Resource Conservation and Recovery Act, it decided to regulate all facilities that could contribute to the problem. Thus treatment/storage/disposal (T/S/D) facilities are not only highly scrutinized but also subject to permit provisions requiring corrective action for all hazardous waste components at the facility. The corrective action requirement includes remediating areas that are no longer active. If the T/S/D facility has used other property in the site and a hazardous waste is being released there, the permit will also include offsite cleanup provisions. Since T/S/D facilities must have a permit, the corrective action condition, though not strictly an enforcement tool, is a powerful weapon for the EPA.

Criminal Enforcement

In environmental cases, the distinction between criminal and civil violations is slim. For example, under the Clean Water Act, negligence—ordinarily a tort—can be the basis of a crime. Generally, though, a violation is viewed most seriously when it is knowing, reckless, or willing. The EPA makes the decision about how to proceed, and lately it has filed criminal cases more and more often. In the last few years, the number of investigators and criminal attorneys within the EPA has increased to accommodate prosecuting more offenders.

Civil lawsuits still have clear advantages: the criminal process guarantees in the Constitution do not apply, the burden of proof is lower, and information will be easier to obtain. Nevertheless, criminal cases generate significant press coverage because of public interest in the penalties and in the possible incarceration of people involved. Criminal cases also communicate a clear message: environmental compliance is not optional.

Criminal penalties may range in the millions of dollars, with the highest penalties reserved for repeat offenders and corporations. But the EPA's best weapon in criminal cases is not penalties but the power to put offenders in jail. Under the new sentencing guidelines, federal courts are incarcerating record numbers of environmental violators. The person who goes to jail may be the one who actually committed the offense or the chief executive officer or other official in a business.

Natural Resources Damages

Natural resources damages, a type of damages available under environmental statutes, are relatively new. Their object is to compensate the federal and/or state government for loss of vegetation, wildlife, and uses of the environment due to pollution. The oil spill caused by the *Valdez*, for example, resulted in large natural resource damages.

One major difference between natural resources damages and ordinary penalties is the destination of the funds. According to statute, when penalties are collected by the government, the money goes into the general treasury funds. Natural resource damages, however, go into a fund specifically created to benefit the impacted environment. The enforcer of the natural resource damages provisions is also different. Instead of the EPA, the Secretary of the Interior has the right to enforce for damage to land; the Coast Guard for damage to sea.

Citizen Enforcement

If the EPA or the state environmental agency, using its prosecutorial discretion, decides to allow a particular violation to slide, it may have solid reasons for doing so. However, the infraction, along with all the evidence associated with it, still exists. To the people in the affected community, ignoring the violation may not be acceptable. In that case, they may be able to file a suit to compel enforcement. A past violation by itself is not sufficient for a citizen suit, however. The Supreme Court has held that the suit must allege continuing violations.

Most environmental statutes recognize the right of a citizen to enforce the law if the government declines to do so. Public interest groups, such as the Sierra Club, the Natural Resources Defense Council, and the Environmental Defense Fund, often initiate this type of action, which is called a citizen's suit. A citizen's suit may be brought by an individual or group of individuals within the affected environment as well as or instead of public interest groups.

Before a citizen's suit can be brought, sixty days notice must be given to the state and federal agencies involved, the violator, and the Department of Justice. The agencies, usually the EPA and the state environmental agency, evaluate the allegations to determine whether they will sue the regulated party themselves instead of allowing the citizen's suit to proceed. If the government sues, the citizens may intervene in the lawsuit but cannot initiate their own independent suit.

Citizen suits are often based on information contained in, and obtained from, government records through use of the Freedom of Information Act. The government itself may be named a defendant along with the violator. Another type of citizen suit is one against the EPA administrator for failure to do something the law requires him or her to do. These cases are often brought when the deadline for promulgating regulations is not met. Even if they do not go to trial, they are very effective in establishing, through settlement, deadlines that are enforceable by the court.

CONCLUSION

Over the last three decades, environmental issues have risen to the top of our consciousness. Clean water and air, freedom from negative long-term effects of chemicals we use, and responsible approaches to creating and disposing of waste have become as important to us as our personally owned resources. Whether the reasons for our concern are selfish or altruistic, we are beginning to understand that human activity has had a significant impact on the world.

From one perspective, we humans have been an extraordinarily successful species. We have improved our quality of life and remained ever on the move, ever growing in number. We have used our resources as if we were buying on credit, spending freely with no thought to how we would pay the bill.

Many other species have come and gone on the earth over its long history, and it is doubtful that any of them knew why. Humans alone are capable of seeing the direction we are heading as a species. Within the last few decades, we have attempted, through environmental legislation, to correct our course. But it is difficult to convince anyone of the need to change practices that have short-term benefit until the price of ignoring their effects is fully revealed. Thus, most of our environmental statutes are reactive; they grow directly out of environmental disasters we have created.

Fortunately we have a wonderful planet that has given us life and forgiven us much. We can see our footsteps and imagine the future. The spirit of international cooperation in addressing common environmental issues will grow because it must. If we continue to address our environmental problems responsibly, we will leave a better world to our children, and they, to theirs.

ACID RAIN A term used to describe abnormally acidic rain. Although any form of precipitation—snow, hail, fog, and others—can be acidic, many people use the words *acid rain* instead of the more comprehensive phrase, *acid deposition*, to describe this phenomenon. The two phrases will be used interchangeably here.

The problems associated with acid rain are often severe, damaging both natural habitats and man-made structures. Trees and vegetation cannot tolerate highly acidic water, so they show damage quickly before they die. Water bodies, such as lakes and streams, receive not only precipitation, but also run-off. Over time, the change in acidity causes major reductions in fish, aquatic plants, and other aquatic populations. Buildings erode due to acid deposition.

Acidity is measured in terms of pH, a scale that defines the degree of acidity or alkalinity of a solution. Using the scale, a 7 is neutral, showing no signs of either extreme. Numbers lower than 7 indicate acidity, while those above 7 reflect alkalinity. Each descending or ascending number represents a tenfold change in acidity or alkalinity.

Normal rain tends to be slightly acidic from natural causes, but acid deposition is significantly more acidic. The normal pH range of rain water should be between 5.3 and 6.0. Acid rain in the United States has been measured as low as 4.1. It results largely from two pollutants emitted during fossil fuel burning: **sulfur dioxide** (SO_2) and **nitrogen oxides** (NO_x). The exact correlation between these emissions and acid rain is disputed, but a link has been established. The primary emitters of large quantities of SO_2 and NO_x are electric utilities.

Acid deposition has been a topic of debate and study since the early 1970s, when scientific investigation verified that acid precipitation was occurring. Acid deposition has had profound effects in Europe, particularly in Germany. In the United States, the problem is most pronounced east of the Mississippi River, where it has affected fish and lakes, forests, crops, soil, and building surfaces. Canada, too, is plagued with acid rain. For years a controversy has raged between Canada and the United States because the acid precipitation falling in Canada appears to originate at U.S. power plants.

The source of acid rain is difficult to pinpoint, since the pollutants are carried long distances by air currents and accumulate to create the problem. For example, a power plant gets a permit to release a certain amount of the pollutants. Other electric utilities with their own permits are emitting the same pollutants simultaneously. If they are located in the same air current, the combined pollutants may be enough to trigger acid deposition, even though each plant stayed below its permitted limit.

In 1990, the **Clean Air Act** was amended to add a section, Title IV, that deals with acid rain. In the **Clean Air Act Amendments of 1990,** Congress faced the problem of acid rain, taking the issue away from President Bush [see **Bush, George Herbert Walker**], who had committed only to study the situation. Although he and President Reagan [see **Reagan, Ronald**] expressed concern for Canada, neither had moved toward a diplomatic solution.

Two of the goals of Title IV are to greatly reduce emissions from the 1980 levels, with a goal of 10 million tons reduction of SO_2 and 2 million tons of NO_x emissions by the year 2000. The reductions are to be phased in gradually.

Market-Based Emissions Control

Some of the emissions control measures in the act are market-based, a very different philosophy from earlier approaches. Traditional pollution control measures, which have been called *command and control* regulations, set numerical limits for pollutants by regulation or permit and require that emissions be controlled at the point of release. In order to comply with these requirements, a company must install pollution control equipment, such as a scrubber, filter, incinerator, or neutralizer.

Although Title IV applies only to electric utilities, other pollution sources may opt into the program. If they do, they become eligible for allowances, but they also become subject to all the other details of the provision.

The controversial market-based approach in the Clean Air Act Amendments of 1990 treats discharges of SO_2 as a type of asset called an *allowance,* defining one allowance as one ton. Title IV requires the **Environmental Protection Agency** (EPA) to give allowances of SO_2 to utilities; in fact, utilities are listed by name in the act. The EPA also holds a number of allowances itself, which it must offer at a public auction.

If a utility does not use its allowance, it may hold it, trade it, sell it, or offer it at the EPA's auction. A trade is not effective until it is registered with the EPA. A new utility may purchase allowances from the EPA, but in order to qualify, it must show that it tried and failed to obtain allowances on the open market. Allocations for new power generators are specifically set aside for that purpose and are not included in the auctions.

The first deadline for reductions of SO_2 is 1995, though extensions until 1997 may be granted to utilities that are developing alternative power sources, with emphasis on renewable energy, as well as clean coal technology. Permits will be issued for businesses that are regulated, and they must establish a continuous emission system to monitor emissions. The final deadline for reductions in SO_2 is 2000, with extensions available only until 2003. The total annual allowances are capped at 8.95 million tons of SO_2.

The penalties for exceeding allowances are very steep. The violator must pay the permitting authority $2,000 per ton without demand, and its next year's allowance will be reduced by the excess amount. In addition, it must pay the penalties that the EPA or state agency can assess for violating the permit.

The allowance provisions of the Clean Air Act Amendments of 1990 received a mixed response. Many people believe the command and control measures have had very limited success in reducing pollution. Some environmental organizations, such as the National Wildlife Federation, have lobbied for the market-based approach, hoping to find a more effective system of pollution control. However, treating pollution as a commodity bothers many environmentalists.

Reduction of NO_x

NO_x and SO_2 reductions are treated differently. Emission limits apply to various specified units, like coal-fired burners and boilers, but no allowances like the SO_2 allowances will be set. The NO_x emission limits are also phased in.

One peculiarity of NO_x control is the restriction placed on the EPA. The EPA cannot require more stringent technology than low-NO_x technology or a technology equivalent in cost. Also, the permitting authority can relax the standards if it can show that the technology does not exist to meet the emission limits.

ADMINISTRATIVE AGENCY   An administrative division of government created either by the executive head of the government (the president for federal agencies, the governor for state agencies) or by the legislative branch. Some agencies may have no power to regulate, as in the case of advisory councils. Others have the authority to perform all three functions of the government: legislation, execution, and judgment. This latter type of agency is a regulatory agency and must get its mandate through a statute.

Although Congress enacts laws concerning the environment, it leaves most of the details and all of the enforcement and execution to administrative agencies. States operate in the same manner. Thus, the statute itself is only the starting point when determining which laws apply to a particular issue; the federal and state regulations are critical components of that analysis and often make up the bulk of the applicable law.

The **Environmental Protection Agency** is a regulatory agency, as are most state environmental agencies. Other agencies that deal with environmental issues include the National Oceanic and Atmospheric Agency, the **Agency for Toxic Substances and Disease Registry,** the **Coast Guard,** the **Corps of Engineers,** the Fish and Wildlife Service, the National Advisory Council on Historic Preservation, the Bureau of Land Management, the Office of Surface Mining, and the Nuclear Regulatory Commission. Many other agencies also contribute to environmental regulation.

ADMINISTRATIVE LAW JUDGE (ALJ)   A person hired by an **administrative agency** to oversee and recommend a decision in cases where the regulated person has a right to a formal **hearing.** Administrative law judges are selected through competition and a merit system. The Administrative Procedures Act of 1946 defines their roles and preserves their independence. They cannot be removed from office except for good cause. In the case of the **Environmental Protection Agency** (EPA), the ALJs are not assigned to a particular regional office but travel to various locations to hear the cases.

The EPA is directed by several statutes to provide formal hearings for people subject to **administrative penalty order**s if the orders involve an amount specified in the statute. A hearing is held if the respondent to the order requests one. Information concerning the right to a hearing and how to ask for one must be included in information accompanying the proposed penalty order.

Administrative hearings may be formal or informal. If they are formal, they are subject to the Administrative Procedures Act of 1946, and an administrative law judge will hear the case and make the decision. ALJs control the hearing process, making sure the person involved is given an opportunity to be heard. The filings and testimony become a part of the record so that the decision can be reviewed by the administrator and, if necessary, by a court. Testimony may be submitted in written form, if the ALJ wishes, or it may be given at the hearing.

After the hearing, the parties submit proposed findings of fact and conclusions of law to the judge, who may adopt one of them or write his or her own. The agency administrator is not required to agree with the ALJ, so the judge's decision will be couched as a *recommended decision*. The administrator must affirmatively accept it in order to make it an order or an *initial decision*, which will become final after a certain period of time unless the administrator rejects it.

Many agencies other than the EPA employ ALJs. In contrast to judges within the court system, ALJs have experience and knowledge in the substantive issues the agency deals with. Therefore, their decisions are given a great deal of weight. See also **Administrative Procedure Act; Clean Air Act; Clean Water Act.**

ADMINISTRATIVE ORDER (AO)   This document, issued by an agency administrator, designates how a regulated person must act in relation to a statute, regulation or permit. It contains a description of the agency's allegations and sets out its requirements, which may include deadlines for complying with terms of a permit, interim limits to be met, and demands for compliance with the statute.

Because an administrative order is a means of enforcement, a statute must authorize it. Administrative orders are an effective means of dealing with violations because they do not require a formal **hearing,** can be issued relatively quickly, and address the noncompliance directly.

The regulated person is entitled to present information before the order is finalized, but this is generally done in a meeting rather than a hearing. At the meeting, the parties discuss the violations and the reasons for them. If the regulated party is claiming the agency is wrong, it may submit information to be considered. Often the order issued after a meeting will reflect an understanding between the parties and become a consent order, to which both parties agree. See also **administrative penalty order.**

ADMINISTRATIVE PENALTY ORDER (APO) A document that requires a regulated person to pay a penalty for violating the law or the terms of a permit. Congress instituted administrative penalty orders in some statutes because they provide a quick, cheap, and efficient way of enforcing the law when the violation is not significant enough to warrant a lawsuit. The agency administrator may only assess a penalty if the statute being enforced provides for it, and the maximum penalties allowable in a penalty order will generally be smaller than if the case were taken to court.

Because an administrative penalty order demands the payment of money for an alleged violation of environmental law, the person subject to it is entitled to a **hearing** before the order becomes final. Thus the order is prepared initially as a *proposed penalty order*, and at that point the regulated person must be informed of the right to a hearing. Administrative penalty proceedings may be instituted by the **Environmental Protection Agency** (EPA), but the **Corps of Engineers** and **Coast Guard** also have that right when they are enforcing certain environmental laws.

Administrative Penalty Provisions in Environmental Laws

The first major environmental statute that provided for administrative penalties was the **Toxic Substances Control Act** (TSCA). The **Administrative Procedure Act** and the EPA's own Consolidated Rules of Practice provide the structure for the procedure. Under the **Clean Water Act** (CWA) revisions of 1987, the administrator issues a proposed penalty order. Two classes were established, Class I and Class II, and the formality of the hearings depends on the class of penalty. Class I penalties are lower than Class II. The maximum penalty under Class I is $25,000, but a Class II penalty may be as high as $125,000. Therefore, if a Class II penalty is sought, the alleged violator is entitled to more procedural protections than if a Class I penalty is at issue. Typically, the administrator will also issue a compliance order, requiring the alleged violator to begin complying with the law, at the same time the penalty order is proposed.

The **Oil Pollution Act** (OPA) specifies two penalty options for violators: the Clean Water Act's penalties or alternative measures based on a fee per barrel of oil. The Coast Guard and the Department of Transportation are among the agencies with power to assess a penalty for these violations. The **Emergency Planning and Community Right-To-Know Act** (EPCRA) and the **Comprehensive Environmental Response, Compensation, and**

Liability Act (CERCLA) have similar schemes for penalties in some sections. A Class I penalty may be no greater than $25,000; a Class II penalty may be up to $25,000 per day.

The **Clean Air Act Amendments of 1990** added the flexibility of the Clean Water Act administrative penalty provisions to the **Clean Air Act** (CAA). The penalty under this statute can be as large as $200,000, provided that the attorney general agrees with the EPA administrator. This new section replaces an earlier, less comprehensive portion of the CAA that allowed penalty assessment. See also **administrative law judge; administrative order.**

ADMINISTRATIVE PROCEDURE ACT (APA) A law enacted in 1946 to provide procedural guidance for administrative agencies [see **administrative agency**]. It has never been significantly amended. The major topics addressed in the law are requirements for publication of agency documents in the *Federal Register;* participation by interested parties in rulemakings and adjudications; availability of policies, interpretations, formal opinions, and administrative manuals; formal adjudications; open meetings; and scope of review by the courts.

The most frequently mentioned aspect of the APA is the formal **hearing** guidelines. The APA established the role of the **administrative law judge** (ALJ), and it describes the type of evidence that may be considered at a hearing and defines unacceptable conduct. However, the APA sets forth the fundamental notion of due process in other areas as well. Agencies must publish in the *Federal Register* notices of their organization, rules of procedure, substantive rules, internal processes, and any changes. They must prepare an index of other available information if it is not published, such as policies and interpretations, manuals, and formal opinions, and if the documents are not produced for sale, the agency must reproduce them at cost for interested parties. In rulemakings, which precede binding regulations, the agency must notify the public in advance of the topic; the time, date and place of the rulemaking; the legal authority for the proposed rule as well as its terms and substance; and avenues for public comment.

The **Environmental Protection Agency** (EPA) is bound by many of the terms of the APA. Since so much of law is specified in regulations, the notices in the *Federal Register* are critical to understanding where the agency is headed. The access to internal EPA documents provided by this statute also gives the public a better understanding of the agency's position on a variety of topics. See also **administrative penalty order.**

AGENCY FOR TOXIC SUBSTANCES AND DISEASE REGISTRY (ATSDR)   In the **Superfund Amendments and Reauthorization Act** (SARA), Section 110, Congress established the ATSDR within the Public Health Service. It reports directly to the Surgeon General of the United States. The ATSDR works with many different health agencies and the **Environmental Protection Agency** (EPA) to develop a registry of serious diseases resulting from exposure to toxic substances, to research and maintain a library of literature and studies on health effects of toxic substances, and to develop a list of areas closed to the public or restricted because of toxic substance contamination. It also provides medical assistance in public health emergencies and does research and screening to determine the relationship between exposure to toxic substances and illness.

The ATSDR has a number of duties, but in relation to **Superfund** sites, it completes a health assessment and delivers it to the EPA. It can establish a registry of exposed persons, along with medical surveillance and treatment, and research relationships between exposure and illness. Working with the EPA, it developed a list of the 100 most commonly occurring **hazardous substances** at **National Priority List** sites. It is required to report to Congress on a number of issues. See also **Comprehensive Environmental Response, Compensation, and Liability Act.**

AIR PERMITS   A type of license for air pollution sources. Until the **Clean Air Act Amendments of 1990** (CAAA), the federal program for air pollution control was limited to preconstruction permits for major emissions sources under the **New Source Performance Standards** (NSPS), **Prevention of Significant Deterioration** (PSD) or nonattainment provisions of the **Clean Air Act** and regulations.

In 1990, Congress significantly amended the Clean Air Act to include an integrated permit program for air pollution sources. When it is fully functional, it will deal not only with the preconstruction phase but also with operation.

Under the permit program, called Title V, the states are to be the permit authority. The method of implementing the program follows:

1. The **Environmental Protection Agency** (EPA) promulgates rules about the contents of the program (completed in June 1992).

2. States submit their plans to the EPA (due by November 1993).

3. The EPA either accepts or rejects the state's plan. If it is rejected, the EPA may act for the state.

4. States may revise their plans to address the EPA's concerns;

5. When its plan is accepted, a state begins its pollution reduction program immediately, though it could take five years to get an individual state's program up and running. After approval of the plan, the state has three years to issue permits.

Emissions sources covered by the program include major stationary sources, sources regulated by the National Emission Standards for Hazardous Air Pollutants, sources listed by or opting into the acid deposition provisions in Title IV, and other regulated sources. Until the program is working, permits required by Phase I of Title IV (**acid rain**) and preconstruction permits will be issued separately.

The air permitting scheme will be similar to the successful water permitting system. Applicants will be required to pay an annual fee, which is to be used by the state for costs associated with the program. The permits will include emission limits; requirements for continuous emission monitoring systems (CEMS); reporting and inspection requirements, including an annual certification from the source that it is in compliance with its permit and the law; and a compliance schedule if the source is not in compliance. Along with the permit application, the source must also include a description of how it will comply with the terms of the permit. That requirement and the requirements for annual compliance certification and the CEMS are enhancements to the water permitting system.

Permits will be issued for a specified period of time. The EPA may veto a permit, revoke, or modify it; the EPA may also enforce the terms of the permit if it decides the state is not acting properly.

The public will be given notice of proposed permits. Citizens may obtain copies of any document required of the permittee, and they may comment during the prepermit phase or use the information they gather for a lawsuit for violations after the permit is issued.

Contiguous states also have the right to comment on any proposed permit for a source within 50 miles of their border if they think the source will violate their standards. Permitting states do not have to agree with neighboring states, but they do have to listen and consider their comments. See also **major source; National Ambient Air Quality Standards; nonattainment areas; Prevention of Significant Deterioration; state implementation plans.**

AIR POLLUTANT   Any type of substance or matter that enters the ambient air. *Ambient air* means open air, so air within a confined area, such as a building, is not included. The **Clean Air Act** (CAA) regulates air pollution, which it defines to include biological, radioactive, physical, or chemical agents within its definition of pollutants. In addition to specifying the pollutants, the Clean Air Act and its regulations tackle sources of the problem.

For example, air quality control districts were set up under the CAA, and air quality limits were set for substances called **criteria pollutant**s: **sulfur dioxide,** carbon monoxide, nitrogen dioxide [see **nitrogen oxides**], **ozone,** lead, and small **particulate** matter, designated PM_{10}. The methods of reducing the pollutants involved state implementation plans and preconstruction permits for new major stationary sources and major modifications of existing sources. The new integrated permit program provided under the **Clean Air Act Amendments of 1990** will also include operating permits.

Air toxics [see **hazardous air pollutants**] are covered under a different section of the Clean Air Act; mobile source emissions fall under a new section of the Clean Air Act Amendments of 1990, as do the constituents of acid deposition [see **acid rain**]. See also **air permits; mobile sources; Prevention of Significant Deterioration; state implementation plans; visibility.**

AIR POLLUTION CONTROL TECHNOLOGY   Methods used to reduce the amount of air contaminants discharged from a source. "Sources" originate **air pollutant**s. Examples of sources include industrial plants, automobiles, and numerous small businesses, such as dry cleaners. Technology is the application of knowledge to a particular problem.

Air pollutants appear in two types: particles (called *particulates*) and gases. Selection of proper mechanisms hinges on their form and, in the case of gases, their chemical composition.

When air pollution was first regulated, most regulators focused on particulates. Particulates impact visibility by contributing to smog, and they affect breathing. Because of government emphasis, technology to reduce particulates developed sooner than it did for gaseous air pollution.

Controlling air pollution at the source may be accomplished at three different times in a process. The first is the beginning: substitution of materials or fuel may impact the creation of air contamination. Second, changes made to the process itself can eliminate the formation of pollutants. Finally, at the end of the process, the air pollutants may be captured and destroyed or reduced to an acceptable level.

To illustrate the first option, a printing company may be using petroleum-based inks and generating air pollution during the printing process and when cleaning equipment. By switching to a vegetable-based ink (most commonly soy-based), pollution will be drastically reduced.

Process design controls are called "in-process" technology. An example would be a system that captures solvents in a closed system, cleans them, and returns them to use within the process.

The treatment of air pollution at the end of the process, known as end-of-pipe treatment, occurs when pollutants are captured and treated before release to the atmosphere. For example, a scrubber may be added at the end.

Add-on or end-of-pipe treatment has been the method of choice for many years. The major reason is cost: it is cheaper to change an industrial system at the end than to redesign an entire process. However, with the air emission limitations becoming more stringent, industries that want to build new plants (or modify old ones) are forced to consider air pollution control while designing their structures.

Several types of technology used for air pollution control are examined below. Particulates and gaseous emissions are treated separately since they must be the focus of a chosen method. However, many air pollution streams contain both particulates and gases, so treatment may involve more than one technology.

Technology Applied to Particulates

Particulates are differentiated by their size, concentration, and some physical properties (like density). Use of specific control equipment follows an analysis of the particulate's characteristics. Four categories of equipment address most air particulate pollution: cyclones, fabric filters, wet scrubbers, and electrostatic precipitators.

Cyclones operate as one might expect. The incoming pollutant stream is forced into a vortex spin. The coarser particulates fall out and are collected.

Fabric filters operate in the same manner as straining a liquid through a cheesecloth. The filter, a bag often made of cotton, fiberglass, or teflon, acts as a surface upon which the particulates collect as the air stream is pushed through. The dust cake is removed periodically.

Wet scrubbers use a spray liquid to remove particulates from an air stream. The liquid is introduced counter-current to the air flow.

Electrostatic precipitators use electricity to separate the particulates from the air stream. The particulates are given an electrical charge and then they are attracted to an oppositely charged plate, where they collect until removed as a dust cake.

Technology Applied to Gaseous Pollutants

Gaseous pollutants vary according to their chemical composition. For that reason, analysis of the proper control technology is more complex and not as easily broken out into categories as particulate control technology. However, certain processes recur within treatments to remove gaseous pollutants. They are adsorption, absorption, catalytic oxidation, and thermal oxidation.

Adsorption is the collection of gases on the surface of a solid or liquid. The layer is extremely thin, and the gases are held until released (desorbed). This process is used to hold gases for recovery or destruction. Desorption may be accomplished by using hot air or steam. One of the most common and effective adsorbing media is activated charcoal. It can be reused after regeneration.

Absorption involves assimilation of the gas into a liquid. It is not a surface phenomenon, as adsorption is. The gas must be capable of being dispersed in the liquid. In some cases, a chemical reaction may also be engineered by the selection of a liquid that will absorb the gas. Examples of commonly used absorbing liquids are water, caustic, sodium carbonate, and certain nonvolatile oils.

Catalytic oxidation is primarily a thermal (heat) process, but it uses a catalyst to enhance the efficiency of the thermal unit. The technology operates at lower temperatures than a thermal oxidizer. Catalytic oxidizers operate within a range of 400° to 1100° Fahrenheit. They are quite efficient in treating volatile organic compounds. A catalyst is a substance that enables a chemical reaction to occur faster or under different conditions than those normally required. The catalyst itself does not change during the reaction. A mixture of metals is the common catalyst for a catalytic oxidizer. It is placed at the bottom of the unit and is designed to allow maximum surface contact. Honeycomb patterns are not uncommon.

Thermal oxidation requires more fuel to destroy air pollutants because it operates solely on the heat provided. The temperatures of a thermal oxidation unit (commonly called an incinerator) is at least 1500° Fahrenheit. Thermal oxidation is cheaper to set up, but more expensive to operate, than a catalytic oxidizer. Their efficiency of destruction is roughly the same.

AIR QUALITY CONTROL REGIONS   Areas designated by states to cover the geographical interior of the state. The regions are demarcated after taking air currents and distribution patterns for pollutants into consideration.

Several attempts to regulate air pollution had been made before the modern revisions of the **Clean Air Act** (CAA) occurred in 1970. When the act was passed in 1963, it stated goals and little else, spreading responsibility between the Department of Health, Education and Welfare (HEW) and the states. In 1967, it was amended to provide more guidance for the states. It instructed the states to designate air quality control regions where air pollution was a problem and discussed ambient air quality standards and implementation plans. However, nothing was mandatory; air quality standards did not exist on a national level, and HEW had virtually no power to enforce.

When the Clean Air Act was overhauled in 1970, it gave the newly created **Environmental Protection Agency** (EPA) responsibility for air pollution control and much more power to enforce the law than HEW had had. The EPA was tasked with the job of establishing the ambient air quality standards and the deadlines for complying with them. States were required to formulate implementation plans demonstrating how they intended to meet the new standards, and the plans had to be submitted to the EPA for approval.

From the beginning, the Clean Air Act, unlike some other major environmental laws, recognized the states' interest in controlling air pollution within their borders. After the EPA designated the air quality standards, the states not only had to name the air quality control regions, but also had to determine whether an individual region met those standards. A region's success in meeting the standards was categorized as non-attainment, attainment, or unclassifiable. The regions might attain the goal for one pollutant but fail to meet the standard for another. The **Clean Air Act Amendments of 1990** divide the **nonattainment areas** into five categories: severe, serious, extreme, marginal, and moderate. The deadline for attainment is based on the designation of the region. But the deadlines for attainment were not met; they were changed again in the 1977 and 1990 revisions.

The 1970 CAA also introduced the regulation of new sources, **hazardous air pollutant**s, mobile source emissions, and a broad enforcement scheme. Not only does the CAA emphasize technology, it forces it. Starting with best available technology (BAT) in the 1970 version, the Clean Air Act has been modified to include reasonably available control technology (RACT), lowest achievable emission rate (LAER) and best available control technology in 1977. In 1990, maximum achievable control technology (MACT) was established for hazardous air pollutants. Some of the goals of the regulations were unachievable when first set, but technology has been developed to meet the standards. The EPA operates a clearinghouse to distribute information on technology. See also **air permits; criteria pollutant; National Ambient Air Quality Standards; New Source Performance Standards; state implementation plans.**

AIR QUALITY STANDARDS   See **National Ambient Air Quality Standards.**

AIR TOXICS   A term used interchangeably with **hazardous air pollutant**s. The federal hazardous air pollutant program has existed since 1970, but many regard it as a failure. The **Clean Air Act Amendments of 1990** have restructured the law and given new direction to the **Environmental Protection Agency.** See **hazardous air pollutant** for a complete discussion of this topic.

APPLICABLE OR RELEVANT AND APPROPRIATE REQUIREMENTS (ARARs) Standards used to determine the extent of cleanup necessary at a **Superfund** site. Superfund sites are **hazardous waste** sites that are so badly contaminated that the federal government has put them on a list (the **National Priority List**) because they pose a danger to human health or the environment. At these sites, the government forces the individuals or companies that may have contributed to the problem to clean up the mess. Once the actual work begins, the **Environmental Protection Agency** (EPA) must decide what results will be satisfactory. A crew cleaning up large amounts of lead in the soil, for example, must know when they can stop—that is, how much lead, if any, will be allowed to remain in the soil? The EPA may determine that the site will be considered clean when the excess is removed, neutralized, or contained. A number of guidelines are used to decide cleanup goals, such as the nearness of the site to populated areas, use of the groundwater in the presence of intercepting water bodies, and the federal and state statutes and regulations that make up the ARARs.

The first word in the acronym ARARs is the word "applicable." It refers to legal requirements that apply precisely to a problem at the site. For example, if the groundwater is part of a public water supply, the **maximum contaminant levels** found in the **Safe Drinking Water Act** and the associated regulations must be met. If surface water is being treated and discharged, it has to meet the requirements of the **Clean Water Act.** Air emissions must comply with the **Clean Air Act.** If the state where the Superfund site is located has stricter standards, the applicable requirement will be based on state law.

Applicable standards may also pertain to the type of pollution control used during the cleanup, if a law or regulation exists that specifies it. For example, if hazardous waste is being burned in a cleanup, the EPA regulations may require that the incinerator have a particular piece of control equipment to ensure that **hazardous substances** are not released during the combustion process.

"Relevant and appropriate requirements," the second part of the ARARs acronym, describes standards that do not specifically apply to the conditions at a Superfund site but should be used because a similarity exists. For example, if the groundwater is not used as a public water source, the Safe Drinking Water standards are not applicable, but the government could use them because they are relevant.

ARARs are used in the Superfund program's cleanup process to determine what type of remediation and control technology must be used. The Superfund Amendments and Reauthorization Act (SARA) of 1986 added ARARs to the statutory list of items that had to be included in the regulations for cleanup of Superfund sites. Those regulations, revised many times since 1980, are called the **National Contingency Plan** (NCP). They provide a blueprint for dealing with remediation of hazardous waste sites. According to statute, remedial actions cannot be inconsistent with the National Contingency Plan.

When the EPA began using ARARs as standards for cleanup—prior to the Superfund Amendments and Reauthorization Act—it left itself a way to escape the harshness of strict compliance. The rigid use of ARARs at Superfund sites could result in costly and possibly unnecessary cleanup, so the EPA used what it called an alternative concentration limit (ACL) in those situations. In order to justify using an alternative to ARARs, the EPA had to be convinced that the contamination on site would not impact a drinking water source or cause a health or safety problem.

When the Superfund law was amended, Congress shrank the EPA's ability to use alternative concentration limits. Since then, they have practically disappeared. SARA requires the use of ARARs. An exemption from their use may be obtained, but only if the president determines that it is merited based on specific conditions.

Superfund sites are the worst of known environments. Each site is unique, and the EPA must evaluate every one individually. The process of determining how the site should be treated is called **Remedial Investigation/ Feasibility Study** (RI/FS). It is during this procedure that the ARARs are identified.

ASBESTOS   A group of minerals that are, chemically, a type of silicate with fibrous qualities. Asbestos has been used in a variety of ways because of its special properties: it is heat, fire, and electrically resistant; it impedes noise; acids and alkalis do not affect it.

Although asbestos use has been documented back to ancient times, it became commercially popular beginning in the nineteenth century. Products incorporating asbestos range from protective clothing and brakes to building materials such as thermal insulation, wallboard, tiles, and mastic.

The most enduring use of asbestos is that of building materials. Until the mid-70s, builders used asbestos liberally.

Asbestos is quarried or mined. Crushing and blowing separates asbestos from the extracted rock. Generally, it is white, but it can be light green, blue, or yellow. The sharp microscopic fibers are small enough to be inhaled, and when they are, they remain in the lungs, making lifelong exposure to asbestos a cumulative problem.

In its natural state, asbestos fibers may be friable, which means they can be easily crushed with hand pressure. After they are incorporated into another material, the friability varies. Friability is a crucial issue in decisions about how to deal with asbestos. The EPA and other environmental professionals refer to materials that contains more than one percent of asbestos as **asbestos-containing materials** (ACM).

The public first became aware of health effects of asbestos through a study of ship workers and asbestos miners. The results showed an increase in three types of ailments after exposure to asbestos: asbestosis (a lung disease), mesothelioma (cancer of the pleural lining of the lungs), and lung cancer. The likelihood of asbestos-related lung problems is significantly higher for smokers. Though no one could quantify the risk directly to the exposure of the workers, the link between inhalation of asbestos fibers and health effects had been established.

A number of laws and three separate federal organizations as well as state and local agencies regulate asbestos. The federal organizations are the **Environmental Protection Agency** (EPA), the Department of Transportation (DOT), and the Occupational Health and Safety Administration (OSHA). Each has distinct duties.

The Department of Transportation determines how asbestos is transported, labeled, packaged, and placarded. The EPA regulates emissions of asbestos fibers to the atmosphere, asbestos management in schools, uses of asbestos, and its disposal. Finally, the Occupational Safety and Health Administration concerns itself with worker safety, both in the workplace in general and in asbestos abatement projects and construction activities that may disturb material containing asbestos.

The environmental laws involving asbestos are the **Clean Air Act,** the **Toxic Substances Control Act,** the **Clean Water Act,** the **Comprehensive Environmental Response, Compensation, and Liability Act,** and the Solid Waste Disposal Act. The most significant of these laws are the Clean Air Act and the Toxic Substances Control Act.

Asbestos is designated a **hazardous air pollutant,** and the type of activity regulated under the Clean Air Act is associated with construction and demolition projects. Since the EPA is required to deal with ambient air pollution, environmental regulations protect the public against air emissions. If construction or demolition projects will disturb a specified amount of friable asbestos-containing material, the material must be managed according to the EPA's rules. It is assumed that buildings erected prior to the mid 1970s contain asbestos-containing material. Though asbestos in building materials was eventually phased out, some asbestos-containing material was used in buildings even after that date. Asbestos is sometimes found in vinyl floor tiles, the mastic that secures the floor tiles, and roofing materials in buildings erected as late as the mid 1980s.

The EPA promulgated regulations under the Toxic Substances Control Act to ban the use of asbestos-containing material in many products other than building products. In the case of *Corrosion Proof Fittings v. Environmental Protection Agency,* the court found the ban was unsupported, sending the EPA back to the drawing board and invalidating the ban.

In 1986, the Toxic Substances Control Act was amended to add Title II, which deals with asbestos in schools. The name of the law is the **Asbestos Hazard Emergency Response Act** (AHERA). In addition to identification and removal of certain asbestos-containing material, this statute requires reinspection, an operation and maintenance program, and education of school employees. A loan and grant program was established under a different statute to assist the schools with the expenses involved in asbestos removal.

AHERA also required the EPA to complete a study of the asbestos problem and report to Congress. One of the issues to be considered was whether the asbestos in schools program should be extended to public and commercial buildings. In its report, the EPA did not make that recommendation. Since the EPA does not seem intent on regulating asbestos in public and commercial buildings, OSHA is gathering comments on the question of whether it should do so. Workers, particularly maintenance, custodial, and other service personnel, may be exposed because of their jobs, since no federal law requires identification of asbestos-containing material in public and commercial buildings.

Lawsuits involving companies that manufactured asbestos-containing building materials have crowded the courts for over a decade. Many of the suits become class action suits, and the defendants are often more than one company.

ASBESTOS HAZARD EMERGENCY RESPONSE ACT (AHERA)

A statute enacted in 1986 that requires action to deal with **asbestos** in schools. Although the **Environmental Protection Agency** (EPA) had regulations under the **Toxic Substances Control Act** requiring the identification of **asbestos-containing material** (ACM) and notification of its location, Congress had complained that the law lacked substance.

AHERA ordered the EPA to develop comprehensive asbestos regulations for schools, including requirements for inspections, reinspections, response actions to friable ACM, development of operation and maintenance plans, standards for education and protection of school employees and building occupants, asbestos management plans (which must be available to the public and submitted to the governor), and labeling of ACM that remained in routine maintenance areas.

Not only were the schools to be subject to the AHERA standards, but asbestos contractors (both inspectors and abatement workers) and laboratories doing the analysis of samples were regulated. An accreditation program had to be established for each category. Either the state or the EPA was to provide for education and continuing education, testing, and approval. Because AHERA contains a number of explicit details that cannot be found elsewhere, most asbestos contractors and environmental consultants follow AHERA's provisions for accreditation, sampling, and work.

AHERA also required the EPA to complete a study on several topics and report to Congress about the findings. The report recommended more training to increase the number of asbestos abatement and inspection workers, development of procedures for dealing with thermal insulation, improved enforcement of standards, and an assessment of the AHERA in schools program.

AHERA has been a model for asbestos-related work even when it does not involve a school, though it is only binding on work in schools. However, the cost of asbestos abatements and management of asbestos can be significant. School abatement plans and other requirements of the law are the responsibility of the local educational authority, though schools with financial problems may qualify for assistance under the Asbestos School Hazard Abatement Act of 1984. Also, if a governor of a state can convince the EPA that a school district is meeting the goals of the law with standards that are no less stringent than the federal ones, the AHERA requirements may be waived.

ASBESTOS-CONTAINING MATERIALS (ACM) Any product or substance that contains more than 1 percent **asbestos.** The EPA regulates the types of asbestos designated as regulated asbestos-containing materials (RACM). RACM includes friable asbestos and asbestos-containing materials that will become friable or have a high probability of becoming friable during sanding, grinding, cutting, or other types of construction or demolition activities. Only friable asbestos can become airborne, threatening the health of the public. A material is considered friable if it can be easily crumbled or reduced to powder by hand pressure when the substance is dry.

The **Clean Air Act** authorizes the **Environmental Protection Agency** (EPA) to name and regulate **hazardous air pollutant**s. The standards the EPA sets are called **National Emission Standards for Hazardous Air Pollutants** (NESHAPs); asbestos is one of the pollutants subject to the standards. The NESHAP for asbestos deals only with construction and demolition projects: projects that could disturb specified amounts of ACM. Since friability is an issue, the EPA regulates not only ACM that is friable at the beginning of the project, but any ACM that will or probably will become friable during the work.

The EPA amended the regulations for construction and demolition projects in November 1990 and clarified many requirements. One helpful addition was clearer descriptions of asbestos-containing material that is not friable during its normal life. Two different categories were established for such products, and they will only be regulated if they fit the definition of RACM. See also **Clean Air Act Amendments of 1990.**

BEN A computer program used by the **Environmental Protection Agency** (EPA) to calculate the economic benefit of delayed compliance with environmental laws. The program was developed to provide standard variables, such as interest rate, inflation rate, discount rate, and investment tax credit. If available, specific information can be substituted for the standard variables.

Compliance with environmental laws is expensive. Often it involves installing and maintaining equipment or using control methods that may be costly. But the penalties for noncompliance can be even more expensive. A regulated entity faces a maximum penalty of $25,000 per day per violation for most federal violations. But even that is not always enough to encourage compliance. The reasoning is familiar: if you don't get caught, you can put off the cost of compliance indefinitely. Meanwhile, other regulated entities are following the legal requirements. As a consequence, they have incurred expenses a violator has not, since money spent for compliance is money not available for other business uses. Thus, a violator could easily gain an economic advantage by spending its money elsewhere.

To address this problem, the EPA has issued penalty policies. Starting with the statutory maximum penalty, the EPA makes adjustments to the penalty based on factors such as ability to pay, gravity and duration of the violation, history of compliance, and economic benefit. The EPA has long taken the position that a penalty cannot be reduced below the economic benefit realized from noncompliance so that there is no incentive for violation.

The BEN model takes some of the pain out of calculating the economic benefit. The inputs cover the initial cost of installing the required equipment—whether it is a one-time expenditure, whether it is tax deductible—its operation and maintenance costs; noncompliance date and date of compliance; useful life of the equipment; the marginal tax rate for the business; the inflation, discount and interest rates.

With all these factors taken into consideration, it sounds as if a penalty calculated by BEN would be indisputable. It is not, though, because the result is wholly dependent on the input. Therefore, even the conclusion reached through BEN may be subject to negotiation, particularly when the violator could have achieved compliance through several methods and the EPA has used the cost of the most expensive one for the input. If the violator is in compliance at the time the penalty is calculated, determining the economic benefit is simpler. Actual costs can be used as the inputs for the program, along with the assumption that the regulated party should have implemented the modification earlier.

Economic benefit is sometimes a difficult concept for some regulated parties to grasp and hotly contested even by knowledgeable businesses. They contend, basically, that they did not realize an economic benefit from noncompliance. Often they bring out their books to prove that they did not divert compliance funds elsewhere. If they had already budgeted for environmental expenses then decided to use the money elsewhere, the benefit would be clear. Most of the time, though, the compliance delay will be the result of not borrowing the money, either from an outside source or another internal account. Rarely will a windfall be apparent because of delayed compliance. However, during the period when compliance was deferred, all associated costs were postponed. A penalty that does not recognize this component of compliance tends to reward those who delay and discourages law-abiding businesses.

 BEST AVAILABLE CONTROL TECHNOLOGY See **air pollution control technology; air quality control regions.**

 BEST AVAILABLE TECHNOLOGY See **air quality control regions; Clean Water Act.**

BHOPAL On 3 December 1984, a Union Carbide plant in Bhopal, India, released approximately 30 tons of methyl isocyanate into the air. Two thousand people died immediately, and estimates eventually rose to 3,500. Over 200,000 people were injured from the gas. Five years later a survey of the immediate community revealed that up to 70 percent of the inhabitants were ill or disabled.

The government of India sued Union Carbide. When the case was settled, Union Carbide paid 470 million dollars in exchange for release of all claims against it. It denied liability, saying an employee deliberately caused the discharge.

Soon after the Bhopal catastrophe, a plant in Institute, West Virginia, released aldicarb oxime. Later, in Basel, Switzerland, the Sandoz chemical factory warehouse burned, instantly sending more chemicals into the Rhine than are normally released in a year.

Reaction to these disasters was strong. It was obvious, after these two incidents, that accidents like these could destroy life quickly and without warning, and that many people are vulnerable. The public outcry reached Congress and resulted in a significant change in the **Superfund Amendments and Reauthorization Act** (SARA). It had become apparent that cleanup and control of pollutants as they are normally managed would not benefit communities with potentially dangerous chemicals close to them. The focus shifted to planning, information, and emergency response to unexpected releases of harmful chemicals. The section of SARA that deals with this topic is Title III, and many practitioners refer to it as SARA Title III. The full name of the law reveals its intent: the **Emergency Planning and Community Right-To-Know Act** (EPCRA).

EPCRA requires businesses to file information on the chemicals it uses or makes, prepare emergency action plans, disclose the amounts of chemicals it releases, and cooperate with authorities. It establishes state and local emergency planning organizations and sets up a system to coordinate emergency response. See also **State Emergency Response Commission.**

BIOCHEMICAL OXYGEN DEMAND (BOD) The measurement used by scientists to determine the effect of pollutants discharged into water bodies.

Aquatic life requires oxygen, but some pollutants encourage the growth of microorganisms and bacteria that deplete the amount of oxygen available for larger creatures. The **Clean Water Act** establishes a permitting program, called the **National Pollutant Discharge Elimination System,** under which dischargers are issued permits with limits on the types of effluent released into surface waters.

One frequent parameter within such permits is biochemical oxygen demand. BOD is a calculated number that results from multiplying fats, proteins, and carbohydrates by specified numbers, or the permittee may rely on generally accepted published values. The numbers reflect the amount of dissolved oxygen used over a five-day period to break down the material. Because of the five-day span, the parameter listed on a permit is often called BOD5. The permit will establish a limit on the amount of pollutants with biochemical oxygen demand so the dissolved oxygen does not reach critical levels.

Pollutants that demand and use dissolved oxygen are organic materials. They may be materials discharged by food canning operations, for example. However, the most commonly released pollutant with a high biochemical oxygen demand is sewage. See also **water pollution control technology.**

BIOREMEDIATION　See **cleanup technologies.**

BIOTECHNOLOGY　The use of science and technology to modify species, establish them in new locations where their characteristics are advantageous to humans, and alter them genetically for specific purposes.

For thousands of years, humans have altered the genetic makeup of organisms through selective breeding. But now, newer technologies such as gene splicing, gene fusion, and DNA recombination can accelerate changes and even create entirely new genetically engineered microorganisms called *designer bugs.* They have many applications in agriculture, pharmaceutical and chemical manufacturing, and environmental cleanup.

Although genetic engineering is a relatively new form of biotechnology, the **Environmental Protection Agency** (EPA) has already taken an interest in it. It is not alone. Several other agencies have an interest in genetic engineering as well. The Food and Drug Administration, the Federal Department of Agriculture, and the National Institutes of Health cooperate to deal with this evolving science. The Office of Science and Technology Policy (OSTP), an organization that works closely with the president, has also influenced regulatory practices.

In 1986, the federal agencies concerned with biotechnology issued a cooperative statement that outlined how they interacted, where their authority originated, and what they would regulate. Guidance and policy statements, interpretations of jurisdiction, and discussions of the issues have been the basis of the early regulations. Rules for development of new microorganisms have not yet been established. Though both the Department of Agriculture and the EPA focus on these issues, the discussion here will focus on the EPA.

The EPA uses two primary laws as the basis of its regulations: the **Toxic Substances Control Act** (TSCA) and the **Federal Insecticide, Fungicide, and Rodenticide Act** (FIFRA). TSCA covers new chemical substances and those determined by the EPA to have a significant new use. FIFRA sets procedures for licensing of pesticides and gives the EPA authority to gather information about them. In addition, other environmental statutes could be used to address particular concerns, such as the **Clean Air Act,** the **Clean Water Act,** the Resource Conservation and Recovery Act, and the **Comprehensive Environmental Response, Compensation, and Liability Act**. However, these statutes have not yet been at the forefront of environmental review of this issue.

FIFRA jurisdiction is perhaps easier to see than TSCA jurisdiction. Since many of the organisms being developed function as pesticides, FIFRA applies without stretching definitions. When the EPA began using FIFRA to regulate genetically engineered microbes, it issued guidance, along with an information packet.

A person who wanted to obtain an experimental use permit would notify the EPA, supply it with the information requested and supplementary information upon demand. If the permit is granted, testing may go forward. Testing means, in most situations, that the microbial pesticide will be released into the environment to prove its worth.

The Office of Science and Technology Policy published a policy statement to establish criteria for federal agencies to follow when deciding what type of discretionary jurisdiction to exercise. Tension between the desire for scientific advance and protection of the environment is apparent in the statement. Basically, the OSTP, in conjunction with former Vice President Dan Quayle and the Council on Competitiveness, determined that a risk-based analysis should be used, and the analysis must not be unreasonable. The focus is to be the product, its characteristics and risks, not the process that created it. For example, if the product is to be used as an insecticide, the proper review would be done by the EPA under the Federal Insecticide, Fungicide, and Rodenticide Act. If, on the other hand, the product is to be used as a food additive or substitute, the Food and Drug Administration would review it. Performance-based standards instead of design standards are to be used in considering the permit application. The focus is whether the product achieves its purpose, and not how it was created. Regulatory review is to be minimized to the extent possible. However, public health and welfare are to be protected.

In February 1993, the EPA issued proposed rules for FIFRA that followed the policy statement. It decided, after requiring experimental use permits (EUPs) for genetically altered microbial pesticides, that many should be exempt from notification and EUP components of FIFRA. The EPA believes the history of registered microbial pesticides has demonstrated they are safe in small-scale testing projects. Therefore, the need for a permit will be determined based on risks, but will usually not be required if EPA rules are followed.

The EPA uses TSCA as a catch-all for microbes that are not pesticides and do not fall under other TSCA exemptions. Although TSCA is limited to regulation of chemical substances, the EPA has seized jurisdiction of genetically engineered organisms by breaking down organic substances into their smallest component: the identifiable molecule, which is technically a chemical substance. To date, this interpretation of the EPA's right to regulate under TSCA has not been tested.

Under TSCA, the agency gets a notice called a **premanufacturing notification** (PMN) before the organism or chemical is manufactured. Information must accompany the PMN if it is available. The EPA can request more data and testing; it may also want additional information about the environment into which it is to be released. The procedure gives the EPA an opportunity to prescreen the substance. See also **cleanup technologies; water pollution control technology.**

BUBBLE CONCEPT   When federal air pollution permits were first issued, it was not uncommon for a single facility to have numerous permits because each piece of equipment was viewed as an isolated pollution source. The idea of regulating the emissions of the facility as a whole—as if there were a dome or bubble over it—was attractive to industry. It allowed a company to vary its processes and still stay beneath the allowable total, even if one or more of the individual pieces of equipment exceeded the permitted limits. The concept was resisted by the **Environmental Protection Agency** (EPA) in the beginning, but it has gradually won acceptance. The **Clean Air Act Amendments of 1990** authorize emission allowances and emission trading, and permit a facility to shift allowances from one source to another.

In some locations, a new facility may be able to begin operations by purchasing emissions that are not being used by an existing source. But in nonattainment areas—that is, areas that have not achieved the standards set by the Environmental Protection Agency (EPA) for specific pollutants— a new source will probably not be permitted to use all of the allowances it purchases. So if a source wishes to emit only 100 tons of a particular pollutant, it may have to buy an allowance of 150 tons. This is a way of retiring some of the allowances so the area can attain compliance. If it wants to emit more than 100 tons, the new source will have to obtain credits from another facility within the same air control region. This is an extension of the bubble concept as it was originally conceived, because the entire area is within the bubble. For that reason, the emissions for a given air control region are frozen. See also **air permits; air quality control regions; Clean Air Act Amendments of 1990; emission trading.**

BURFORD, ANNE GORSUCH (1942–) Administrator of the **Environmental Protection Agency,** appointed by Ronald Reagan [see **Reagan, Ronald**] in 1980. She resigned under fire in 1983 after refusing to turn over papers to Congress (under the Reagan administration's orders) and was cited for contempt of Congress.

The Reagan administration was openly hostile to environmental regulation. Reagan's agenda from the beginning was to cut regulation and help private business, and his appointees were spokespersons for that philosophy. Like James Watt [see **Watt, James**], who worked to privatize federal lands, and her husband Robert Burford, who opened federal lands to low fee public grazing, Burford's agenda also favored private industry. A number of industry representatives were brought into the EPA under Burford's direction.

Mrs. Burford stated her mission plainly: reducing the "overburden" of environmental regulations. She did not encourage enforcement efforts. Rita Lavelle [see **Lavelle, Rita**], chief of the **Superfund** program under Burford, allowed the program to become so inefficient that Congress conducted an inquiry into the **hazardous waste** program. Eventually, Lavelle resigned and went to prison for six months for perjury.

Besides James Watt, Reagan's widely disliked Secretary of Interior, Lavelle and Burford received the most uncomplimentary attention from the press. They were not alone in their gutting of environmental enforcement, but they took much of the heat. See also **Comprehensive Environmental Response, Compensation, and Liability Act; Ruckelshaus, William D.**

BUSH, GEORGE HERBERT WALKER (1924–) The 41st president of the United States and self-designated "environmental president." His environmental record was weak, but it was significantly better than Ronald Reagan's [see **Reagan, Ronald**]. One of the major accomplishments during the Bush years was the passage and signing of the **Clean Air Act Amendments of 1990,** sweeping changes that strengthened the act considerably.

CALIFORNIA COASTAL COMMISSION V. GRANITE ROCK
CO. A 1987 case in which the U.S. Supreme Court determined that states may regulate on federal public lands as long as the purpose of the regulation is based on environmental concerns and not merely limiting on land use.

CARSON, RACHEL (1907–1964) Aquatic biologist and author of four books, including *Silent Spring*, the book credited with starting the modern environmental movement. In *Silent Spring*, Carson argues that pesticide use, notably **DDT** applications, had far-reaching effects on the food chain. By the time Carson wrote her warnings, some birds were in danger of extinction due to the thinning of their eggshells caused by ingesting DDT. Because of the wide distribution of *Silent Spring*, international awareness of the dangers of pesticide persistence in the environment increased until, in 1972, DDT was banned in the United States and in many other countries. The first major revision of the **Federal Insecticide, Fungicide, and Rodenticide Act** was enacted that year as well. Carson's work is thought to have brought about these changes.

CHARACTERISTIC WASTE A waste that is designated hazardous because it exhibits one of four qualities: toxicity, ignitability, corrosivity, and reactivity. **Hazardous waste**s are regulated by the **Resource Conservation and Recovery Act,** which sets forth only general guidelines. It defines hazardous wastes as those that, when improperly managed, cause an increase in mortality, irreversible or incapacitating illnesses, or pose a substantial hazard to human health or the environment. Assigned the task of fleshing out the statute, the **Environmental Protection Agency** listed specific wastes as hazardous (**listed wastes**) and

determined what characteristics of other wastes would make them hazardous. The criteria had to be quantifiable, so that people could determine when a waste became hazardous.

Wastes must be tested to determine whether they meet the criteria set out in the regulations for hazardous wastes. The characteristic wastes cause one or more problems unless they are handled carefully. Ignitable wastes can cause a fire or feed one; corrosive wastes can escape metal containers, corrode other containers and release other wastes, and cause damage to tissue; reactive wastes are unstable and react with other wastes; wastes that can leach toxic materials into the groundwater can impact large areas. As science is better able to test and quantify other aspects of wastes that fit Congress's definition, new characteristics may be added.

CHERNOBYL   The largest nuclear power plant disaster in history occurred at Chernobyl in the Soviet Union in April 1986. Human error led to an explosion that blew off a huge lid, destroyed much of the concrete containment around a reactor, and spewed radioactive fallout into the atmosphere. At first, the Soviet Union played down the incident, but when the Swedish government, among others, measured the large amounts of radioactivity in the air, the USSR admitted a major problem had occurred. All of Europe, large portions of the Soviet Union, and the Scandinavian countries were eventually affected. Though the number of victims is unknown, estimates have ranged from thousands to one million or more.

CHESAPEAKE BAY FOUNDATION, INC. v. GWALTNEY OF SMITHFIELD, LTD.   This case determined one of the restraints on citizen suits, primarily that a citizen must claim ongoing violations in the complaint. A subsidiary rule, developed in a later case with the same name, requires an ongoing violation for each claim made.

For example, if a factory violates its permit by discharging too much arsenic and lead but corrects the conditions so the problem cannot recur, a citizen may not be able to bring a lawsuit. However, if the condition has not been corrected and the factory has simply had no violations for a year, a citizen may be able bring a successful suit by stating that violations are intermittent. To obtain penalties for both violations, the citizen would have to mention each pollutant (arsenic and lead) in his complaint.

These restrictions limit citizens more than they limit government. The **Environmental Protection Agency** has the right to sue for past violations without regard to whether the violator has committed additional violations, even if the offender has fixed the problem and is not likely to have a new problem. See **citizen suit.**

CHLOROFLUOROCARBONS (CFCS) A class of manmade chemicals used as aerosol propellants, refrigerants, fire suppressants, and in the production of packaging materials. CFCs are composed of chlorine, fluorine, and carbon and were originally thought to be a miracle solution to many problems. Unfortunately, the stability of these chemicals has caused significant damage to the environment, resulting in an international effort to phase them out.

CFCs do not break down naturally; they accumulate in the upper atmosphere and react with ultraviolet rays. As ultraviolet radiation reacts with the CFCs, chlorine is released, as well as fluorine. Once the chlorine and fluorine are liberated, they impact **ozone.** Ozone is a form of oxygen that is comprised of three atoms of oxygen. It is formed in the upper atmosphere as oxygen molecules (with two atoms of oxygen) are broken apart by ultraviolet radiation and then combine with other oxygen molecules. The bond that holds ozone together is weak, and both chlorine and fluorine are highly reactive. They attack and destroy the ozone molecules.

The current concern about CFCs has resulted primarily from their role in depleting stratospheric ozone, though some scientists claim CFCs also contribute to **global warming.** This phenomenon is a warming of the earth due to solar energy that cannot escape from the earth's atmosphere. CFCs are thought to be even more effective than carbon dioxide in trapping radiation.

Because the problems caused by CFCs are global, two major international conferences have been held to address them: the Vienna Conference on Substances Which Deplete the Ozone in 1985 and the Montreal Conference on Substances Which Deplete the Ozone in 1987. The latter conference was the most successful, leading to the **Montreal Protocol,** an agreement signed by over one hundred nations. Developed countries readily agreed to implement the Montreal Protocol, especially in the light of evidence that the problem is worse than it appeared at the time of the Montreal conference. Developing countries, on the other hand, balked at the agreement. They wanted the economic opportunities CFCs had provided for the developed nations. To resolve this conflict, the developed nations have agreed to share their technology with the developing countries.

The United States regulates CFCs under two statutes, the **Toxic Substances Control Act** and the **Clean Air Act Amendments of 1990.** The Toxic Substances Control Act (TSCA) lists CFCs as toxic and prohibits their use in aerosols. However, the most powerful statute in this area is the Clean Air Act Amendments, which were adopted in 1990 to include an entire section on regulating chemicals that deplete the ozone. Under the act, most CFCs will be banned by 1996.

Substitutes for CFCs are not readily available, though. Scientists created hydrochlorofluorocarbons (HCFCs), hoping they would cause less damage, but they too have been implicated in ozone depletion and are on the list for elimination. In order to prevent other harmful substances from being introduced as substitutes for the phased-out CFCs, the United States established the Significant New Alteratives Program to monitor new compounds.

CITIZEN SUIT   A lawsuit brought by a person or organization against someone who is accused of violating environmental laws or against the **Environmental Protection Agency** (EPA) for not doing a nondiscretionary job. Citizen suits must be authorized by the law that prohibits the violation, but many environmental statutes contain provisions for citizen suits.

Most citizen suits have been brought under the **Clean Water Act,** probably because evidence of violation is given routinely to the EPA in required reports, and citizens can obtain the reports simply by requesting them. Citizens cannot collect the fines, though; since they act in place of the government, any fines collected go to the U.S. Treasury. If, however, the citizen settles the lawsuit, the settlement agreement may provide for some payment to the citizen or group. Attorneys' fees and other costs are typically awarded if the citizen takes the case to court and wins.

Requirements for Citizen Suits

All of the citizen suit provisions in the various environmental laws require sixty to ninety days notice to both the government and the person alleged to be violating the law before a complaint may be filed. This requirement allows the government to review the situation and decide whether it should bring the suit itself. Or, if the government itself is the target of the lawsuit, as it would be if EPA failed to issue regulations within a time limit set by a statute, it gives the government a chance to act.

After notice is given and the waiting period expires, the lawsuit may be filed by a person who claims to have been harmed by the defendant's action. *Person* in legal terminology is broadly defined; a person can be an individual or a public interest group, a business, or a trade organization. Courts have been very generous in finding that a person has an interest in stopping the violations.

Another requirement for a citizen suit is set forth in an important case, ***Gwaltney of Smithfield, Ltd. v. Chesapeake Bay Foundation:*** the suit must claim that the violations are ongoing. Though the citizen bringing the lawsuit need not show that the violations are continuous, the suit must claim that they are at least intermittent or likely to recur. The EPA, however, is not limited by this requirement. It can sue for past violations, even though the problem has been corrected and the offender is complying with the law at the time the suit is filed.

Finally, citizen plaintiffs must show that some harm is related to the violation. Again, courts are fairly generous on this point. The violation must be connected in some way to the harm, but the violator does not have to be the only person who contributed to the pollution. For example, if a company discharges more oil and grease than its permit allows and a film is seen on the river, that is enough to connect the company to the harm, even if other companies also violate their permits.

CITIZENS TO PRESERVE OVERTON PARK V. VOLPE (OVERTON PARK)

CITIZENS TO PRESERVE OVERTON PARK V. VOLPE (OVERTON PARK) A suit brought against the Department of Transportation to force the secretary to consider alternative siting for a highway in lieu of going through Overton Park. Overton Park is a municipal park in Memphis, and the statutes in question prohibited use of federal funds to build highways through public parks if feasible and prudent alternatives existed. Volpe, the Transportation Secretary, had not stated any reasons in his decision to support the building of the highway.

Overton Park is primarily an administrative law case. It established the authority of courts to review agency decisions and discussed the various standards of review under the **Administrative Procedure Act.** That law defines requirements for administrative agencies, including the types of **hearings** and publish participation permitted during certain formal agency procedures. It also specifies what standards the courts are to use when deciding whether a particular agency has overstepped its authority.

The citizens in *Overton Park* obviously wanted a formal rule-making procedure and an in-depth review of Volpe's decision. The agency, the Department of Transportation, felt the secretary had unlimited discretion to make his decision.

Because the statutes themselves did not require a formal record, the Supreme Court did not require one. However, the Court found the statutes to be quite clear in directing the agency to consider alternatives to going through parks. No record of that analysis was available; thus, the Court could not determine whether such an analysis took place.

The standard of review adopted by the Supreme Court was the one most commonly applicable to agency actions: was the action of the secretary "arbitrary and capricious"? That standard is the least difficult of all review standards to meet. Nonetheless, the Court could not answer the question because it had no administrative record before it.

Rather than vacating the secretary's decision and sending it back to the Department of Transportation to start over, the Supreme Court sent the case back to the district court. The Supreme Court made suggestions as to how the district court could gather enough information to decide whether the secretary had given proper consideration to the statutory limits. Testimony could be taken or formal findings prepared by the secretary.

The major holding emerging from this case is still valid. The court determined that actions by an agency are always reviewable by a court unless the statute prohibits it or the agency's power to regulate is so broadly written that the actions are up to the discretion of the agency. To be reviewable, however, the agency must have sufficient evidence of how it reached the decision.

CLEAN AIR ACT   The federal statute that controls **air pollutant** discharges. Revisions to this law have been important, culminating in the **Clean Air Act Amendments of 1990.** This entry will cover the basic structure of the act up to the 1990 changes, which significantly altered many aspects of the statute.

Before the Clean Air Act was passed in 1963, the only federal law dealing with air pollution was the Air Pollution Control Act of 1955, which focused on research and financial assistance to states. The Department of Health, Education and Welfare (HEW) was the key agency under both laws, but even in the 1963 statute its role was weak, limited to establishing air quality standards that were not binding on the states. Congress attempted a restructuring of the act in 1967. The new amendments required the states to establish air quality regions, air standards, and to develop plans to reach the standards. But again, the changes did not carry the nation toward cleaner air. When the **Environmental Protection Agency** (EPA) was created in 1970, Congress seized the opportunity to write environmental statutes for the new agency to enforce. The Clean Air Act Amendments of 1970 led the way to modern environmental law. The act was amended again in 1977; the following discussion deals with the statute through those revisions.

The Core of the Program: National Ambient Air Quality Standards

With the 1970 amendments, basic assumptions in the law were changed, and the Clean Air Act came into its own. It had become clear that the states would not regulate air pollution voluntarily. Congress, acknowledging that a stronger federal role was necessary, gave the job to the EPA and required that the agency develop **National Ambient Air Quality Standards** (NAAQSs) for certain pollutants. This time the standards were mandatory.

Ambient air was not defined in the Clean Air Act, but the EPA defined it in its regulations as any air outside buildings that is generally accessible to the public. The *Natural Resources Defense Council v. Train* case upheld the agency's definition.

The act requires that the EPA set two types of standards for ambient air quality: primary standards, designed to protect human health (with an ample margin of safety); and secondary standards, designed to protect public welfare. The standards are to be reviewed every four years and modified as necessary. Pollutants regulated initially included carbon monoxide, nitrogen dioxide [see **nitrogen oxides**], **particulates**, **ozone**, **sulfur dioxide**, lead, and hydrocarbons, although hydrocarbons are no longer part of the standards. Most of the secondary standards are identical to the primary ones.

This time states did not get to choose whether they would go along with the new federal limits. They were required to designate air quality control regions within their states and submit a state implementation plan (SIP) to the EPA showing how the state would achieve the National Ambient Air Quality Standards.

If, as has often been the case, an air quality control region cannot achieve all of the standards, it is declared *nonattainment* for the pollutant it has not controlled. At that point, the state must either demonstrate that its implementation plan will bring the area into attainment or revise its plan. If the EPA believes the plan is inadequate, it may, at any time, require a revision. This required revision is described as a *SIP call*. Plans must also be amended whenever the statute requires it.

Congress included a deadline for meeting the NAAQSs in the 1970 act, but for the most part, the standards were not met. The 1977 revisions extended the compliance deadline but gave the EPA no discretion to extend it further. Still, over seventy cities missed the 1987 deadline for compliance. So when it was again time to review the act in 1990, Congress took its task very seriously.

Regulating Existing Sources of Air Pollution

State implementation plans include several methods of air pollution control: technology changes, end of process control equipment, and restrictions on new sources. Most of the regulations are implemented through permitting. Air pollution standards are often technology-based, with baffling names such as "best available control technology" and "lowest achievable emission rate."

Existing major stationary sources of air pollution must meet reasonably available control technology. The traditional manner of reducing pollutants at an existing facility is retrofitting, which means improving existing technology. Often it simply means adding control equipment to the end of the process, such as adding an incinerator to burn volatile components of a discharge.

Regulating New Sources

Congress established several programs in the Clean Air Act to control sources of air pollution: **New Source Performance Standards, Prevention of Significant Deterioration,** and nonattainment permitting. All of these programs focus on *major stationary sources.* Generally, a major source is one capable of emitting 100 tons or more per year of a regulated pollutant. A *new source* may be a completely new construction or a major modification of an existing source.

The issue of when a change to an existing facility becomes subject to permitting was discussed in the *Wisconsin Electric Power Co. v. Reilly* case (generally called the *WEPCo*). In that case, the company had begun a massive reconstruction of its plant. The EPA determined that the changes were significant enough to require regulation under the new source provisions; the company argued that the construction was only a routine replacement of equipment and therefore a **New Source Review** should not be required. The case had important implications for utilities, but other industries also watched with interest.

The court upheld the EPA's right to consider the work a major modification but did not agree with its manner of calculating the potential to emit. As a result of the case, the EPA wrote regulations to clarify the criteria for New Source Review, and its position is no longer as harsh as its original determination.

New Source Performance Standards

Certain businesses, including most industrial processes, have so much potential to release air pollutants that limits on their emissions are stated in federal regulations. New companies falling within one of these categories must meet these standards if they begin construction after the date the regulations are proposed. So far, the EPA has listed sixty-one such categories and created regulations for them. Examples include portland cement plants, municipal waste combustors, incinerators, copper smelters, steel plants, glass manufacturing plants, and industrial surface coating.

New Source Review in Attainment Regions

Even if the operation isn't listed within the established categories, new major sources (or modifications of existing sources) must go through a review and permitting process. The stringency of permit requirements will depend on whether the area is an attainment or nonattainment region.

In attainment areas (areas that have met the National Ambient Air Quality Standards), new sources must show they will not cause the air quality to worsen to the point of becoming nonattainment and that they will meet the technology level required for control.

Prevention of Significant Deterioration

The Clean Air Act regulates maintenance of air quality through the Prevention of Significant Deterioration (PSD) provisions. Once an air quality region meets the standards, the state is required to maintain them.

Under this part of the law, each air quality region is designated as a Class I, II, or III area, and the class determines how much deterioration is allowed. (This does not mean that the state can allow the region to become nonattainment.) Class I areas are national parks. For the most part the rest of the nation is Class II, which means that a small amount of degradation is permitted as long as the NAAQSs are met. At this time, there are no Class III areas.

New source review in an attainment area includes obtaining a permit if the operation could discharge 250 tons per year of any regulated pollutant or 100 tons per year if the source fits within certain categories. Major modifications or reconstruction of existing facilities are also subject to the program. New sources in attainment regions must use best available control technology (BACT). The states, with guidance from the EPA, determine what is best, taking cost into consideration.

Nonattainment Permits

If a new source will be located in a nonattainment area [see **nonattainment areas**], the applicable technology is called the lowest achievable emission rate (LAER). Because the area already has a problem, smaller sources are considered major and subject to permitting. Sources that could discharge 10 tons per year of the pollutant in question or 100 tons per year of any regulated pollutant fall into the major category in nonattainment areas. For example, if the region is nonattainment for particulates only and the source can emit 10 tons or more of particulates per year, it must have a permit; but if it can release 10 tons or more of sulfur dioxide and nothing else, it will not be considered a major source.

Offsets and Bubbles

In nonattainment regions, the state may require the new source to obtain reductions from other plants in the area to offset the additional emissions it will contribute. If the new source itself has other plants in the area, it is possible for it to achieve this goal itself by shutting down operations, changing control equipment, or installing other technology at one of its own plants. Otherwise, the permit hopeful may have to purchase credits or cooperate with other sources.

When a new source wants to build in a nonattainment area, it is sometimes required to obtain reductions from existing sources that exceed the amount of pollutant it will emit. The excess is called an offset. For example, if a company wants to build and will have the capacity to emit 10 tons of sulfur dioxide in a nonattainment region for sulfur dioxide, it may be required to get another source to reduce the same emissions by 11 tons. The ratio will be greater in areas that have bigger problems. The purpose of these offsets is to improve air quality rather than simply maintaining the status quo.

An offset applies to a reduction at a different facility, but a bubble involves a single facility or complex at which adjustments are made from more than one emission source within a company in order to bring the entire business into compliance. Bubbles were controversial when finally sanctioned by the EPA. Allowing a source to shift processes around or control one emission point tightly so more of the same pollutant can be allowed to escape from another was determined to be permissible, but not everyone agreed.

Chevron U.S.A. v. Natural Resources Defense Council was the case that finally determined that the EPA could allow bubbles. The court decided the statute gave a lot of discretion to the EPA to establish permits and get the nation into compliance with the Clean Air Act. How the agency accomplished this, the court stated, was a matter of policy.

Mobile Sources

The 1970 Clean Air Act introduced control of vehicular pollution. Design of vehicles was the primary focus in the beginning; Congress required and the EPA implemented changes in fuel usage, emission controls, and reduction of hydrocarbons and carbon monoxide. As in many environmental provisions, availability of technology was not considered, so vehicle manufacturers were forced to create the methods of control.

Hazardous Air Pollutants or Air Toxics

In addition to more common pollutants, the Clean Air Act also addressed hazardous air pollutants. The regulatory program was designated the National Emission Standards for Hazardous Air Pollutants, and the EPA administrator was directed to list the pollutants to be regulated in this fashion. By 1990, only a few had been listed: vinyl chloride, benzene, asbestos, coke oven emissions, beryllium, mercury, inorganic arsenic, and radionuclides. Congress changed the program in 1990 to list 189 substances as air toxics and bring them under the regulations. See **Clean Air Act Amendments of 1990.**

CLEAN AIR ACT AMENDMENTS OF 1990 The latest revision to the **Clean Air Act.** Although the 1990 amendments left the National Ambient Air Quality Standards alone and preserved the core of the act, they added new programs to address problems that had never been managed before. This entry discusses those changes.

Acid Rain

The Clean Air Act Amendments (CAAA) established a program to reduce the pollutants that can cause **acid rain**: **sulfur dioxide** and **nitrogen oxides**. Because the largest amounts of those pollutants come from utility companies, they are regulated under the provisions. Other sources of sulfur dioxide emissions may choose to be subject to them.

The object of the acid rain requirements is to reduce sulfur dioxide emissions by 10 million tons from 1980 levels, and nitrogen oxides by 2 million tons. Electric utilities have been given allocations specifying the amount of sulfur dioxide they may emit, and the allotment will be reduced in 2000. Nitrogen oxides will be controlled by use of improved control equipment, and the **Environmental Protection Agency** (EPA) is required to set emission limits for different types of boilers and steam generating units.

The most controversial part of the CAAA is found in the acid rain provisions. In 1970 the United States had opted to manage pollution through what is often called the *command and control* approach: set standards and force businesses to control the emissions. This approach had some success, but Congress built a new scheme into the acid rain provisions. Limits are set in the form of allowances, permits to emit a specified amount of a particular pollutant. Allowances must be purchased before they may be used. Businesses subject to the law may purchase or trade allowances, either by approaching other companies or by participating in the EPA's allowance auction. The EPA keeps a small reserve of allowances to sell to new utilities that are unable to obtain allowances on the open market.

The idea of using market-based strategy to control pollution angers people who believe that companies must be ordered to comply with the law. They argue that selling a pollution credit is immoral and that the only way to cut pollution is to punish companies that emit more than they should. However, the market-based acid rain provisions do not allow unchecked pollution. Utilities that exceed their allowances are not only subject to penalties, but they must also subtract the amount of their excess emissions from their next year's allowances.

Stratospheric Ozone Protection

The United States signed the **Montreal Protocol,** which committed many nations to reduce their emissions of the substances that deplete **ozone.** See **chlorofluorocarbons.** When the Clean Air Act was amended in 1990, Congress added a section that phases out the chemical compounds considered to be the most damaging to the ozone layer. The Amendments list a number of substances to be reduced and divides them into two classes, depending on their potential for harm. Production of Class I substances such as halons, carbon tetrachloride, and methyl chloroform must cease by 2002. Production of Class II substances (hydrochlorofluorocarbons) is forbidden after 2030. The amendments allow the EPA to accelerate these deadlines, and it has already moved to do so. They also address venting of gases during servicing of air conditioning equipment, reducing the production of regulated substances until they are eliminated, labeling products with ozone-depleting substance in them, and establish a program to find acceptable alternatives. Regulated materials used for fire suppression, military defense, or medical purposes may be exempted by the EPA if suitable substitutes do not exist.

Nonattainment Regions

The amendments retain the older provisions involving nonattainment, but Congress added many new requirements, hoping to finally bring the regions into compliance. The first change involves a finer distinction among the regions and how far out of compliance they are from the **National Ambient Air Quality Standards** for each pollutant. Nonattainment regions for ozone, for example, may be extreme, severe, serious, moderate, or marginal. The more serious the problem, the more controls are required. States with nonattainment regions must amend their **state implementation plan**s to include information about the actual emissions, adoption of reasonably available control measures, provisions to show reasonable further progress, a permit program, identification of new source emissions that will be allowed, and any other measure necessary to achieve compliance.

Because the EPA had been lax concerning offsets in nonattainment regions, Congress established new ratios in the law. If a new source wants to locate in a nonattainment region, it must obtain reductions from another source in the area—which was true under the 1970 Clean Air Act—but under the amendments, the amount of the offset increases as the severity of nonattainment increases.

Ozone is the pollutant that most commonly causes violations of the National Ambient Air Quality Standards, and the amendments prescribe numerous revisions to state plans to attain the standard. They set up a rolling scheme: each nonattainment region is required to meet the minimum, but the requirements increase as the classification worsens. Examples of the criteria to be met in extreme areas are inspection and maintenance of motor vehicles, vapor recovery for fueling, clean fuel fleet programs, reasonably available control technology revisions, employer trip reduction plan requirements, and transportation control measures. In ozone nonattainment regions, the degree of nonattainment determines the number of years the state has to come into compliance. Extreme areas, for example, have 20 years, but marginal areas have only 3. (Only the South Coast Management Air Quality Region in California is classified as extreme.)

Two other pollutants, carbon monoxide and **particulate**s, are subdivided into classes: serious and moderate. All **nonattainment areas** for particulates were initially classified as moderate, though the EPA may alter this classification. Nonattainment regions for the remaining pollutants regulated by the NAAQSs, nitrogen dioxide, lead, and sulfur oxides, were not included in the categorization scheme because they are not as troublesome. However, states with nonattainment regions must still revise their plans.

Often the difficulty of achieving compliance with the standards cannot be addressed by one state. Air moves across state borders, and states have been baffled by attempts to deal with the problems alone. The Clean Air Act Amendments of 1990 authorize states to have the EPA declare an air transport region. They then work together with the other state or states involved to solve the nonattainment puzzle.

Air Toxics

The Clean Air Act was less than successful in dealing with **hazardous air pollutants**. Only a few substances were controlled through the EPA's regulations, and many battles were fought over them. With the Clean Air Act Amendments of 1990, Congress took the problem out of the hands of the EPA and compiled its own list of 189 hazardous air pollutants. It then ordered the EPA to develop standards. Any person may petition the agency to have substances added to or deleted from the list, but the EPA may delete a substance only after finding that it is "not reasonably anticipated to cause adverse health or environmental effects."

Duties assigned to the EPA include listing major categories of sources of the hazardous air pollutants, and then later listing area sources that, although they may not be major, can contribute to an area problem. For hazardous air pollutants, sources considered major are often smaller than for other types of pollutants. The definition includes any source capable of emitting 10 tons per year of any one hazardous pollutant or 25 tons of any combination.

The technology required for control of hazardous air pollutants is called maximum achievable control technology (MACT). Regulations are to be health-based and do not consider cost. The EPA must determine what technology satisfies the requirement and publish its determination.

Comprehensive Permitting

One additional provision of the amendments should benefit the businesses that need permits: comprehensive permits. Under this provision, one permit rather than many separate permits will cover all of the requirements for the source. Submission of a completed application serves as an interim permit until the final one is issued.

Under this new revision, it is possible for the permittee to be shielded from enforcement. To be eligible for a permit shield, the source must be in compliance with the permit, the permit must include all applicable requirements of the Clean Air Act, and the agency must state explicitly that the permittee is not subject to other provisions. The easiest route for the permitting agency is to set specific limits, then state that the permittee must also comply with any other applicable provisions. It is difficult to imagine a change in this policy, since it protects the permitting authority in case it missed something during the permitting process.

Enforcement Provisions

The amendments also increased the amount the EPA may assess under the administrative penalty sections of the Clean Air Act and changed most criminal offenses into felonies. For the first time, EPA inspectors have the power to issue field citations for violations.

CLEAN WATER ACT   The common name for the Federal Water Pollution Control Act, the statute that controls pollution in surface waters in the United States. Enacted in 1972, the Clean Water Act has been amended several times but retains the most important aspects of the original law.

History

In the early history of water pollution control, power lay in the hands of the states; they were supposed to establish water quality standards and enforce them. The federal government, through the Health, Education, and Welfare Department, had a role only in research and distributing money. It used the **Refuse Act of 1899** to control discharges but ran into many obstacles. So Congress overhauled the system in 1972 and assigned the job of overseeing it to the **Environmental Protection Agency** (EPA).

Basic Structure

The Clean Water Act prohibits any person from discharging a pollutant from a point source into navigable waters without a permit. The key terms in this statement are defined broadly. *Person* includes an individual, company, municipality (or other government), partnership or organization. *Discharge* is any type of release, accidental or purposeful. *Pollutant* covers any substance other than clean water, including heat, chemicals, and dyes. A *point source* is any discernible manner of carrying the discharge. It can be a sewer, a pipe, a ditch, or anything that brings the discharge to the water. Finally, *navigable waters* include streams, marshes, lakes, or virtually any surface water that eventually leads to a river or ocean. In other words, a ship does not have to be able to travel on it for a body of water to be protected.

The Clean Water Act does not protect groundwater and has limited applicability to ocean discharges. See **Safe Drinking Water Act** and **Marine Protection, Research, and Sanctuaries Act** for discussions of those topics.

Under the Clean Water Act, the EPA established one of the most suc-cessful permitting schemes in environmental regulation. The act autho-rizes the **National Pollutant Discharge Elimination System** (NPDES). Public wastewater treatment plants (called publicly owned treatment works, or POTWs), industrial plants, and anyone else who wants to discharge some-thing into the water must apply for and receive permits in order to do so lawfully.

Types of Pollutants

The Clean Water Act regulates three types of pollutants: conventional, nonconventional, and toxic. Conventional pollutants are the most common, often discharged in municipal wastewater: **biochemical oxygen demand** (BOD) substances, which require a great deal of oxygen to degrade and can cause the water to become oxygen-poor; total suspended solids that have not broken down; and fecal coliform bacteria from human wastes.

Toxic pollutants are those that have been found to cause health prob-lems. They were the subject of an early lawsuit, *Natural Resources Defense Council v. Train*, which the EPA settled. The lawsuit was based on the EPA's failure to regulate toxic pollutants as required by the statute. Because of the agreement reached with the **Natural Resources Defense Council**, the EPA listed 65 categories of toxic chemicals (also called priority pollutants) and created standards for 34 industries. The toxic pollutants were incorpo-rated into the Clean Water Act in the 1977 amendments.

Nonconventional pollutants are the middle of the spectrum, generally discharges from industrial plants that do not fit into the other two catego-ries. They are subject to tighter controls than the conventional pollutants, but not as stringent as the toxics.

Regardless of the type of pollutant to be discharged, a permit is neces-sary. The permit may be issued by the EPA or the state, if the state has gained authority from the EPA to run its own program.

Permits

The permit specifies all the conditions the discharger must meet and gen-erally throws in a catch-all requirement as well: that the permittee must comply with the law. The permit will set specific limits for the pollutants to be discharged, require reports on a regular basis, and state that all appli-cable regulations must be followed. Two restrictions will always apply: federal effluent standards and state water quality standards. A permittee must meet the federal numerical maximum for discharges. However, water quality standards are designated by the states; they determine what the use of the receiving water is or should be and can require more stringent limits on pollutants.

National pollutant discharge elimination permits are issued by the federal government, unless the state has submitted a plan to the EPA and received the authority to issue them. If the state has permitting ability, the EPA oversees the process and may veto applications or sue the permittee for violations.

Because the stated objective of the Clean Water Act is to eliminate pollutants, permits tend to become stricter over time. One clause in the act states that water quality may not be degraded, so permits must not allow the water quality to worsen. The government also may require that the discharges decrease so that the water quality will improve.

The system has been self-regulating: Permittees monitor their discharges and report quarterly on the results of their testing. They must also immediately notify the permit agency if a problem occurs. To make sure the reporting is accurate, the forms require a signature of an authority who can swear to the truth, and it is a crime to file a false report.

Violation of a permit is therefore easy to prove. Furthermore, anyone who is interested in obtaining the records can get them by making a request under the **Freedom of Information Act.** Clean Water Act violations have been the most common basis for **citizen suit**s, due to the accessibility of the information about discharges.

Defenses to permit violations are quite limited: bypass, upset, and Act of God. A bypass is an intentional circumventing of the treatment system to avoid a disaster, like harm to humans, destruction of the plant, explosion, and similar problems. Upset is an unavoidable problem with the system that cannot be controlled; and an Act of God is a natural disaster or climactic condition that could not be foreseen.

Technology Standards

Like other environmental laws, the Clean Water Act establishes technology standards for treatment. In short, the effect of the standards is to establish a control hierarchy: conventional pollutants require less control than nonconventional pollutants, and toxic pollutants must be most tightly controlled. Also, existing sources must meet lower standards than new sources. For existing sources, the best practical control technology available (BPT) is required for nonconventional pollutants; best conventional control technology (BCT) is required for conventional pollutants. For toxic pollutants, the best available technology that is economically achievable must be used.

Other terms used to describe a level of treatment apply to conventional pollutants: primary treatment, secondary treatment, and advanced or tertiary treatment. All sources of conventional pollutants are now required to meet the secondary treatment standard, which includes the use of gravity, separation, biological treatment, digestors, and many types of methods to reduce the amount of pollutants released to the surface waters. Advanced treatment addresses specific targets to clean the effluent further.

When the agency is dealing with a new source, the rules change because the whole construction project can be revised to include process changes, treatment within the system, and many other design changes. If toxic pollutants are involved, cost is not one of the considerations, and the best available demonstrated technology (BDT) must be used.

Fundamentally Different Factors

When attempting to get a permit, a discharger who cannot meet the technology standards set by the agency may be able to claim that it should have a different limit because of differences in its design. This is true only of existing sources, and the Clean Water Act has been amended to restrict the use of this variance. Cost of complying is not a sufficient reason for changing the standard for a source.

Indirect Dischargers

Not all sources that discharge effluents send them directly to a regulated water body. Many send their wastes to publicly owned treatment works, which are typically municipal wastewater plants. The **Clean Air Act** regulates these discharges through requirements for pretreatment. The purpose of pretreatment is to make sure that waste sent to the plant does not disturb its normal operation, harm it, or pass through the plant without treatment. The most common name for this type of source is *industrial user.* General provisions regulate indirect discharges, and certain industries have additional requirements.

In this situation, the person holding the national pollution discharge elimination permit is the municipality, village, town, or other political subdivision. That person functions as the control authority for the indirect discharger and must set limits, surcharges, and fines, and may issue its own permits as well. Since failure to control an industrial user can cause the treatment works to violate its own permit, the wastewater plant must enforce the limits for its protection.

Construction Grants

One of the principle roles of the federal government in the early days of regulation was to provide money to states and political subdivisions so they could build treatment plants to treat wastewater. This function carried through to the 1972 Clean Water Act and was a significant portion of the EPA's job until the program was changed in the 1987 amendments. Now the states receive money from the federal government, but they must establish a revolving fund and administer the money themselves. Those states that use federal money must pay some money back and charge enough interest from sources who borrow to keep the state funding program going.

Wetlands

Wetlands and marshes are considered waters of the United States, regulated by the Clean Water Act. The actual delineation of a wetland is done by the U.S. Army **Corps of Engineers** based on an analysis of hydrology, plant life, soil conditions, and water cover over the soil for a certain portion of the year. Section 404 of the Clean Water Act deals with dredge and fill operations in wetlands.

Primary authority for issuing permits under Section 404 rests with the Corps of Engineers. The Corps receives permit applications, reviews them, and issues or denies the permits. The EPA has the right to oversee the permit issuance and may veto the permit. If the Corps and the EPA do not agree, the matter is referred to the Council on Environmental Quality.

To understand the permitting requirement in wetlands, it is necessary to view the term *discharge* in a broad sense. Putting pilings in a wetland is considered a *fill;* plowing furrows in wetlands causes a discharge of the soil that is displaced; storing sand dredged in wetlands is both *a dredge and a fill* operation. All of these activities require a permit. A person who brings soil into a wetland to convert it to dry land needs a permit.

The Corps has issued general permits to deal with certain projects, such as developing small residential properties. If a general permit exists and the undertaking falls within the description of the permitted activity, an individual permit is not necessary.

Both the Corps of Engineers and the EPA have authority to enforce the law against violators, but generally the Corps handles such problems. The two agencies operate under a memorandum of agreement, which states one of their primary goals: no net loss policy of wetlands.

Stormwater Runoff

Until the 1987 revisions to the Clean Water Act, stormwater was not usually regulated under the permit system, although some industry permits included stormwater collection and treatment. However, stormwater can contribute significant amounts of pollutants to waterways, so Congress decided to deal with this problem.

Stormwater in cities collects oil and other contaminants from streets and parking lots, and in many industries, when it washes over the premises it carries industrial wastes with it. Because it usually moves randomly as runoff, it has not been considered a point source. The solution has been to bring stormwater runoff under the National Pollutant Discharge Elimination System and require permits for the types of runoff most likely to affect the surface water, including discharges from large municipalities, industrial activities, and some construction projects.

Oil and Hazardous Substance Discharges

The Clean Water Act, under Section 311, deals with discharges of both oil and hazardous substance and establishes liability for them. The **Oil Pollution Act** of 1990 added more guidelines to deal with oil discharges. Part of that statute amended the Clean Water Act.

Section 311 prohibits onshore and offshore facilities and vessels from discharging oil or **hazardous substances** into the water. It authorizes administrative penalties and significantly higher civil penalties if a lawsuit is brought and allows the government to act to correct the damages (which the responsible person must pay for).

The key to this provision is the requirement for planning. Owners or operators of a facility or vessel that could discharge oil or hazardous substances into surface waters must develop contingency plans for dealing with the worst spill that could occur. They must train employees to respond, create a communication system to pass information to all who need to be notified, identify the person in charge, send the plans to the president (or his designated agent), and review and update the plans as necessary.

State Squabbles: Water Quality Near State Borders

States have the right to designate the water quality of rivers or water bodies within their borders, and they generally draft regulations to protect them. Occasionally a source in a neighboring state will apply for a permit and the downstream state will object because it believes the discharge will affect its water quality.

The most important case on this issue, *Arkansas v. Oklahoma,* involved an EPA-issued permit. Oklahoma claimed that issuing the permit to Fayetteville for its wastewater treatment plant would violate its prohibition for degradation of the river in its state. The EPA heard the arguments and rejected them; the **hearing** office rejected the appeal. Oklahoma took the case to the Circuit Court, which decided the case in an interesting fashion. First, the river did not meet the water quality standards set for that water. So, the court reasoned, any discharge of pollutants would increase pollution and contribute to violation of the water quality standards. Therefore, no permit could be issued. The Supreme Court reversed the decision and chastised the court for substituting its own opinion for the EPA's. The EPA had determined that the contribution of the source would not measureably degrade the water quality in Oklahoma, and the Supreme Court thought the EPA's decision was entitled deference.

States have been trying in recent years to regulate the influx of pollutants from out of state. This becomes a constitutional battle because of the conflict between the state's right to protect public health and safety and the federal power to control interstate commerce.

CLEANUP TECHNOLOGIES   Various methods used to destroy, alter, or dispose of **hazardous substances** and **hazardous waste.** Because of the **Environmental Protection Agency**'s involvement in cleaning up hazardous waste sites, it is often in the position to determine which technology should be used. This entry will briefly describe the cleanup technologies available.

Although the selection of cleanup technology seems to be separate from the legal questions, it is a major concern argued in cases involving **Superfund** site cleanups. Environmental attorneys must be familiar with waste treatment in order to participate productively in negotiations and lawsuits.

One of the biggest problems both regulators and neighborhoods face is how to deal with hazardous waste that is affecting the environment or health of the community. Generally, the impacted persons want the waste taken away. That type of action reassures the community more than a cleanup that takes place on the property. But waste dug up from one site and carted to another is likely to generate anger from the community scheduled to receive it, and the transportation of hazardous waste can increase the exposure of the public and the environment far beyond the immediate vicinity.

For those reasons, the government favors on-site treatment. If the dangers of the waste can be neutralized without expanding the sphere of impact, the public benefits. Such reasoning does not impress an enraged community that has waited, most likely for years, for the government to begin dealing with the waste and making their lives safer and healthier. Ultimately competing interests will help shape the remedial plan.

For example, one preferred treatment is incineration on site. Communities often fight incineration, as they typically fight treating the waste on-site and leaving it there. Yet to remove the waste and dispose of it elsewhere involves the dangers inherent in transportation of hazardous waste, plus involving a different community. Meetings with community members will help the agency understand and address their concerns to the extent possible. Additional controls may be added, and the community may be given information on testing and progress.

The effectiveness of the treatment depends on the type of waste, its location (water, air, ground, or groundwater), its concentration, and the goals set by the government. Particular methods may work only in limited circumstances, but the science of hazardous waste treatment is constantly expanding, with new techniques emerging to meet the demand.

In the simplest terms, treatment technologies fall into just a few categories: chemical, thermal, mechanical/physical, and biological treatment. Another technique for dealing with waste, though not a cleanup method, is containment. Often several techniques are combined, and the waste goes through multiple processes.

Containment

The oldest—and now the least favored method of dealing with hazardous waste—is containment. The term may be used to describe landfilling or leaving waste where it is already buried and making some attempt to keep it from migrating. The 1986 **Superfund Amendments and Reauthorization Act** made it clear that containment without treatment was to be avoided when possible.

Another law that limits the use of containment is the **Resource Conservation and Recovery Act,** which prohibits landfilling of virtually all hazardous wastes. See **corrective action.** When it is impossible to relocate hazardous wastes or when a licensed hazardous waste facility closes, a *cap* may be created over the area. The cap, a layered cover engineered for such sites, is designed to keep water from percolating into the wastes and carrying them elsewhere. Generally trenches and drains will be placed around the outside so the runoff and seeping fluids can be captured and treated.

Thermal Treatment

Incineration (burning wastes at high temperatures) is quite effective in dealing with many types of waste. Although regulators frequently favor incineration, public interest groups and community members are often distressed by the possibility that air contaminants from the incinerator will add to the existing problem. However, air contaminants can be captured and destroyed, provided the incinerator has the proper mechanisms for destruction. Efficiency of incineration depends on the construction of the unit. Heat may also be used to volatilize certain compounds, causing them to leave the waste mixture. Often such action necessitates use of other technology to make sure contaminants don't escape into the air.

Thermal treatment can also convert some compounds into fuel, or it can melt wastes and trap them in a glass-like matrix. The latter process, called vitrification, can be done in the ground if the situation is favorable. Otherwise, it is completed in equipment similar to that used to create glass.

Chemical Treatment

The purpose of chemical treatment is to chemically alter the waste so it is no longer harmful. In one method, called ion exchange, chemical reactions create new compounds that are less toxic. Dechlorination, a treatment limited in application, removes chlorine atoms by use of chemical reagents. Carbon, often used to absorb certain compounds, is used to capture volatile organic compounds with consistent success. Another way to lower toxicity is to add chemicals that react with the hazardous wastes to neutralize the waste's harmful qualities.

Physical/Chemical Treatment

Wastewater treatment has utilized technology in this classification for some time, and the methods are beneficial in hazardous waste treatment as well. Waste is divided into sizes by screening, air separation, flotation, or magnetic properties. The amount of waste can then be reduced by dewatering, thickening, filtration, and centrifuges. Soil can be cleaned by soil flushing or soil washing, using a washing solution, which adds chemical treatment to the physical one.

Another way to clean soil, *vapor extraction,* works well with compounds that will become airborne. It is commonly used for gasoline spills. Wells are placed in the ground, air is pumped in, then sucked out and treated before release. To enhance the effectiveness of this technique, heat may be applied, steam may be injected, or the ground may be warmed through radio frequency waves. This technology, too, combines both physical and chemical treatment.

Biological Treatment

Biological treatment has been used for years to manage wastewater. Microorganisms, either naturally occurring or genetically engineered, eat the waste, transforming it into less harmful waste. Bioreactors used in wastewater treatment include tanks, aeration, and trickling filters. In a trickling filter, the microorganisms are on the filter and the wastewater is forced into contact with them.

Land farming (also called solid phase bioremediation) occurs either on the ground or in shallow tanks. The waste is spread, microorganisms are added, and tilling takes place periodically. A variation of land farming is soil heaping, in which the organisms, nutrients, and air must be injected into a mound of soil. Composting is yet another form of biological treatment.

Biological treatment of hazardous wastes has grown more and more common. Its greatest successes have been scored wastewater treatment and organic compound cleanup, but gasoline and other fuel spills are also effectively treated by using microorganisms. A significant advantage of using microorganisms is that they can often be effective without moving the waste. But the process does require monitoring, because the bugs need nutrients, water, and air, and they generally work best in warm temperatures.

Radioactive or Mixed Waste

Mixed waste consists of both radioactive and nonradioactive wastes. The first step in its treatment is to separate the two. The nonradioactive portion then undergoes appropriate treatment. However, no one has found a way to treat radioactive waste to accelerate its breakdown into normal waste. So the only treatment possibility for the radioactive portion is containment.

COAST GUARD   The organization responsible for enforcing federal maritime laws. During peacetime, the Coast Guard operates under the Department of Transportation; during wartime, it is under naval command.

The Coast Guard's domain spans the high seas and the coastal waters within the territorial jurisdiction of the United States. Since its purpose is to enforce applicable federal laws, the Coast Guard deals with the **Clean Water Act,** the **Oil Pollution Act** of 1990, the **Marine Protection, Research, and Sanctuaries Act,** the **Superfund Amendments and Reauthorization Act,** and similar laws.

It responds to emergencies involving oil spills and other discharges at sea and takes the lead in enforcing the law, including assessing penalties for environmental violations. The Coast Guard also develops contingency plans to deal with potential releases. If a discharge occurs within its jurisdiction, the on-scene coordinator will be a representative from the Coast Guard.

COASTAL ZONE MANAGEMENT ACT   A statute first enacted in 1972 to preserve the coastal waters, shores, intertidal areas, and marshes. It authorizes grants to coastal states for coastal zone management and encourages all levels of government to assist in preservation. The primary authority for promulgating and enforcing the regulations and the statute is vested in the Department of Commerce, acting through the **National Oceanic and Atmospheric Administration.**

COMMAND AND CONTROL   A name given to the most common method of pollution control in the United States. Limits for pollutant discharge are set, either by regulation or on an individual basis, then incorporated into individual permits. If the requirements of the permit are not met, enforcement follows.

When environmental law first appeared, command and control seemed to be the only approach available. Facing an array of serious environmental problems, the government elected to make standards fairly uniform throughout the nation. Public participation in the regulatory process was limited to commenting after the regulations were proposed or when a permit was being considered. Some people maintain that the command and control approach is still the only viable option.

Still, the environment continues to have problems, so experimental approaches are finding their way into the statutes, and only time will reveal whether they succeed in advancing a cleaner environment [see **Clean Air Act Amendments of 1990**].

Negotiated rulemaking is an experiment with the beginning phase of command and control. The idea is to get people representing industry, government, and the public involved earlier in the process—when the **Environmental Protection Agency** (EPA) is considering a regulation. Though certain designated participants become official members, other people may attend and make comments as well.

Once the EPA decides, based on the committee's work, that a rule is necessary, the committee members work together to write it. Because the composition of the committee is so broad, this process is long and difficult and results in regulations that are not totally satisfactory to anyone. But such is the nature of negotiation.

Another approach being tested is market-based, incorporated into the Clean Air Act Amendments of 1990. Under this system, units of permitted pollution are considered assets that can be marketed. The holder of a permit may sell excess units to another business that needs them. At the extreme, a permit could be issued that would be fully transferrable, as opposed to belonging solely to a named permittee. It is too early to see the impact of this new strategy. Many praise it; many condemn it as a license to pollute.

COMPREHENSIVE ENVIRONMENTAL RESPONSE, COMPENSATION, AND LIABILITY ACT (CERCLA) The law that deals with cleaning up abandoned **hazardous waste** sites in the United States. The statute was written in response to the public outcry about **Love Canal** (1978), a highly publicized toxic waste site. It was first enacted in 1980, with a major amendment, **Superfund Amendments and Reauthorization Act,** in 1986. Commonly called **Superfund,** the law is now undergoing revisions.

This statute is the most controversial of all major environmental laws, primarily because it is perceived as unfair and cumbersome. Most laws that have large penalties and expenses associated with them require some type of wrongful action by the person being required to pay. CERCLA does not. It merely requires some type of connection of the hazardous waste site. Although the law allows certain defenses, they are severely limited.

The fundamental goal of Congress in enacting Superfund was to clean up abandoned hazardous disposal sites. Therefore, it does not matter that the disposal occurred in a lawful manner at the time, or that the site (usually a landfill) had a permit, or whether a little or a lot of hazardous waste was put there by any particular person. Anyone connected with the hazardous waste site faces the prospect of being responsible for the entire cleanup. Called *joint and several liability,* this type of accountability means that everyone is answerable for all of the waste, both individually and as a group. However, despite the plain directive of the law, courts do appear to be rebelling against gross unfairness. An appellate court held in *In re Bell Petroleum Services, Inc.,* that if a person can prove a reasonable basis founded on volume for allotting responsibility among the parties, the agency may not recover all its cleanup costs from one party. Another court determined in *United States v. Broderick Investment Co.* that the environmental harm to groundwater could be divided geographically and refused to find the defendant liable for the entire site.

In addition to providing for cleanup of hazardous waste sites, CERCLA includes requirements for emergency planning and response. See **Emergency Planning and Community Right-To-Know Act; natural resources damages claims.**

Potentially Responsible Parties

Under CERCLA's definition, a person, business, government, or other organization, can be forced to cleanup the site if it owns or operates the site, if it owned or operated the site during the time of the disposal, if it transported or arranged for transportation of **hazardous substances** to the site, if it owned the waste in the beginning, or if it completed the disposal. In legal terms, anyone within these classifications is a potentially responsible party [see **potentially responsible parties**].

To illustrate how this works, assume Bob owned a farm. He decided in 1960 to allow the city of Municipal to use a portion of it for a landfill, so he got a license from the state of Disarray. Industry put all of its ethyl-double-bad-stuff waste in barrels. Then it contacted Hauler to get rid of it. Hauler took the waste to Bob's landfill. Hauler also picked up old transformers from Power Company, used oil and batteries from Service Station, and occasionally some waste from Lead Smelter. In 1970, Bob decides he's tired of operating a landfill, so he stops taking waste. In 1975, he sells the property to Tom. Tom found out a problem existed because the EPA sent him a letter notifying him that groundwater in the area was contaminated and that the problem came from his property. The EPA told him later to help with an investigation and cleanup of the property.

The potentially responsible parties for this site include Bob, Municipal, Power Company, Service Station, Lead Smelter, Hauler, Industry, Tom, and anyone else who contributed to the hazardous substances disposed of at the landfill.

Structure of Law

The Comprehensive Environmental Response, Compensation, and Liability Act details a number of procedures that the **Environmental Protection Agency** (EPA) must follow. It also leaves many details to be developed by that agency in the form of regulations. The regulations the EPA created are an important segment of the law in Superfund practice.

In a capsule, the process starts with identification of a potential Superfund site. The statute requires disposers to notify the EPA of disposal activities, but some sites are discovered because of a complaint. After the initial notification, the EPA makes a preliminary assessment, and a site investigation follows if necessary. Then the site is evaluated by the agency under the **Hazardous Ranking System,** a scheme set up by the EPA. The government looks at many aspects of the site: the type of substances disposed, problems that have developed around the site, the potential for migration of waste, and the possible effects on the surrounding area. Only if the potential for problems is great will the EPA nominate the site as a Superfund site. However, even if the property does not score high enough to be on the national list, it may be listed by the state in which it is located. After a notice and comment period, the site is listed unless public comments demonstrate the site should not be. Periodically the EPA publishes a list of Superfund sites (the **National Priority List**) in the *Federal Register,* a daily journal of all federal agency action. Because of the impact a listing has on a piece of property, interested persons can contest the EPA's proposal before it is listed.

Once a site is listed as a Superfund site, the EPA makes a choice about how to proceed. The agency itself can do whatever is necessary to remove the threat (a removal action) or it can order a potentially responsible party to complete the removal action. If the EPA does the work, it can later sue the potentially responsible parties for its costs [see **cost recovery**]. The same power can also be used by the EPA to deal with emergency spills.

The next step is to identify as many potentially responsible parties as possible. The EPA will send out notice letters requesting information to anyone it thinks may be involved. CERCLA requires a response from the recipient.

The government must then begin an in-depth investigation of the site. Two phases of this process are usually linked together: the remedial investigation and the feasibility study. Superfund lawyers refer to this combination as the **remedial investigation/feasibility study** (RI/FS).

The remedial investigation focuses on the extent of the problems at the site. Groundwater is studied, soil sampling completed, borings of disposal areas tested, and the general physical, geological, and hydrological characteristics determined. A remedial investigation normally takes between eighteen months and three years to finish. The feasibility study examines the available waste technologies that could be used to deal with the problems. It includes options, effectiveness projections, and cost estimates. Generally, a feasibility study can be completed within three to six months.

The EPA then examines the information in these two documents and makes a decision about what should be done at the site. Then a **record of decision** (ROD) is published, which addresses the evidence gathered, discusses the options (including those not accepted by the agency) and selects a remedy. The next step is the remedial design, in which specific engineering plans are prepared. The final step, implementation, is called the remedial action.

When the site has been cleaned to the extent the government thinks is sufficient, the EPA will propose the deletion of the site from the National Priority List. For years, sites on the list just stayed there while everyone grappled with the law, but now deletion notices are common.

Dealing with the Process

Due to the cost of cleaning up Superfund sites, potentially responsible parties are not inclined to march in and face up to liability without a fight. The situation pits everyone against everyone else—the more persons available to share in the costs, the less any one party has to pay. Also, courts are prohibited from reviewing many of the early decisions the EPA makes. For example, if a potentially responsible party receives an order, it cannot challenge the order in court immediately. It must first obey, then later try to get its money back or ignore the order and face paying four times the amount of the order if it loses.

A potentially responsible party (or a group of parties) may enter into agreements with the EPA to do portions of the work. Many believe it is cheaper to do the work themselves than to rely on the government. The government's costs, they reason, are likely to be higher. But the downside of negotiating an agreement is that stipulated penalties will be included in the agreement, so the potentially responsible party may be liable for missed deadlines. The EPA will also insist on the power to oversee the work, with the parties to the agreement liable for all the oversight costs. If a potentially responsible party does the work at a site, it can then sue any other potentially responsible parties to recover its costs. It will win if the work is consistent with the **National Contingency Plan** (NCP). That plan, a set of regulations promulgated by the EPA that governs all Superfund cleanups, is critical to actions taken at a Superfund site.

Potentially responsible parties at a site often form groups (usually called steering committees) that work with the EPA and the Department of Justice to determine how work is to be done and liability allocated. The objective is a consent decree that describes specifically what will be done.

Parties who have contributed significantly less waste to a site than the major contributors may be able to work out an agreement with the government to pay some determined amount and then walk away from the site. These persons are called *de minimis* or *de micromis* parties. Before the EPA will enter into such an agreement, it must be fairly certain of the status. It will also make these persons pay extra because of the unknown total costs of the remedial action.

The Superfund

CERCLA's nickname, Superfund, comes from the fund Congress established to deal with hazardous waste sites. When it was first set up, the

Superfund was much too small, but each time the law has been amended, Congress has increased the pool of money available for cleanup.

The Superfund may be used for the EPA's expenses, for cleanup, for removal actions, to recover EPA's costs, and to force potentially responsible parties to clean up a site. The EPA strenuously avoids using the fund if there are any persons who can pay for the cleanup, but it is allowed to pay the portion of the cleanup costs that covers people who are bankrupt, will not settle, or cannot be found. See **orphan's share.**

Money for the fund comes from taxes on chemical and petroleum industries, environmental taxes on certain corporations, and general tax receipts. The amount available has ranged from $1.6 billion to $8.5 billion. Cleanup costs at a typical Superfund site are approximately $25 million, so the fund would quickly be drained if the EPA did not try to force other parties to pay for the work. Of the 1,295 sites listed or proposed on the National Priority List, construction of all necessary work for cleanup has been completed for about 290 sites. Many of those sites will remain on the list for years, while the selected remedy operates.

Legal Controversies Surrounding CERCLA

Practically no one likes the Superfund statute or the way it is administered. Public interest groups as well as neighboring communities complain about the slowness of the program. It takes a great deal of time to prepare all the preliminary studies and get into the remediation itself. In addition, legal fees are extremely high. It is not uncommon for the potentially responsible parties to involve their own inhouse attorneys, outside counsel, and counsel that represents a group of the parties who have joined together to settle the case. On the government's side, teams from both the EPA regional office and EPA headquarters as well as litigators from the Department of Justice are involved. The U.S. Attorney may also assign a local attorney, and the state in which the site is located will also be represented. When dealing with fifty or more potentially responsible parties, the legal fees can hit millions quickly.

The remediation chosen by the EPA will impact the parties financially, so they must add expert technical advisors to the group of attorneys to evaluate and dissect the government's plans, design the remedy, and testify if necessary. It is possible for a group of potentially responsible parties to convince a court that the government's remedy is not appropriate. *United States v. Hardage* is an example of such a case, in which the court chose the remedy proposed by the potentially responsible parties.

The threshold question after a remedy has been selected is this: what is the appropriate level of cleanup for the site? Again there is a battle from two sides. The community often wants the site cleaned to a pristine level while the parties to the lawsuit—and a growing group of the public—believe that goal is unrealistic. There is a point in a cleanup when the site swallows money with little benefit to the environment.

The truth is that a large portion of the money spent on Superfund cases is not spent on restoring the site. Instead, it is poured into attack and counterattack, drawing out the process for years.

Another point of contention is the perception that EPA or Congress will exempt certain classes of people from the pool of potentially responsible parties, leaving others to pay their share. For example, cities are often parties to Superfund lawsuits because they managed, owned, or sent waste to a hazardous waste site. Congress is being pressured to delete municipalities from available parties for cleanup. Current owners and operators of a Superfund site, too, may have to pay for cleanup, even if they did not cause any problems there. Including these people in the group of potentially responsible parties has, until recently, subjected banks and other loan agencies to liability if they foreclosed on contaminated property. Through a number of court decisions interpreting a CERCLA provision for lenders, it is now possible for lenders to avoid liability. The EPA attempted to give more guidance on this subject in a rule, but the D.C. Circuit Court of Appeals struck it down, saying the EPA does not have the authority to tell the courts how to interpret the law.

The statute itself allows a new owner of property to avoid being held responsible for a cleanup if it completes an appropriate investigation of the property prior to acquiring it. If the buyer investigated the property and found no problem, he or she is considered an innocent purchaser and can use that defense to avoid contributing to cleanup costs. If the investigation reveals a problem, though, the defense is lost. See **innocent purchaser.**

The problem for buyers is deciding how much probing is enough. An independent standards organization has released guidelines for property buyers, but whether this will establish the defense remains to be seen. Also, even when the property owner did not contribute to the contamination, the EPA's position has been that the owner must pay something, perhaps as a de minimis party. Thus far, the EPA has been successful in maintaining that stance.

🏛 **CONSENT AGREEMENT**   Settlements are common in environmental practice. The type of consent agreement reached in a settlement depends on whether the case is in court or the agency is handling the alleged violation itself. A consent agreement will be either a consent decree or a consent order.

Consent Decree

These agreements are worked out between the defendant to a lawsuit and the plaintiff (usually the government in environmental cases) and then filed with a court. When the government notifies a business that it will be sued, it may at the same time open the door to settlement. The parties meet to discuss the claims and proposed penalties, actions, or other relief, and negotiate. In this manner, many of the EPA lawsuits are settled at the same time the complaint is filed.

Because a lawsuit is the triggering mechanism, a consent decree involving the EPA must be approved by three offices: the regional EPA, the EPA Headquarters, and the Department of Justice. Also, a consent decree cannot be entered as final until it goes through a period of notice and comment to allow interested parties to object. This process is called the lodging of the consent decree. After the notice and comment period, the EPA and other parties make a motion for entry of the decree, which then becomes an order of the court.

Consent decrees usually have much lower penalties than those initially sought in the complaint, because the EPA normally asks for the maximum amount allowed under the law but has much discretion to reduce the penalty when negotiating. Some of the matters considered by the EPA in settlement discussions are duration of the noncompliance, severity of the violation, history of violations, economic benefit resulting from noncompliance, good faith efforts to comply, and similar matters.

The EPA obtains several benefits from settling a case, most obviously time and manpower savings. Often it also obtains stipulated penalties, written in a way that requires the defendant to pay without being asked if it violates the consent decree.

The defendant also stands to gain from settlement, particularly when the complaint has not yet been filed. Publicity for environmental violations is not welcomed by many companies. But if the consent decree and complaint are filed simultaneously, public exposure is lessened.

Normally defendants will also profit by reducing financial exposure as well as legal fees.

Consent decrees rarely contain an admission of liability, since that would expose the defendant to other lawsuits. If noncompliance was based on technical problems, defendants can negotiate a schedule for remedying the problem. The decree normally reserves the government's right to sue for a violation of the statute but the government seldom takes that step unless the defendant ignores the consent decree.

Consent Order

This agreement may be negotiated with an **administrative agency** when the agency issues or plans to issue an administrative complaint, **administrative order,** or **administrative penalty order.** Consent orders have many of the same features as a consent decree, but neither the Department of Justice nor a court is involved. If a penalty is proposed, it is limited by the amount allowed for an administrative penalty proceeding, which generally is less than is available in a court.

CONSTRUCTION GRANT   Money given to wastewater treatment plants to enable them to update their facilities to comply with the deadlines specified in the **Clean Water Act.** Municipalities in particular often lacked the funds to build plants that could meet the new federal demands when the Clean Water Act was passed.

For many years, the EPA administered the construction grant program, taking applications and dispensing the money. However, Congress concluded the program was swallowing money and time that the agency did not have. In 1987 the law was amended and a state revolving fund was established in the amendments (the Water Quality Act of 1987). The EPA was given the task of dispensing money to the states to help them establish loan programs for water treatment plants. To qualify for the money, each state had to develop and submit a grant program to the EPA and contribute 20 percent of the necessary money for the fund. The revolving funds are intended to be used as loans, which the recipients must repay to the states to keep the program in operation. So construction grants are now given to the states to distribute instead of directly to the person building or modernizing a plant.

CONTINUOUS EMISSION MONITORING (CEM) A method of continuous testing for air emissions. The **Clean Air Act Amendments of 1990** order this type of monitoring for sources that emit **acid rain** pollutants (**sulfur dioxide** and **nitrogen oxides**). Continuous emission monitoring may also be required by a state when it issues permits for other types of air pollution sources to operate within its borders. Though the new CEM requirement adds considerable cost to air pollution control, it enables the discharger to quickly spot problems in a process or control equipment so they can be fixed before significant amounts of pollution escape.

Information obtained from continuous emission monitoring must be supplied to the EPA or state as specified by regulations. If a source cannot provide data to prove it is complying with the law, the EPA can assume it was operating in an uncontrolled manner during that time period.

CONTRIBUTION RIGHTS Under the **Comprehensive Environmental Response, Compensation, and Liability Act,** persons who clean up a **hazardous waste** site may sue other **potentially responsible parties** to force them to pay a portion of the cleanup costs. This provision of the statute eases the burden of the strict joint and several liability of the law.

A contribution action may be brought in conjunction with a **cost recovery** lawsuit, or it may follow one. The case law is murky on contribution, with courts often treating it as cost recovery is treated—that is, the person suing for contribution must prove that their cleanup work is consistent with the National Contingency Plan.

In determining the right of contribution, the courts will evaluate the defendant's participation in creating the hazardous waste site. To decide how much contribution is required, the court will look at the volume of waste, its toxicity, the activity that involved the defendant in the site (ownership of property or waste disposal), the degree of care exercised, and cooperation with the government.

One benefit of settling a case for **Superfund** cleanup with the government is contribution protection. The statute itself provides that if a potentially responsible party has settled, it cannot be liable to another party for those matters addressed. Thus contribution protection can be quite attractive to persons who are involved in a multi-party cleanup.

CONTROL TECHNIQUE GUIDELINES (CTGs)   Under the **Clean Air Act Amendments of 1990,** the EPA may develop guidelines to aid states in determining what control technology is reasonably available for certain industries. Once that determination is made, states must amend their **state implementation plan**s to require permittees to use reasonably available control technology.

The guidelines do not make a particular technology mandatory. They simply demonstrate the existence of affordable and obtainable methods of controlling emissions. When states amend their plans, they may select technology other than that recommended by the EPA, as long as their method achieves similar emission reductions to that chosen by the EPA in the guidance.

CORPS OF ENGINEERS (COE)   An organization within the U.S. Army that deals with wetlands issues and wetlands permits under the **Clean Water Act.** The Corps of Engineers is a unique military organization. It designs and builds structures for the military during wartime, but it is also responsible for flood control, improvements of waterways, and some civil building as well.

In the area of environmental law, the Corps of Engineers determines where wetlands currently exist and is the primary permit authority for dredge and fill operations in wetlands areas. It is also responsible for the **Marine Protection, Research, and Sanctuaries Act** (commonly known as the Ocean Dumping Act).

Regulations for wetlands permits are issued by two authorities: the EPA and the COE. The Corps rules deal primarily with the process of issuing permits; the EPA sets the substantive requirements for obtaining one. Therefore, the Corps issues permits based on its interpretation of the EPA's rules, which may lead to conflict.

To facilitate interaction between the two agencies, the EPA and the Corps have entered into a memorandum of agreement, which sets forth the basic groundrules. The Corps makes the initial determination concerning the existence of a wetlands area (a process known as a wetlands delineation). When a violation is suspected, it usually does initial investigation and determines whether a violation has occurred. It may issue orders to cease and desist actions taken without a permit, or it may take a violator to court.

The **Environmental Protection Agency** is not a passive partner in the wetlands protection, however. It reviews permit applications and provides comments to the Corps. In some cases, the EPA may choose to enforce when the law has been violated. It also has the right to veto a permit the Corps of Engineers has issued when it believes that (1) its regulations have not been followed or (2) resources will suffer adverse impacts after mitigation is completed. In such cases, the matter may be referred to the **Council on Environmental Quality** (CEQ) for assistance in resolving the matter. The secretary of the Army and administrator of the EPA will confer, but the final decision rests with the EPA. The veto power has been used fairly successfully by the EPA, but a permit applicant can still turn to the courts for a review of the veto.

The Corps of Engineers must also coordinate with a number of other agencies while doing its job, so it has agreements with the National Oceanic and Atmospheric Administration, the **Coast Guard,** the Departments of Commerce, Interior, Transportation, and Agriculture. See also **taking; wetlands.**

CORRECTIVE ACTION The **Resource Conservation and Recovery Act** governs, among other things, permitting at facilities that treat, store, or dispose of **hazardous waste**. To ensure that permitted facilities are not breeding grounds for new hazardous waste sites, the law requires not only state-of-the-art engineering from the date of the permit forward, but also cleanup of current or previous releases. This is called corrective action.

Any part of a **treatment/storage/disposal** facility may be considered a discrete unit for the purposes of managing hazardous waste; it is called a solid waste management unit (SWMU). Units include lagoons, tanks, waste piles, landfills, and other types of containments. Permits must require corrective action for any unit from which hazardous waste or hazardous constituents have been released. All hazardous waste treatment/storage/disposal facilities must have a permit to operate, whether they already existed when the law took effect or are built after the requirements for facilities were enacted. Existing facilities were generally defined as those in existence on November 1980.

New facilities need a permit before construction begins; existing facilities submit an application and then operate as an "interim facility" until a permit is issued or the interim status is revoked. Two different sets of regulations apply to interim facilities and permitted facilities, but they are the same in the important details, such as monitoring, reporting, training, emergency response, and corrective action. Major modifications of a facility or its activity must go through the permitting process as well.

Basically, the government will conduct an assessment when a permit application comes in, and in many ways the process is similar to a **Superfund** assessment [see **Comprehensive Environmental Response, Compensation, and Liability Act**]. The permit itself will require corrective action for future releases and a plan to correct any current problems with a schedule for compliance. It will also require financial assurance from the permittee.

The **Environmental Protection Agency** (EPA) has finalized some regulations on corrective action. One of them deals with a *corrective action management unit.* This regulation is important not only in treatment/storage/disposal facilities, but also at Superfund sites. Prior to the regulation, wastes could not be moved or consolidated on a site, even if that proved to be the wisest action, because placement of hazardous waste on land is prohibited by the land ban. Now, though, a site may be designated by the EPA regional administrator as a corrective action management unit. Placing waste within that unit does not constitute land disposal. However, a corrective action management unit can only be used to manage wastes from the remedial action. Design, site monitoring, groundwater monitoring, closure, and postclosure procedures must be approved by the EPA.

COST RECOVERY   A lawsuit brought by the government, and in some cases, a private party who has incurred expenses to respond to a release or threatened release of **hazardous substances**. The defendants in such lawsuits are parties who are potentially responsible for the problem. See **Comprehensive Environmental Response, Compensation, and Liability Act; potentially responsible parties.**

The section of the Comprehensive Environmental Response, Compensation, and Liability Act (CERCLA) that authorizes cost recovery is Section 107. The plaintiff must prove (1) that a release occurred or is likely to occur (2) from a facility or vessel, (3) that a hazardous substance was involved, (4) that the defendant or defendants are potentially responsible, (5) that the costs of responding were incurred as a result, and (6) that the actions of the plaintiff were either consistent with the **National Contingency Plan** or not inconsistent with it, depending on whether the plaintiff is a private party or the government.

Although the statute provides for joint and several liability, courts are beginning to allow defendants to offer evidence concerning apportioning the liability. In *United States v. Alcan Aluminum Corp.*, the Third Circuit Court of Appeals stated that in appropriate circumstances, the defendants should be allowed to prove the harm is divisible and the damages can, therefore, be alloted. *In re Bell Petroleum Services, Inc.*, took an even stronger position, stating the government cannot ignore such evidence if it is provided.

Cost recovery lawsuits are the most commonly brought suits under CERCLA. Defenses are limited: an act of God, act of war, or an act of a third party without any connection to the person named as a potentially responsible party. Thus, in a cost recovery suit, a corporation that bought a company after it disposed of a hazardous substance might be responsible for the actions of the predecessor. The corporate officers could be potentially responsible for the acts of the corporation, and a lender could be responsible for a site contaminated by the borrower. Also, almost any type of interest in real estate, e.g. ownership, lease, or use permit, could result in liability if the property is discovered to be a **hazardous waste** site.

Costs that can be obtained through this process include investigative, removal, administrative, cleanup, and enforcement. When the government is involved, the costs can be recovered even if they appear unwise, as long as they are not arbitrary and capricious, a difficult standard to meet.

Whatever response was taken, it must also comply with the National Contingency Plan. However, the government's actions cannot be inconsistent with the Plan, while the private individual's actions must be consistent with it. The difference is this: if the government is the plaintiff, the court will assume the actions are consistent and the defendant has the burden of proof, but if a private party is the plaintiff, the burden of proving consistency is on that party.

Claims against the Superfund

The Comprehensive Environmental Response, Compensation, and Liability Act allows any person who has spent money during a response action to make a claim against the **Superfund** for reimbursement. As a practical matter, this provision has not been useful to private parties, but the EPA has established regulations to streamline the process.

Generally, the government will not entertain a claim made by a **potentially responsible party** unless the party has already started negotiating a settlement. Since the Superfund is designed to fund cleanups for which emergency action is necessary or potentially responsible parties are not available, the EPA has been reluctant to use the Superfund to reimburse persons who are legally responsible for cleanup.

However, a private party may be ordered to do a cleanup and later prove it was not a potentially responsible party, or it may be acting out of public interest. In order to qualify for payment from the fund, private parties must first get preauthorization to respond. The EPA will issue a document with terms and conditions in it, and the private party must follow them. Documentation of actions and costs can then be submitted to the EPA as a claim. It will be approved only if the site had sufficient priority to consider using the Superfund to clean it up.

Legal Issues

Basic legal conflicts continue to surround the cost recovery provision of CERCLA. Because most cases settle, many of the issues raised have not been resolved.

Although other provisions of CERCLA require a release of a specified amount of a hazardous substance before it must be reported, the cost recovery provision does not state a threshold amount. It would be conceivable for a penny, which contains copper, a hazardous substance, to trigger liability for an entire cleanup. Some courts have dismissed without a qualm arguments concerning the amount of a hazardous substance contributed, but the Fifth Circuit Court of Appeals indicated in *Amoco Oil Co. v. Borden* that the plaintiff should be able to justify why the response costs were incurred.

A threshold issue in cost recovery actions—as in actions to require the abatement or remediation of a hazardous waste site—is identification of the potentially responsible parties. The government has been successful in catching almost everyone with any connection to the hazardous substance, but the biggest battles involve liability dependent upon relationships. For example, heirs to contaminated property, parent corporations to the target company, lenders that foreclose on contaminated property, owners of property previously contaminated, and successor corporations that acquire a company after the problem was created may all be listed as potentially responsible parties.

Another issue arises primarily in cost recovery actions brought by private parties. Since the statute requires responses to be consistent with the National Contingency Plan, private parties have a difficult burden to bear. The National Contingency Plan was revised in 1990 to indicate that substantial compliance is necessary and that the actions must result in a CERCLA-quality cleanup.

For private parties, then, the activities should include worker protection, documentation, obtaining permits, evaluation of the site and study of feasible methods of cleanup, release reporting, identification of the **applicable or relevant and appropriate requirements,** remedial design and implementation, and selection of remedy. The imperative parts of the actions are these: (1) the cleanup must protect human health and the environment, (2) it must utilize permanent and alternative technologies to the extent possible, (3), it must attain the applicable or relevant and appropriate standards, (4) it must be cost effective, and (5) meaningful public participation must occur.

COUNCIL ON ENVIRONMENTAL QUALITY (CEQ)   An organization created in 1970 by the **National Environmental Policy Act** (NEPA) to advise and recommend national policies to improve the environment. The CEQ has acted as a presidential advisor and, over the years, has been criticized for failing to play a larger role.

The CEQ establishes the regulations for an **environmental impact statement** (EIS) required by the National Environmental Policy Act. It coordinates positions of cabinet officers and independent agencies on environmental issues and assists the president in preparing an annual report on the environment.

CRITERIA POLLUTANT   An air contaminant for which a **National Ambient Air Quality Standard** has been set pursuant to the **Clean Air Act.** These pollutants include lead, **sulfur dioxide, nitrogen oxides**, carbon monoxide, **particulate** matter of 10 microns or less, and **ozone**. The criteria in the term refers to the limitation, but the pollutants were chosen because the administrator of the **Environmental Protection**

Agency determined that a standard was necessary for them in order to protect the public health.

The selection of a criteria pollutant hinges on its persistence. A toxic **air pollutant** is more dangerous, but a criteria pollutant tends to be generated from a multitude of sources, both mobile (cars) and stationary (industrial plants). For that reason, criteria pollutants are both more common and more difficult to control.

CUYAHOGA RIVER   In 1969, the Cuyahoga River caught on fire in Cleveland, Ohio. It was not the only river to burst into flames, though. During that decade, three other rivers also burned. However, the Cuyahoga River became a symbol of the deteriorating condition of rivers in the United States, and it is often cited as a precipitator of the first comprehensive water pollution law, the **Clean Water Act.** The fire was caused by uncontrolled dumping of oil and chemicals into the river. When hot slag was accidentally discharged into the river, it ignited the flammable mixture and caused a fire.

DDT An acronym for dichloro-diphenol-trichloroethane, an extremely toxic pesticide that was widely used from 1939 to the early 1970s. At the time it was developed, it was considered a valuable tool for agriculture. But problems with DDT use slowly became apparent. Because it accumulates in fatty tissues of wildlife and breaks down slowly, DDT passes through the food chain easily. It is also highly toxic to fish and birds. By causing eggshells to thin, DDT brought some species of birds to the brink of extinction.

The use of DDT was banned in the United States by **administrative order** in 1971 and in Europe later in the 1970s. However, developing countries are still using it because they can obtain it elsewhere. In some countries, the levels of DDT in human tissue and mother's milk is far above the acceptable levels. Even in the United States, it persists in tissue of animals, fish and birds today, and is a common contaminant in groundwater. See also **Carson, Rachel.**

DE MINIMIS The term used in environmental law to describe a small deviation from the norm or from what is required. For example, a permittee that is allowed to discharge five milligrams of sodium per liter of wastewater would describe five and a half milligrams as a *de minimis* violation.

DE MINIMIS/DE MICROMIS **PARTIES** Persons who sent only small amounts of waste to a particular **hazardous waste** site. Under the terms of the **Comprehensive Environmental Response, Compensation, and Liability Act** (CERCLA), anyone who has any connection with a hazardous waste site may be liable to clean up the entire problem. See **potentially responsible parties.** At many hazardous waste sites, however, parties whose contributions were minimal may be considered *de minimis* or *de micromis* parties and allowed special settlement options.

According to the **Environmental Protection Agency** (EPA), *de minimis* parties at various sites have contributed amounts equal to .07 to 10 percent of total waste, with a mean of 1.059 percent. *De micromis* parties contributed even less. The EPA determines who *de minimis* or *de micromis* parties are at any given **Superfund** site.

Benefits of Being Designated a *De Minimis* or *De Micromis* Party

The Comprehensive Environmental Response, Compensation, and Liability Act has frightening aspects to it. Fault has nothing to do with liability, and once a person is named as a potentially responsible party, he may be responsible for cleaning up the entire site.

As an example, suppose that in 1978 a symphony orchestra disposed of several containers of cleaning fluid, a hazardous substance [see **hazardous substances**], at a landfill that is now an abandoned hazardous waste site. The EPA has the right under the statute to require the orchestra to clean up the entire site. If the orchestra is named as a potentially responsible party, it could be forced into years of negotiations and litigation costs, not to mention expenses for the work done at the site.

But it is likely that the EPA may decide not to pursue the orchestra. Even so, the musicians' nightmare is far from over, because the law allows any party that has acted to clean up the site to sue other potentially responsible parties for contribution to the cleanup. It also allows lawsuits by parties to recover their costs. Thus the orchestra could be forced to pay even though the EPA itself had declined to bring it into the cleanup activities.

Fortunately, CERCLA provides relief to small contributors of waste at Superfund sites through the *de minimis* and *de micromis* designations. However, the EPA has to take action to provide it. If a party is determined by the agency to be a *de minimis* party, the EPA can work out an agreement with that party early in the cleanup process. The agreement may be either a consent decree or an **administrative order.**

Settlements with *de minimis* parties are advantageous to both the EPA and the parties. The EPA reduces the number of parties involved, gains instant cash for the Superfund or the cleanup, and can point to some resolution in the case. The *de minimis* parties escape from the proceedings, pay a determined amount, and obtain protection from the government against other parties that might otherwise sue them later. Thus, if the EPA decides the orchestra is a *de minimis* party and settles with it, other parties at the site cannot sue it for a share of their cleanup costs. The orchestra will pay once and walk away from the site.

The settlement amount required from a *de minimis* party is based on the government's estimate of the costs to clean up the hazardous wastes. If the government has not yet selected a remedy at the site, it will consider the costs at similar sites to obtain a figure. The *de minimis* party must then pay the percentage for which it is determined to be responsible. Frequently, though, the cleanup costs more than was originally thought, and in that case, the government has the right to sue the parties for the additional costs. However, the government will trade that right in the settlement agreement if the party pays an additional sum called a premium. The premium usually ranges from 50 to 100 percent of the calculated cost. Therefore, if the government decides a party's share of a cleanup is $1,000, the party will pay an additional $500 to $1,000 to obtain a covenant not to sue. The EPA guidance makes it clear that the amount of the premium will determine how broad the covenant not to sue will be.

Determining *De Minimis* Status

The most recent guidance on settlements with *de minimis* contributors of waste to Superfund sites describes how the EPA determines who may qualify. Besides the volume of waste contributed, the EPA considers its toxicity.

At any site hazardous enough to be on the federal list, much of the waste is toxic. The issue, then, is whether the waste contributed by a specific party is significantly more toxic or has potential for significantly greater hazardous effects than other waste at the site. Because the emphasis is on early settlement, the EPA may not have enough information at the time to accurately calculate the volume of waste contributed by a given party. Therefore, the EPA may estimate.

Once the calculations or estimates of total wastes are made, the EPA considers individual contributions. Sometimes a facility has no idea it is a potentially responsible party until the EPA notifies it. If it has evidence it contributed relatively small amounts of waste, it can present that to the EPA. Based on the total volume of waste, the EPA will set a cutoff for *de minimis* parties. If a party can show it is below that amount, which has traditionally varied from .07 percent to 10 percent, it can try to cash out of the cleanup.

Another class of *de minimis* parties is landowners. The current landowner of a Superfund site may be liable for cleanup of the property, whether or not he helped create the problem. However, the statute provides a defense to liability: the **innocent purchaser** defense.

The importance of this provision is illustrated in the following example. A local company took industrial wastes to a local farm where the farm owner allowed the wastes to be dumped in a lagoon. Later the farm owner died and the property was sold. The new owner did not know about the arrangement with the now-defunct company, had never allowed dumping, and had done nothing to cause a problem. But, unless he can *prove* his innocence, he may be liable for the entire cost of the cleanup.

If the landowner can prove his innocence, the statute will absolve him from all liability. However, the defense is one which must be proven, and that typically requires going to court. Given the lengthy litigation procedures involving Superfund sites, a landowner could expend great sums of money before being allowed to present a defense. The EPA has now issued a guidance document for settlement with current landowners designed to save innocent purchasers from litigation costs by giving them an opportunity to settle earlier in the process.

The Comprehensive Environmental Response, Compensation, and Liability Act was amended in 1986 by the **Superfund Amendments and Reauthorization Act.** In addition to spelling out the defense that can prove innocence, a provision was added allowing settlement with landowners if the settlement involves only a minor portion of the response costs. Before it can settle with a landowner, the EPA must determine that (1) the owner did not conduct or permit the property to be used for creation, transportation, storage, treatment, or disposal of any hazardous substance; (2) the owner did not contribute to the release or threat of release of a hazardous substance; and (3) the owner did not have actual or constructive knowledge about transportation, generation, storage, treatment, or disposal of hazardous substances at the property.

There are a number of possible readings of this settlement provision. The EPA has interpreted it to mean that the landowner must prove the same things to the agency that he would have to prove in court. This interpretation is the most favorable to the government, but the EPA's power to settle such cases is entirely discretionary, so the landowner does not have much leverage. If the EPA decides to enter into negotiations, it will attempt to determine whether the landowner can prove he is an innocent purchaser. The more evidence of innocence he can provide, the guidance states, the better his settlement terms will be. A settlement might require little more from the landowner than providing access and not interfering with the cleanup. On the other hand, the landowner might have to pay a portion of the cleanup costs. The major advantage of settling with the government, however, is the contribution protection the landowner would receive against other potentially responsible parties. See **contribution rights.**

De Micromis **Parties**

The EPA has created a subclass of *de minimis* parties called *de micromis* waste contributors, those that have sent "minuscule" amounts of hazardous waste to a listed site. In the past, the government has rarely pursued such parties, even though the statute authorizes it. The cost of suing everyone who may have sent something to a hazardous waste site is seldom justified when the government can simply sue the parties it believes contributed the most and/or are capable of paying the bill for the cleanup.

Thus the law does not excuse a person because he sent only a tiny amount of hazardous waste to a site, but the EPA may choose not to sue a person because the effort is not justified by the contribution. So, for example, a party who sent a can of used oil to a site one time may be ignored in favor of industries that sent large volumes of hazardous waste to the site. However, the statute is written in terms of joint and several liability, which means the used oil contributor could be responsible for cleaning up the entire mess. His liability, then, could simply seethe and wait while the EPA forces other parties to do the work and pay for the cleanup. After some of the work is finished, the parties that have paid can sue anyone else who is a potentially responsible party under the law, including the person who sent one can of used oil to the site. What often happens is the parties who have settled or paid for part of the costs will send letters to other parties, demanding a contribution.

The EPA determined that often persons who get such letters do not understand that they are not dealing with the government; nor do they realize that the government can give them relief. As a result, the EPA recently issued guidance on entering into settlements with *de micromis* parties based on this major premise: the EPA does not want potentially responsible parties determining how to enforce the law or who will pay for cleanup. Thus, if the EPA is aware of the letters, it can offer settlement orders or decrees to *de micromis* parties; the parties themselves can also come forward and ask for relief. The EPA is not required to seek out the parties, though, just as it is not required to settle with them.

Because the amounts of *de micromis* settlements will be extremely small in the big picture, EPA policy does not allow any negotiations. The *de micromis* parties must accept the document as it is written, paying a portion of the cleanup costs to receive both protection against other parties and a covenant not to sue from the government. Premiums are not necessary in this case.

In determining which parties are the *de micromis* parties, the EPA considers the toxicity of the waste they contributed along with the volume. The EPA estimates that at a site where all the wastes are similar, a *de micromis* party's share would be about .001 percent. But at a site where there is a lot of variation in waste, the *de micromis* party may have contributed larger amounts of waste with lower toxicity. At those sites, the cutoff could be as high as .1 percent of the total volume at the site.

The EPA has not used *de minimis* settlements as much as many would like, but the public's impatience with the Superfund program has begun to have an impact: emphasis is now being placed on working out agreements with small contributors as early as possible in the process.

DEBARMENT   A procedure developed to prevent chronic violators of the **Clean Water Act** and the **Clean Air Act** from obtaining federal contracts. Also called *listing*, debarment can be either mandatory, in the case of a criminal conviction against a business or a person supervising a business, or discretionary, if the violation is civil rather than criminal.

Once violations of the Clean Air Act or Clean Water Act have been established through a court judgment or administrative action, the **Environmental Protection Agency** (EPA) may, at its discretion, begin the procedure to debar the facility from government contracts. First the EPA submits a recommendation for listing to the listing officer. Then the owner, operator, or supervisor of the facility is notified of the proceeding. Unless the facility requests a **hearing** before a case examiner, it is debarred when its name is published in the *Federal Register* on the List of Violating Facilities. A debarred facility may not hold government contracts.

In cases of discretionary debarment, removal from the list is automatic, ordinarily after a year. In mandatory debarments, however, the facility remains on the list until it is formally removed. Before removal can take place, the listing officer must be notified by the assistant administrator of the EPA that the problems have been corrected. Alternatively, the case examiner or administrator may file a decision to remove.

DELANEY CLAUSE   A provision in the Federal Food, Drug, and Cosmetic Act (FFDCA) that prohibits unsafe additives in processed food and bans additives that have been shown to cause cancer (carcinogens) in animals or humans. This ban against carcinogens has created a conflict for the **Environmental Protection Agency** (EPA) in administering this and the second statute that regulates pesticides, the **Federal Insecticide, Fungicide, and Rodenticide Act** (FIFRA).

Generally, when the EPA decides whether to allow a substance to be marketed, it must weigh the benefits of its use against the risks. Thus, when the EPA registers a pesticide, it completes a risk-benefit analysis and establishes tolerances for pesticide residue on raw agricultural products. But *any* residue from a pesticide considered carcinogenic is prohibited by the Delaney Clause. It is possible, then, for a farmer to use a registered pesticide according to directions, to achieve an EPA-approved level of residue, and still not be allowed to sell or process his crop if the pesticide is considered cancer-causing—no matter how small the risk. (Pesticides are considered additives in processed food.)

Pesticides are toxic by design, created to kill weeds, insects, rodents, fungi, and other organisms harmful to agriculture. But the goal in pesticide development is to make products that aid agriculture without posing unacceptable risks to humans. Because the sophistication of measurement and growing accuracy of projections have exposed potential risks far more clearly than in the past, it is increasingly difficult to find benign substances. Today, pesticides are found in drinking water sources and in meat, vegetables, and fruits—even when no pesticides were applied to them directly. Determining the extent of people's exposure to them is a difficult task. As new pesticides are developed, safety standards are becoming more stringent, but older, more dangerous pesticides remain on the market. Some people fear that they will be the only ones available if new pesticides cannot be registered due to ultimate prohibitions on residues in food.

Because of the problems it creates, the EPA tried to modify the Delaney Clause in 1988 by issuing interpretive regulations that would allow four registered pesticides to be used even though they had been shown to cause cancer. The EPA argued that they would pose only a minimal [see *de minimis*] risk. In the case of *Les v. Reilly*, the court found the EPA's regulations contrary to law: the EPA has no authority to allow cancer-causing substances in processed foods, regardless of the degree of danger.

The EPA is currently working with the Food and Drug Administration and the Board on Agriculture of the National Research Council to refine methods of setting tolerances for pesticides in food. Many solutions have been proposed that would address the conflict created by the Delaney

Clause, but only a revision of the statute by Congress will be effective. When the congressional debate occurs, social pressures for safe food, particularly for children, will have to be weighed against the benefits of pesticides to agriculture.

DELEGATION The process through which power to act or regulate is given to another person or agency by the one authorized to act. For example, Congress enacts statutes that state its general objectives, then delegates the authority to fill in the details of the statute through regulations to an agency like the **Environmental Protection Agency** (EPA).

Delegation is common in environmental law. When the EPA was first created and environmental statutes became common, the EPA was responsible for most actions required by the laws. Some authority was given to states, but the country was facing what many believed to be a crisis, so enforcement authority centered in the federal government. During the Reagan administration [see **Reagan, Ronald**], however, emphasis shifted to decentralization and paring down government programs.

The **Clean Air Act** was the first major environmental law to create a system for delegation of programs. The **Clean Water Act** followed, and now others are being delegated as well. If authority is to be delegated to the states, a statute will specify the requirements the state must meet before the EPA will relinquish its control. The process is similar for all environmental laws. First, the state must request the delegation. To qualify, it must have an agency and sufficient employees to enforce the provisions of the law, and state law must authorize the agency to act and to assess penalties. Next, the agency must promulgate rules that are at least as stringent as the federal rules. The state's program is then reviewed by the EPA. If the state has satisfied all requirements, the EPA will delegate the program.

Delegation doesn't always stop at the state level. Often states choose to allow county and local agencies to handle some of their responsibilities. For example, an air quality district may deal with all of the permitting and programs that protect air quality within its region.

Once a delegation is made, the delegating agency retains power to oversee the recipient agency. Furthermore, the delegator may step in and enforce the law if the other agency does not. The EPA, for example, can check state records, review permit applications submitted to the state, demand changes to the state program, take the state's authority away, or sue a violator within the state.

DERIVED-FROM RULE   A rule issued by the **Environmental Protection Agency** (EPA) that applies to wastes generated in the process of treating **hazardous waste**s.

The **Resource Conservation and Recovery Act** (RCRA) is the statute that deals with solid and hazardous waste. Pursuant to that law, the EPA has issued three lists of hazardous wastes, and for those wastes not listed by name it has established the characteristics that classify a waste as hazardous [see **characteristic waste**].

One question arising from the treatment, storage, or disposal of hazardous wastes is how to classify the residue from those activities. If a hazardous waste is burned, what is the status of the ash? If a chemical is applied and a leachate is caught, is the leachate also hazardous?

The EPA's derived-from rule starts with the assumption that any waste generated from treatment, storage, or disposal of hazardous waste is also hazardous waste unless it is exempted. It is exempted only if it is delisted or it no longer exhibits the characteristics of a hazardous waste. The first exemption is available only for wastes derived from listed wastes, the second only for wastes that were originally hazardous because they were ignitable, corrosive, reactive, or failed the toxic characteristic leaching procedure (a test required by the EPA). For example, if hazardous waste A, a listed waste, is burned, the ash is hazardous unless the owner of the ash gets the EPA to exempt it. However, if hazardous waste B is hazardous because it is corrosive, the ash from its burning will be hazardous only if it remains corrosive. A related rule, the **mixture rule,** states that if a listed waste is mixed with another waste, the resulting waste is hazardous. The way to escape the hazardous label in this case is through delisting.

The purpose of these rules is to ensure a listed waste and its by-products do not slip out from under the regulations controlling hazardous waste treatment, storage, or disposal until the EPA determines that they are no longer hazardous.

In 1991, the D.C. Circuit Court of Appeals determined that the EPA did not go through the necessary rule-making process when it created the derived-from and mixture rules. In *Shell Oil Company v. EPA*, the challenge was both to the substance of the rules and the procedure that created them. The court did not rule on the substance because it did not have to. Instead, it determined that the initial notice of rulemaking did not mention either rule and that the rules were not a logical outgrowth of the proposal. The original proposal dealt with establishing criteria for identifying hazardous waste characteristics and listing particular wastes as hazardous. That public notice, which resulted in five massive public meetins and even more comments through formal submission in writing, did not mention the possibility of regulating mixtures or derived-from wastes. The court suggested, however, that the EPA reinstate the rules on an emergency basis while it completed the proper steps. The rules were reinstated by the EPA on an interim basis on 3 March 1992. After they were reinstated, EPA treated the rules as if they had always been valid. Thus, although the circuit court found them to be flawed, the EPA's position sought to eliminate any lapse in the rules from the time they had first been promulgated.

An administrative case, decided by the **Environmental Appeals Board** in 1994, determined that EPA's retroactive application of the rules was not permissible. The board reasoned that once the court invalidated the rules, they did not exist from the time of creation in 1980 until they were reinstated in March 1992.

In a later notice (20 May 1992), the EPA solicited comments on two different approaches to identifying hazardous waste. Either of these approaches would exempt some derived-from wastes and mixtures from hazardous waste classification without requiring a delisting process. One proposal is a concentration-based approach to identification: if the mixture or other waste is below a certain concentration, it is no longer a hazardous waste. The other expands the current system of identifying wastes by their characteristics to define when a waste enters or exits the hazardous waste system [see **characteristic waste**]. Refining the hazardous waste identification system will ease the burden on both the EPA and the regulated public. It will allow the EPA to focus more on the substance of the regulations than on threshold identifications, and help generators of waste avoid lengthy delisting processes. However, Congress added a rider to the Deparment of Veterans Affairs and Housing and Urban Development and Independent Agencies Appropriation Act that required the EPA to promulgate revisions to the mixture and derived-from rules. The law prohibited the agency from making revisions effective before 1 October 1993. The EPA withdrew its earlier proposal.

On 22 March 1995, the EPA entered into a consent decree with the Environmental Technology Council. Approved 12 May 1995, the decree requires the EPA to propose a replacement rule by 15 August 1995 and promulgate a final rule by 15 December 1996. The first deadline has been missed.

DIRECT DISCHARGER   A person, company, or other entity that sends wastewater to a water body without going through a treatment plant run by someone else. The most common direct dischargers are **publicly owned treatment works,** the entities that treat sewage for communities. Industrial facilities may also have their own systems to treat wastewater and release it directly without further handling, but they often send their water to publicly owned treatment works after initial treatment. See **pretreatment; industrial user.**

Anyone who is directly discharging wastewater into waters of the United States must have a permit for the pollutants being released. For all waters within the boundaries of the United States except wetlands, the permit is called a **National Pollutant Discharge Elimination System (NPDES) permit,** available from the **Environmental Protection Agency (EPA)** or a state agency [see **Clean Water Act**]. For **wetland**s, permission is granted by a Section 404 permit, referring to the section in the Clean Water Act that governs **dredging and filling.** It is available from the U.S. Army **Corps of Engineers.** Ocean Dumping permit authority is shared by the Corps of Engineers and the EPA. See **Marine Protection, Research, and Sanctuaries Act.**

DREDGING AND FILLING   The **Clean Water Act** controls dredging, filling, and other activities that may disturb or change a water body by removing or placing material within it. Although this provision of the law may appear to have limited application, it has been extended both in activities and locations regulated.

Dredge and fill activity includes not only disposal, but intentional (and unintentional) placement of dirt, pillars, debris, and other materials in waterways. These activities often become an issue when developers convert wetlands to dry land. Plowing within a wetlands is also considered filling, since dirt from the furrow will fall to either side of the blade.

Some activities within waters or wetlands are exempted from permitting if specified impacts are avoided. Maintenance, temporary roads, and a few agricultural projects fall within the exemptions. Also, the U.S. Army **Corps of Engineers** or a state may issue general permits. If an endeavor fits within the terms of a general permit, an individual permit need not be obtained [see **taking**].

The Corps of Engineers has primary responsibility for this provision (Section 404) of the Clean Water Act. It issues individual and general permits for dredge and fill operations. Through interpretation of the law by the EPA and the Corps, endorsed by the courts, the need for a permit extends to **wetland**s as well as rivers, streams, and other waters.

DRINKING WATER STANDARD   Limits the amounts of particular contaminants in the public water supply system. The **Environmental Protection Agency** (EPA) is authorized by the **Safe Drinking Water Act** to set primary standards for 83 contaminants, most of which have been completed. The standards are stated in terms of **maximum contaminant levels** (MCLs).

There are two types of standards: the National Primary Drinking Water Regulations and the National Secondary Drinking Water Regulations. The primary regulations are designed to protect the health of the public; the secondary standards address aesthetics such as odor and appearance. Only the primary standards are enforceable, and drinking water standards apply only to public water supply systems. A public water system is one that provides piped water for human use to an average of at least 25 persons or connections to 15 locations.

In establishing the maximum contaminant levels, the EPA first sets goals at a level where no adverse health effects are known or anticipated to occur, allowing an ample margin of safety. For contaminants that do not cause cancer, the goals are based on a reference dose (determined through tests) and assume that an individual will drink two liters of water from the same source every day for seventy years. For carcinogens, the EPA sets the goal at zero.

The primary standards are set as close to the goals as feasible, taking into consideration the best technology and treatment techniques available. The EPA must use field conditions (as opposed to laboratory analysis) as the basis for its determinations, and cost of treatment must be taken into account. If the EPA decides it cannot determine the appropriate maximum contaminant level, it can require specific types of treatment.

Secondary standards are advisory only; states may use them in their own laws if they choose, but the EPA cannot enforce them. An example of a contaminant with a secondary standard is fluoride, which discolors teeth, mottling them or turning them brown. Because fluoride does not actually damage teeth, a primary standard was not necessary to protect the health of the public, so the EPA declined to issue one. This decision was unpopular in many communities.

DUE DILIGENCE   See **innocent purchaser.**

EARTH DAY A day in late April dedicated to environmental awareness. The first Earth Day, on 22 April 1970, is often cited as the catalyst for legislative action to remedy environmental problems.

Wisconsin Senator Gaylord Nelson gave a speech in late 1969 advocating a "teach-in" for environmental issues. The public's enthusiastic reaction surprised him, and soon he had to hire a staff to field calls about his idea. Although President Richard M. Nixon was not pleased with the concept, political pressure convinced him to allow participation by various federal departments, including the Department of Interior. Eventually a day was set for the "celebration."

The first Earth Day was called a communist plot by some—the Daughters of the American Revolution, for example—and criticized by radical groups as an attempt to cloud other issues. Nevertheless, it was a huge success, with over 1,500 colleges and 10,000 schools participating. The message to Congress was clear: the environment is important to the American people.

Earth Day is still celebrated yearly. International as well as American environmental groups take part, offering information, workshops, and exhibits.

EARTH FIRST! This radical environmental group with no paid staff, organizational structure, or formal leadership prefers to be called a movement. Founded in 1980 by David Foreman and others, Earth First! sees the system of environmental regulation as flawed and corrupt. A clenched fist is its symbol; its motto is "No compromise in the defense of Mother Earth."

Earth First! members advocate direct action against property and machinery. This practice is called monkey wrenching, after a book called *The Monkey Wrench Gang*, written by Edward Abbey and published in 1976. (Its plot involved efforts to blow up a dam and free a river.) In 1985 Foreman published a related book, *Ecodefense: A Field Guide to Monkeywrenching*.

He left the movement in the early 1990s. He stated in his book, *Confessions of an Eco-Warrior*, that he no longer believes Earth First! represents his views. It has moved toward "anti-capitalist rhetoric and an overwhelming emphasis on direct action to the exclusion of other traditional Earth First! techniques." [p. 219] He continues to believe in conservationism and biocentrism.

Earth First! has been associated with numerous direct actions, such as spiking trees (to make logging them impractical), sabotaging oil exploration equipment, and ramming whaling ships. Members have also engaged in sit-ins and chained themselves to trees. However, according to spokespersons, the organization does not engage in direct action as a group and does not necessarily endorse it. Even so, the Federal Bureau of Investigation has targeted members of Earth First! in many investigations. In one undercover operation alone, the FBI spent two million dollars to gather evidence against Foreman and others.

EFFLUENT LIMITATION   A standard for discharges of contaminants into waters of the United States from a **direct discharger.** Numerous effluent limitations have been established under the **Clean Water Act.**

At first, limits on effluents were set only for the most common pollutants, such as total suspended solids, fecal coliform, ammonia, oil and grease. However, the wastewater from a number of industries discharging toxic pollutants was not being regulated. The **Environmental Protection Agency** (EPA) had been tasked by the 1972 Clean Water Act to establish effluent limitations for industries. However, it hesitated to do so because it interpreted the Clean Water Act as giving no consideration to technological feasibility or cost. So, as has often been the case, the EPA was sued. In a consent decree with the **Natural Resources Defense Council,** the EPA agreed to issue effluent limitations for 21 major industries. The 1977 revisions to the Clean Water Act included the terms of the consent decree as part of the statute.

Effluent limitations for toxic pollutants must take into account any health impacts and provide an ample margin of safety. Cost of treatment is not an issue, as with the provisions of the **Clean Air Act** provisions. Thus the effluent limitations may force the development of technology, since the standards may not be reachable with available methods.

ⓘ EMERGENCY PLANNING AND COMMUNITY RIGHT-TO-KNOW ACT (EPCRA)

The statute designed to notify the public and appropriate agencies about **hazardous substances** and **extremely hazardous substance**s used, manufactured, or stored at a facility, and to plan to deal with releases of such substances. It was enacted in 1986 as part of the **Superfund Amendments and Reauthorization Act** (SARA) and is often called SARA, Title III.

In December 1984, a large amount of toxic gas was released from Union Carbide's plant in **Bhopal,** India. Shortly afterward, the incident nearly repeated itself in Institute, West Virginia. As a result, members of the public became understandably concerned about hazardous substances in their communities. New Jersey provided the first legislative reaction to public pressure, but Congress was not far behind with EPCRA. The system it established was extensive, covering reporting, planning, and creation of local and state bodies to oversee the plans.

Community Responsibilities: Emergency Response Plans

The law starts with integrated planning. Each state is required to designate a **State Emergency Response Commission** (SERC), which is then responsible for defining emergency planning districts and appointing Local Emergency Planning Committees (LEPC).

Any facility that handles extremely hazardous substances in amounts greater than the "threshold planning quantity" (stated in regulations) must notify the Local Emergency Planning Committee and name a facility representative. The initial deadline for these actions has passed, but if a facility begins handling extremely hazardous substances after the deadline, it must notify within 60 days.

After the Local Emergency Planning Committee has identified the local facilities that handle extremely hazardous substances, it must review the information and develop a plan to respond to an emergency within its area. The plan must identify the facilities involved, routes used to transport extremely hazardous substances, and risk-related facilities such as power stations, schools, hospitals, natural gas facilities, etc. It must describe procedures to be followed in response to a chemical release, a strategy to notify the public in an emergency, and evacuation plans. The committees must also specify how they will determine whether a release occurred and the probable area affected. All emergency equipment and facilities within the area must be listed, along with their location and the person responsible. Finally, a training program must be developed and described.

Completed emergency plans are submitted to the State Emergency Response Commission, which reviews them and determines whether they are sufficient. The state committees also receive information when a release occurs.

Emergency Release Reporting

Another section of EPCRA requires facilities to report releases of hazardous substances and extremely hazardous substances if the amount released is above an established amount (called a reportable quantity) and exposes persons off the site of the facility. Reports must go to the local and state committees and the fire department. In addition, if the material released is on the list of hazardous substances regulated by the **Comprehensive Environmental Response, Compensation, and Liability Act,** the facility must notify the National Response Center.

The initial notification may be made either by telephone or in person, but a written report must follow. If the release is from a vehicle, simply calling the emergency number, 911, or the operator is sufficient for the first report. Notification must include enough information for the **emergency response** team to begin working on the situation: chemical name, amount, whether it is an extremely hazardous substance, time and duration of the release, precautions necessary, potential health effects and medical attention necessary, and what environmental media (air, earth, water, groundwater) were affected. The facility contact's name and phone number must be released.

Speed of reporting is critical to response and emphasized in the law. If a facility does not have all the information required, it cannot delay notification to gather it. Large penalties have been assessed for slow reporting.

This reporting requirement applies to emergency releases only. Releases that occur in normal circumstances are reported differently. The reporting requirement does not apply to continuous releases of hazardous substances, which must be initially reported to the same organizations as the emergency release, but in a written form. Facilities must follow up in a month with another report, and then provide an annual notice and evaluation.

Community Right-To-Know Provisions

Three sections of EPCRA require informing the community. The first section is very broad, covering many employers. It uses a provision of the

Hazard Communication Standard, regulations established by the Occupational Safety and Health Administration, to determine threshold reporting requirements.

The Hazard Communication Standard is often called the Worker's Right-To-Know. Employers who use **hazardous chemicals** in their business are required to train their employees about using them safely if the employees are likely to be exposed to them. One of the critical elements of this training and information program is providing copies of **Material Safety Data Sheets** for hazardous chemicals to their employees. These sheets, supplied by the manufacturer or distributor of the hazardous chemical, give vital information, such as chemical name, routes of exposure (such as inhalation, ingestion, skin), hazards associated with the chemical, and emergency treatment.

EPCRA states that employers required to provide Material Safety Data Sheets to their employees must also provide copies to the state, local emergency committees, and the fire department if they have more than a specified quantity of a hazardous chemical. The employer may supply either the data sheets themselves or a list of the hazardous chemicals. This information must be revised as necessary.

A company required to file the list above must file an annual inventory of chemicals as well. The inventory may be simple (called a Tier One form), or the planning agencies may require more information (a Tier Two). Required information includes identification of the substance, amount, location, and daily average of the amount of the substance at the facility.

Toxic chemical release inventory reporting is also required from certain industries if they have ten or more full-time employees and use more than the threshold planning quantity of an extremely hazardous substance in their businesses. "Extremely hazardous substances" are listed by the **Environmental Protection Agency** (EPA). The list includes a minimum trigger for reporting, called the "Threshold planning quantity." These reports are made to the state and the EPA. A national database is used to input the data.

Trade Secrets

With the amount of reporting required under the statute, manufacturers find it difficult to protect trade secrets. EPCRA gives limited protection for trade secrets. However, in an emergency, the facility must provide whatever information is needed to facilitate response.

The specific identity of a hazardous ingredient in a formula or process may be protected if no emergency exists, as long as the facility has taken the proper steps to claim the formula or process as a trade secret. Information on the location of hazardous substances and extremely hazardous substances may also be protected, but the state and local governments must be provided with the information so they can respond to emergencies.

Waste Reduction

If a facility is subject to the **toxic release inventory** requirements, it must also follow the **Pollution Prevention Act**'s mandate to file a report discussing its waste reduction efforts. This new law puts emphasis on reducing waste at the source: new processes, treatments, or raw materials. The report is also public, so the attitude of the facility can be compared with its output toxic chemicals.

Information and Lawsuits

When EPCRA was enacted, one of industry's greatest fears was that reports would be used in personal injury cases. To some extent, the fear is justified. Any interested person in a given community now has access to information concerning chemical releases and what was done in response to them. So when a suit is filed, the plaintiff's lawyer no longer has to recreate much of the evidence about the release itself. As a result, the number of toxic tort lawsuits filed has grown dramatically over the past decade, and availability of information has contributed to the impetus. Industries know that they now operate in a fishbowl. Whether this statute will further encourage litigation remains to be seen.

The central issue, though, is the ability of the community—and the facility itself—to respond to releases. The success of these efforts will depend not only on how well facilities meet their reporting obligations, but more importantly, on how well they plan to avoid a release in the first place.

EMERGENCY RESPONSE   An action taken to remove a threat to humans or the environment immediately after the release of a hazardous substance [see **hazardous substances**], an **extremely hazardous substance**, or oil.

The key to effective emergency response is planning. Thus, under the **Oil Pollution Act** of 1990, operators of vessels are required to develop a plan to deal with emergency spills or leaks, train their employees to respond, and communicate with the agencies responsible for the area. Similarly, the **Emergency Planning and Community Right-To-Know** Act details numerous steps a facility must take to inform the response agencies and the public about potential exposures from the facility.

Agencies that may be involved in emergency response include the **Environmental Protection Agency,** the **Coast Guard,** the **Corps of Engineers,** local planning agencies, state agencies, and the National Response Center. However, the primary actor is the person or facility that caused or allowed the release. That person is closest to the emergency and can act more quickly and effectively than an agency.

EMISSION A discharge of gases, solids, or liquids from a source. The term is most commonly used in environmental law to describe discharges to the air, but it can include releases to water or ground. Inherent in the term is the assumption that some type of pollutant is involved.

Emissions either come from a conduit, such as a pipe or stack, or escape from a process. The latter type of emissions are called fugitive emissions. See **Clean Air Act** and **emission trading.**

EMISSION TRADING Any method of reducing **emissions** from one source to compensate for new emissions from another. Trading may be limited to one facility, or it may stretch as far as anywhere within an air district. The owner of the original emission limits (the permitted amount) may use trading to meet his own limits, yet still expand a facility, or sell or trade reductions (called *credits*) to another facility.

Four major categories of emissions trading exist: bubbles [see **bubble concept**], netting, emission offsets, and emission reduction banking. Bubbles, most common of the four, allow existing plants or groups of plants to increase emissions at one source in exchange for decreasing them at another. The bubble concept comes from imagining a bubble enclosing an entire facility, then measuring total emissions instead of focusing on one discharge point. Example: A plant has four stacks. The manufacturing process makes it difficult to control emissions for stacks 1 and 2, but the plant can make stacks 3 and 4 perform better than is required by the permit. If the controls on stacks 3 and 4 can make up for the excess emissions at stacks 1 and 2, the entire plant may be treated as a bubbled facility. Total emissions cannot exceed the aggregated amount for the four stacks.

Netting applies to modifications of existing major facilities. The **Clean Air Act** requires facilities of certain sizes to go through **New Source Review** before they modify. If the modifications will not increase emissions or the increase will be insignificant, the source does not have to go through all of the requirements for New Source Review. Instead, the net effect is considered. A preconstruction review must take place, and the source is not exempt from the **New Source Performance Standards** or the regulations for **hazardous air pollutants**. See **national emission standards for hazardous air pollutants**.

Emission offsets are used by states to allow growth in an area. An offset requires a reduction in one source to offset the increase in other emissions. The sources need not be in the same immediate vicinity, but they must be in the same air quality region. Depending on the status of the air quality for the pollutant involved, different standards will apply.

Emission reduction banking is aptly named. It means that a facility accumulates emission reduction credits, which can be stored for later use in bubbles, offsets, or netting transactions. If the state allows it, the owner of the credits can also sell or trade the credits.

Purpose of Emissions Trading

The ultimate goal of emissions trading is to provide flexibility for industry. At the facility level, the operator may shift resources to control emissions without increasing the total amount released, so emissions trading can sometimes result in innovative approaches to pollution control. The netting approach reduces agency review requirements but puts the burden on the facility to control emissions and avoid triggering the requirement for full review. Emission offsets and banking give the state flexibility in allowing new sources without sacrificing air quality. They also introduce marketing into air pollution: sources can sell their reductions, trade them, use them, or give them away. Numerous restrictions apply to these mechanisms, however, and the EPA maintains ultimate responsibility for approval.

Restrictions on Emissions Trading

Emission reduction credits are specific to the pollutant involved. (For example, **sulfur dioxide** credits can only be used for sulfur dioxide emissions.) The EPA also requires that emission reduction credits meet four criteria: they must be surplus, enforceable, permanent, and quantifiable. Only reductions that are not required, relied upon by the state to meet federal requirements, or used to meet other regulatory requirements are considered surplus. The reductions must be established in relationship to the baseline emissions allowed for the area.

ENDANGERED SPECIES ACT (ESA)   A conservation statute enacted in 1973 to protect endangered and threatened animals, fish, and plants. The Department of Interior is charged with regulatory responsibility, but power to enforce it is delegated to the Fish and Wildlife Service (a branch of the Department of Interior).

The Fish and Wildlife Service lists (and removes from the list) endangered and threatened species. It is also responsible for developing regulations to protect them.

The Endangered Species Act prohibits activities that affect endangered species, such as importing or exporting them, taking, possessing, or selling them. It allows the Fish and Wildlife Service to put similar restrictions on threatened species. Exemptions to the prohibitions in the law can be obtained for "incidental takings" and scientific experimentation. An incidental taking occurs when an activity is not directed toward the animal, fish, or plant, but it will happen as a result of another activity. For example, if a person needs to build a facility in a certain location that is the habitat of a threatened or endangered species, the development can destroy the habitat, resulting in the death of the animal—even though the intent of the development was not to possess or harm the animal. If taking is allowed, the person who is allowed to "take" the species must mitigate or compensate for the damage done. A common solution is creation of an alternative habitat and moving members of the species.

ENVIRONMENTAL APPEALS BOARD (EAB)   An arm of the **Environmental Protection Agency** (EPA) created specifically to hear administrative appeals. The EAB came into existence on 1 March 1992. The EPA explained its action in the *Federal Register* notice by stating it would ease the burden of increasing appeals and inspire confidence.

The Environmental Appeals Board consists of three judges appointed by the EPA. They must be "senior career government attorneys." The EPA is represented by its own attorneys in appeals; the opposing party may represent itself or hire an attorney.

A majority vote is required for an opinion, but two judges constitute a quorum. If a tie results, the final vote is the administrator's. Usually the board's opinions are based on the record and written briefs, but the judges may schedule and hear oral arguments. Formal decisions may be issued.

The number of administrative proceedings have increased significantly since statutes have given the EPA power to issue **administrative penalty orders**. Since it is quicker and more efficient to issue orders than to sue a violator, the EPA often prefers the orders. But as the number of orders multiply, so does the number of people who contest the decisions.

An illustration of the procedure: A permittee violated its water discharge permit three times in a month. The EPA issued a proposed order, assessing a penalty of $75,000. Permittee asked for and had a **hearing**, but the EPA issued a final order that assessed $50,000. The permittee could at this point file an appeal of the order, and it would be heard by the Environmental Appeals Board.

Before the Environmental Appeals Board existed, appeals were heard by the regional administrator or delegated to judicial officers of the agency. Delegations were permitted, but the delegation was not done in the rules themselves. In the new rules, the EAB was given the power to hear appeals.

Appeals can only be sent to the administrator if the board directs it. The idea is to reduce the burden on the administrator, so the parties cannot go around the board by appealing directly to the administrator.

The EAB can hear appeals of permit decisions as well as enforcement orders. It has power to rule on cases arising from virtually every environmental statute existing today, including **Clean Air Act, Clean Water Act, Resource Conservation and Recovery Act,** and the **Toxic Substances Control Act.**

ENVIRONMENTAL ASSESSMENT   An evaluation of the condition of real property, any improvements on it, and surrounding properties to determine whether it has environmental problems. Sometimes called an environmental site assessment, it has become common in commercial transactions.

Real Property and the Comprehensive Environmental Response, Compensation, and Liability Act

The driving force behind environmental assessments is the desire to be an **innocent purchaser.** Under the **Comprehensive Environmental Response, Compensation, and Liability Act** (commonly called **Superfund**), owners or operators of contaminated property may be forced to clean it up, even if they didn't cause the contamination. However, if a person can prove he is an innocent purchaser, he may be able to escape liability.

To do so, one of the things the landowner or operator must do is make "all appropriate inquiry into prior ownership and uses of the property, consistent with good commercial and customary practice." That requirement has solidified into an environmental assessment.

Hazardous waste site cleanup is not the only consideration, however. Some environmental situations would not create liability under Superfund but could cause extraordinary expenses, nonetheless. For example, asbestos in building materials will not trigger Superfund liability, but if the building is going to be renovated, the asbestos may have to be removed. Removal of asbestos is extremely expensive, and prospective building owners who address asbestos in the assessment will not be unpleasantly surprised later.

Similarly, petroleum storage tanks—particularly underground tanks— can leak into the soil or groundwater. Although petroleum is not covered by Superfund, the prospective owner could face hundreds of thousands of dollars cleaning up a petroleum spill under the **Resource Conservation and Recovery Act.** As a consequence, most environmental assessments include investigations about tanks.

Contents of Environmental Assessments

Each property and transaction is fact-specific. A potential buyer, lender, or lessee must consider the situation to know what is appropriate. In some cases, it is prudent to hire an independent environmental consultant to complete the assessment. In others, an in-house screening might suffice.

In general, the elements of an environmental assessment are (1) a records search, (2) interviews, (3) a site visit, and (4) communication of the results. The depth of investigation should intensify as problems arise.

Records that must be searched include databases or government records indicating **hazardous waste** releases, Superfund sites, releases from tanks, facilities that treat, store, or dispose of **hazardous substances**, and information about reported releases currently under investigation. Also, chain of title and deeds must be researched to make sure the property does not have environmental liens and that past owners are not associated with industrial activity. Violation notices, aerial photos, and fire code maps are other sources of information.

Interviews with the owner, tenants, neighbors, local government officials, and other available sources are invaluable sources of information to fill in the gaps. It often helps to have the owner, supervisor, or major tenant present when the site visit is completed.

But a true picture of the property and its environment cannot be gleaned by looking at records or talking to people. The site visit is critical to the process. During the visit, the person doing the assessment should look for signs of contamination, storage of hazardous substances or wastes, outlets for **air pollutant**s, note the health of the vegetation, and use his sense of smell as well as his sight. It is also important to notice what the vicinity is like. If it is heavily industrial, that would be important to consider because the area is more likely to be contaminated. If a landfill is next door or nearby, caution is advised.

Finally, the information must be packaged so the person reading the report can see what was done during the assessment. If an independent environmental consultant did the assessment, it should be an in-depth report, complete with professional interpretations. If it was done as a screen, the reader may have to interpret the raw information.

Occasionally, the steps above will not make a purchaser comfortable enough to go ahead with the deal without testing. For example, if the property had underground tanks in the past and no one knows whether they are still present, testing may be appropriate.

Examples of Activities Involving Environmental Assessments

Loan Involving Existing Dry-Cleaning Establishment

If a lender is loaning money to a dry-cleaning company and takes the business and property as collateral, the lender may eventually become the owner of the property. Dry-cleaners have a number of hazardous substances associated with them, so the lender should not only complete the standard evaluation, but also investigate the past and current disposal practices of the dry-cleaner thoroughly.

New Commercial Development in Former Industrial Zone
The developers could cause a release of hazardous substances or might later find out the land is contaminated, subjecting them to liability. Businesses in industrial areas often use, store, and dispose of hazardous substances or wastes, so the developers should do a significant amount of investigation before they purchase the land. Testing may be necessary, depending on the prior use of the property and surrounding uses.

Acquisition of Buildings and Property Formerly Used for Manufacturing
The purchaser may be acquiring problems not apparent immediately, so an environmental assessment should be tailored to cover the potential problems. Hazardous waste-handling activities should be investigated, and sampling of soil and groundwater is advised.

Asset or Business Acquisition
Buying the assets of a business or acquiring the company outright often subjects the purchaser to liability if a cleanup is necessary. Depending on the number of sites, the complexity of the deal, and the nature of the business, the purchaser should gather as much information as he can about the sites and the compliance history of the target company.

Purchase of Undeveloped Land for a Commercial Building
If the purchaser does not find any problems in the records, interviews, or site visit, this type of environmental assessment will be a simple one. Even so, the buyer should not assume the property is clean unless the investigation is completed.

Standards for Environmental Assessments

Over time, most in-depth assessments have evolved to include standard elements (records searches, site visits, interviews, and reports). However, the actual components have varied, and environmental consultants often take different approaches.

In 1993, the American Society for Testing and Materials, a private organization that has developed many widely used standards, issued two documents for environmental site assessments. One is for transaction screens, a scaled down version of a full-blown assessment; the other is for a Phase I assessment.

A transaction screen does not have to be done by an environmental professional. It is based on a questionnaire and encompasses all of the elements mentioned before with the exception of a report. The questionnaire is, in a sense, the report. It contains no opinions of the person who filled it out.

The Phase I assessment must be done by an environmental professional. Each step in the assessment process includes more data, and the required report must also contain professional opinions about the data collected.

Both of the standard practices are voluntary. Also, they are flexible so they can be used in many circumstances. The purpose of the standard practices is to help landowners prove they are innocent purchasers.

ENVIRONMENTAL AUDIT   An examination of a facility's or company's compliance with environmental laws and regulations. Audits may focus on one location, as in the case of an **environmental assessment,** or they may be broader and cover many facilities.

Reasons for Environmental Audits

Audits may be done prior to an acquisition of a company to determine whether liabilities may be hiding in the wing. In situations involving financing, they are usually required by the lender. Another type of audit is done by companies to determine whether they have problems they have not yet addressed. Depending on the type of business, audits may take days or weeks to complete. The results can be used to find problems, determine the cost of compliance, or identify methods to prevent pollution and reduce waste. The process can be used to train employees and sensitize them to environmental issues.

Benefits of Environmental Audits

Environmental violations subject the violator to numerous penalties. Today, it is not uncommon for the **Environmental Protection Agency** (EPA) to bring criminal charges, and even in cases that remain civil, penalties can be as high as $25,000 per day per violation.

When the EPA discovers a violation, it chooses whether to enforce the law or not. Since the agency is responsible for overseeing many statutes and thousands of facilities, it is inclined to select cases to enforce based on the message it will give to similar facilities. History of violations is considered, so companies benefit if they check their own compliance records and avoid building a negative record.

Both the EPA and the **Occupational Safety and Health Administration** have power to inspect regulated facilities. Audits can reveal weaknesses and give the business an opportunity to correct them before the regulators appear.

Another purpose of an audit is to minimize criminal liability and corporate exposure. Environmental laws are so broadly written that often the EPA can select either criminal or civil enforcement. Thoroughly investigating and addressing areas of concern reduces the chance of either option being exercised.

Corporate officials, directors, and managers may be named as defendants right along with the company. Companies can be fined; people can go to jail. A strong system of checking for compliance along with follow-up shows commitment to environmental compliance. That in itself may assist the company and the individuals.

The U.S. Sentencing Guidelines operate to standardize the types of penalties levied on criminal defendants. One factor that lightens the sentence is the existence of an auditing program.

Finally, if the EPA enforces, it can require the company to undergo an audit. They are common not only in administrative actions but also civil suits.

Disadvantages of Audits

Well-designed investigations require time, money, and manpower. Audit teams must be given enough freedom to examine anything that is compliance related. Specialists may be necessary, if the business does not already have expertise in-house. Also, the audit must be properly managed.

Because audits usually have little to do with the primary purpose of the business, they may be disruptive to the company. Records will have to be searched, processes examined, and interviews conducted. The audit teams can affect the productivity of employees and managers.

The most difficult issue for many companies is the documentation. Identifying a problem in a report raises the awareness of the business. If it is not corrected, the offense may become a criminal offense because a "knowing" violation is occurring.

Also, when documents are created, they can easily become evidence in a lawsuit. Some companies attempt to address this problem by having an attorney oversee the work of the audit team, hoping they can claim a privilege against disclosure if necessary later. Another approach is to have the audit teams identify only facts, without statements of violations or recommended action. The Department of Justice issued a document about using such evidence against a company or person when the audit was voluntary. The main focus is what happened after the audit.

Examinations of compliance can be quite useful to achieve and maintain compliance. It is crucial, however, for the company to have a commitment to correct problems after they are found. Otherwise, the benefits of an audit are greatly overshadowed by the liabilities.

ENVIRONMENTAL DEFENSE FUND (EDF)   A membership organization dedicated to addressing environmental problems. Its slogan is "The Power of Positive Solutions." EDF has been a powerful force in shaping environmental law since Fred Krupp and others formed it in 1967. Its members lobby for legislation, get involved in developing regulations, and use lawsuits against violators and the government. Its staff consists of both ecologists and lawyers, which gives it the capability to both analyze scientific data and litigate. Though it is not the only organization to recognize the benefits of the marriage of law and science, it has used both disciplines effectively.

The EDF, along with the **Natural Resources Defense Council,** has successfully challenged the **Environmental Protection Agency** when it did not produce regulations required by statutes, disputed the content of regulations, and forced agreements by aggressive actions. It has also been active in **citizen suit**s, taking companies to court for violations when the agency did not enforce the law.

One difference between EDF and some of the deep ecology groups such as **Earth First!** is its willingness to work with the people who are subject to environmental regulation to craft alternative approaches. An example of unconventional cooperation occurred through the influence of Krupp, who developed a task force to find a substitute for the polystyrene used for McDonald's packaging. Eventually, the company converted to paper. The EDF also provided the Bush [see **Bush, George Herbert Walker**] administration with the system of credits that eventually became part of the **Clean Air Act Amendments of 1990.** The EDF saw market-based pollution credits, vigorously opposed by many environmental groups, as an acceptable alternative to the old method of pollution control. See also **acid rain.**

ENVIRONMENTAL IMPACT STATEMENT (EIS) A report required by the **National Environmental Policy Act** that analyzes the effects of a proposed "federal action" on the environment, suggests alternatives, and frequently examines methods of correcting (mitigating) any damages that might result. Through this process, Congress forces public officials to consider the consequences of actions on the environment, resulting in informed decisions. The EIS procedure is public, so the agency does not operate secretly.

An EIS must be prepared for "federal actions" unless the agency can demonstrate that the project will have no significant impact on the environment [see **finding of no significant impact**]. Any project that requires a permit from a federal agency is considered a federal action.

Guidelines for an EIS

The primary authority under the National Environmental Policy Act is the **Council on Environmental Quality.** That agency creates the regulations and oversees their implementation. The council has developed a recommended format and requires the following information: a discussion of environmental impacts, adverse environmental impacts that cannot be avoided, alternatives to the project, the relationship between short-term uses and long-term productivity, and irreversible commitments of resources. Of all the elements, the alternatives section is the most important.

Mechanics of an EIS

When a federal action is proposed, the agency involved must publish a notice of intent in the *Federal Register.* If more than one agency is involved, the agency with the most involvement becomes the lead agency.

Scoping is the next step, in which the agency determines the scope of the EIS. The agency must invite the public as well as the state, other agencies with expertise or concern, local governments, and affected tribal governments to participate in the process, along with the affected party and interested persons. During the scoping, the agency eliminates issues, determines the significant ones, sets limits on time and process.

The agency then reviews information in the first document prepared to determine whether the EIS was required (the environmental assessment). It begins to gather information from many sources and prepare the report. The agency must respond to any comments it gets and they must be attached to the EIS. After the agency prepares a draft and it goes through a period of public notice and comment, it is finalized. Then the agency must consider it, along with mitigation and alternatives, when it makes its decision.

Exclusions

If an agency proposes legislation, an EIS must be prepared within 30 days of transmittal to Congress. Usually it is only a draft. However, if the president originates the proposed legislation, no EIS is required, since executive office actions are not included in the definition of federal actions. Another exclusion is appropriations bills, which means that cutting the budget of an agency with environmental responsibilities does not require an EIS.

ENVIRONMENTAL PROTECTION AGENCY (EPA) The primary agency for overseeing environmental compliance in the United States. It was created in 1970 by President Richard M. Nixon in Reorganization Plan No. 3, which transferred to it the powers of fifteen agencies and parts of agencies. The EPA started with a staff of 6,000 employees and a budget of $455 million.

The EPA is headquartered in Washington, D.C., and also has ten regional offices. It is headed by an administrator, appointed by the president. Assistant administrators supervise various organizations within the agency, such as the Office of Air and Radiation, the Office of Enforcement and Compliance Monitoring, and the Office of Solid Waste and Emergency Response.

Because of its origin, the EPA is an executive agency, not an independent one. Discussions of elevating it to cabinet status have been going on for a decade, but no change has resulted. Instead, most of the EPA's influence comes from the regional offices. Each has a regional administrator, appointed in consultation with the senior senator and governor of the state where the office is located. Although policy is set in D.C., implementation of the programs comes from the regions. The regional offices also enforce the law and work closely with states within their regions.

Though statutes have added responsibilities to the original charter of the combined agencies, the structure of the EPA continues to reflect the segments into which its work was originally divided. For example, pesticide and toxic functions are separate from water, and even water is divided into pieces: groundwater is detached from surface water. These divisions make it difficult for the EPA to assess compliance and complicate industry's dealings with the agency. The EPA has been drifting toward what is called multimedia enforcement, in which violations involving air can be combined with **hazardous waste** or water complaints. Total integration of the programs, however, seems unlikely.

Once the EPA was founded, environmental laws were pushed through Congress. Inherited responsibilities faded in comparison to the new mandates. For example, the EPA had only 120 days after it began to churn out regulations.

The blackest days for the EPA occurred during Ronald Reagan's administration [see **Reagan, Ronald**]. An avowed opponent to regulation, Reagan appointed people to environmental posts who were sympathetic to his point of view. In 1981 he appointed Anne Burford [see **Burford, Anne Gorsuch**] as EPA administrator, and she filled other high-level positions in the agency with political appointees.

Under Reagan, the EPA's enforcement efforts ground to a halt; the creation of regulations were slowed to a crawl. Furthermore, he slashed the budget of the agency until even Burford complained: the EPA lost 29 percent of its budget and a quarter of its staff during Reagan's first two years.

In 1983, Congress began an investigation of the EPA and alleged abuses, focusing on the program funded to clean up hazardous waste sites. It found evidence of private, illegal meetings with industry, settlements that covered only minor portions of cleanups at hazardous waste sites, and other misconduct. See **Comprehensive Environmental Response, Compensation, and Liability Act.**

When the congressional **hearing**s were finished, Rita Lavelle (head of the **Superfund** office) [see **Lavelle, Rita**] was sentenced to six months in jail for perjury. Anne Burford resigned, along with twenty other people she brought in. Reagan swiftly appointed William Ruckelshaus, who had been the first administrator of the EPA. He worked to bring the agency back to a level of competency and pride.

The EPA has functioned for more than twenty years. Even though many federal programs have been assumed by the states, its workload increases with every environmental statute Congress enacts.

EXECUTIVE ORDER   A directive issued by the president to executive agencies and published in the *Federal Register* after it is signed. Executive orders reflect the philosophy of the president toward agency structure and the regulatory process; they also set priorities and give the agencies direction. Since most federal agencies are within the executive branch, executive orders exert a great deal of influence on regulatory action.

The most infamous of the executive orders that impacted the **Environmental Protection Agency** was Executive Order 12291, issued by Ronald Reagan [see **Reagan, Ronald**] on 17 February 1981. The order anticipated his strategy of making regulations more difficult to promulgate: it prohibited regulatory action unless the potential benefits of the action exceeded the potential costs.

After Executive Order 12291, every proposed regulation had to be scrutinized by the Office of Management and Budget (OMB), and what had been merely one consideration in the rulemaking process became a crucial element. The OMB review focused on figures. Since the price tag associated with environmental benefits is hard to calculate, many regulations were effectively killed because of the review process.

EXTREMELY HAZARDOUS SUBSTANCE (EHS) An acutely toxic substance enumerated on the **Environmental Protection Agency's** (EPA) list of Extremely Hazardous Substances by authority of the **Emergency Planning and Community Right-To-Know Act.** The list serves as a reference, informing facilities of their responsibilities under this statute. In addition to the name of the substance, the list gives two other necessary pieces of information. First, it states the threshold planning quantity; second, it specifies a reportable quantity.

The threshold planning quantity is the amount of the substance that triggers requirements to report its existence to emergency planning agencies. The reportable quantity figure determines the amount of the EHS released to the environment that must be reported. Chlorine, for example, has a threshold planning quantity of 100 pounds; nicotine, 100 pounds; and mustard gas, 500 pounds. A facility with any of those EHSs in the amount specified must file information for emergency response planning.

Reportable quantities has also been established for the same chemicals: chlorine, 10 pounds; nicotine, 100 pounds; and mustard gas, 1 pound. Therefore, if a facility spills 10 or more pounds of chlorine, 100 or more of nicotine, or 1 or more of mustard gas into the environment, it must report the spill to the responsible agencies.

Initially 406 substances were listed as extremely hazardous; the list was later reduced when the EPA found that some of the substances listed were not acutely toxic. Recently, however, it has proposed adding 313 substances to the list.

FEDERAL INSECTICIDE, FUNGICIDE, AND RODENTI-CIDE ACT (FIFRA)

The primary federal statute regulating pesticides. Although this law has existed since 1947, it has changed significantly through the years. Original responsibility for pesticide regulation resided in the Department of Agriculture until the **Environmental Protection Agency** (EPA) was created in 1970. The EPA was then given the authority to implement the law, and FIFRA's contemporary framework was established in the 1972 amendments, which overhauled and strengthened the law. Initially it focused only on mislabeling. It now covers registration, labeling, testing, and use of pesticides. A pesticide is defined as any product that is designed to control pests, including unwanted vegetation.

The biggest impacts of pesticides are localized, affecting groundwater and surface water. For this reason, most states and many local water agencies regulate pesticide use, and often the state assumes the federal program. State laws may be (and usually are) more stringent than FIFRA.

Components of FIFRA

Registration of Pesticides

Before a pesticide can be sold or distributed in the United States, it must be registered with the EPA and with any states requiring registration. Federal exceptions exist for experimental use or for companies shipping pesticides among their own facilities. To register a pesticide, the applicant must supply evidence that it is safe for its intended use, along with the name and address of applicant, name of pesticide and formula, a copy of labeling and directions for use, all claims to be made for the product, and other data requested by the EPA.

The EPA has little authority to refuse a registration, however. Registration must be approved if claims are justified and other information is correct, unless the EPA determines unreasonable adverse effects to the environment will occur when it is used according to common practice. Before it can issue a finding of "unreasonable adverse effects," the EPA

139

must weigh the benefits of the use of the pesticide, including social and economic ones, against the risk to humans and the environment.

Advances in scientific methods have greatly increased the amount of data available to a contemporary applicant compared to an early pesticide user. Many older pesticides have not been subjected to the same type of scrutiny as newer pesticides because they were simply allowed to stand on old registrations. However, the 1988 amendments added a provision requiring re-registration. Registration of pesticides is now effective only for five years unless the applicant re-registers. Also, any pesticide on the market prior to the creation of the EPA is required to re-register and submit the type of information that is now required for initial registration.

Me-Too Registrations and Featherbedding

Occasionally, a pesticide may be introduced that is similar or identical to an already registered product. In those cases, the EPA is required to expedite review of the application. These are called me-too pesticides, and the process is referred to as featherbedding. The applicant for a me-too product may rely on data produced by another pesticide maker, but he or she must compensate the data owner.

The EPA is not involved in the compensation aspects, so the applicant must deal with the registrant of the original product. Generally, the formula agreed upon provides that the producer of the me-too pesticide pays for the cost of the research and a royalty.

Classes of Registrations

A pesticide may be registered for general use, restricted use, or a combination of the two. General use pesticides can be applied by anyone and sold with few conditions. Restricted use pesticides are those that the EPA determines will pose an unreasonable risk to the environment unless restrictions are imposed. Only a certified applicator or someone working directly under his supervision may apply them. Pesticides that have a mixed registration are treated as general use products in some circumstances and as restricted in others. For example, when used on one crop, a pesticide may be comparatively safe; another crop may absorb more of it. In that case the pesticide must be applied with greater precision by a certified applicator.

States and local water agencies can restrict use of pesticides even further through their own registration processes. Texas, for example, has added another category to the three listed above: state limited use pesticides. It includes some of the older pesticides that have not yet gone through the re-registration process and imposes requirements similar to those in the restricted use classification.

Re-Registration of Pesticides

The 1988 Amendments to FIFRA accelerated the process of re-registering pesticides. To start the process, the EPA listed all active ingredients subject to re-registration. The registrants then notified the EPA whether they intended to re-register. In order to re-register, they would have to identify missing and inadequate information and commit to supply it within 12 months of listing. Then the EPA reviews the updated information for comprehensiveness and asks for more, if necessary. The final stage, which may take another year, is agency examination of the documentation and decision about eligibility for re-registration.

Labeling

Labeling, according to the law, is any written or graphic material that accompanies the pesticide. The EPA has published regulations that specify labeling requirements, providing standard language and describing the information that must be included, along with packaging specifications. The EPA examines labels during the registration process. Afterward, it can also check to ensure that the labels continue to carry the proper information.

If a pesticide is misbranded, the EPA can take action to remove it from the market. Misbranding includes a number of problems, such as making false claims, packaging the pesticide in a way not authorized by the regulations, labeling it as one pesticide when it is another, failing to give the registration number or any other information required by the EPA, and omitting proper instructions for its use.

User Restrictions

Federal law requires certification of people who apply restricted pesticides. To a certain extent, this is a self-certification process, but the applicator must have training and be competent in the use and handling of pesticides. The statute does not allow the EPA to require an examination, however. Behind this restriction was the fear that farmers might be prohibited from becoming certified because they failed the test. States usually administer the pesticide programs, though, and it is common for states to specify training, testing, and continuing education for certified applicators. Dealers are also required to keep records of their sales and may not sell restricted pesticides to people who are not certified.

Applicators are themselves subject to recordkeeping requirements. The federal government requires that they keep records of the type of pesticide, date, amount, concentration, and location where it was applied. State requirements often add many details to the recordkeeping requirements, such as soil type, weather conditions, and time of day applied.

Protection of Confidential Information

Much costly research goes into the development of pesticides, so the pesticide industry has feared release of information it considers confidential ever since the federal government began regulating pesticides. To address their concerns, provisions for protecting trade secrets have long been a part of the law. To claim a trade secret, the applicant must notify the agency of the claim when the data about the pesticide is first supplied. Protection is only extended to formulae and manufacturing processes.

In environmental law, though, the overriding concern is for the public and environment, and that priority necessarily leads to release of information if an emergency occurs. See also **Emergency Planning and Community Right-To-Know Act.** Assuming an emergency does not exist, the EPA can notify the registrant that it intends to release certain information in 30 days: the pesticide's effect on the environment as well as production, distribution, sale, and inventory information. Disclosure of this type of information can be done if the EPA believes it is necessary in order to carry out the provisions of the statute. The registrant then has those 30 days to go to court to prevent the release of the information. The burden of proof concerning the trade secret claim rests on the registrant.

Storage, Disposal, and Transportation of Pesticides

The EPA regulates all aspects of moving, containing, and disposing of pesticides. It also deals with disposal of pesticides that are canceled or suspended. To assist in orderly transfer and handling of pesticides, the EPA can require records and reports about pesticides from dealers, producers, and applicators. States often have stricter requirements for transportation and disposal of these substances. Though states cannot interfere with interstate commerce, they are permitted to regulate the movement of pesticides through their territory, as well as their final disposition, if it will occur within their borders.

Canceling or Suspending a Registration

Suspension

Of the two types of action, canceling or suspending a registration, suspension is the quickest. The ban is immediate, but it must be accompanied by a cancellation order. The suspension may be ordinary or an emergency one. For an ordinary suspension, the EPA must be acting to prevent an imminent hazard to the public. Public includes fish and wildlife, and a hazard may be considered imminent even if the effects will not be seen for years. In *Environmental Defense Fund v. Environmental Protection Agency*, the Court verified the Environmental Defense Fund's contention that a crisis does not have to exist before the EPA can issue a suspension. The test is whether there is substantial likelihood of serious harm.

To initiate an ordinary suspension, the agency must issue a notice accompanied by findings about the imminent hazards. Suspension remains in effect until after the **hearing** is completed and final decision is made. The registrant must request a hearing within five days of receipt of notice or its right to a hearing is waived. If requested, the hearing must be held within five days after the request is received, and a decision must be issued no later than seventeen days after evidence is presented.

An emergency suspension does not require prior notice to the registrant, though the registrant is entitled to an immediate review of the order. Because this is the strongest reaction to a perceived risk, the EPA must examine the seriousness of threatened harm, urgency, probability that harm will result, benefits of continued use of the pesticide during the suspension process, and available information on the risk.

Cancellation

If the agency does not have enough evidence to support suspending a registration but believes a pesticide is a threat to humans or the environment, it can initiate cancellation proceedings. Cancellation may also be used to gather information when the safety of a pesticide has been questioned, to respond to issues raised in a **citizen's suit,** or to close out a registration that has expired if the pesticide is not re-registered.

Prior to cancellation, a notice called an Intent to Cancel must be served on the registrant. The registrant is entitled to a hearing and, as in a suspension, has the burden of proof. If the cancellation proceeding is primarily initiated to develop information, the notice is structured differently to indicate the purpose of the hearing.

The order could take effect thirty days after it is issued, but generally hearings and challenges will delay it. It may take years to complete.

During the cancellation process, the pesticide can be manufactured and sold.

Pesticide Recalls

After a pesticide is canceled or suspended, the issue shifts to what to do with the pesticide that has already been distributed. Usually, it may be used until the supply is exhausted, but the EPA has the right to demand a recall. If the recall is mandatory, the EPA specifies how it will be done. In voluntary recalls, the registrant supplies the EPA with a recall plan. FIFRA provides for compensation for end users who have suffered because of the recall, but any other losses must be recovered directly from the seller.

Conflicts between FIFRA and the Food, Drug, and Cosmetic Act

The EPA has responsibility under the Food, Drug, and Cosmetic Act to establish tolerance limits for pesticide residues in processed agricultural products. A provision within that law, the **Delaney Clause,** sets the limit for a particular group of chemicals—those that may cause cancer—at zero. Conflicting with that mandate, however, is the EPA's obligation to determine through risk analysis which pesticides may be marketed. Thus, a pesticide that presents a low risk of causing cancer may be permitted for use in agriculture, but then the crops cannot be processed because of its residue. See Delaney Clause for further discussion.

Biological Pesticides

One application of **biotechnology** is biological pesticides. These pesticides are not created from combinations of chemicals but result from genetic engineering. Like other pesticides, they must be registered with the EPA and they are subject to the same type of regulations.

Use of biological control in agriculture and horticulture is not a new concept. Existing birds, insects, and plants have long been used to limit unwanted species. Genetically engineered organisms, in contrast, are life forms that have been genetically altered to serve a specific purpose. Those introduced as methods of controlling pests fall within the scope of FIFRA.

Scientific Advisory Committees

When the EPA proposes to cancel a pesticide or to adopt new regulations, FIFRA requires the involvement of a scientific advisory committee. Such committees are not part of the EPA but consist of six members nominated by the National Science Foundation and six by the National Institutes of Health. The EPA administrator chooses seven people from among those nominees to make up a scientific advisory committee. These committees listen to evidence at hearings, issue findings, and review regulations. Their recommendations and findings are given to the EPA, but the agency is not required to agree with them.

Worker Protection

By agreement with the **Occupational Safety and Health Administration** (OSHA), the EPA has authority to issue regulations for worker safety involving pesticide application. The EPA has issued regulations dealing with farm workers. Employees not covered by those regulations are covered by the general OSHA regulations, which require employers to provide a safe working environment. That might mean, for example, providing protective equipment such as masks or breathing apparatus when the employee is working with pesticides that could cause respiratory problems.

FEDERAL WATER POLLUTION CONTROL ACT See **Clean Water Act.**

FINANCIAL RESPONSIBILITY Problems associated with **hazardous wastes**, oil spills, and leaking underground **storage tanks** can be expensive and difficult to remedy. For that reason, Congress placed provisions in the **Resource Conservation and Recovery Act** and the **Oil Pollution Act** requiring certain businesses and people who deal with them to demonstrate that they have the means to fix any problems they create. The term used to describe this demonstration is *financial responsibility*. This requirement is in addition to technical requirements for facilities engaged in hazardous waste operations.

Owners and operators of underground storage tanks and hazardous waste **treatment/storage/disposal facilities** can prove financial responsibility in a number of ways, including self-insurance, letter of guarantee, liability insurance, letters of credit, surety bonds, state-required mechanisms, state trust funds, and other trust funds. The amount of financial responsibility required depends on a number of factors. In the case of hazardous waste facilities, the assurance must be sufficient to correct any problems, close the facility, and monitor it. If oil is being transported or an offshore facility is handling oil or **hazardous material,** the amount is determined by the number of gross tons of cargo handled. For underground storage tanks, the amount depends on the size and type of operation.

A few examples of the financial requirements demonstrate their impact. Under current law, every hazardous waste treatment/storage/disposal unit must be closed at some point, since each particular unit has a limited life. Therefore, the owner or operator must determine how much it will cost to close (that is, properly shut down) the facility and maintain the financial ability to pay for the closure when it occurs. The amount required is based on the current regulations and estimated costs at the time it is first calculated, but if the estimate goes up in a following year, it must be adjusted. The estimate is calculated annually. Whether money must be set aside depends on the type of financial assurance used to satisfy the requirement. If the company uses self-insurance, it must simply have the capability of paying out the amount required. The prior year's financial reports must verify the company's ability to do that.

The primary purpose of financial assurance for vessels, offshore facilities, and underground storage tanks is to ensure clean up of releases. Therefore, the owner or operator must employ some mechanism to cover one-time events and assume responsibility for cumulative events occurring over a year. Each year, the owner or operator must meet these conditions. Vessel owners must provide for $1,200 per gross ton if they handle hazardous materials and $600 per gross ton if petroleum is involved. For offshore facilities, the amount is $150 million; for deep-water facilities, $350 million, but the Department of Transportation can lower these amounts. Underground storage tank financial responsibility varies according to the type of owner or operator and the number of tanks. If an owner or operator is a petroleum marketer, the amount is $1 million per occurrence; others must provide $500,000 per occurrence. Projected occurrences are determined in the same manner as insurance companies determine risks when writing policies. Neither the statute nor the regulations provide guidance on this point. Annual aggregate amounts range between $1 million and $2 million.

Tank owners or operators and vessels must obtain insurance or use one of the other mechanisms to show financial capacity, but they are not required to submit information unless the government asks for it or a release occurs. Only hazardous waste facilities must automatically demonstrate financial responsibility to the federal government. States often assume responsibility for overseeing operators of hazardous waste treatment/storage/disposal facilities, and they, too, may require a demonstration of financial responsibility [see **delegation**]. However, states have different approaches. Some require submission of a form explaining how the owner or operator meets its financial responsibility. Others want a copy of the mechanism. Most simply follow the federal regulations.

Owners and operators of underground storage tanks and vessels, offshore facilities, and deep-water ports must keep financial mechanisms in effect while in operation. For a stationary site, closing the facility ends the need for the financial mechanism. Also, transfer of the facility or vessel moves the requirement to the new owner.

FINDING OF NO SIGNIFICANT IMPACT (FONSI)   The **National Environmental Policy Act** requires federal agencies to consider the impact of all major federal actions that significantly affect the environment. In the beginning of any major project, the agency proposing the action must go through a screening process called an **environmental assessment** to determine whether an **environmental impact statement** (an in-depth evaluation) must be done. The agency may decide after the environmental assessment that the action will not cause a serious consequence to the environment. In most situations, it then issues a finding of no significant impact (FONSI).

The key elements that trigger the need to follow the steps outlined in the National Environmental Policy Act are these: the action must be (1) federal, (2) major, and (3) likely to have a significant effect on the quality of the environment. Some actions are easily identified as federal actions, but others may be less obvious. If the federal government is building a highway, for example, the project is clearly a federal action. However, the federal government is peripherally involved in many projects, such as state highways, since it issues federal permits and awards grants. That sort of federal involvement is sufficient to make the proposed permit or grant a federal action.

Not all federal actions will require a finding of no significant impact before the agency can decide not to do a complete analysis. Each agency has its own regulations describing how the National Environmental Policy Act will be implemented. They specify what type of agency actions will not be subject to the law's requirements because they cannot cause meaningful distress to the environment. If the proposed action falls within these categories, an environmental assessment is not necessary.

Assuming the federal action is not within the excluded classifications, the FONSI discusses why the proposed action will not have a significant impact on the environment. It must be accompanied by the environmental assessment or a summary of it. In some cases, the FONSI must be available to the public for 30 days before the action starts. If the action usually merits an environmental impact statement or if the type of action is the first of its kind, public access and opportunity to comment is required. Although the public does not have to be included in the environmental assessment process to the same degree required for an environmental impact statement, the agency benefits from public participation. Public involvement at the early stages lessens the likelihood of attacks on the action later if the agency issues a FONSI.

FREEDOM OF INFORMATION ACT (FOIA) This statute, enacted in 1967, makes governmental information available to the public. It is now part of the **Administrative Procedure Act.** It specifies two types of material that must be disclosed upon request: agency information and any other record, with limited exceptions.

To obtain information under the Freedom of Information Act, a person must request it in writing. He or she does not have to explain why the information is needed. There are only two requirements: the information must be reasonably described so the agency knows what is wanted, and the request must comply with the agency's published rules about time, place, fees, and procedures. Generally, the agency will have a strict timetable in producing the information. It can charge copying fees if it wishes. Agencies often provide copies free if only a few pages are involved, but charge for larger numbers of pages.

The two categories of accessible information are very broad. Agency information includes the following: opinions following a **hearing,** unpublished policy and statements of interpretation, and staff manuals and instructions. Almost any other information the agency collects or creates may be obtained as well. For example, the **Environmental Protection Agency** (EPA) issues permits for water pollution discharges, and it requires all permittees to submit regular reports about the discharges and special reports when an unusual event occurs. If a local public interest group wanted any or all of that information, it can obtain it by making a request under the Freedom of Information Act.

Exceptions to Disclosure

Nine classes of information are exempt from the disclosure requirements of the Freedom of Information Act: (1) national defense and foreign affairs, (2) internal personnel rules and practices, (3) trade secrets, (4) inter- and intra-agency memos, (4) personnel and medical files, (5) investigatory records, (6) results relating to examination of financial institutions, (7) geological and geophysical data, (8) information required by statute to be withheld, and (9) commercial and financial information.

Exemptions are not normally mandatory. Thus, the agency can release information it is not required to disclose. Often, the administrator or secretary of the agency sets the policy for disclosure, and the employees of the agency follow it. Some administrations are more open than others and will provide virtually any records it has. Others scrutinize requests carefully and claim exemptions for anything arguably falling within an exemption classification.

If an agency denies a request under the Freedom of Information Act or fails to reply, the person seeking the information can go to district court and ask for an order. The agency has the burden of proving the records are exempt or do not exist.

FOIA and Environmental Records

Environmental laws frequently require permits for polluting activities. They also mandate reports and registration, even when permits are not necessary. The result of the inpouring of paperwork is collection of massive amounts of records. An interested party can target an industry or a particular business and obtain information it can then use to sue, as evidence in an ongoing lawsuit, or to put pressure on the Environmental Protection Agency to enforce. See **citizen's suits.**

Since the Freedom of Information Act does not require the requesting party to give reasons for its request, businesses can also use the information to obtain information about competitors. Although trade secrets are protected to an extent, the protection is limited, and most of the information provided to the EPA will not fall into an exemption.

Freedom of Information Act inquiries are enormously helpful to citizen groups and public interest groups. Once the information is analyzed, the groups are informed enough to determine whether a fight is worthwhile. The Freedom of Information Act also provides a way for an interested person or organization to find out through agency records how an agency views different laws. Regulations are often complex, and the regulated community can only read what is published in the *Federal Register* and interpret the words. However, the agency may issue memos interpreting the regulations, or it may have produced guidance documents for employees. These documents are invaluable to people who are trying to use the rule, and they are available under FOIA.

GENERATOR   In environmental law, the person or business that creates **hazardous waste** or disposes of hazardous waste. The designation *generator* is important under two laws: the **Comprehensive Environmental Response, Compensation, and Liability Act** (CERCLA), and the **Resource Conservation and Recovery Act** (RCRA).

Generators under CERCLA

CERCLA specifies who may be required to clean up hazardous waste sites; generators are one of the categories specified. Generators, like other people who can be held responsible for a cleanup, are jointly and severally liable for the cleanup. That means any one of them may have to finance the entire remedial action.

An example to illustrate the breadth of the term may be helpful. Company A uses solvents in its operation. After the solvents have been used a few times, they become wastes. Company A, then, is a generator, having created the hazardous waste. Company B is a lender with a security interest in Company A. Company A defaults on the loan, and Company B forecloses. After taking possession of the operation, Company B gets a waste hauler to come and get the solvents. Company B is also a generator. Finally, Company A's property is a mess, and **hazardous substances** have been disposed of in a lagoon. Company B gets an environmental company, Company C, to handle the cleanup. Company C does not know much about actual cleanup, because it has never done one before. So Company C sends property off to another site, signing the manifests as the owner of the waste. Company C is also a generator.

Generators under RCRA

The focus of the Resource Conservation and Recovery Act is not the same as that of CERCLA, the **Superfund** law. RCRA established a method for dealing with waste from the time it is created through the time of disposal called a *cradle to grave* system. Generators under RCRA are not identified for the purpose of financing the cleanup of an abandoned hazardous waste site, but to manage the storage, disposal, and handling of hazardous waste. However, once identified as a generator under RCRA, the person will remain a generator if a problem occurs in the future.

RCRA sorts generators into three groups, based solely on the amount of hazardous waste generated at a facility during a month: small quantity, conditionally exempt small quantity, and large quantity generators. The two types of small quantity generators are subject to few requirements. A conditionally exempt small quantity generator creates or disposes of less than 100 kg of hazardous waste or 1 kg of extremely hazardous waste in a month. This generator is exempt from almost all requirements. Small quantity generators may dispose of up to 1,000 kg of hazardous waste or 10 kg of extremely hazardous waste in a month. These generators are not subject to short-term storage limits, manifesting, recordkeeping, or reporting requirements of RCRA. The large quantity generator (more than 1,000 kg of hazardous waste generated per month), however, is required to follow all of the requirements in the statute. Furthermore, states may demand more of each classification, particularly when the waste is being imported from another state.

General Requirements

Characterization
The first step in determining what type of regulations apply—if any—is analyzing what each waste stream is. A number of methods may be used to make this decision.

Hazardous waste will either be **listed waste** or **characteristic waste.** If it is listed (that is, if it is one of the substances that has been placed on the list of hazardous wastes), it may not be treated as nonhazardous waste unless the **Environmental Protection Agency** (EPA) delists it. Dilution, neutralization, or other means of treating a hazardous waste will not, by themselves, transform a hazardous waste into a nonhazardous waste. This policy may change, though, because the EPA has recognized the limits of this approach.

Characteristic waste exhibits one or more of these traits: ignitability, corrosivity, toxicity, or leachability. The reason for treating these wastes as hazardous is apparent: disposal without treatment can cause damage to the environment and threaten water supplies. Unlike listed wastes, characteristic wastes can be made nonhazardous simply by treating them. The aim of treatment is to eliminate the hazardous characteristic.

Waste is analyzed by running laboratory tests. These tests can be rather expensive, but if the generator does not know how the waste was produced or whether it exhibits one of the characteristics of hazardous wastes, the only way to find out is through scientific analysis. If the generator knows what substances were used in a process, it may be possible to narrow the focus of the tests to look for certain chemicals and specific characteristics. Results of testing or the reasons for determining that the waste was hazardous or nonhazardous must be retained for at least three years.

Notification and Entering the System

Once a generator knows it has hazardous waste to dispose of, it must notify the EPA and obtain an identification number unless it is otherwise exempt. If the generator has more than one site, each facility must obtain a different number, since the identification number applies to only one location.

The generator number becomes a tracking mechanism. It must be placed on shipping documents called manifests, which are extremely important to the RCRA scheme of regulating hazardous waste. The manifest, a multipage document, originates with the generator, then accompanies the waste through transport and disposal. When the generator gives the waste to the transporter, the transporter leaves a copy with the generator; the transporter then takes the waste to the treatment/storage/disposal facility, and the transporter receives a copy. The disposal facility must also send a copy to the generator. Generators are responsible for reporting to the EPA if they do not receive the manifest back from the final resting place of the hazardous waste, and they must maintain the copies for at least three years.

Storage

Containers must be marked so their contents can be easily determined. The date the hazardous waste is first placed in the container must be clearly marked, and generators that keep hazardous waste on site for more than 90 days will generally become subject to rules that are much more rigid. However, some small generators may accumulate hazardous wastes for longer periods of time.

Storage containers must comply with the Department of Transportation rules for **hazardous materials**, which set out marking, labeling, placarding, and packaging instructions. All hazardous waste containers must be kept closed when not in use, and generators must inspect them for leaks and condition at least weekly. Hazardous wastes may not be placed in containers that are incompatible with them, and incompatible wastes, such as an acid and a base, may not be stored close to each other.

Records
The federal government requires reports to be filed every two years, but states often want annual reports. Both federal and state reports describe the disposal activity of the generator and identify the type of waste generated. If the generator exports hazardous waste, an annual report must also be filed, and again, the EPA must be notified of problems involving unreturned manifests through an exception report. Manifests and waste determinations must be maintained by the generator. All records should be kept at the site for at least three years, although they are often retained longer.

Emergency Response
Because hazardous wastes are dangerous, generators must develop an emergency response program for the employees. Training in handling the substances is required, and information must be posted on what to do in case of a release or other situation where employees or others may be exposed. Emergency contacts must be chosen as well.

The surrounding community is also entitled to information concerning the dangers at the facility, and the public is usually notified through the procedures established by the **Emergency Planning and Community Right-To-Know Act.** Fire departments and other emergency response personnel must be informed of the presence of the hazardous waste in case they are called to the site.

GLOBAL WARMING The gradual increase in the earth's temperature due to certain gases that trap heat and prevent it from escaping into the atmosphere. Scientists have been gathering evidence on the effect for years, but it has not yet been clearly established by those who claim that it is imminent, and other scientists strongly contest the theory.

Carbon dioxide, methane, nitrogen oxide, and **chlorofluorocarbons** (CFCs) accumulate in the earth's atmosphere, breaking down slowly and trapping heat at the earth's surface. That effect, called the greenhouse effect, has been proven necessary to sustain life on earth. The greenhouse effect itself is not bad; it is beneficial. However, the proponents of the global warming theory caution that the atmosphere is now being pumped full of gases that hold heat in. As a result, they project temperature increases between 2 and 9 degrees in the next century.

Global warming is not a new theory. The greenhouse effect was identified in 1827 and studied intermittently since that time. One scientist during the nineteenth century claimed that the increase in coal and wood burning due to the industrial revolution would cause the earth's temperature to warm.

Warming and cooling temperatures have not, however, been limited to the time after the industrial revolution. Even the amount of carbon dioxide in the atmosphere, which has been measured in core samples taken from glaciers, has varied markedly through centuries. Therefore, there is a certain amount of natural deviation that must be screened out before determining cause and effect. Some natural reasons for temperature swings include changes in the earth's position in relation to the sun, variations in sun's radiant energy, volcanic eruptions, meteor impacts, changes in reflectivity of the earth, differences in land and ocean area and shape, and composition of the atmosphere. These issues bring into question the validity of assumptions behind computer models.

However, some of the relevant factors have been clearly demonstrated. The rise in the earth's population, agricultural activity, and industrial enterprise have increased the proportion of the heat-trapping gases in the atmosphere, and the use of CFCs has complicated the situation. All of these influences together result in an increase in heat-trapping gases.

Since the industrial revolution, the amount of carbon dioxide, methane, and **nitrogen oxides** in the atmosphere has drastically increased. Agriculture and ranching are largely responsible for increased methane, since rice cultivation and cattle raising release large amounts. The growth in population contributes to increases in carbon dioxide, since carbon dioxide is a by-product of breathing. Additionally, as population has expanded, reliance on carbon-rich coal and other fossil fuels, as well as deforestation, have multiplied carbon dioxide output. Burning coal, particularly the lower grade coals, and the combustion of other fossil fuels contribute nitrogen oxides and carbon dioxide, as well as **sulfur dioxide**. CFCs were added to the mix in the 1950s. The controversy among scientists focuses on these questions: Will the additional gases cause global warming? If so, how much? Has global warming already begun? Computer modeling suggests a relationship between the greenhouse effect and global warming, but the models fail to take a number of factors into consideration, such as the effect of ocean evaporation and cloud cover.

Legal Response

Given the existing evidence, Congress and past presidents have been unwilling to take a stand on this issue and have taken no direct action to deal with global warming. However, some of the measures in the **Clean Air Act Amendments of 1990** should automatically reduce some of the greenhouse gases. For example, the Montreal Protocol, an international conference in which the United States participated, agreed to reduce CFCs. Congress implemented the agreement through a new section in the amendments to the Clean Air Act, which phase out both production and use of CFCs and totally eliminates their use by 2000. It also gave the **Environmental Protection Agency** the right to move the deadline forward, which it has done. Another new provision was added to the Clean Air Act to reduce **acid rain** but should affect global warming as well. The section places utilities under restrictions for releases of sulfur dioxide and nitrogen oxides, the two compounds primarily responsible for acid rain.

Whether these emission reductions will simply slow the process of accumulating greenhouse gases, have little effect, or somehow reverse it remains to be seen. The population of the earth continues to increase, and developing countries often resist attempts to restrict their uses of resources—natural and manmade—when developed countries had free use of them for so long.

GREENHOUSE EFFECT   See global warming

GREENPEACE

An international organization founded in 1971 to protest nuclear testing. Since then, it has expanded its mission to include fighting for marine mammals and dealing with other environmental concerns, such as toxic waste reduction and protection of tropical forests. Greenpeace bases its tactics on the Quaker philosophy of "standing in harm's way"; it uses nonviolent resistance to accomplish its goals, as well as lobbying for legislation and educating the public.

The first incident involving Greenpeace took place in the Pacific Ocean, where Greenpeace members sailed small boats into a testing site to stop the nuclear tests. Later, in 1985, French agents blew up a Greenpeace ship called the *Rainbow Warrior*, killing a Greenpeace photographer. This event created a storm of public outrage and resulted in a sharp growth in membership for the organization.

Though Greenpeace is now known primarily for its Save the Whales campaign, that program came about when members encountered whales during their primary mission of nuclear protest and became fascinated with them. Other marine life such as sea lions and dolphins soon came to their attention as well, and protecting them merged with Greenpeace's original goals.

One Greenpeace member, Paul Watson, led other members to destroy a whaling ship. Because the action did not comply with the nonviolent notion of the organization, they were asked to leave. Watson founded the Sea Shepherd Conservation Society in 1977, a radical environmental group that considers sabotage a legitimate weapon.

Greenpeace has two separate divisions: Greenpeace USA and Greenpeace Action. The latter runs numerous campaigns, research studies, and education. Examples of a few of the campaigns include the Ocean Ecology Campaign, to strengthen protection for marine mammals and other inhabitants of the ocean; the Toxics Campaign, to stress reduction of toxic waste and encourage recycling and pollution prevention; and the Atmospheric and Energy Campaign, to stop production of **chlorofluorocarbons,** decrease air pollution and greenhouse gases [see **global warming**], and reduce use of fossil fuels in favor of renewable energy sources.

HAZARD **C**OMMUNICATION **S**TANDARD **(HCS)** A regulation created by the **Occupational Safety and Health Administration** (OSHA) to protect workers who may be exposed to **hazardous chemical**s at work. It is often called the Worker's Right-To-Know.

The standard requires employers who use or create hazardous chemicals to establish a written program describing how the HCS will be met. Employees must be trained (and retrained any time a new chemical is introduced or they change jobs) and provided with information concerning the chemicals in the workplace. The employer must follow proper labeling procedures, provide access to the informational sheets the manufacturer or importer prepares (**material safety data sheets**, or MSDSs), and establish an emergency response system.

Since hazardous chemicals are everywhere, the HCS does not require separate training or programs for every chemical used in the workplace. Exceptions to the requirements include household chemicals if used in the same way and with the same frequency as those purchased for personal use, such as cleaners or copier toner, and articles that are manufactured in a particular form to do a particular job and do not expose an employees to hazardous chemicals when they are used as intended, such as a lead-acid battery.

Hazardous chemicals are those chemicals that pose physical or health hazards. A physical hazard is a property of the chemical itself, such as flammability, explosion potential, instability, and reactivity. Health hazards include any potential harmful effects on people, such as chemicals that cause irritation, sensitization, corrosion, toxicity, cancer-causing, and attack certain organs.

The Hazard Communication Standard requires proper labeling of the chemicals. The label must contain information about the identity of the chemical, directions for use, and warnings about physical and health hazards. For more detailed information about the chemical, the material safety data sheets must be consulted.

Material safety data sheets are prepared by the manufacturer or importer, but the employer using the hazardous chemical must obtain them if they are not included with the chemicals when they are received. Material safety data sheets must be maintained where the chemicals are being used or they must be readily accessible, as through computer access.

Information that must be on the material safety data sheets is as follows: identity of the chemical, physical and chemical characteristics, physical and health hazards, primary routes of exposure, permissible exposure limit, sources that represent the chemical as hazardous or carcinogens, safety precautions and control measures, emergency and first aid procedures, date of preparation and name and address of preparer. Because the details can be critical in an emergency situation, employers must train employees in locating the sheets and reading them. They must be available at all times during working hours.

Training is a major component of the Hazard Communication Standard. Employees are to be taught about the existence of the standard and dangers associated with working with hazardous chemicals. Education also must discuss how chemicals are introduced into the body, importance of labeling, and how to read material safety data sheets. Employees who need personal protective equipment (such as masks, gloves, or goggles) must be trained in their use. They must have specific instruction on the chemicals they will be dealing with and whom to contact in an emergency situation. In some states, retraining must be done annually.

Required recordkeeping varies from state to state but generally documents who was trained along with a copy of the materials used. Many states have a single statute concerning the right to know, and it includes both community and worker rights. In the federal system, a community's right to know is overseen by the **Environmental Protection Agency.** The law and regulations fall under the **Emergency Planning and Community Right-To-Know Act.** The worker's right to know, in contrast, falls under the Occupational Safety and Health Administration's jurisdiction, and the rights are established by regulations, not a statute.

HAZARDOUS AIR POLLUTANT A chemical, compound, or **particulate** that Congress has placed on a list of pollutants that can cause health problems when discharged to the air. In 1970, the **Environmental Protection Agency** (EPA) was given the responsibility of listing hazardous air pollutants. However, only eight had been listed by the time the **Clean Air Act Amendments of 1990** were passed, so Congress legislated its own list, including 189 substances.

History

The 1970 **Clean Air Act** mandated control of hazardous air pollutants. The EPA's job was difficult, however. Before it could list a substance as a hazardous pollutant, it had to determine that it would cause health problems, what the standard should be to minimally protect the public, and then add an "ample measure of safety."

Health-based standards, such as those built into the 1970 Act, precipitated another problem. If health was to be the only consideration, how could cost or technological feasibility be factored into the equation? Public interest groups took the position that it could not be. The standard for a hazardous air pollutant, according to those groups, had to be zero.

The EPA had trouble determining which pollutants should be listed. At first, many people believed that the only significant exposures to hazardous air pollutants were in the workplace and the Occupational Safety and Health Administration was responsible for workplace safety. Another law changed that perception.

In 1986, when the **Superfund** law was amended, the **Emergency Planning and Community Right-To-Know Act** became part of it. That law required public disclosure of releases, as well as planning for them. The Toxic Release Inventory was established; in it, information became available to the public and lawmakers for the first time.

The first Toxic Release Inventory of all reported releases of hazardous air pollutants reported under the Emergency Planning and Community Right-To-Know Act was prepared in 1989. In 1990, Congress knew much more about the existing levels of exposure to various **air pollutants**. The listing problem was taken from the EPA, at least initially, and Congress created its own list. However, the EPA administrator can add or delete substances from it after making specified findings.

Technology-Based Standards

A source considered major for hazardous air pollutants is much smaller than a major source for other types of air pollutants. If a source emits 10 tons per year of any one hazardous air pollutant or 25 tons per year of any combination of hazardous air pollutants, it is considered major. That means it is subject to more regulation than other sources.

Since the concept of basing control levels on health concerns had caused so much trouble, the 1990 Amendments moved to a technology-based standard like those used in other statutes. The level of control necessary for hazardous air pollutants became the technology required to get the maximum reduction in emissions or maximum achievable control technology (MACT). To determine what that means numerically, the EPA looks at the available technology and determines what the best technologies are. Then it sets standards based on what those controls can achieve.

According to the 1990 amendments, the EPA is to look first at technology. Later, consideration of health is to be factored in. See **National Emission Standards for Hazardous Air Pollutants.**

HAZARDOUS AND SOLID WASTE AMENDMENTS (HSWA)   A major revision to the **Resource Conservation and Recovery Act** passed in 1984 to address concern that the **Environmental Protection Agency** (EPA) was not adequately dealing with **hazardous waste.** Unlike many environmental statutes, which leave the details to the EPA, HSWA added numerous specific requirements to the statute itself. Congress included provisions to force the EPA to deal with small quantity generators of hazardous waste, phase out use of land disposal for hazardous waste, and control underground injection and boilers using hazardous waste. It also added a comprehensive program to regulate underground storage tanks.

The Hazardous and Solid Waste Amendments broadened the EPA's authority to require cleanup of hazardous waste facilities, brought many more people under the requirements, and authorized **citizen suits.** The law set deadlines for regulations and then created provisions that would take effect if the EPA had not acted by the deadlines. Called hammer provisions, they were more stringent than the EPA would have pushed through the system. The hammer provisions put pressure on the agency by forcing more interested parties into the regulatory process.

An example of lesser known hammer provisions in HSWA involved small quantity **generators.** The EPA had been unable to come up with regulations under the 1976 RCRA, so it did not regulate persons who create hazardous waste in amounts between 100 and 1,000 kg per month. HSWA required the EPA to promulgate regulations for small quantity generators by 31 March 1976, or all small quantity generators would have to prepare manifests (documents for transportation and disposal of hazardous waste), retain copies of them, and file reports if the manifests did not return to them signed. It was estimated the number of regulated small quantity generators would increase from approximately 60 thousand to 130 thousand when these hammer provisions took effect, since they had not been covered by the existing regulations.

Congress also created a hammer provision related to minimizing or eliminating land disposal of hazardous waste [see **land disposal restrictions**]. It therefore created a scheme to prohibit land disposal of liquids, imposed minimum technical requirements for existing and new landfills and surface impoundments, and phased in restrictions on disposal of certain wastes in land disposal units. This provision is the most famous hammer in the statute.

The land disposal restrictions were to be phased in on certain dates, with an absolute prohibition of land disposal unless the waste met treatment standards established by the EPA, the EPA granted an exemption, or the disposer could demonstrate the waste would not migrate during the time it remained hazardous. Since EPA had not developed treatment standards (or considered exemptions) when the law was enacted, this provision forced them to act or deal with the consequences.

HSWA also brought millions of underground **storage tank** owners under federal regulation. Over time, underground storage tanks have been the favored method of storing petroleum products such as gasoline, diesel fuel, and oil. Older tanks were usually made of bare steel, which corrodes and attracts electricity, weakening the structure. Eventually, they leak and may contaminate not only the soil, but both groundwater and surface water.

In 1984, the number of underground storage tanks was estimated at between 2.8 and 5 million. In 1985, 100,000 of them were thought to be leaking, and 350,000 were projected to leak in the future. The first order of business for the EPA was to determine where underground storage tanks were located. Tank owners were required by HSWA to file a notice with the EPA about the tanks they owned. The EPA was then directed to develop regulations for management of underground storage tanks and their contents.

Corrective action was another important addition to the Resource Conservation and Recovery Act through HSWA. Abandoned hazardous waste facilities are addressed under a different law, the **Comprehensive Environmental Response, Compensation, and Liability Act.** However, many facilities remain open, closing only a unit that is full and moving on to a new one.

HSWA states that all permits for a **treatment/storage/disposal facility,** except those classified as **interim status facilities,** must compel corrective action. (The law gives the EPA the right to order corrective action, even for interim facilities.) That condition means that releases of hazardous waste must be cleaned up as the need arises, not simply after the facility is closed and the owner moves on. If a waste unit has caused damage off the property, the EPA may order cleanup there as well. See **solid waste management unit.**

HAZARDOUS CHEMICAL   A chemical regulated by the Occupational Health and Safety Administration through the **Hazard Communication Standard.** The requirements set forth in the standard were established to protect workers in the workplace.

The person responsible for determining whether a chemical is a hazardous chemical is the manufacturer or importer of the chemical, and the process is called a hazard determination. To make a determination, the manufacturer or importer must identify and consider all available scientific evidence. If at least one credible study reveals a health or physical risk, it is sufficient evidence to label the chemical hazardous.

HAZARDOUS MATERIAL   A substance designated as hazardous by the Secretary of Transportation because it may cause an unreasonable risk to health, safety, or property when transported in a particular quantity or form. Hazardous materials are regulated under the **Hazardous Materials Transportation and Uniform Safety Act.** Examples of hazardous materials include explosives, radioactive materials, substances that can cause disease, flammable liquids or solids, oxidizers, corrosives, and **hazardous waste**s. A list is published in the Code of Federal Regulations.

HAZARDOUS MATERIALS TRANSPORTATION AND UNIFORM SAFETY ACT (HMTUSA)   The statute that governs transportation of **hazardous material**s. Passed in 1990, it replaces the Hazardous Materials Transportation Act and covers not only transporters, but everyone who offers a hazardous material for transportation and people who manufacture, test, or repair shipping containers for hazardous materials.

State and local agencies determine which routes may be used for transportation of hazardous materials, and the law specifies what the agencies must consider when establishing them. They must examine and evaluate the population density, type of highways, type and quantity of hazardous materials, emergency response capabilities, results of consultation with affected persons, terrain, alternative routes, and effects on commerce.

The statute requires permits for carriers of some types and quantities of hazardous materials. In addition, vehicles must be placarded in certain cases and shipping papers showing what is being transported and who can be contacted for further information must be carried with the shipment. Shipments of hazardous materials must be packaged according to the regulations and properly marked. Responsibility for these details falls on the person offering the material to the transporter. Containers used for packaging hazardous materials must withstand specified tests, and manufacturers, reconditioners, and testers of the containers are required to follow the transportation regulations.

All parties subject to the HMTUSA must train employees involved in transportation of hazardous materials. They also have recordkeeping requirements and are subject to inspections and investigations by the Department of Transportation.

A special agency of the Department of Transportation, the Research and Special Programs Administration, is tasked with developing many of the transportation rules. It promulgated the most important regulations for the transport of hazardous materials, the HM-181, from which the requirements mentioned above are taken. The Department of Transportation has jurisdiction over highways, railways, air and water transportation. Different forms of transportation require different precautions and are addressed in the regulations.

Federal law involving transportation of hazardous material stems from the U.S. Constitution and the right to make laws concerning commerce. If a state or local law or regulation differs with federal law and makes it impossible to comply with both or if the state or local law is not consistent with federal law, federal law prevails.

Hazardous Waste Transportation

Both the Department of Transportation and the **Environmental Protection Agency** (EPA) have jurisdiction over the transportation of **hazardous waste**. The EPA's power comes from the **Resource Conservation and Recovery Act,** in which a system of "cradle-to-grave" hazardous waste management was established. Generally, a transporter of hazardous waste must have an EPA identification number and a manifest, a document with required information and tracking requirements, must accompany the waste. If the hazardous waste is also a designated hazardous material, it must be shipped according to the Department of Transportation regulations as well.

The EPA and DOT have entered into an agreement called a Memorandum of Understanding. Under it, the EPA is responsible for investigating midnight dumping and possible environmental violations, and providing the DOT with information about transportation violations. The DOT's obligations include conducting inspections and investigating situations reported by the EPA and giving the EPA information about possible environmental violations.

Both agencies have enforcement authority. Although they could both enforce against the same person for the same set of facts, the EPA and DOT try not to duplicate efforts. Instead, they are connected by liaisons and free with information.

Radioactive Materials

Three agencies deal with radioactive shipments. The Department of Energy ships commercial radioactive waste and defense nuclear waste for storage as well as weapons. The Nuclear Regulatory Commission regulates the commercial activities of nuclear power plants and certifies as safe the containers for those materials. Finally, the Department of Transportation has the power to control most radioactive shipments, with the exception of the DOE's defense nuclear material. The Nuclear Regulatory Commission and the Department of Transportation have agreed the DOT may require non-DOE waste to be transported in certified containers. The DOE is allowed to self-certify containers based on Nuclear Regulatory Commission standards.

Major Change Made by HMTUSA

The most sweeping change to prior law regarding transportation of hazardous materials was to require the use of international standards for transportation of hazardous materials. The United Nations provided recommendations for the change, and international hazardous standards are now used for packaging, hazard classification, and handling specifications. The new requirements, implemented through HM-181, a regulation, provide objective criteria for determining what risks a hazardous material poses. They also move away from design packaging to performance-oriented packaging and adopt international principles. As with many new standards, costs increased when they took effect.

Before the international standard was adopted, the risk posed by a hazardous material was difficult to gauge. If a material is flammable, does that mean it will burn at 100 degrees? 73 degrees? 140 degrees? Now, a hazardous material will not only have a packing classification that indicates what the danger is, it will also have a group code to describe the amount of risk. For example, for combustible liquids, group I liquids (those with boiling points under 95 degrees Fahrenheit) pose the biggest threat of fire. Group II substances have flashpoints under 73 degrees; and Group III, between 73 and 140 degrees.

For packaging, the move from design standards has simplified container preparation. Before the change, certain wood might be required, with specified widths, thickness, spacing, and nailing criteria. Now the regulations state what types of risks the package must withstand. Another benefit of using performance standards in packaging is that they allow use of new materials instead of freezing criteria and limiting packaging to materials available at the time the regulation went into effect.

HAZARDOUS RANKING SYSTEM (HRS) The method used by the **Environmental Protection Agency** (EPA) to evaluate the dangers posed at a site where **hazardous waste** has been disposed. The system is spelled out in the regulations, and it is amended from time to time. The evaluation is designed to help the agency decide which sites should be placed on the **National Priority List,** the list of **Superfund** sites. If a site is on the list, the EPA may use federal funds if necessary to eliminate a threat to health or the environment. If a site is not on the list, use of federal funds is severely limited.

General Concepts in the HRS

Throughout the ranking process, the EPA's purpose is to determine the likelihood of exposure to or release of **hazardous substances** and the type of threat the site poses. The EPA determines the score or rank by looking at four different pathways for release: soil, air, groundwater, and surface water. Its evaluation includes some common elements for all four pathways.

First, the source of the danger is considered. The agency must identify the hazardous substances available to the various pathways, the sources at the site, and overall contamination. Second, the likelihood of release or exposure is evaluated, including contamination that has been observed and, if no release has occurred, the potential for contamination or release. Movement of hazardous substances is also considered. The EPA must find answers to a number of questions: What is the possibility of a hazardous substance being leached from the soil into groundwater or running off into surface water? How certain is the movement of contamination from groundwater to surface water? This sort of inquiry will focus on the hydrogeology of the area, the soil type, and other relevant factors. Third, waste characteristics are rated. Toxicity, mobility, quantity, and persistence are considered in this calculation, along with the likelihood that the substance will accumulate in organisms.

Finally, the targets are scored. This element considers the likelihood that the community will be exposed to the contaminants. For example, the population may be exposed to the hazardous substance because it uses an impacted aquifer as a source of drinking water. Some soils conduct contamination more quickly than others because they are more porous. These and similar factors increase the public risk.

How the System Works

The EPA comes into the picture when a person or a state notifies it that hazardous substances may have been disposed of at a particular site. An investigation follows, usually in the form of a preliminary assessment. If the preliminary assessment shows a possible release or threat of release, a site inspection will generally be conducted. If the agency determines that the site may pose a risk, it may move the site to the ranking process. However, the EPA may act immediately if the dangers appear imminent.

Once the site is being evaluated, the regulations are quite specific about how the scores are to be calculated. The person working on the ranking will consider numerous factors for each pathway, resulting in a number for that pathway. Then the total score is calculated using a formula: the sum of the squares of each pathway score divided by four. The result will range between 0 and 100. If the score is high enough, the site is proposed for inclusion on the National Priority List. If it is not, the site may be listed by the state, but it will not be eligible for a federal remedial action unless the state names the site as its first priority for cleanup.

HAZARDOUS SUBSTANCES Chemicals, pollutants, mixtures, or wastes regulated by the federal government under the **Comprehensive Environmental Response, Compensation, and Liability Act.** The list of hazardous substances includes **hazardous waste**, toxic or hazardous water pollutants, hazardous air pollutants, imminently hazardous substances and mixtures subject to the **Toxic Substances Control Act**, and any other substance listed due to the Comprehensive Environmental Response, Compensation, and Liability Act (**Superfund**).

Petroleum, crude oil, and natural gas are three major exclusions from the definition of hazardous substances. The EPA takes the position that the exclusion covers petroleum as it is being refined, extracted, transported, and stored. However, if it is used and picks up contaminants during the use, the end product may no longer fall under the exclusion.

Before the EPA may intervene in a cleanup under Superfund, a hazardous substance must be released or the threat of release must exist. The list of potentially hazardous substances is very long, but other facts limit the EPA's authority to act. For example, a release that occurs inside a workplace is excluded, as is engine exhaust. Normal use of fertilizer is also carved out of the definition, although land applications of other hazardous substances would be considered releases.

Since Superfund was enacted for the purpose of responding to abandoned hazardous waste sites and emergency releases, Congress placed additional restrictions on the EPA's use of its Superfund powers, even though the substances involved are hazardous substances. The agency may use Superfund, however, if an emergency exists.

The EPA is not permitted to use Superfund to respond to naturally occurring substances in their unaltered forms or those that are altered solely through naturally occurring processes, excluding naturally occurring radioactive materials. Another constraint involves products that are part of the structure of buildings, such as asbestos. Yet another is a release into public or private drinking water supplies due to deterioration of the system through normal use, a provision that covers potential lead contamination.

Although Congress decided in the situations specified that the EPA would not use Superfund powers or money to deal with a release, it did not eliminate the hazardous substances from regulation. So if asbestos, lead, or radioactive material is disposed of, the EPA can react to the situation. It cannot, however, enter a building or a public utility and demand the removal of asbestos or lead pipes, nor can it dig up areas with naturally occurring radon and force a cleanup.

Many statutes regulate the discharges of hazardous substances. Superfund is a tremendously powerful statute, but it is not the only one with teeth. For example, petroleum is not included in the definition of hazardous substance, but petroleum stored in tanks is regulated by the **Resource Conservation and Recovery Act.** Releases in workplaces that do not affect the outside environment are subject to the **Occupational Safety and Health Act.**

HAZARDOUS WASTE A hazardous substance regulated by the **Resource Conservation and Recovery Act.** Under that law, waste must be *solid waste,* but that term includes not only solids, but semisolids, liquids, and contained gases.

One definition of hazardous waste is a solid waste that may cause or significantly contribute to mortality or serious illness because of its concentration, quantity, physical or chemical characteristics. Hazardous waste is also solid waste that can cause a substantial hazard to health or the environment if it is improperly stored, treated, transported, disposed of, or managed.

The term hazardous waste does not include useful substances that have not been discarded or abandoned, even though they are hazardous. However, a substance does not have to be thrown away or burned before it is considered waste; its useful life must be over. It may also remain at the place it was created and still be a hazardous waste.

The Resource Conservation and Recovery Act exempts some materials from its definition, even though they might otherwise qualify as hazardous wastes. For example, household waste, agricultural wastes returned to the ground, mining overburden returned to the site, and utility wastes from coal burning are all excluded.

Wastes may be hazardous either because the specific substance is listed as hazardous by the EPA, or simply because it has characteristics, such as corrosivity, ignitability, reactivity, or toxicity, that make it hazardous. Therefore, a person can find out whether a waste is subject to the hazardous waste regulations by checking the lists and testing the substance for the four characteristics of hazardous wastes. See **characteristic waste; listed waste.**

The requirements for dealing with hazardous waste are extensive. If certain materials are recycled, they may not be subject to all of the regulations. For example, spent lead acid batteries, scrap metal, used oil, and precious metals are exempt from many requirements if they are recycled. Since the recycling process for hazardous wastes may also generate hazardous waste, the recycler will be subject to the hazardous waste regulations.

HEARING   In administrative law, an opportunity to present evidence to an agency, such as the **Environmental Protection Agency** (EPA). Hearings may be formal, similar to trials, or they may be as informal as a meeting or an invitation for written comments. The nature of the hearing depends on the type of action the agency is proposing and the statute or statutes involved.

Constitutional Safeguards

The Fifth Amendment to the Constitution is the source of the right to a hearing. That provision states that "no person shall be deprived of life, liberty, or property without due process of law." Although the Fifth Amendment is often considered in the criminal area, it also applies to government actions that take away liberty in ways other than putting someone in jail, such as eliminating a person's right to practice a profession. It also prevents the government from taking property without weighing the individual's rights.

Administrative agencies make decisions every day that impact the people they regulate. Not all of them require a hearing, but many do. The first question is whether one of the protected interests (life, liberty, or property) is involved. If so, then the agency must conduct some type of hearing.

To comply with the Fifth Amendment's mandate, two things must occur: the individual must have notice prior to the time the agency acts; and the hearing must give the individual the opportunity to be heard. These two steps must precede the agency's action unless a serious situation exists that will harm the public or the environment and the agency cannot wait. For example, the EPA may immediately stop the sale and distribution of a pesticide if an imminent danger exists. See **Federal Insecticide, Fungicide, and Rodenticide Act.** However, when the agency does act before a hearing can take place, it is required to hold a hearing soon after the emergency action.

Constitutional scholars debate what is meant in the Fifth Amendment by focusing on a major issue: what is the *process* that is *due*? When agency action is involved, courts consider three questions to decide the answer:

(1) What is the private interest? (2) What is the risk of making a mistake that deprives the individual of the interest if the agency's procedures are followed? (3) What is the government's interest?

Assuming no statute tells the agency how it must provide the opportunity to be heard in a particular case, administrative agencies have a great deal of latitude in deciding what to do. If a government employee is notified that he or she will be fired and why and allowed to meet with the employer to contest the firing, that process may be enough protection as far as the Constitution is concerned. Another example of a government action that may require a hearing is a reduction in benefits. A hearing for a welfare recipient may be no more than a chance to protest in writing, or it may take the form of a meeting with a caseworker to discuss the cut.

On the other hand, sometimes the courts hold that if the individual has a right to sue, file a claim with the agency, or go through other steps to regain what has been lost, the need for a prior hearing is not as important.

Statutes and Hearings

As administrative agencies have multiplied and their powers increased, Congress has added its own requirements to laws to make sure individuals do not lose their Constitutional protections. The **Administrative Procedure Act,** the law that forms the backdrop to agency action, is only one source of direction for the agency in this matter.

The Environmental Protection Agency has power under major statutes to choose between a lawsuit and an administrative proceeding when it finds violations of the law. Generally, it chooses administrative action rather than litigation through the court system because the process is easier and quicker. Many agency actions are not subject to a formal hearing process, but administrative action that impacts an individual who is alleged to be a violator must involve the opportunity to be heard.

A person charged with violating an environmental law such as the **Clean Air Act** or the **Clean Water Act** faces penalties and/or orders for compliance. A compliance order is significantly different from a penalty order, however, because the facility should have spent the money to comply before the order is issued. The effect of such an order does not penalize the facility as much as it equalizes the cost of owning a facility with the costs other facilities have paid to comply. If the agency action is only for compliance, the "hearing" is likely to be an informal meeting with an agency official and will be held on request. Occasionally, the meeting will be recorded.

If the EPA combines the compliance order with a penalty action, the violator must pay a penalty in addition to the cost of correcting the problem. Thus, a penalty action is closer to a government lawsuit for damages. To ensure that the agency allows the accused party an opportunity to present evidence before the penalty is assessed, Congress has set up particular requirements concerning the type of hearing that must be held. In general, the higher the proposed penalty, the more formal the hearing must be. See **administrative penalty order.**

Hearing Officers

In administrative hearings, both formal and informal, people who will hear the case are employees of the agency involved. The main restriction on the hearing officer is that he or she may not be involved in the case being heard. In federal environmental actions, the hearing officer is usually a lawyer or an **administrative law judge.** After the hearing, the officer will make recommendations to the regional administrator concerning the case. The administrator may adopt the position of the hearing officer or may choose another. As the hearings become more formal, the decisions themselves becomes more formal. Instead of an informal recommendation, the hearing officer will issue findings of fact and conclusions of law, which are then submitted to the regional administrator.

Formal hearings resemble trials but in many respects are conducted less rigidly. The administrative law judge hears motions, holds prehearing conferences, and ultimately listens to the evidence. Evidence is broadly admissible, and much evidence that would be excluded in a trial is allowed in an administrative hearing. The Administrative Procedure Act stipulates that cross examination of witnesses must be sufficient to allow "full and true disclosure of the facts." However, the judge may require written testimony in lieu of oral.

Public Hearings

Some agency proposals affect not only the person directly involved, but also the community or other members of the public. For that reason, proposals are published and contain a means of asking for a hearing. Members of the public may request hearings, attend them, and present evidence concerning the issue.

An example: if a industry wants a permit to discharge pollutants into a river, the public may want the opportunity to support the industry or argue against the permit. The EPA will accept comments on proposed permits, but it may also determine that a public hearing is warranted. If a hearing is held, a hearing officer will go to the community and hold an open forum. Later, recommendations will be made concerning the action.

Rulemaking

The EPA, as well as other agencies, issues rules. Some merely interpret or clarify an agency position. Other rules become the law; they are called legislative rules. Legislative rules must go through a notice and comment period.

The primary reason rulemaking is restrained through the notice and comment requirement is that administrative agencies are not elected officials so are not directly accountable to the public. Public notice and opportunity to comment on rules keeps the agency from acting in a vacuum and provides a record that a court can review later to determine whether the rule is arbitrary and capricious.

Informal hearings on proposed rules are common. The proposal is published along with the basis and purpose of the rule. Then the public is informed about how to submit comments. A public hearing may or may not follow. If the statute requires a formal hearing, one must be held, and this type of hearing then becomes a part of the record. In either situation, the agency must consider and respond to comments submitted at the end of the process.

INDUSTRIAL USER   An industrial firm that does not discharge wastewater directly into a stream or other water body but uses a public treatment facility to treat its waste before it is discharged. An industrial user is also referred to as an indirect discharger. See **direct discharger.** Because industrial users often produce a different type of waste than that normally treated by a **publicly owned treatment works,** they are subject to **pretreatment** standards under the **Clean Water Act.**

There are two types of pretreatment: general and categorical. All industrial users must meet the general standards. Categorical standards are industry specific and apply primarily to 34 industries (approximately 700 subcategories are included) and 65 toxic pollutants.

Development of Pretreatment Standards

The Clean Water Act of 1972 created a lot of work for the **Environmental Protection Agency** (EPA) but gave it insufficient guidance on toxic pollutant regulation. The section that dealt with toxic pollutants made it difficult for the agency to assign a particular substance to the priority pollutant list. When the EPA did list a substance, it had the burden of proving it belonged there. Consequently, the agency focused its attention on conventional pollutants.

Conventional pollutants such as alkalinity/acidity, biochemical oxygen demand, and suspended solids, are the primary pollutants released from publicly owned treatment works. The decision to regulate them was important, but more hazardous industrial pollutants remained largely unregulated. So the **Natural Resources Defense Council** sued the Environmental Protection Agency for its failure to address toxic pollutants. The EPA settled the case, and the resulting consent decree established the toxic pollutant regulatory scheme. In the settlement, the parties identified the primary toxic pollutants, polluting industries, and methods of regulating them. Basically, the EPA was asked to develop programs to address 65 categories of priority pollutants (including 129 specific chemicals) and 34 categories of industries. More than 70 percent of industry was affected by the agreement. The consent decree also required the use of best available technology when setting the standards.

Congress amended the Clean Water Act in 1977 to reflect the terms of the agreement. The 1977 amendments also established a procedure for removing or adding substances to the priority pollutant list and increased the EPA's enforcement authority. The consent decree was modified to accommodate the changes in the statute.

General Pretreatment Standards

The premise behind pretreatment is that pollutants must be treated, not simply dumped into a system unprepared to deal with them and thus allowed to escape management. The pretreatment standards anticipate and prevent an industrial user from skirting the permit process to escape pretreatment. Even if an industry obtains its own permit to discharge wastewater into a treatment system, it must meet pretreatment standards before the discharge.

The general standards prohibit an industry from interfering with the ability of a publicly owned treatment works to treat domestic wastewater. The prohibition includes dumping solids or thick liquids that disrupt flow; dumping petroleum products, highly alkaline wastes, and pollutants that cause physical reactions to workers at the treatment plant; creating fire or explosion hazards; and raising the water temperature high enough to inhibit biological action. Even if the pollutants added are the same as those normally treated by the plant, large amounts or high concentrations can upset the balance and cause violations of the treatment plant's permit. Industries that process food, for example, frequently discharge large amounts of conventional pollutants.

Another prohibition of the general standards is contributing pass-through wastes, although the categorical standards deal with this problem more directly. Pass-through waste is exactly what it sounds like: waste that goes through the system without treatment. If a particular waste is sent to a plant incapable of dealing with it, it remains untreated.

Categorical Pretreatment Standards

The categorical standards were first established in the NRDC consent decree, and they have changed very little since they were agreed upon. Three specific pollutants have been removed from the original 129 on the list of priority pollutants, but the 65 pollutant categories remain, as do the 34 industry categories. Priority pollutants include chromium and its compounds, lead and its compounds, asbestos, benzene, and cyanides. Industries covered by the categorical standards include canned and preserved seafood processors; sugar processors; textile mills; cement manufacturers; organic chemical, plastics, and synthetic fiber producers; inorganic chemical manufacturers.

Industrial users must pretreat their waste before they send it to a publicly owned treatment works unless the plant is capable of consistently removing the pollutants the industry contributes. A large treatment plant—one with a total design flow of 5 million or more gallons per day—must have an approved pretreatment program if it accepts incompatible wastes from industrial users.

Enforcement

Both federal and state governments can enforce the pretreatment regulations. However, the EPA generally holds the permittee (the publicly owned treatment works) responsible for violations of its permit, even if an industry caused them. Thus the treatment works, typically owned by a city or similar jurisdiction, is required to prevent industries from sending incompatible wastes to it. This arrangement results in cities issuing permits to industrial users, testing for quality control, and offering financial incentives to pretreat. If the treatment system is large enough, it must have an approved pretreatment program detailing the procedures.

If the city does not control the industrial user's input, it will frequently wind up the defendant in a lawsuit, along with the industry causing the violation. The threat of federal intervention is helpful in many communities, since the polluting industry may be important to the city as a major employer of its inhabitants. Often, when the EPA brings a lawsuit involving a small city and one primary industry, it finds itself fighting not only the industry but the city's fear of reprisal from the industry. Many cities resort to assessing taxes based on the volume or toxicity of industry waste instead of holding the industries to pretreatment requirements. This tactic can result in more income, but it often fails as a means of control. The most common threat made by the industry is moving to another location, crippling the small town economically. Such threats create the fear necessary to gain the city as an ally, but they are often based on an untrue assumption: the industry will not have to pretreat its waste in another jurisdiction. Unsophisticated cities are, however, vulnerable to this possibility and fear the worst.

INNOCENT PURCHASER A person who is not liable as an owner or operator of contaminated property because he investigated the property prior to acquiring it and did not discover the contamination. The term is important under the enforcement scheme of the **Superfund** law, the **Comprehensive Environmental Response, Compensation, and Liability Act** (CERCLA). It was added as a defense in the 1986 **Superfund Amendments and Reauthorization Act,** but the defense is hard to prove.

Background

CERCLA created an unprecedented liability system. The law's primary purpose, to clean up abandoned **hazardous waste** sites, depended on finding people to pay for the work. Although some money is available to the federal government, it has never been sufficient to address all of the identified sites. The law therefore held many classes of people strictly liable for cleanup. For the purpose of the innocent purchaser defense, only one of those categories is critical: the owner or operator who acquired the property or an interest in it after the contamination occurred.

The issue originated in the 1980 version of CERCLA. One defense to against liability was that the release or threat of release of a hazardous substance was caused by the act of a third party who did not have a contractual relationship with the owner. However, a contractual relationship includes any agreements that passed title or possession of the property to someone else. So a person who bought a piece of contaminated property would never be able to show that an unrelated third party was responsible. Inevitably, a contractual relationship would exist between the new owner or operator and the past owner. Therefore, a current owner or operator who had nothing to do with past waste disposal activities at a site could not escape liability. Under CERCLA, the terms *owner* and *operator* are very broad, including persons who lease or have a permit to use the property, and may extend to a leaseholder. A facility may, therefore, have a number of "owners" and/or "operators." Each one must complete his own investigation to obtain the innocent purchaser defense.

The Patch Approach to Clarification

When Superfund was reauthorized, Congress decided to allow some parties to be declared innocent. But instead of dealing with the issue head-on, it added some language to the definition of contractual relationship. In short, there are two requirements in the innocent purchaser defense: (1) the property had to be acquired after the disposal activities; (2) when the property was acquired, the defendant did not know and had no reason to know about **hazardous substances** on, in, or at the facility. The definition does exclude inherited property and government entities that acquire the property by an involuntary transfer. The burden of proof is on the defendant and must be established by more than 50 percent (preponderance of the evidence).

The definition does not stop there, however. It goes on in another paragraph to describe how innocence is demonstrated. If the defense rested only on knowledge, a party could avoid the issue by not asking about prior use. Congress was not willing to let the landowner off so easily and decided to require some investigation to show the defendant had no reason to know about the hazardous substances. To show that he or she had no reason to know, the defendant "must have undertaken, at the time of acquisition, all appropriate inquiry into the previous ownership and uses of the property consistent with good commercial or customary practice in an effort to minimize liability." In addition to meeting the conditions in the definition, the defendant must also show that he or she exercised due care with the hazardous substances and took precautions against foreseeable acts of other persons. Presumably, this requirement would apply only after the presence of the hazardous substances was detected, since the innocent owner would not be aware of them when taking possession.

Preacquisition Environmental Assessments

Within the commercial real estate field, the hope of establishing innocence has created the practice of conducting **environmental assessment**s prior to acquiring an interest in property. Many environmental companies jumped on the bandwagon, and the more reputable ones tended to agree on the elements necessary for an investigation. An environmental assessment typically includes the following: a title search, usually back at least 50 years; an examination of aerial photographs; a search of public records on spills and other recorded environmental problems; a site visit; interviews with the property owner and other individuals who may know about the history of the site; and consideration of land use on surrounding properties. If the initial results suggest a problem, the prospective buyer may investigate further through a variety of tests, including soil and groundwater samples.

Even though commercial practice has evolved to include environmental assessments, the potential buyer still has no assurance that he has done enough. Many legal scholars have concluded that it is impossible to obtain the innocent purchaser status because the court will hold that if the purchaser did not discover the problem, he did not look hard enough.

Cases directly considering the defense are rare, but they will be more important in the future. Since the defense was only created in 1986 and it takes years to take a Superfund case through the courts, the issue is only beginning to be heard. The cases thus far have determined that commercial buyers must undertake some type of inquiry. A site visit is required, and the buyer cannot ignore obvious signs of contamination or commonly known facts. Also important is the time of acquisition; a person who bought property in the 1950s will not be held to the same standard as one purchasing property today.

The issue usually comes to the attention of a court when the government makes a motion to have parties declared liable pursuant to CERCLA. Then the party claiming the defense must offer sufficient evidence to allow a court to grant a cross-motion. In practice, this is more difficult than proving the defense in a trial.

A motion for summary judgment, which is the type of motion at issue, is a request to have the court enter judgment for the moving party without the necessity of proving the point. Courts can only grant such a motion in exceptional circumstances, however. To do so, they have to assume that the facts most favorable to the opposing party are true and then conclude that the moving party is still entitled to win as a matter of law.

The burden of proof at trial is a preponderance of the evidence, so the owner of the property must convince the jury or the judge that it is more likely than not he did the necessary inquiry. Unfortunately, taking the issue to court is expensive, not only in terms of litigation fees but also because the owner will be subject to cleanup costs in the meantime.

A few examples of cases considering the defense may be instructive. In *United States v. Serafini*, a 1988 case decided in Pennsylvania, the court would not grant summary judgment to the government even though the purchaser had not visited the site it purchased. Since the property was acquired in 1969, the court believed the government needed to establish more than the lack of a visit.

The situation was this: a partnership named Empire bought a property in Pennsylvania. It had been leased to the city for waste disposal, and 1,141 drums were visible on the property. When the government cleaned up the property, it sued the partnership and the partners.

The government tried twice again before it presented the evidence the court wanted to see. Through affidavits and depositions, it demonstrated the commercial practice in Pennsylvania in 1969 did include a visit to the site before acquisition. In 1990, the court granted summary judgment for the government, finding the Empire Group could not establish it was innocent.

In 1988, in *Wickland Oil Terminals v. Ascarco, Inc.*, the Northern District of California Court found the preacquisition investigation was deficient. Slag piles containing lead and other heavy metals were visible on site, and the contamination was widely known. Also, the previous owner had received notices of violation, and the new owner knew about them.

Standard Practices for Environmental Assessments

The American Society for Testing and Materials (ASTM), an organization that sets voluntary standards, recently published two standard practices for environmental assessments. One is a transaction screen (E 1528-94); the other is called a Phase I Site Assessment (E 1527-94). These two documents ASTM were drafted with input from users (those who will need the document), providers (those who will complete the assessments), and attorneys. They address only issues that would arise under CERCLA except for one addition: they do consider petroleum underground storage tanks.

The transaction screen is the more controversial of the two standard practices, at least to the providers. It is basically a questionnaire, and it need not be completed by an environmental professional. It is designed to be the environmental site assessment when no potential problems are flagged during the screening process. The Phase I environmental site assessment gathers more information than the transaction screen and relies on professional opinion; it must be conducted by an environmental professional.

The ASTM has attempted to fill in the gaps of the statute by outlining "good commercial or customary practice," and its work has determined what is acceptable for environmental assessments today. Although the ASTM standard practices are not endorsed by the government, they are tremendously helpful and specifically designed to assist the buyer in becoming an innocent purchaser.

Settlement

Short of litigation, the other way out of a Superfund lawsuit is settlement. The EPA takes the position that an innocent purchaser is eligible for settlement as a *de minimis* party and has published guidance for settlements with current landowners.

Authority for settlement with landowners is found in CERCLA. The provision appears to allow for settlement with not-so-innocent landowners as well as innocent purchasers. The owner must not have conducted or permitted generation, transportation, storage, treatment, or disposal of any hazardous substance and must not have contributed to the release or threat or release through an act of omission. The EPA, however, interprets the provision to call for the innocent purchaser defense and requires that the landowner provide evidence. The better the evidence, the EPA document states, the better the settlement terms.

INSPECTION An on-site investigation of a facility to determine compliance with a regulation, permit provision, or statute. One potential conflict with an agency's right to inspect is found in the U.S. Constitution. The Fourth Amendment states:

> The right of the people to be secure in their persons, houses, papers, and effects, against unreasonable searches and seizures shall not be violated, and no Warrants shall issue, but upon probable cause, supported by oath or affirmation and particularly describing the place to be searched and the person or things to be seized.

The protection of the Fourth Amendment extends to businesses as well as individuals. Therefore, in many situations, agencies must obtain warrants for their searches if consent is not given for inspections. Furthermore, a statute must give the power for inspection to the agency. Environmental statutes routinely contain language allowing inspections and other methods of gathering information. However, the EPA has not directly tested the scope of that authority. If refused entry, the EPA goes to court for a search warrant.

The **Occupational Safety and Health Administration** (OSHA) did test its power to search without a warrant. In *Marshall v. Barlow's, Inc.*, a 1978 case, the Supreme Court held that Congress could not authorize warrantless searches of businesses not highly regulated. The business involved was an electrical and plumbing contractor. However, some businesses, such as mines, automobile junkyards, and firearms dealers, have traditionally been regulated more tightly than others. In situations like these, the Supreme Court determined a warrant was not necessary.

The requirement that an agency get a warrant is not great protection for the business or person involved. For a criminal case, the government must show probable cause that a crime was committed and that the person who committed the crime or other evidence of the crime is located at the site to be searched. For administrative searches, the agency must show only that the inspection is part of a neutral scheme to enforce the statute. It's not difficult to obtain an administrative search warrant.

There are two instances when no administrative search warrant is required: emergencies and public view. Thus, fire officials who respond to a fire alarm may investigate for evidence of arson after the fire is extinguished, *Michigan v. Tyler.* Also, inspection of grounds through aerial photography, *Dow Chemical Co. v. U.S.*, or taking smoke measurements on site have been upheld as constitutional, *Air Pollution Variance Board v. Western Alfalfa Corporation.*

To eliminate the question of authority to inspect without a warrant, many environmental agencies put the right to inspect within the terms of permits they issue. It is unclear whether that step totally eliminates the warrant requirement, but most inspections occur with consent. Refusal to admit an inspector can backfire, and companies recognize that. If consent is withheld, warrants are easily obtainable.

INTEGRATED RISK INFORMATION SYSTEM (IRIS)

A database, created and maintained by the **Environmental Protection Agency** (EPA), that provides health information on specific substances. It reflects the EPA consensus opinion on the substances and includes information on hazard identification and a determination of how likely a substance is to increase the occurrence or severity of an adverse health effect. The database also provides dose response or information about the relationship between dose and the effect. IRIS is used by the EPA when developing site-specific information. The public may provide information to the IRIS database and access the data.

INTERIM STATUS FACILITY

A **treatment/storage/disposal facility** (facility that handles **hazardous waste**) in existence on 19 November 1980. A facility built after that date and not regulated when it was built is also an interim facility for a time after the **Environmental Protection Agency** (EPA) decides to regulate it. The **Resource Conservation and Recovery Act** (RCRA) establishes, among other things, a permitting system for hazardous waste treatment/storage/disposal facilities. The law was first passed in 1976, with significant revisions in 1984. Existing facilities must apply for a permit and provide notice to the EPA or the state, if the state is responsible for compliance. See **Hazardous and Solid Waste Amendments.**

Facilities built after the deadlines specified must have a permit before they may begin operation. However, Congress recognized that the EPA would have difficulty issuing permits due to the volume of permit applications it would need to process. Rather than shutting down existing facilities, Congress created interim status so they could continue operation while the permit was pending. To claim interim status, the facility does not have to provide the government with as much information as new facilities do in the initial application, but before it gets a permit, it must provide the same type of documentation. Interim status facilities lose that designation if the permit is denied or granted; if the facility refuses to supply information requested by the government; or if the right to operate is terminated by any other means.

The difference between permitted and interim status facilities is insignificant as far as technical requirements are concerned; the regulations are nearly identical. However, if the owner begins using a different part of the facility to store, treat, or dispose of hazardous wastes, that area is not covered under the interim facility umbrella. It must be permitted before operation, and the regulations that apply are those for permitted facilities.

LAND DISPOSAL RESTRICTIONS (LDRs) The prohibitions against waste disposal in, on, or under the ground that were built into the 1984 **Hazardous and Solid Waste Amendments** to the **Resource Conservation and Recovery Act.** During the legislative process, Congress decided that it was time to eliminate land disposal of **hazardous wastes** and liquids. The amendments aggressively address this issue.

Land disposal includes not only landfilling, but also placement into injection wells, salt beds, domes, or caves, landfarming (spreading the waste on the ground); dumping; lagoon disposal; and similar activities. Collectively, the land disposal restrictions are commonly known as the *landban.* Apparently unwilling to trust the **Environmental Protection Agency** (EPA) to generate regulations within a reasonable time, Congress composed its own list of hazardous wastes based on those listed by the state of California. It also built in its own deadlines and consequences so that the law would operate automatically. These provisions are called *hammers.*

Hammers work in this way: Congress tells the Environmental Protection Agency to promulgate regulations by a certain date, then specifies what rules will go into effect if the EPA has not acted by that date. Hammers place a lot of pressure on the EPA, because the automatic rules are conservative—that is, they provide for more severe restrictions than the EPA would be likely to require. Thus businesses impacted by a hammer will push the agency into action, and public interest groups may also get involved. Furthermore, the EPA may be subject to a **citizen suit** if it fails to act.

Basically, the law prohibits land disposal of hazardous wastes that the state of California had listed in 1987, unless the EPA determines otherwise. Before the enactment of the Hazardous and Solid Waste Amendments, California had taken the lead in determining which wastes were hazardous. The list it developed was called the "California list." Dioxin and specified solvents were banned from land disposal, effective 1986.

Congress directed the EPA to divide all other federally **listed wastes** into thirds, prioritized by volume and toxicity. If the EPA did not promulgate regulations for their disposal by specified deadlines, bans would follow. For the first third, the deadline was August 1988; for the second third, June 1989; for the final third, May 1990.

Most of the land disposal restrictions built into the Hazardous and Solid Waste Amendments are called *soft hammers*: disposal of the wastes in question was allowed if the disposal facility was in technical compliance with the regulations and it certified that the disposal was the only practical alternative. But the final hammer, which followed the ban on the last third of the listed substances, was a *hard hammer*. It prohibited all land disposal of any of the mentioned hazardous wastes if the EPA had not completed its review and regulatory requirements.

EPA's Authority

Primarily, the EPA was required to evaluate the hazardous wastes and ban them unless they were treated. However, the EPA could grant variances from the landban and allow land disposal if no migration of the waste would occur. Another task for the EPA was establishing treatment standards for the wastes. The EPA was to establish regulations specifying acceptable methods of treatment and levels of concentration that would reduce the probability of health and environmental impact, effective the same day that the land disposal restrictions were applied to the particular waste.

Although the statute's requirements pushed the EPA hard, they were effective: the regulations have been promulgated. Regulations now replace the ban in the Hazardous and Solid Waste Amendments. In general, the EPA exempted small quantity generators from some restrictions along with farmers who disposed of waste pesticides. A waiver or extension may be granted by the EPA, but otherwise, the hazardous wastes banned from land disposal must be treated according to the standards. Hazardous wastes that may not be land disposed may not be stored either, unless they are being accumulated for treatment. If they are stored, other requirements for storage must be met.

Requirements for Generators and Facilities

The **generator** of hazardous waste has a number of responsibilities if the waste is subject to the landban, but most of the requirements apply to any hazardous waste. The generator must analyze the waste and specify waste codes. The waste code is specified in the regulations, and it depends on the composition and nature of the waste. Further, the generator must certify whether the waste meets the treatment standards. If the waste is subject to land disposal restrictions, that fact must be pointed out, along with notice of any variances or extensions granted by the agency. Finally, the generator must keep documentation of testing information, as well as all other information accompanying the waste.

If the hazardous waste contains more than one waste prohibited from land disposal, the generator must meet each treatment standard that applies. Leachate that accumulates from waste piles is considered to contain all of the listed wastes in the pile, and all treatment standards that apply must be followed.

Treatment facilities must conduct period tests of wastes. They must also document treatment residues or extract of residues to show that they meet the standards specified for the waste. Copies of the documentation go to the land disposal facility along with the treated waste. Land disposal facilities are required to verify the information they receive from the person who treated the waste. They must also test the waste and keep records of their results.

Cleanups and the Land Disposal Restrictions

A peculiar problem arose when the landbans took effect. When a cleanup of hazardous waste was being conducted under the **Comprehensive Environmental Response, Compensation, and Liability Act** or the Resource Conservation and Recovery Act, the government could not pick up waste from one part of a facility and consolidate it, confining it on site. Nor could it dig up the waste, treat it, and put it back. Either action violated the land disposal restrictions. It became clear that the new regulations were not designed for cleaning up facilities. They were, instead, meant to control land disposal as the hazardous waste was generated. If the minimum technology requirements and land disposal restrictions were applied to **Superfund** sites or hazardous waste **treatment/storage/disposal facilities,** not only would the cleanup costs be significantly increased, but the person doing the work would be forced to leave the waste where it was, incinerate it, or move it offsite.

The EPA decided to amend the regulations to deal with these difficulties. It wanted to encourage onsite treatment, because moving hazardous waste increases the risk of exposure to it as well as possible releases. Also, given the changes in technology and control, the EPA determined that consolidation of hazardous wastes into a better-designed area might be preferable to leaving it where it was.

Out of the proposals and comments on this issue, the EPA created the concept of *a corrective action management unit* (CAMU) [see **corrective action**]. These units, which are areas of land rather than tanks, containers, or incinerators, must be designated by the regional administrator. They may not be used for new wastes brought to the site, only to manage remediation wastes, those generated by the cleanup of contamination from wastes originating at the facility. By rule, the EPA has determined that remediation wastes may be placed into such a unit without being subject to the land disposal restrictions or having to meet the minimum technology requirements of the Resource Conservation and Recovery Act.

Prior to designating a corrective action management unit, the EPA must publish its intention in a publicly available notice. The agency must evaluate a number of factors in the document, including the benefits and/or detriments associated with placement of remediation wastes in the unit; the type of management to be done after the unit is closed and wastes remain in place; and the extent to which treatment technologies may reduce the toxicity, mobility, or volume of wastes.

The cost savings generated by this change in the regulations is projected to be between $17 and $27 billion dollars. But aside from the dollars saved, the EPA believes the measure will facilitate cleanup and minimize risks connected with leaving the waste where it is.

LAVELLE, RITA (1947–) Administrator of toxic waste programs for the **Environmental Protection Agency** (EPA) during the first Reagan administration [see **Reagan, Ronald**]. Lavelle was hired by Anne Burford [see **Burford, Anne Gorsuch**]. She was fired by President Reagan on 7 February 1983. In 1982, Congress began an investigation into EPA operations that focused on the **Superfund** program, which Lavelle administered. She was convicted of perjury for lying to Congress during the investigation and sentenced to six months in prison. She served only four.

LENDER LIABILITY In environmental law, the term refers to a lender becoming a **potentially responsible party** under the **Comprehensive Environmental Response, Compensation and Liability Act (Superfund)** or responsible for cleanup under the **Resource Conservation and Recovery Act** (RCRA). Of the two statutes, Superfund figures more prominently.

A bank or other lending institution that holds a security interest in property (such as a mortgage) or a business (such as a lien against the inventory) may become the owner of the secured property if the borrower defaults on the loan. Before Superfund, lenders' only concern with the property was its value. Once Superfund was enacted, however, owners and operators of contaminated property were thrown into the group of people who can be forced to clean up the site. Therefore, a bank must plan both its lending and foreclosure activities carefully to avoid cleanup responsibility.

The limited defenses to the broad liability include "an act of a third party," but the third party may not be a person with whom the current owner has a contractual relationship. Since a written agreement is typically executed when a loan is granted, a lender cannot rely on the third party defense. However, the law specifically excludes lenders from being owners or operators under one condition: that they do not participate in management of the vessel or facility. They may hold indications of ownership, though, to protect the security interest, such as the paperwork associated with a mortgage.

Lender liability under the Resource Conservation and Recovery Act has focused on the underground storage tank provisions. The owner or operator of an underground tank has numerous responsibilities: meeting technical standards, reporting releases, cleaning up in the event of a release, and proving **financial responsibility.** See **storage tank.** In RCRA, the security exemption language is similar to that used in Superfund. It applies, by its words, only to exempt lenders as owners from cleanup. It does not address meeting technical standards or financial responsibility.

The Lender as Owner

As is typical in legal cases, the plain language of the statute has not obliterated lender liability. In the 1990 case *United States v. Fleet Factors,* an appellate court included language that indicated that a lender could be liable if it had the capacity to control **hazardous waste** disposal, even though it did not exercise it. The *Fleet Factors* case sent panic through the financial community. Lenders were afraid to foreclose on properties or intervene in a lesser way to protect their financial interest. After they made enough noise to be heard, the **Environmental Protection Agency** (EPA) created a rule about lender liability. In it, the agency provided some tests for lenders to follow to retain the security interest exemption in the statute.

But before the rule was promulgated, other cases made it to appellate courts. Taken together, they spelled out much of what was in the rule. For example, a lender could not be involved in hazardous waste handling decisions. Day-to-day management of operations was also action that would cost the lender the exemption. The lender could, however, participate in financial decisions and could even exercise some control over the company's management personnel. If the lender took title to the property, it was expected to attempt to resell it within a reasonable time. Failure to do so changed the character of the transaction from security interest to investment property.

Fleet Factors turned out to be a bad representative case in any event. Four decisions were published over time, as the case bounced from court to court and motion to motion. But the defendant had taken some egregious actions at the site. Fleet Factors had foreclosed on a business. After the foreclosure, its agents went to the site and removed asbestos from pipes in an uncontrolled manner and crushed drums containing hazardous waste with a forklift. The court held, ultimately, that the postforeclosure activities of the lender eliminated the protection of the lender exemption. Fleet Factors seemed determined to be an owner of the property.

Attack against the Lender Liability Rule

The EPA published its lender liability rule for Superfund liability in April 1992, and it was immediately challenged by a number of parties. Their attack was successful, and the rule was declared invalid in the case of *Kelley v. Environmental Protection Agency,* decided 4 February 1994.

The reasons for a heavy assault are apparent: people who still remained in the pool of responsible parties felt it was unfair to give lenders more protection than the statute already gave them, and state governments and public interest groups felt the agency had gone too far to remove a potential funding option for cleanups. The D.C. Circuit Court of Appeals was split in its opinion in the case (two voted for the majority opinion and one dissented). Interestingly enough, the decision turned entirely on administrative law and not on the substance of the rule. The EPA had argued through reference to a number of separate provisions that Congress had intended for it to define the terms of the law and that the EPA had authority to create the rule. The EPA contended that the rule was interpretative and not legislative in nature and should be given deference.

The D.C. Circuit rejected all of the agency's arguments. It decided that Congress had not given the EPA power to limit liability, define it, or set up a "comprehensive regulatory regimen to address the liability problem facing secured creditors." Determining what the statute said and meant was not the EPA's job, but the duty of the judicial officer. The court suggested that the EPA go back to Congress and ask for an amendment to the law to allow what it wanted to do.

During the period before the rule was struck down, cases involving lenders continued to be heard. Some courts used the EPA rule to determine the result; some referred to the rule and also to cases to back their decision; and some explicitly refused to use the rule, relying on case law and the statute as authority.

For some time the financial community has been pressuring Congress to amend the Superfund law to provide more protection for it. A variety of approaches have been put forward in the reauthorization bills that are pending. The easiest solution for Congress, though, is to explicitly delegate the power to the EPA to create the rule.

On 13 June 1994, the EPA proposed a rule under the Resource Conservation and Recovery Act to protect lenders who have security interests in underground storage tanks. It is similar in many ways to the Superfund rule. But since a different statute is involved, a court will have to determine whether the EPA has sufficient authority under RCRA to promulgate this rule.

Under RCRA, the lender is protected from liability as an owner if it does not exercise day-to-day control. However, if it forecloses on property with a storage tank and allows the tank to remain in service, the lender becomes an operator and will be required to follow the regulations. The proposed rule specifies that a lender can avoid liability under certain conditions. First, before foreclosure, the lender may not control the borrower's compliance with the environmental rules applicable to the tank. Second, it may not operate the borrower's enterprise and simply refuse to handle the environmental implications of the business. The EPA does not forbid inquiry about the borrower, however. The lender may investigate the tank and site before it loans money, and it may also require compliance with environmental laws and check on the property from time to time.

Like the Superfund rule, the proposed RCRA rule puts emphasis on resale: the lender must list the property within 12 months of foreclosure. To avoid becoming an operator, the lender must also empty the tank within 15 days after foreclosure. Lenders must report releases, but they are not required to clean up contamination or meet the technical requirements for tanks if they have emptied them. If a lender does not empty the tank, the lender loses the exemption.

LISTED WASTES The **Resource Conservation and Recovery Act** (RCRA) regulates solid and **hazardous waste**s from the time they are considered discarded until they are finally disposed of. The focus of the statute is on hazardous waste and petroleum products stored in underground storage tanks.

RCRA recognizes two different categories of hazardous wastes: those that are listed by name and those with characteristics considered hazardous. Three separate lists of hazardous waste have been developed, and any substances included on those lists are considered listed wastes.

A hazardous waste must meet two criteria. First, it must be *solid waste,* but that term includes contained gases, liquids, and semisolids as well as solids. Next, it must pose a significant danger to human health or the environment. The statute speaks in terms of a solid waste that can cause or significantly contribute to an increase in death or serious irreversible or incapacitating reversible illness. Also, if improper disposal or handling of the waste will cause it to adversely impact health or the environment, it is hazardous. However, the statute itself excludes some types of waste from the solid category, and some from the hazardous category.

To determine which wastes are hazardous, the EPA must look at the quantity, concentration, physical, chemical, and infectious properties of the waste, taking into account its persistence, accumulation in tissue, toxicity, and degradability in nature, along with other hazardous characteristics. The EPA came up with two methods for the waste generator to determine whether a waste is hazardous. If the waste has hazardous characteristics, such as toxicity, ignitability, corrosivity, or reactivity, it must be handled as a hazardous waste. If the EPA has listed it on one of three lists, based on its own evaluation of the substance's characteristics, it automatically falls under the hazardous waste regulations unless it is delisted by the agency. See also **characteristic waste.**

Over 400 wastes have been placed on the lists. The first list consists of wastes from nonspecific sources; the second covers specified sources; and the third includes commercial chemical products that have been discarded. Each waste has a hazardous waste number. The designation for wastes on the first list is an F before the number—*F wastes.* These wastes include spent solvents, wastewater sludges, and wastes from production of certain acutely **hazardous chemical**s, regardless of their origin. Specific source hazardous wastes are *K wastes.* This list encompasses wastes from wood preservation processes, petroleum refining, ink formulation, and production of pesticides, explosives, and organic or inorganic chemicals, among many others. The third list deals with chemical wastes discarded in nearly pure form.

The prefixes are either P for acutely hazardous wastes—*P wastes*—or U for toxic wastes—*U wastes*. Typically, these wastes result from spills during processing, the containers that hold the chemicals, the product itself, or off-specification products.

Once a waste is listed as hazardous, the only way to remove it from the numerous requirements for its management and disposal is to have it delisted by filing a petition with the EPA. In it, the party requesting delisting must demonstrate that the substance does not meet the criteria for which it was listed and that it is not hazardous under other criteria. The public must be notified of the petition and allowed to comment. The EPA must grant or deny the petition within 24 months after it is deemed complete by the agency. If it is granted, the delisting applies only to the waste from the particular facility where the testing proved it is nonhazardous.

LOCAL EMERGENCY PLANNING COMMITTEE (LEPC)
See **Emergency Planning and Community Right-To-Know Act.**

LOVE CANAL
A **hazardous waste** site in Niagara Falls, New York. Discovered in the mid-to-late 1970s, the site was highly publicized and focused national attention on what had become of the by-products of industrialization. In 1980, Congress passed the first statute to deal with abandoned hazardous waste sites. That law, the **Comprehensive Environmental Response, Compensation, and Liability Act,** authorized the federal government to address the problems and started a fund (the **Superfund**) to help finance cleanups until the responsible parties could be forced to take care of the sites.

History

Between the years 1942 and 1953, Hooker Chemical and Plastics Corporation (now Occidental Chemical Corporation) disposed of its hazardous waste at a dump site at Niagara Falls. Government documents estimate that approximately 21,000 tons of waste were placed in the area. In 1953, Hooker deeded the property to a New York school district for a dollar. The deed attempted to limit Hooker's future liability for its past activities at the property.

A housing development and schools were built in the area after the transfer occurred. Soon, chemicals began to ooze to the surface. The residents became concerned by the unusually high number of illnesses in their population. One woman, Lois Gibbs, set the wheels in motion. She had moved to the community in 1974 with her husband and one-year-old son. He developed asthma, a blood disease, and a urinary tract disorder. Later, Mrs. Gibbs had a daughter, who also developed the blood disease.

A local news reporter wrote a story in 1978 that discussed buried chemicals and the types of illnesses they could cause. Gibbs read the article and began to investigate the connection. She tried to get the school closed, but failed. Local environmental organizations were at a loss when she contacted them for guidance. She carried a petition through the community and discovered that health problems were not limited to children. Gibbs organized the Love Canal Homeowners Association, and members began a struggle to get the government to pay attention to the Love Canal situation. They appealed first to the governor, then to the president.

The governor declared a state of emergency on 2 August 1978, and the first group of Love Canal residents, representing 240 homes, was evacuated that year. Two years later, the government evacuated another 500 homes in the vicinity. President Carter declared a federal environmental emergency for Love Canal in 1980.

All but two homes were destroyed. The initial buy-out was financed by the state and federal governments, but the government looked to Hooker and its successor to foot the bill. By 1990, over $14 billion in claims had been filed against the company.

Lois Gibbs eventually moved to the Washington, D.C., area and founded an organization called Citizens Clearing House for Hazardous Waste to help communities faced with similar circumstances. Her children recovered from their illnesses after they were removed from the area.

The Remedies

Love Canal was one of the first Superfund sites. The New York State Department of Environmental Conservation took the lead in the cleanup, with the **Environmental Protection Agency** (EPA) providing assistance. They focused on several different aspects of the site. First, they tried to stabilize the source of the contamination. Wastes were consolidated, and an elaborate drainage system was built to catch the leachate from the chemicals. A waste treatment plant then treated the leachate. Forty acres were capped— covered with layers of low-permeability soil and liners—to prevent most precipitation from seeping into the wastes, thereby reducing the amount of leachate. Signs were posted and fences erected to keep people out of problem areas. The sewer system was temporarily cut off, because the outfalls and pipes had been carrying contaminants to Love Canal, and rehabilitated by the EPA and New York in 1985. It was hydraulically cleaned and dredged, the sediments were contained, and access to the contaminants was limited. Later, the soil removed from the storm and sanitary system was incinerated on site.

In 1988 the state government declared the area safe for habitation in most areas, and the Environmental Protection Agency cleared the sale of new homes to buyers in 1990.

During rehabitation, the school board wanted to reopen the schools, but there were hot spots (areas of higher contamination) at one of the schools (93rd Street). In 1988, the EPA had decided to excavate, stabilize, consolidate and cap the area, but the school board believed parents would be opposed to leaving the contamination where it was. The EPA reopened the issue in 1991. To assist in the rehabilitation of the area, the EPA amended its earlier decision to allow the hot spots to be dug up and taken offsite for disposal. Backfilling using site soil was approved. Approximately 7,000 cubic yards of soil will be removed, and the property will then be capped.

Love Canal cases have been in the court for years. The Department of Environmental Conservation announced that Occidental has agreed to pay over $100 million dollars toward the cleanup, which does not include other claims or future liability.

The events at Love Canal brought the public eye-to-eye with disposal problems throughout the country. Public outrage about chemical disposal and its effects has resulted in increased government intervention, not only in cleaning up the problem after it occurs, but also in managing hazardous wastes as they are created. See **Resource Conservation and Recovery Act.**

MAJOR SOURCE   Under the 1970 **Clean Air Act,** a pollution source is considered a major source if it is stationary and has the potential to emit 100 tons per year or more of a regulated **air pollutant.** The **Clean Air Act Amendments of 1990** made the definition more inclusive by lowering the threshold of 100 tons per year for certain facilities: those that emit hazardous air pollutants or those located in an air district that has not attained the national air quality standards for the pollutant they discharge. See **hazardous air pollutants; National Ambient Air Quality Standards; National Emission Standards for Hazardous Air Pollutants; nonattainment areas.**

A stationary source may consist of more than one building. For purposes of determining the status of the facility, the government aggregates all facilities managed by the same person if they are near each other. The pollutant tonnage considered is not what the source actually emits but what it is capable of emitting. This figure is based on facility design: how much pollution would the source generate if it were operating at peak capacity? In some situations, if the source owner or manager agrees to limit plant operations so that it does not exceed certain levels, and if those levels are enforceable by the government, the **Environmental Protection Agency** (EPA) may consider actual emissions instead of potential emissions when deciding whether or not the source is major. Several courts have also determined that if the source is modifying its facility, the EPA should consider past operating practices to calculate future emissions.

Hazardous air pollutant dischargers are considered major sources if they have the potential to emit 10 tons per year or more of one hazardous air pollutant or 25 tons per year of any combination of hazardous air pollutants. In nonattainment areas for any of the **criteria pollutant**s (**ozone, nitrogen oxides, sulfur dioxide,** lead, and small **particulate**s), a source may be considered major at a level as low as 10 tons per year if it discharges the pollutant the area is having trouble with.

Once a facility is designated a major source, a permitting requirement for operation as well as other restrictions are triggered. All of the pollutants it emits will be regulated. For example, if a plant discharges 100 tons per year of nitrogen oxides but is below that amount for sulfur dioxide, it is still a major source. When the permit is written, it will include limits for sulfur dioxide as well as nitrogen oxides. A new major source or existing major facility that wants to modify its plant or operation is also required to go through preconstruction review and permitting before it can begin construction. Minor sources are not regulated to the same degree.

MARINE PROTECTION, RESEARCH, AND SANCTUARIES ACT (MPRSA)

A law enacted in 1972 to deal with ocean dumping, oceanic research, and protection of specified ocean areas. Commonly called the Ocean Dumping Act, MPRSA applies to discharges from vessels within the U.S. territorial seas, which extend three miles from the coastline, and to all U.S. vessels and persons, even if they are outside U.S. waters. Certain discharges are totally prohibited by MPRSA: industrial wastes, sewage sludges, high-level radioactive materials, and radiological, chemical or biological warfare agents. However, this particular law does not govern oil discharges.

The most common waste discharges allowed by the statute are those of dredged spoils. The U.S. Army **Corps of Engineers** issues permits for dumping the spoils, but the **Environmental Protection Agency** (EPA) designates allowable dump sites. Ocean incineration also requires a permit. The EPA has limited incineration permits to researchers. Even so, public opposition to incineration has caused the EPA to deny most applications. Burial at sea and sinking of vessels would require a specific permit under MPRSA if the EPA had not issued a general permit for those activities. The general permit allows dumping of small quantities of material that has a minimal effect on the environment.

Penalties for violating the Marine Protection, Research, and Sanctuaries Act can reach a maximum of $50,000 per day. In addition, the vessel can be seized, and the owner may face up to a year in prison.

MPRSA also established a marine sanctuary program. The Secretary of Commerce (acting through the **National Oceanic and Atmospheric Agency**) may designate areas that should be protected. A number of matters must be considered during the process, such as natural resources and ecological quality, historical and archaeological significance, current uses, existing federal and state control, and the ability to identify the area. A number of agencies must be involved in the decision process, and public **hearing**s are required. The governor of a state that will be affected by the designation may veto it within 60 days. Once an area is designated as a sanctuary, permits are required for activities not consistent with the designation. For example, if an area is designated a sanctuary for recreation, recreational activities would be allowed but commercial fishing would require a permit.

MATERIAL SAFETY DATA SHEETS (MSDSs)   Under the **Occupational Safety and Health Act** and the **Hazard Communication Standard,** these data sheets are required to contain information that must accompany **hazardous chemical**s to the workplace. The sheets do not have to be in a particular form, although the **Occupational Safety and Health Administration** (OSHA) has developed some guidelines. They must, however, contain specific information.

The law holds the importer or manufacturer responsible for preparing the material safety data sheets and supplying them to purchasers either before or concurrent with the first shipment of the hazardous chemical. Thereafter, they need not be supplied unless they are requested or have been changed or updated.

Employers are required to obtain material safety data sheets for any hazardous chemicals in the workplace. Some exceptions exist, though, primarily because the law excludes specific items from the category of hazardous chemicals that would otherwise fall under the definition. No material safety data sheet is required, for example, for a product that can be purchased for household use and is used in the workplace in a similar manner and in similar quantities. A bottle of acetone might fall in this exception. Personal drugs and tobacco are also excluded from the law's coverage. Other items are not considered hazardous chemicals because of their construction; these are called articles. A battery is a good example of the article exemption: it works because of the way it is made, and it does not release the electrolyte under normal use and operating conditions.

When material safety data sheets are required, the manufacturer or importer must identify the hazardous chemical by both its common and chemical names. The sheet must state the substance's physical and chemical characteristics, outline the physical and health hazards associated with it, whether it is a carcinogen, the permissible exposure limits, and detail the primary routes of entry (like skin, mouth, or inhalation). Further, it must include precautions for safe use and handling, control measures necessary (such as use of masks, gloves, or ventilation), and describe emergency and first aid measures to be used if a problem occurs. The manufacturer or importer must also date the sheet and include the name, address, and telephone number of someone who can provide more information. The manufacturer or importer must also keep a copy on file.

Employers are required to obtain the sheets if they were not provided. They must train employees how to read them and keep a copy of the sheets in a central location so they are available to workers during normal working hours.

MAXIMUM CONTAMINANT LEVELS (MCLs) The limits set on drinking water contamination that determine whether a supplier can deliver water from a specific source without treatment. The current law regulating drinking water is the **Safe Drinking Water Act,** and it provides authority for the **Environmental Protection Agency** (EPA) to set standards.

The Safe Drinking Water Act does not apply to every drinking water source; it governs only public water supply, which is defined as water piped to fifteen or more service connections or at least twenty-five individuals. Thus, a private well is not covered.

Under the Safe Drinking Water Act, the EPA is required to establish two sets of regulations: the National Primary Drinking Water Regulations and National Secondary Drinking Water Regulations. The primary standards provide health-based protection. Secondary standards deal with aesthetics, such as odor and color.

Before it sets the maximum contaminant level for a particular constituent, the EPA sets a goal. This goal is a lofty value that reduces risk of problems to zero and then adds a buffer called "an adequate margin of safety." The goal for contaminants that do not cause cancer is based on an assumption that a person drinks two liters of water a day from the same source for seventy years. The goal is the level at which this person would have no significant risk of negative health effects. For carcinogens, the goal is automatically zero. But the goals are not enforceable. They are used as a guide for the limits that will become the standards; the maximum contaminant level is set as close as feasible to the goal. Each source of drinking water has its own peculiarities. The EPA must arrive at levels that are attainable through use of the best available treatment technology. Cost is considered in the determination, since many public water suppliers serve small communities and are not wealthy. When the maximum contaminant level is set, the EPA must reveal what type of technology it based the standard on.

Maximum contaminant levels are stated in terms of milligrams per liter. For example, chromium and arsenic both have a maximum contaminant level of 0.05 milligrams per liter. Mercury's MCL is 0.002 milligrams per liter.

Before 1986, maximum contaminant levels were the only type of drinking water standards created by the EPA. The law has been amended, however, and the National Primary Drinking Water Regulations include two different methods of complying with the law. A maximum contaminant level may be specified or, if it is not technically or economically feasible to determine the maximum contaminant level for a pollutant, the EPA may require a specific treatment technology. When treatment technology is substituted for numerical limits, the EPA must outline the treatment procedures to be used and other criteria to ensure that the drinking water is safe.

Variances and exemptions from the established maximum contaminant levels may be granted by the EPA or the state agency, since the agency is required to consider cost of compliance, availability of technology, and quality of the raw drinking water source. These provisions are designed to assist smaller public water suppliers. Even so, the EPA's reluctance to grant exemptions or vary the requirements for a public water supply are understandable. When a variance is granted, the agency must oblige the source to eventually meet the standards, and neither a variance nor an exemption can be granted if the water supply will pose an unreasonable risk to health. Furthermore, a request for a variance or exemption is subject to a public **hearing**.

When a public water supply fails to meet the National Primary Drinking Water Regulations, whether they are stated as maximum contaminant levels or treatment technologies, the water supplier must notify the customers and the government. If the risk is serious, announcements must be made on radio and television. Otherwise, a notice in the newspaper is sufficient if followed by mass mailing.

Maximum contaminant levels also serve as important cleanup criteria when a public water supply has been contaminated by **hazardous substances** or oil. They are often part of the negotiations even when the groundwater is not used as a drinking water source, because they are considered relevant standards. See **applicable or relevant and appropriate** regulations; Comprehensive Environmental Response, Compensation, and Liability Act.

MIXTURE RULE   A principle created by the **Environmental Protection Agency** (EPA) to prevent people from diluting **hazardous waste** in order to avoid regulation. The EPA's standard motto in this area is "the answer to pollution is not dilution." According to this rule, if a hazardous waste is mentioned by name in the EPA regulations, adding any other substance to it results in a mixture that is also a hazardous waste.

The mixture rule, as well as the **derived-from rule,** was invalidated in the case of *Shell Oil Company v. Environmental Protection Agency.* Later the **Environmental Appeals Board** determined that the effect of the *Shell Oil* decision was to erase the two rules from the time they were created in 1980 until reinstatement by emergency rule on 3 March 1992. The case before the Environmental Appeals Board was *In the Matter of Hardin County* (1994).

MOBILE SOURCES   This term includes motor vehicles and aircraft that are regulated as pollution sources under the **Clean Air Act.** Mobile sources contribute carbon monoxide, hydrocarbons, **nitrogen oxides**, and **particulate** pollution to the air. Before unleaded gasoline was introduced, they also emitted lead.

Environmental regulation of mobile sources began as early as 1955, but only small steps were taken until the 1970 Clean Air Act was passed, giving the **Environmental Protection Agency** (EPA) the power to set standards for emissions for new automobiles and to regulate fuels. The Clean Air Act forced automobile manufacturers to develop emission controls and fuel efficiency for cars before the technology for them existed. The deadline for compliance was 1975, a deadline the manufacturers did not meet. When the act was amended in 1977, more realistic standards were set. The goals were not abandoned, but the deadlines were extended.

Today, the federal government controls many aspects of mobile sources: cold start carbon monoxide emissions, vapor recovery systems, emission control devices and diagnostic equipment, and testing of vehicles both before they are marketed and after they have been purchased. Other issues closely related to mobile sources involve fueling, such as fuel additives, vapor recovery from gasoline nozzles, and reformulated or oxygenated gas.

Fine-tuning mobile sources and fuels has greatly reduced air contamination. Still, many areas of the country remain out of compliance with the **National Ambient Air Quality Standards** for **ozone**, nitrogen oxides, carbon monoxide, and particulates. Mobile sources contribute large percentages of the total for all of these pollutants.

As a result, the **Clean Air Act Amendments of 1990** focused not only on motor vehicles but on their use. Congress envisioned the vehicle owner playing a significant role in creating clean air. Methods of control include periodic inspections of the emission control equipment and vapor recovery systems at gasoline stations. Transportation control measures, such as driving restrictions and special lanes for carpools, have become necessary in some places. Large employers and business owners in major metropolitan areas often must develop and implement a plan to reduce the number of cars being driven to work during peak business hours. Many businesses that own ten or more vehicles must phase in fleet vehicles that run on cleaner fuels. See also **nonattainment areas.**

California is required to operate a pilot program to reduce emissions from mobile sources within the state. By 1996, 150,000 vehicles sold must be capable of running on clean fuel. The number doubles by 1999. Other areas of the country were allowed to opt into the program, but they are not required to do so.

MONTREAL PROTOCOL First signed in 1987, the Montreal Protocol is an international agreement to reduce the use and production of chemicals that attack the earth's protective **ozone** layer (stratospheric ozone). Twenty-four nations signed the initial agreement, and others added their signatures later.

The full name of the agreement is the Montreal Protocol on Substances That Deplete the Ozone Layer. It was amended in 1990 by ninety-three nations, accelerating the deadlines for phasing out the target chemicals, **chlorofluorocarbons** and hydrochlorofluorocarbons.

The protocol provides that the first reductions in ozone-depleting substances were to result from a freeze on production levels. In 1989, for example, producers could not create more of the substances than they did in 1986. By 1995, the limit is 50 percent of the 1986 level; by 1997, 15 percent.

The Montreal Protocol requires that production of these substances cease by 2000.

In the United States, the Montreal Protocol became the driving force behind a new section of the **Clean Air Act Amendments of 1990.** The new provisions go beyond the Montreal Protocol, however. Activities are regulated that had never been regulated before, such as air conditioner servicing requirements, training for technicians, labeling of products containing the offending chemicals, and provisions for reclamation of gases from equipment and goods that use these chemicals.

One of the biggest obstacles to widespread acceptance of the Montreal Protocol was the disparity between industrialized nations and developing nations. During the London conference in 1990, the more technologically developed countries agreed to transfer technology to developing nations.

The Clean Air Act Amendments of 1990 establish two classes of ozone depleters. Class I includes the chlorofluorocarbons, carbon tetrachloride, halons, and methyl chloroform. Class II covers the hydrochlorofluorocarbons. Class I substances are to be phased out by 2000; Class II by 2030. If no acceptable substitute is found for an essential use, such as medical devices, aviation, or fire fighting, the ban may be lifted for that use.

To assure the development of alternative chemicals, Congress mandated a program called the Safe New Alternatives Program or SNAP. Under that program, the EPA and industry are cooperating in the search for new chemicals that can substitute for the ozone-depleting substances and will not create new health or environmental problems.

NATIONAL AMBIENT AIR QUALITY STANDARDS (NAAQSs)

Limits set by the **Environmental Protection Agency** (EPA) for **air pollutant**s it believes may endanger public health (primary standards) or welfare (secondary standards). The standards apply to ambient air, not indoor air. They are stated as maximum permissible concentrations in outdoor air.

For many years, the air pollutants regulated by the National Ambient Air Quality Standards have been these: **nitrogen oxides**, carbon monoxide, **sulfur dioxide**, **ozone**, small **particulate**s (called PM_{10}), and lead. The EPA may revise the list as necessary. Hazardous air pollutants and air toxics are not subject to these standards but are regulated separately, under the **National Emission Standards for Hazardous Air Pollutants.**

Steps in Standard-Setting

The process of regulating air pollutants under the NAAQSs begins with listing. In order to list a substance, the EPA must determine that it is an air pollutant, that it is emitted from numerous or different types of sources, and that the **emission**s may endanger public health or welfare. From the EPA's point of view, an air pollutant may be any chemical, physical, biological, or radioactive substance that enters the air. The EPA's definition does not include ozone, since ozone is not directly emitted. Instead it includes the precursors of ozone, such as volatile organic compounds and nitrogen oxides, which combine under certain conditions to form ozone. The National Ambient Air Quality Standards focus on the substances that are common, and these substances are commonly emitted from factories and businesses as well as motor vehicles.

Once an air pollutant has been listed, the EPA must establish limits in terms of yearly average and maximum permissible concentration within twelve months. Air pollutants regulated under the NAAQSs are often called **criteria pollutant**s because standards exist for them. Primary standards address the health concerns created by the pollutant, while the secondary standards deal with public welfare. Examples of issues the secondary standards confront are effects of the pollutant on wildlife, soils, weather, personal comfort, and economic values. Historically, the limits specified in the primary standards have been the same as those in the secondary standards for most pollutants. Review of the standards is required every five years.

The Effects of the Standards

The National Ambient Air Quality Standards determine the acceptable quality of air throughout the United States. Once a standard is set or revised, each state must revise its law to ensure compliance with the standard [see **state implementation plan**].

Air quality impacts not only human health, but also economic development. Industrial growth may be severely restricted by programs designed to improve air quality within an area that has not met the NAAQSs, and governmental control over businesses tightens dramatically as noncompliance worsens. See also **New Source Performance Standards; New Source Review; nonattainment areas; Prevention of Significant Deterioration.**

NATIONAL CONTINGENCY PLAN (NCP) The regulations created by the **Environmental Protection Agency** (EPA) under the **Clean Water Act** to deal with the cleanup of releases of **hazardous substances** and oil to water. When the **Superfund** law (the **Comprehensive Environmental Response, Compensation, and Liability Act**) was enacted in 1980, hazardous substance releases to air and land were added to the plan.

The National Contingency Plan is a comprehensive set of regulations that covers emergency planning, establishes response teams, and provides for obtaining and maintaining response equipment. However, it goes beyond emergency response; it is the blueprint for long-term cleanup of **hazardous waste** sites.

Superfund spelled out the types of issues the EPA had to deal with in the National Contingency Plan: methods of responding to releases, gathering information, and evaluating risks. The EPA was also required to devise a way to learn about releases and potential for future releases. Whenever a Superfund site is recognized as such, all parties involved in the cleanup, including the **potentially responsible parties,** federal and state governments, and persons who voluntarily undertake the work, are required to follow the National Contingency Plan. Failure to follow the NCP results in loss of the opportunity to get other responsible parties to pay their share of expenses. See also **contribution rights; remedial design/remedial action; remedial investigation/feasibility study.**

NATIONAL EMISSION STANDARDS FOR HAZARDOUS AIR POLLUTANTS (NESHAPs)   Regulations that

set standards for **hazardous air pollutants,** also called **air toxics.** They are mandated by the **Clean Air Act,** which was enacted in 1970. However, hazardous air pollutant regulations changed fundamentally with the passage of the **Clean Air Act Amendments of 1990.**

Pre-1990 Law

In 1970 the **Environmental Protection Agency** (EPA) was charged by the Clean Air Act to list **air pollutant**s that "may reasonably be anticipated to result in an increase in mortality or an increase in serious irreversible, or incapacitating reversible, illness." After the pollutants were listed, the EPA was required to develop standards that were stringent enough to protect human health with "an ample margin of safety."

By 1990, the EPA had listed only eight substances as hazardous air pollutants: asbestos, benzene, radionuclides, inorganic arsenic, coke oven **emissions**, vinyl chloride, and beryllium. Standards had been established for all but coke oven emissions, but the standards were not applicable to all of the sources that discharged them.

An article in the *Environmental Law Reporter* lucidly explains some of the reasons for the EPA's failure to do more. First, most people assumed that emissions of hazardous air pollutants affected workers, not the public, and regulation of the workplace is the job of the Occupational Safety and Health Administration. Second, the EPA seemed uncertain what level of control was necessary under the Clean Air Act. Many substances could be said to be hazardous enough to require a zero exposure limit, but if the standards were set at zero, they could eliminate many businesses and products. The law was ambiguous concerning whether the EPA could consider the cost of meeting the standards when it made its determination. Finally, modeling done by the EPA when determining health effects is extremely conservative. It assumes a person is exposed to a constant level of the pollutant twenty-four hours per day in the same location for seventy years. The model does not yield a realistic estimate of minimim controls necessary.

Awareness of the need for more regulation of hazardous air pollutants coincided with the release of the **Toxic Release Inventory** in 1989. The EPA compiled the inventory using numbers reported by industry concerning emissions of **hazardous substances**. Industries had not been required to monitor and report those emissions until the **Emergency Planning and Community Right-To-Know Act** was passed in 1986. But once the inventory had been compiled, the public (and Congress) knew at last that hazardous air pollutants pose health problems outside of the workplace.

Changes in the Program

The Clean Air Act Amendments of 1990 immediately changed the focus of the air toxics regulations from attempting to establish what air toxics were to regulating them, since it included its own list of 189 hazardous substances or classes of substances. (The EPA may add to the list or delete from it by going through a regulatory review.) Congress also determined that the EPA may consider cost of technology when setting the limits.

The amendments also require the EPA to list the types of industries that may be considered **major source**s or area sources of hazardous air pollutants. *Major source* for the purpose of regulating air toxics is any stationary facility capable of emitting ten tons or more per year of one hazardous air pollutant or twenty-five tons or more per year of any combination of hazardous air pollutants. Approximately 7,000 sources are regulated as major sources of air toxics.

Area sources are smaller stationary sources. However, their combined emissions may create a problem within an **air quality control region.** Examples of area sources include wood stoves, dry cleaners, service stations, water treatment facilities, and solid waste disposal facilities. Individually they may not emit enough hazardous air pollutants to place them into the major source category, but together they may contribute significant amounts of air toxics.

Standards under the amended Clean Air Act are technology-based rather than health-based, and most are expressed in terms of emission limits. However, the EPA may promulgate standards based on work practices, design standards, or equipment if emission standards cannot be developed.

The EPA must require major sources to use the maximum achievable control technology (MACT) to achieve compliance with the limits. Contrary to what the term implies, MACT does not usually mean that a specific type of technology is required. Instead, the EPA establishes emission standards after considering what that technology can accomplish. The new emission standards are to be phased in by 2000.

Area sources have a lesser burden. They must comply with emission levels set with reference to generally available control technology or GACT. However, the EPA's first priority is to establish MACT. It is required by the statute to develop an area source program by November 1995. The appropriate control measures will follow the publication of the area source program.

After the appropriate technology has been applied, some risk from the emissions may remain. The EPA is directed to calculate the risk, determine the health significance, consider methods of further control and costs, and examine the actual health effects. Recommendations must be made to Congress based on the EPA's conclusions. If Congress does nothing, the EPA must set emission standards to deal with residual risks by 1998.

NATIONAL ENVIRONMENTAL POLICY ACT (NEPA)

A statute enacted in 1969 that established a national policy concerning environmental considerations and requires federal agencies to consider the environmental impact of major decisions. It also created the **Council on Environmental Quality** (CEQ), an agency charged with developing procedures for other federal agencies to follow in fulfilling the goals of the statute.

Since its enactment, the National Environmental Policy Act has played an important role in development. Federal courts filled in many of the gaps in the law and strengthened it. A 1971 decision, *Calvert Cliffs Coordinating Committee v. United States Atomic Energy Commission*, explained the significance of NEPA: "It makes environmental protection a part of the mandate of every federal agency and department." Congress may exempt (and has exempted) specified actions from the application of NEPA. However, exemptions are rare, and must be explicit. The only federal agency to escape rigid application of NEPA is the **Environmental Protection Agency** (EPA). Although for many actions, the EPA does go through the same process, it has used alternate methods of review. Courts have reasoned that NEPA is not as important to an agency that has environmental protection as its main duty as it is to other agencies.

The statute requires federal agencies to consider the environmental effects when a proposed action is (1) major, (2) federal, and (3) will significantly affect the quality of the human environment. The stipulation that a proposed action be federal is broader than it appears, since the federal government is often involved in a project that appears to be a private or local government endeavor. But if a federal permit is issued, federal funds are involved, or other federal involvement exists, the statute may apply. Costs and responsibility for completing the environmental review are usually passed to the party who will benefit, but the ultimate liability belongs to the federal agency with the most accountability for the project.

The process of review includes an **environmental assessment,** followed by either a report called an **environmental impact statement** or a **finding of no significant impact.** Throughout the study period, public participation is encouraged, and alternatives to the action must be considered during review. The Council on Environmental Quality developed regulations to guide most agencies through the evaluation, though it is not uncommon for agencies to have their own rules on the matter.

NEPA does not dictate the action an agency must take in response to the results of an environmental impact study. An agency may choose to continue with the original proposal without change after going through the procedure, even if alterations would be beneficial to the environment. The statute simply aims to force review of environmental issues; it does not require that the ultimate decision conform to the recommendations.

NATIONAL OCEANIC AND ATMOSPHERIC ADMINIS-TRATION (NOAA) An agency within the Department of Commerce that has numerous environmental responsibilities. It is the primary federal agency involved with the **Coastal Zone Management Act.**

NOAA conducts considerable research and makes recommendations concerning the atmosphere. It works with other agencies to measure **ozone** depletion in the stratosphere and calculates chemical components in the air. Acid precipitation studies are also part of the agency's job.

The oceanic duties carried out by the agency include monitoring marine life and estuary habitats. NOAA designates areas that need special protection in the U.S. territorial seas and coastal areas. It must be consulted by the Army **Corps of Engineers** if a permit to allow dredged material to be dumped into the seas is proposed. See also **Marine Protection, Research, and Sanctuaries Act.**

NATIONAL POLLUTANT DISCHARGE ELIMINATION SYSTEM (NPDES)

The permitting system for discharges of polluted water, established in 1972 by a major overhaul of the **Clean Water Act.** Except for a few exemptions specified in the statute, a permit is required for all discharges from a *point source* to any *navigable waters* of the United States. A point source, according to the law, is a "discrete conveyance" from which effluent is discharged. The definition includes more than one might think. In addition to pipes and conduits, it covers ditches, machinery, and other methods of channeling water. Navigable waters, prior to the 1972 revisions, meant waters that could be navigated by ships. However, when Congress enacted the changes, it made it clear that the term was to be interpreted as broadly as possible. Thus the term navigable waters now includes streams, wetlands, manmade waters, tributaries, storm sewers, interstate and intrastate lakes, rivers, lagoons, and even seasonal pools. The word navigable no longer limits the scope of regulation.

Regulation under the National Pollutant Discharge Elimination System

Congress had always given states the primary responsibility for determining what was necessary to protect their waters, but the result was disappointing. The states did establish water quality standards, but they had little authority to measure pollution or enforce the standards, and except in rare cases, the federal government was relegated to a support role.

The 1972 Clean Water Act moved many responsibilities from the states to the **Environmental Protection Agency** (EPA). The statute set goals for clean, fishable, swimmable water, but its most significant aim was total elimination of pollutant discharges to water. That goal remains in the law today. For the first time the EPA was required to establish national standards for effluents. Technology was to be the key to the limits, but the law anticipated—and forced—better technology as time went on. The law began with a requirement of using best practicable technology for industrial discharges and became more stringent over time, finally dictating use of best available technology. Domestic sewage plants were required to use best conventional technology.

Technology standards are commonly used in pollution control today, but the terms mean little to the lay person. They simply establish the type of technology the agency is to consider when setting standards. The agency sets numerical standards based on what the technology can consistently accomplish.

As may be expected, toxic pollutants are more highly regulated than conventional pollutants. For a number of industries, the regulations specify standards they must meet if they discharge into a **publicly owned treatment works** instead of directly into a water body. For new sources—those that have not begun construction prior to a proposal for a new regulation—the EPA may require not only end-of-pipe treatment of wastewater, but also process or design changes to reduce the amount of wastewater that must be treated.

After the national standards are set, anyone who wants to discharge wastewater must, at a minimum, meet the standards. If a national standard for a particular pollutant does not exist, the permitting authority is required to use best professional judgment in setting the limits. The next step in the process is permitting. Based on the national standards, the EPA issues individual permits for effluent. The system applies anywhere a facility is discharging directly to a surface water; wastewater that is discharged must be treated to levels that will at least meet the national standards. Regulated facilities range from sewage treatment plants owned by municipalities to industries.

Basically, the permitting process begins with a permit application. The applicant must supply information about the type of wastewater it wishes to discharge. The permit authority, usually the state or the EPA, will ask for additional data it believes is necessary. Applications must be made at least eighteen months before the discharge is to begin.

States may, and often do, assume the responsibility for the permit program. To do so, they must develop regulations and request **delegation** from the EPA. Among other things, the state must have the appropriate manpower and enforcement ability to both issue permits and punish violators. However, the EPA retains authority to veto a permit application or to enforce the terms of the permit.

Contents of NPDES Permits

Permits contain the blueprint for the handling of the facility's wastewater discharges, including limits for each regulated pollutant. Permittees must monitor their discharges and submit reports (discharge monitoring reports or DMRs) to the permitting agency. Monitoring and reporting responsibilities will be specified in the permit. The permittee must allow inspections and, in addition to standard reports, must report unusual discharges or conditions. All reports are sent to the agency, but they are also available to the public upon request. Since it is a criminal offense to file a false report, the contents are generally reliable.

The NPDES permit forms the basis of the system for regulating discharges. The EPA or state agency can review the compliance status of a particular discharger by checking the discharge reports; it can also use the reports as a basis for enforcement action. Public action groups or other interested parties can do the same thing [see **citizen suit**].

Permits have a relatively short lifespan: up to five years. This turnover accommodates technical progress and changes in the regulations, with the goal of eliminating pollutants always in the background. At least eighteen months before expiration, the permittee must reapply.

Stormwater Permitting

Until the 1987 amendments to the Clean Water Act, one source of water pollution had been studied but not actively controlled: stormwater. Stormwater is a peculiar problem because it often results from random runoff instead of a specific source. Uncontrolled stormwater can be a significant problem in municipal areas, carrying oil and other contaminants from streets and parking lots into waterways. Stormwater associated with industrial facilities often poses an even greater risk, because it may wash toxic pollutants into the surface waters or storm sewers.

Certain stormwater discharges are now regulated by the NPDES program. The regulations focus on runoff that is likely to be contaminated. Thus, stormwater that flows over an industrial facility where it may pick up pollutants is regulated, as are large municipalities with storm sewers. If a permit is required, it will be one of three types: general, group, and individual. The easiest permit to obtain is a general permit, and the group is next. Individual permits are tailored to a specific site and can be expensive to obtain.

General permits are designed to cover common activities that one permit can effectively regulate, such as controlling run-off from a large parking lot. If a facility finds that its proposed activity falls within the scope of the general permit, it may file a notice of intent to be covered by it. When it no longer needs the permit, it files a notice of termination. Similarly, a group permit for stormwater discharge may be obtained if the situations of two or more facilities are similar enough that they can combine their efforts. The costs of collecting data and obtaining the permit can then be shared. To effectively manage stormwater, permits may require diverting it, isolating facility components that can contaminate it, and treating the stormwater to meet the national standards.

NATIONAL PRIORITY LIST (NPL) The federal list of **hazardous waste** sites, which is prepared by the **Environmental Protection Agency** (EPA) with input from the states, is ranked according to priority. Sites listed on the National Priority List are called **Superfund** sites because they are eligible for federal cleanup funds, and the law that drives the listing is nicknamed Superfund. See **Comprehensive Environmental Response, Compensation, and Liability Act; Hazardous Ranking System; Superfund.**

Not all hazardous waste sites are placed on the National Priority List—only those that rank high enough to be considered a federal priority. States send their list of proposed sites to the EPA, which then evaluates them and chooses only the most serious sites for inclusion on the NPL. (The law requires the EPA to list at least one site from each state in the top 100 facilities.) For that reason, states often have their own lists to deal with sites not included on the NPL.

Listing is a long process that involves examination of many factors. The nearness of the site to human population, potential for drinking water impact, likelihood of direct exposure or airborne exposure, and toxicity of the substances at the site are among the factors considered. The EPA also considers whether the state has the capacity to assume the costs and take the actions required for cleaning up the site.

Before it lists a site, the EPA must provide public notice. Listing will diminish the value of the property itself as well as land values in the vicinity. The potentially responsible parties or current owner may try to stop the listing by voluntarily cleaning up the property. The EPA must also provide public notice before it delists a site, ending its status as a Superfund site. Public involvement in the decision to take a site off the National Priority List is critical, since delisting ends federal government scrutiny of the site.

NATURAL RESOURCES DAMAGES Damages assessed by a court against someone who has discharged **hazardous substances** or oil. Their purpose is to compensate the government for replacement, restoration, and rehabilitation of natural resources. For example, if an oil spill kills fish and otters and coats the shoreline, the appropriate government official may sue for the injury to the natural resources. Natural resources damages do not go to the U.S. Treasury as other penalties for environmental violations do. Instead, they are placed in a fund to directly benefit the injured area. Natural resources damages are authorized under the **Comprehensive Environmental Response, Compensation, and Liability Act** and the **Oil Pollution Act,** as it was incorporated into the **Clean Water Act.**

When natural resources have been harmed by contamination, simply cleaning up the substance may not repair the harm. It may be necessary to replace the lost wildlife or biota. Restoration to its original condition may take years. In the meantime, the public has lost the benefit of the natural resources and is therefore entitled to damages. The person authorized to obtain natural resources damages is the trustee of the natural resource. For federal lands, those trustees are the **National Oceanic and Atmospheric Administration** (coastal waters), the Department of Interior (many national forests, parks and monuments), the Department of Agriculture (national agricultural lands), the Department of Defense (military bases), and the Department of Energy (property managed by that department). For state-owned or state-controlled natural resources, governors name the trustees.

The value of lost resources is calculated according to the methods the trustees have developed in regulations. It includes lost revenues in some situations, but the primary emphasis is on restoration and rehabilitation of the resource. The trustee may also recover the incidental expenses incurred in calculating the loss.

Natural resource damage claims are different from other types of environmental penalties in who may bring the lawsuit. Public interest groups, private parties, and governmental agencies that are not trustees of the resource do not have the right to sue. In these types of claims, the harm is seen as a public injury, and the caretaker of the resource is the one who addresses it. However, private lawsuits may be brought on other grounds, as can be seen from the many lawsuits surrounding the **Valdez** oil spill in Prince William Sound. For example, if fishing is impaired because the oil or hazardous substance resulted in elimination or reduction of the fish, fishermen have a separate claim for the damage and may bring a lawsuit under a different theory.

Releases of hazardous substances and oil must be cleaned up according to the **National Contingency Plan.** Therefore, the cleanup is the first order of business. Assessment of damages must be preceded by compliance with the same requirements the **Environmental Protection Agency** and other parties must follow for other types of cleanups.

NATURAL RESOURCES DEFENSE COUNCIL (NRDC)

A membership organization founded in 1970 to deal with various environmental issues. The group is staffed primarily by attorneys and scientific specialists.

The NRDC's foremost weapon is litigation. Like the **Environmental Defense Fund,** it has sued the **Environmental Protection Agency** and other federal agencies for failing to do what it believes the law requires. Over the years, the NDRC has become a major player in the development of environmental regulations and statutes. Moving into the political structure by lobbying Congress and the EPA has given it additional power, although the more radical environmental groups criticize organizations that work within the existing system. Another of the NRDC's activities is education. It provides information to the public and publishes environmental material.

NAVIGABLE WATER See **Clean Water Act; National Pollutant Discharge Elimination System.**

NEGLIGENCE In law, negligence is a type of conduct that can be the basis of liability. It is a tort, a term that commonly describes a civil (as opposed to criminal) wrong. However, an action that is a tort may also be a crime.

The concept of negligence dates back to early English law, so negligence has been well-defined—at least in theory. In practice, negligence must be proven. The person who is harmed must prove all the elements of the tort through facts. To prove negligence, the injured party must show that (1) the accused (the defendant) had a duty to do something or a duty to refrain from doing something; (2) the defendant failed to meet the duty; (3) the breach of duty is the proximate cause of an injury; and (4) the person bringing the lawsuit is the one injured. If any of these components are missing, the injured party may not be able to prove negligence.

Environmental law has incorporated the theory of negligence in several respects. Some statutes specifically state that negligence may be the basis of a criminal lawsuit against a person. However, it is more commonly used in individual or class action suits.

To illustrate, assume Landowner has a brook running through his property. Landowner often fishes in the water, both for relaxation and food. Manufacturer, who owns property about a block away, makes pesticides and stores them in a building near the brook to await transportation. One day Manufacturer drops a drum of pesticide from a forklift and the drum cracks. The contents run into the water and later wind up being carried through Landowner's property. Landowner catches a fish and eats it. He gets very ill because the fish has been poisoned by the pesticide. Assuming that Landowner makes the connection, the elements of negligence are present: (1) Manufacturer has a duty to handle pesticides carefully so the environment and people are not harmed; (2) Manufacturer has breached that duty; (3) as a direct result of that breach, an injury has occurred; (4) Landowner has suffered an injury.

Sometimes the duty is supplied by a statute. For example, companies must obey the **Clean Water Act** and the terms of their permits. The release of a pollutant into the stream is an unpermitted discharge and certainly was not anticipated in a permit. Therefore, Landowner would not have to prove Manufacturer had a commonsense duty to be careful but could simply show that the duty is required by law.

Environmental torts are new, so they are still evolving. In many cases, the theories are confused and the label of negligence may be replaced in some instances by **trespass** or **nuisance.** The example above might be brought as a nuisance because Manufacturer interfered with the peaceful enjoyment of Landowner's property. It can also be a trespass, because the chemicals moved from Manufacturer's to Landowner's real estate. See also **strict liability; toxic tort.**

NEGOTIATED RULEMAKING A relatively new procedure used by the **Environmental Protection Agency** (EPA) and other agencies to create regulations. If the agency believes a proposed regulation would be improved by the participation of interested parties, the EPA may announce its intention to begin a negotiated rulemaking. To be effective, participants must represent the broadest possible spectrum of interested parties, including industries that will be affected, public interest groups, and governmental officials. The number of individuals involved is limited to 25 except in rare circumstances, but the designated representatives are supposed to solicit comments from their peers so that they actually reflect the views of the segment they represent. The committee establishes its own groundrules, which may cover everything from the scope of the negotiation to its termination and what will be required for a consensus. A facilitator, who may or may not be a member of the EPA, will chair the meetings and give advice.

The purpose of the negotiated rulemaking is to resolve as many issues as possible before a regulation is proposed and speed up the process of promulgation. Members of the committee enter into an agreement concerning the consensus. Many times the agreement specifies what the EPA's proposed regulation will be and in return, members agree not to submit adverse comments. Committee members usually agree that they will not sue the agency on the final rule if it is the result of the negotiations. However, the agreement by the committee members does not affect the rights of anyone who was not a member.

Negotiated rules can benefit all interested parties. The process requires people with different perspectives to listen to each other and try to fashion a solution. Often creativity is stimulated by open debate, and the resulting rules are made by consensus. However, the negotiation may also fail because the members may not be able to reach a consensus on important issues. If that is the case, the committee may terminate the effort, or it may narrow the issues to those on which agreement can be reached.

NEW SOURCE PERFORMANCE STANDARDS (NSPS)
Air pollution regulations that apply to new or modified stationary sources in approximately 65 specified categories, such as portland cement plants, fossil fuel steam generators, steel-making facilities, petroleum refineries, glass manufacturers, incinerators, and many others.

The minimum level of technology to be used by these facilities in controlling their **emission**s is *best demonstrated achievable technology* (BDAT). The **Environmental Protection Agency** (EPA) sets emission limits in the regulations by considering how much control can be accomplished by the best system of demonstrated controls. If the EPA cannot determine emission limits, it is permitted by the **Clean Air Act** to require specified work practices, equipment, or design instead.

New Source Performance Standards also apply if an existing facility is undergoing significant reconstruction. The EPA generally looks at the amount of capital going into the project to determine whether the work is repair and maintenance or reconstruction. If the cost will equal 50 percent or more of the cost of a new facility, the EPA will require the source to meet the New Source Performance Standards.

In *Wisconsin Electric Power v. Reilly* (*WEPCo*), a court reviewed the issue of what types of modifications trigger the New Source Performance Standards and the **Prevention of Significant Deterioration** regulations. In this case, the company was engaging in a large project to extend the useful life of the equipment. It argued that it was simply repairing existing equipment, not modifying the plant. The court disagreed. The company was committing large amounts of money, totally overhauling the equipment, and extending its useful life. In the end, emissions would increase. The NSPS was, the court held, properly applied to the modified facility.

The reason for requiring compliance with the NSPS when a major modification occurs is evident: the time to upgrade technology is when the source is being modified. If the work is truly in the nature of maintenance or repair, it will preserve the status quo.

NEW SOURCE REVIEW A process for determining what type of air pollution control a new major stationary source must have to qualify for an installation and operation permit. New Source Review is also done for major modifications of existing sources.

Whether a source is considered a new source depends on when construction begins. If a regulation is proposed and the source begins construction after the proposal, it is considered new. If construction has already started and a new regulation is proposed, the source is considered an existing source. The consequence of being considered a new source is that the owner must follow the latest proposal, and invariably that requires more control of air emissions.

The New Source Review process begins with the owner or operator submitting information to the appropriate agency concerning the amount and type of emissions anticipated after construction. (Existing sources that are making modifications must go through the same procedure if the increase in emissions is considered significant.) In areas that have not attained the **National Ambient Air Quality Standards,** new sources must use technology that will result in the lowest achievable emission rate, called LAER, if they will contribute major amounts of a pollutant that the air district is having trouble controlling. For example: A can-coating operation will emit 100 tons per year of volatile organic compounds in an area that is nonattainment for **ozone** [see **nonattainment areas**]. If the nonattainment is serious enough and the facility will discharge 25 tons per year, it may have to go through a preconstruction review.

Nonattainment areas have emission offset requirements as well. An emission offset is a mechanism to ensure that an **air quality control region** continues to make progress toward complying with the national standards. It means that the new source will have to obtain greater reductions from other sources than it intends to emit. The amount of the offset necessary will depend on how far the area is from meeting the national standards.

For example, a business wants to locate a new facility in a nonattainment area for carbon monoxide. If it meets the lowest achievable emission rate, it will release 100 tons per year. However, unless it takes certain steps, the business may not be allowed to build the facility because the air control district is already out of compliance. Adding 100 more tons per year of carbon monoxide would increase the problem. So, even if the business owner goes to other facilities in the air control region and gets them to agree to add controls to their operations that will cut the amount of carbon monoxide they emit by 100 tons per year, air quality will not improve. But if the new source owner can get them to agree to reduce the amount they discharge by more than 100 tons per year, the air control district may approve the new source, because overall, the quality of air in the area would improve.

Emission offsets are simpler when the source already exists and it wants to modify. It may go ahead with construction if it can reduce the pollution from its own operation. Suppose a company is located in a nonattainment area for ozone. It is a major facility, putting out 100 tons per year of volatile organic compounds. It wants to change its process so it can improve business. If it simply adds the equipment it wants to use, it will increase emissions by 50 tons per year. The owner decides to cut emissions from all of the company's other units so the company can get permission from the state to make the changes. To qualify, the source will have to meet the offset requirements, so it must cut existing pollution by more than 50 tons per year. Otherwise, it will have to go to other facilities in the area and get them to reduce their emissions.

New major sources and major modifications of existing sources in attainment areas (air quality control regions that meet the National Ambient Air Quality Standards) are also subject to review prior to construction. The program that applies in those areas is called **Prevention of Significant Deterioration** (PSD).

One of the differences between New Source Review in nonattainment versus attainment areas is the trigger for review. In nonattainment areas, a proposed facility may be considered major (and therefore subject to the permitting process) when it emits much less than the same proposed facility in an attainment area. Attainment areas have already met the requirements of the federal government for the pollutants, so their primary concern is keeping that status. They may allow growth of industry and therefore pollution, but only if they can maintain air quality good enough to meet the standards after the growth. They are not permitted to allow significant reductions in air quality, even if they have better air quality than the standards require. For that reason, in attainment areas, a source must either be capable of emitting 250 tons per year of a regulated pollutant or, if it falls into certain categories, 100 tons per year of a pollutant to be considered a major source.

Another distinction between New Source Review in nonattainment and attainment areas is the type of controls the sources must use. Again, the level of control in nonattainment areas is lowest achievable emission rate. In attainment areas, the source must use best available control technology (BACT). The difference is one of degree, with the lowest achievable emission rate being—at least theoretically—more desirable from the government's perspective. Both types of technology are somewhat flexible, since cost, availability, and application in the particular situation are all considered by the state in deciding what measures are sufficient. However, neither best available control technology nor lowest achievable emission rate may require less control than definitive standards set elsewhere by the **Environmental Protection Agency** (EPA) [see **New Source Performance Standards**]. The EPA publishes information on available technology.

An evaluation of a new source could be required under the non-attainment review and under the Prevention of Significant Deterioration program. For example, an air quality district may be in compliance with the National Ambient Air Quality Standard for lead and **particulate** matter but in nonattainment for **sulfur dioxide**. In that case, a major new source that will discharge lead and sulfur dioxide in significant amounts will have to go through both types of review before construction.

NITROGEN OXIDES (NO$_x$) One of many combinations of nitrogen and oxygen. Nitrogen oxides are regulated under the **Clean Air Act** in provisions concerning both **acid deposition** and **National Ambient Air Quality Standards.** Uncontrolled **emissions** of nitrogen oxides, such as **sulfur dioxide**, can combine with water in the atmosphere to form **acid rain.** They also precede the formation of **ozone** at ground level and give smog its yellowish color. Nitrogen dioxide is one of the pollutants regulated under the National Ambient Air Quality Standards, but if an **air quality control region** is having difficulty with ozone, it must put additional controls on nitrogen oxides as well as volatile organic compounds.

The sources of nitrogen oxides are many: industry, boilers used in power plants, and internal combustion engines. Motor vehicles [see **mobile sources**] can be a major contributor to nitrogen oxide levels in a municipal area. See also **nonattainment areas.**

NONATTAINMENT AREAS Air quality control regions throughout the United States that have not met the **National Ambient Air Quality Standards.** The standards are designed to ensure that air quality is good enough to protect people's health as well as the environment. They cover common pollutants, such as **ozone**, small **particulates**, lead, **sulfur dioxide**, and nitrogen dioxide [see **nitrogen oxides**].

The **Environmental Protection Agency** (EPA) is responsible for designating air quality regions as attainment or nonattainment. States must submit data to facilitate the determination, and they may request a change in classification of a region. Attainment status is evaluated separately for each pollutant. If an area is designated nonattainment, the pollutant will be mentioned along with the status designation, as in nonattainment for lead, or nonattainment for sulfur dioxide.

The National Ambient Air Quality Standards have been around for years. Congress mandated their establishment in 1970. Unfortunately, much of the country is still having difficulty meeting the levels required. Deadlines have come and gone, and it became apparent when Congress examined the status of the law in 1990 that definitive steps had to be taken or some air quality districts would never meet the standard.

The Clean Air Act Amendments of 1990

When the **Clean Air Act** was revised in 1990 [see **Clean Air Act Amendments of 1990**], Congress took a momentous step toward air quality improvement. It stopped setting dates for compliance that were basically the same for all air districts. Instead, it based the deadlines on the severity of the noncompliance, giving the worst areas more time to meet the standards. For some pollutants, the amendments subdivided the nonattainment areas into categories that reflected the degree of the problem.

Ozone nonattainment areas, for example, are classified as marginal, moderate, serious, severe, or extreme nonattainment areas. Marginal ozone nonattainment areas were required to meet the standard within three years; moderate areas have six; serious areas, nine; and severe areas, fifteen. If the deadline passes and the area is not yet in compliance, it is bumped up into a higher category, though severe areas may not be moved into the extreme classification. Apparently Congress does not believe any part of the country except Los Angeles should be put into that category. Congress also named a large area of the northeast United States as an ozone transport region and allowed the EPA to designate such areas that cover more than one state as nonattainment. The states within the regions must cooperate and regulate to eliminate the problems.

Sanctions may be imposed on states that do not meet their deadlines. In general, the punishment results in loss of federal funds and may require the payment of penalties.

Since the Clean Air Act changed so dramatically in 1990, the states were immediately forced to amend their laws and regulations to reflect the changes. If they do not submit an acceptable **state implementation plan** within a reasonable time, the EPA will impose a federal implementation plan.

Nonattainment Classifications

The pollutant with the most varied requirements and classifications is ozone. As mentioned above, the degrees of attainment for ozone are marginal, moderate, serious, severe, and extreme.

The marginal areas have a laundry list of actions to perform to achieve compliance; moderate areas must do everything the marginal areas must do and more; serious areas must meet all of the duties of the moderate areas and go farther, and so on. Extreme nonattainment areas have the most requirements of all. Los Angeles is the only area of the country classified as extreme nonattainment for ozone. It has twenty years from 15 November 1990 to attain the national standard for ozone.

Carbon monoxide nonattainment areas are either moderate or serious. Moderate nonattainment areas have until 1995 to comply with the national standard; serious regions must reach the standard by 2000. Any moderate area that misses the deadline is automatically reclassified serious. Like ozone nonattainment requirements, carbon monoxide nonattainment requirements increase as the severity of the problem increases. Serious nonattainment regions for carbon monoxide must do everything the moderate areas must do and take other steps as well.

The aim of the National Ambient Air Quality Standards for particulate matter is to reduce the amount of inhalable particles discharged into the air. The EPA has determined the size of inhalable particulates is 10 microns, so it has developed a standard for particulates that size or smaller called the PM_{10} standard. All nonattainment areas for PM_{10} were initially designated moderate, but if they do not meet the standard within six years after being designated nonattainment, they are to be moved into the serious category. The EPA may also redesignate the area earlier if it determines that the region cannot meet the standard by that deadline.

Nonattainment areas for the remaining pollutants, lead, sulfur dioxide, and nitrogen dioxide, are not subdivided into finer categories, and compliance must be reached within five years after being designated nonattainment.

Requirements for Reasonable Further Progress

It would be impossible for any nonattainment area to reach compliance without taking definite steps toward that goal. Therefore, the states involved must design plans that will bring about measureable reductions by specified dates.

States submit initial inventories of air pollution to the EPA. If they are nonattainment for one of the **criteria pollutant**s, they must then create schedules designed to reduce that pollutant incrementally. The schedules establish a series of dates before the deadline by which the pollutant will have been reduced by an acceptable percentage. This system enables the EPA to determine whether the area will reach attainment. If it cannot meet the interim goals, the EPA has the right to bump the area into a different classification.

Within the environmental legal community, the schedules and emission reductions are called demonstrations of reasonable further progress. Permitting of new facilities or changes in traffic could interfere with meeting the interim compliance deadlines, so states must monitor air pollution and be thorough when granting a permit to a new stationary source.

Reclassification

The Clean Air Act itself mandates some reclassifications. If, for example, an air quality district does not meet its statutory deadline, it automatically gets bumped up into another category. However, once an area meets the National Ambient Air Quality Standards, the state may ask the EPA to designate it an attainment area. Similarly, if the state discovers that a nonattainment area is worse or better than it thought, it may request a redesignation. To support a redesignation, the state must submit proof to the EPA.

NONBINDING ALLOCATION OF RESPONSIBILITY (NBAR) A discretionary manner of determining what proportion of the cleanup costs a **potentially responsible party** at a **hazardous waste** site should bear. The **Environmental Protection Agency** (EPA) may do NBAR calculations in an effort to settle a case and get the cleanup underway.

As its name indicates, an NBAR does not forever decide the limit of liability. The **Comprehensive Environmental Response, Compensation, and Liability Act,** the law under which abandoned hazardous waste sites are remediated, provides for joint and several liability; that is, each party is responsible separately and jointly for all costs associated with cleanup. If the lawsuit cannot be settled, the EPA may go back to the statute and claim that the liability need not be apportioned.

The EPA does not have to issue an NBAR; in fact, it seldom does. They are time-consuming to calculate, and the potentially responsible parties will often do their own apportionment of costs as the information is made available. If the agency does complete an NBAR, it is done during the early stages of the response action.

Assuming an NBAR is to be issued, the EPA looks at a number of factors to reach its decision. First, it considers the toxicity, volume, mobility, and strength of the wastes contributed by each party. It also considers the weight of the evidence, ability to pay, litigation risks, public interest, precedential value, and inequities or aggravating factors. An NBAR lists the parties, ranked according to the above factors. It may be issued after the **remedial investigation/feasibility study** is completed, since that phase of the cleanup activity determines what problems exist at the site and what methods could be used to clean it up. See also **National Priority List; Superfund Amendments and Reauthorization Act.**

NONCONVENTIONAL POLLUTANT An odd category of water contaminants regulated by the **Clean Water Act.** The grouping includes all pollutants that are neither conventional nor toxic. The statute itself lists ammonia, total phenols, lead, color, and chlorine as nonconventional pollutants.

The most common water pollutants are called conventional pollutants, and they include suspended solids, biochemical oxygen demand, and pH (acidity and alkalinity). Conventional pollutants were the first type of water pollutants regulated. Toxic water pollutants are those identified as harmful to the living organisms in surface waters. The toxicity may relate to bioaccumulation (storing of pollutants over the lifetime of an organism), immediate effects on organisms, and persistence. These pollutants are listed by the EPA and are often called priority pollutants. Examples include benzene, chromium, and arsenic.

A nonconventional pollutant must be evaluated to make sure it does not meet the criteria for listing as a toxic pollutant, since toxic pollutants are regulated more stringently. Also, the discharger may be eligible for a variance from the standard if it can demonstrate that the facility is fundamentally different from other sources that discharge the pollutant. See also **National Pollutant Discharge Elimination System.**

NONDEGRADATION POLICY A principle in environmental statutes that prohibits an area from allowing a deterioration of the air or water simply because it exceeds the national standards for pollutant control. The **Clean Air Act** has specific provisions to govern growth in **air quality control regions** that have attained the federal standards: the **Prevention of Significant Deterioration** program. See also **National Ambient Air Quality Standards.**

In the **Clean Water Act,** backsliding is prohibited. If a facility is treating its wastewater to a required level, the **Environmental Protection Agency** or state permitting agency may not relax the treatment required when the permit is reissued. Similarly, the Clean Water Act requires states to designate **water quality standards** for waters within their borders. The current use of the water must be preserved, except in extraordinary situations, and once the water quality is improved, the new status of the water is protected as a current use. The state's water quality designations will impact development, because raising the quality of the water will mean that wastewater may have to be treated beyond the national standards.

Nondegradation provisions apply to nationally protected areas as well as state-regulated natural resources. The quality of *outstanding national resource* waters, found in national and state parks, may not be reduced at all. Air quality standards and visibility are also strictly controlled in national and state parks, forests, and wildlife preserves. The effect of this type of policy is to limit growth not only within the protected areas, but also outside them.

NOTICE AND COMMENT A procedure used in administrative law to allow interested parties to review proposed rules and participate in making rules and finalizing proposals. Since environmental law is a type of administrative law, the concept underlies most actions the agencies take [see **administrative agency**].

When the **Environmental Protection Agency** (EPA) wishes to create a new regulation (a process called promulgation), it is required to notify the public. The notice appears in the *Federal Register,* a publication that covers all official activity of federal agencies and is published almost every work day of the year. The *Federal Register* includes notices of proposed regulations, notices of proposed settlements of lawsuits, final regulations, and requests for information. The EPA, like other federal agencies, must record final actions, proposals, and offer the opportunity for interested parties to comment.

Comments on proposed regulations must be answered by the agency, so the final regulation generally has a lengthy preamble in which the EPA responds to the most significant comments. The comments from the public may influence the final form of the regulation. If the regulation will be radically different than the proposal, the EPA must go through the notice and comment process again before issuing the rule.

Notice and comment provisions are protections from unrestrained lawmaking by administrative agencies. Since agencies are specialized and are not elected officials, they could become isolated from voters. Public involvement increases agency accountability and prevents the agency from acting in a vacuum.

Agency activities other than rulemaking may be of concern to the public as well, and they also go through notice and comment. For example, a settlement with the EPA may cut off the rights of an interested party in a lawsuit. Therefore, consent degrees are not entered into court records immediately; they are *lodged*, or placed with the court until the comment period is over.

Concerning remedial actions at **hazardous waste** sites, Congress believes community involvement is crucial in formulating the cleanup plan and eliminating the threats posed by the site's condition. Therefore, the EPA must keep the process open through notice and comment. Virtually all decisions, from placing the site on the **National Priority List** (a list of targeted hazardous waste sites) to removing it after the remediation is complete, are subject to notice and comment.

Permitting of facilities that will discharge pollutants may also affect the rights and interests of the public, an individual, or other facilities in the area. Notices of proposed permits are not placed in the *Federal Register*, but they are published in the local newspaper. The notice will specify where additional information can be obtained and where to submit comments or request a **hearing**.

NOTICE LETTER   One of two types of letters in environmental law. The first is one sent by the **Environmental Protection Agency** (EPA) to inform a company, city, or other party that it is a **potentially responsible party** for cleanup of a **hazardous waste** site. The second is a letter sent to the EPA to notify it that a **citizen suit** will be brought if the EPA does not take some specified action within sixty days.

Notification to Potentially Responsible Parties

In cases involving the cleanup of hazardous waste facilities, the EPA has numerous responsibilities after a site has been designated dangerous enough to require federal involvement. If the situation is immediately hazardous, the EPA may do the work itself or part of it so that it does not pose an immediate threat. See **Comprehensive Environmental Response, Compensation, and Liability Act; National Priority List.**

However, the federal government does not finance **remediation** at hazardous waste sites unless no potentially responsible party can be found. Whether it has already done some work or is merely contemplating it, the EPA must begin a search as early as feasible to locate parties to pay for the investigation and work at the site.

The notice letter is sent to companies, persons, organizations, and cities—in short, anyone with a connection to the disposal of **hazardous substances** at the facility. Also, the statute names the current owner or operator of the site as a potentially responsible party [see **potentially responsible parties**]. Sending the notice letter is a major step in a lengthy process to force the parties connected with the site to bear the cost of evaluating, formulating a remedy, and implementing the remedy selected. See **innocent purchaser.**

The person notified may submit information to the EPA to demonstrate that he or she had no connection with the property or the waste disposal activities. However, the notice letter follows an intense search for potentially responsible parties. Records of waste disposal facilities and other credible information form the basis of the notification. So, when notice letters are sent by the EPA, the preliminary work has been done, and it will be difficult for the person to escape the process. Notice letters are ordinarily issued at least sixty days before a lawsuit is filed. People or companies receiving a notice letter are invited to attend a meeting the EPA will hold to explain what it intends to do. The meeting is open to all of the potentially responsible parties.

Citizen Suits

The other type of notice letter is sent to the Environmental Protection Agency, the state in which the violation occurred, and the party alleged to be the violator. It informs them that an interested party intends to file a lawsuit.

This notice letter must be sent sixty days before a suit is actually filed, with a few exceptions. It may relate to a particular enforcement action the interested party wants the agency to undertake, or it may demand that the agency promulgate regulations. According to the citizen suit provisions of environmental laws, the action the party wants must be nondiscretionary for the agency. Some statutes, such as the **Clean Air Act,** specify which of the EPA's duties are nondiscretionary.

For example, if the agency was given until 15 November 1995 to develop regulations and that date has come and gone without regulations being promulgated, a citizen may sue the agency to force action. On the other hand, if an agency has not prosecuted a violator for a violation of the Clean Air Act, the agency cannot be forced to do so because the EPA has discretion to choose its enforcement actions. In the first instance, the agency will be a party to the lawsuit if it does not act within the sixty days. In the second, the agency may still choose not to prosecute the violator because of other priorities. The citizen will be unlikely to win a lawsuit against the agency itself but can file a lawsuit against the violator after sixty days.

NOTICE OF NONCOMPLIANCE A notice sent by the **Environmental Protection Agency** (EPA) or a state agency to inform the recipient that it is not complying with specified sections of the **Clean Air Act.** The notice is preliminary to payment of a penalty for delayed compliance with one of the specified programs under the Clean Air Act, such as the acid deposition, permitting, and stratospheric **ozone** provisions.

Unlike a number of other enforcement provisions, Section 120 of the Clean Air Act aims to recover the savings a company or other person realized because it did not comply with the law on time. For example, if a business was supposed to limit its **emissions** of **sulfur dioxide** by 15 March and it is out of compliance after that date, the EPA can consider what it has saved by not investing in pollution control equipment. The penalty will depend on the cost of the equipment at the time it should have been installed, the cost of maintaining, testing, and other costs associated with upkeep, and the value of money.

The notice of noncompliance places a duty on the recipient to calculate its own penalty based on the EPA's regulations and begin submitting payments within four months. Payment of the penalty does not eliminate other rights of enforcement the government has. In the example above, the company has not only delayed putting the appropriate equipment into service, it has also been violating the emission limits. The notice of noncompliance does not deal with the emission violations, so the EPA can use a separate section of the Clean Air Act to collect penalties for them.

The notice of noncompliance is unique to the Clean Air Act, but the concept of recovering delayed compliance costs is not. In settlement discussions and penalty calculations for violations of the **Clean Water Act,** for instance, the government uses the economic benefit realized as an absolute bottom line in calculating the penalty. The penalty cannot go below that figure because the statute prohibits it. The penalty policies for settlement reflect the overriding concern that compliance must not be delayed to save money.

NOTICE OF VIOLATION (NOV) A notice from the **Environmental Protection Agency** or a state agency to advise the recipient that the recipient has violated a statute, regulation, or the terms of a permit. NOVs also detail how a **hearing** or a meeting with the agency can be arranged. If the alleged violator does not contest the notice, it will be followed with a **compliance order.** The agency may also issue an **administrative penalty order,** forcing payment of a penalty for the violations.

The notice of violation often precedes a two-way communication that can benefit both the alleged violator and the agency. The recipient of the notice has the opportunity to discuss the reasons for the violation or demonstrate why the notice is in error. If the notice was correct and a violation did occur, the agency and the violator may be able to work out an agreement to eliminate the problems that caused the violation.

NUISANCE Interference with the right to peaceably enjoy the use of one's property. In environmental law, the term nuisance is used as a legal theory to force compensation and to stop the interference. It is a very old theory, dating back to the early British judicial system, but has been used successfully in certain situations. The most widely publicized recent use was by the state of New York to clean up and compensate for the pollution at **Love Canal.**

A nuisance may be public or private. A public nuisance affects the community, so the proper person to bring a lawsuit for a public nuisance is the government. The only time an individual can sue for a public nuisance is when he or she has suffered a peculiar injury, that is, one not suffered by the public at large. Private nuisances interfere with an individual's rights.

An example of a public nuisance is contamination of groundwater. The problem is widespread, affecting the water supply of the whole community, and interferes with the ability of the government to provide water for the citizens. Therefore, the government has the right to sue the person responsible for the contamination. A private nuisance is, for example, the contamination of a private well due to migration of pollution from another property. The individual who owns the well involved could sue for a private nuisance because the injury affects only that person.

Many statutes address contamination, but they do not always authorize a lawsuit. If they do not, the person injured may have to rely on older legal theories. The basis of such lawsuits is a tort, a civil wrong that deals with injuries to personal or public entitlements. Using tort theories increases the likelihood of payment for environmental harm. See also **negligence; strict liability; toxic tort; trespass.**

In environmental law, the theories used as a basis for a lawsuit sometimes overlap. Some nuisances, such as abnormally loud noises, can only be considered nuisances, since nothing physical remains on the property; others, such as a poisoned well or chemical dust falling on a roof, can also be called trespass.

OCCUPATIONAL SAFETY AND HEALTH ACT

A law enacted in 1970 to deal with workplace safety. Environmental statutes focus on ambient air (air outside buildings), surface waters, drinking water supplies, waste management and cleanup: issues that affect the general public. The Occupational Safety and Health Act establishes safety standards in the workplace, but often the problems it addresses are environmental hazards and overlap with environmental regulation. Therefore, the two agencies involved, the **Occupational Safety and Health Administration** (OSHA) and the **Environmental Protection Agency** (EPA), work together on joint concerns and inform each other when they find violations that fall into the other's jurisdiction.

Right-To-Know Provisions

The responsibility for communicating chemical hazards is shared by the EPA and OSHA. The community is informed and prepared for releases to the environment through the **Emergency Planning and Community Right-To-Know Act;** the worker is informed and prepared to work with and respond to emergency releases of **hazardous chemical**s in the workplace through the **Hazard Communication Standard.**

By its own acknowledgment, the Emergency Planning and Community Right-To-Know Act depends on the OSHA provisions. The law requires businesses that must keep **material safety data sheets** to file reports on any hazardous chemicals that are kept in threshold planning quantities (amounts established by the EPA). Therefore, if an employer is subject to the Hazard Communication Standard for its employees, it may have environmental responsibilities as well.

Regardless of the surroundings, the purpose of the right-to-know provisions is to make sure the people who may be injured by hazardous chemicals or substances know what they may be exposed to and are able to react properly if a release occurs. Most states have laws dealing with the same topics, and sometimes the right-to-know law covers both worker and public information.

HAZWOPER

Another area where the concerns of OSHA overlap with those of the EPA is response actions at **hazardous waste** sites and other places where a release of a hazardous substance has occurred. Although the affected water, air, or land may be under the jurisdiction of the EPA, it becomes a workplace as soon as people are involved and is then subject to OSHA rules.

HAZWOPER is the commonly used name for the regulations that govern worker protection during cleanup activities involving **hazardous substances**, hazardous wastes, or hazardous chemicals. It is an acronym for "hazardous waste operations and emergency response." It requires training, personal protective equipment, records, and monitoring so the workers are not exposed to harmful levels of hazardous agents.

Indoor Air Quality

The EPA has studied indoor air quality standards and issued guidance on some issues, such as the presence of radon in buildings. However, it has little authority to deal with air inside structures; its concern is ambient, or outdoor, air. OSHA, on the other hand, has a right to regulate indoor air quality in workplaces subject to its jurisdiction. A sweeping indoor air quality regulation has been proposed, so the issue is gaining momentum. In the meantime, the only standards that exist for workplace safety are those dealing with specific pollutants such as **asbestos,** benzene, methyl chloride, and others. Those standards set worker exposure limits and require the use of personal protective equipment if the limits are exceeded.

Asbestos Standards

OSHA and the EPA also cooperate in regulating emissions of asbestos fibers. Their regulations on abatement and testing are remarkably similar, and the training requirements have been effectively merged. While the EPA is most concerned with the disposal of asbestos and outdoor emissions, such as those that would result from an uncontrolled demolition of a building, it does have authority to regulate in schools [see **Asbestos Hazard Emergency Response Act**]. For the projects it controls, the EPA has established training, certification, processes, and testing protocols.

OSHA focuses on limiting worker exposure to asbestos. Two different standards apply: those designed to cover the worker who is actively involved in operations with a high risk of exposure to airborne asbestos, and those that cover workers who simply work in a building where asbestos is present. Workers in jobs that may require contact with asbestos are covered by the construction standard. That standard protects asbestos abatement workers, custodial staff that may clean up asbestos dust or perhaps disturb it when doing other duties, and workers who must cut into asbestos to get to a building component. The newly updated standards refer to various EPA training courses as the measuring stick for sufficiency of training.

The general asbestos standard applies in workplaces where asbestos is present but the workers are not likely to encounter it in a dangerous form. Limits on the number of fibers in the air are set for those workers as well, and employers and building owners are required to notify workers, monitor activities that can increase airborne asbestos fibers, and keep records of the location of known or suspected asbestos-containing materials.

OCCUPATIONAL SAFETY AND HEALTH ADMINISTRATION (OSHA)
The agency responsible for workplace safety. It promulgates the regulations that determine how the **Occupational Health and Safety Act** applies to specific situations. Like the **Environmental Protection Agency,** the Occupational Safety and Health Administration is a regulatory agency. Thus, its regulations have the force of law. It also has enforcement and inspection authority.

OCEAN DUMPING ACT
See **Marine Protection, Research, and Sanctuaries Act.**

OIL POLLUTION ACT (OPA)
A statute enacted in 1990, after the Exxon **Valdez** spilled oil in Prince William Sound the year before. Congress became convinced that existing law did not properly address preparation, cleanup, and compensation, so it remedied the situation by creating new law.

The Oil Pollution Act deals with oil spills from vessels and from onshore and offshore facilities that could release oil to water. It stresses preparation for emergencies as well as response to spills. Facilities and vessels covered by the law must either prepare plans to respond to spills or stop operating. They must also demonstrate that they are financially capable of cleanup through a **financial responsibility** mechanism, such as insurance, bonds, or trust funds.

Liability under the OPA is strict, joint, and several. That means the court cannot consider fault when deciding someone is responsible for a cleanup. "Fault" in legal terms refers to some action or inaction that causes damage. However, regardless of how carefully a vessel is operated, the OPA holds the owner or operator responsible for any spills from the vessel. Fault is a concept that applies to **negligence,** but not to **strict liability.** Also, the joint and several provision requires everyone responsible for a particular oil spill to be responsible for the cleanup, separately and together. The liability scheme in the OPA is similar in many respects to that in the **Comprehensive Environmental Response, Compensation, and Liability Act.**

Defenses are also limited. An act of God, act of war, or the act of a third party not in contract with the facility or vessel owner are the three defenses. But even if the facility or vessel owner believes it has a defense, it must cooperate with the cleanup. If it does not report the spill, it will lose any defense it may have.

The Oil Pollution Act amended the provision in the **Clean Water Act** that has dealt with oil spills for about twenty years, greatly increasing the limits on liability. Also, the law gives the government the right to sue for **natural resources damages.** Individuals and businesses that relied on the injured natural resources for their livelihoods or had property destroyed may recover their losses. Congress also authorized an Oil Spill Trust Fund, which may be used for emergency response actions. It is financed by a tax on oil producers.

Planning is an important aspect of the OPA. Facilities that may discharge oil to water and vessels that carry oil must create a contingency plan to respond to a worst-case spill. The plan must be realistic, and the facility must train people to implement it. Federal, state, and local governments are also involved in contingency planning in a system much like the one created by the **Emergency Planning and Community Right-To-Know Act.**

The law also sets standards for new construction and requires demonstration of financial responsibility. New construction standards apply to tankers under the new law. By 1995, single-hull tank vessels must be upgraded or replaced by double-hull vessels. Vessels and offshore facilities subject to the OPA must ensure that they are financially capable of responding to an oil spill. They may choose insurance, use a guarantor, start a trust fund, or insure themselves—if they meet the requirements for self-insurance. Financial responsibility must be maintained until the vessel or offshore facility is no longer operating.

Response actions under the OPA may be undertaken by different federal agencies, depending on the location of the spill. If it is within the United States, it may be handled by the **Environmental Protection Agency;** along the coastal areas, the U.S. **Coast Guard** is involved. All response actions, like **hazardous waste** site cleanups, must be consistent with the **National Contingency Plan.**

OPERABLE UNIT   A part of a **hazardous waste** site that is treated separately from the rest of the site to facilitate a remedy. The job of removing, neutralizing, and containing waste can be lengthy and overwhelming at a contaminated site. Operable units make the process more manageable for the **Environmental Protection Agency** (EPA), the public, and the parties who have to clean up the property.

For example, assume that an abandoned hazardous waste facility, HazChem, is targeted for cleanup. During the operation of HazChem, drums of hazardous wastes were dumped into a hole and buried; others were dumped into lagoons. As a result, HazChem has contaminated the groundwater. HazChem also had a storage area, and when the facility closed, containers of hazardous wastes were left stacked inside it.

So that it could phase the work in a logical manner, the EPA could view the facility as consisting of several operable units: the groundwater, the buried waste, the lagoon, and the storage area. Another possibility is that the **potentially responsible parties** can divide the work among them, distributing the cleanup resources to the operable units involved. See **Comprehensive Environmental Response, Compensation, and Liability Act.**

ORPHAN'S SHARE   A term used in cases involving the cleanup of a **hazardous waste** site to describe the proportion of **potentially responsible parties** who are insolvent, no longer in existence, or unavailable and therefore unable to contribute to the costs of **remediation.** It also may be used to describe the portion represented by defendants who have refused to settle.

Although the **Comprehensive Environmental Response, Compensation, and Liability Act** holds each potentially responsible party liable for the entire cleanup, in practice the **Environmental Protection Agency** (EPA) seeks out as many parties as it can find to finance the response action. The goal for the government is to find enough solvent and willing parties to pay 100 percent of the cost of remediation. Potentially responsible parties have an interest in locating as many people with a connection to the waste site as possible. The incentive is clear: generally, the more parties involved, the more money will be available. But that is not always the case.

Abandoned hazardous waste sites are often very old. The company that ran the operation may no longer exist, or the facility may have been run by an individual who has no money. The same situations may apply to many of the businesses that disposed of the wastes. The nonsettlor is as much a concern to the other parties as those who cannot contribute to paying for the work. If a solvent owner, operator, or executive of a hazardous waste site or generator exists, the government can pursue those individuals. Frequently, that ability is exercised; however, many times those people are also insolvent, or they have so little money they cannot finance the cleanup.

When the potentially responsible parties who are solvent are assigned all of the costs for investigation and cleanup, they try to avoid paying the orphan's share. Generally, the parties will argue that the EPA should pick up the orphan's share by using the fund established for cleaning up abandoned hazardous waste sites [see **Superfund**].

Until 1986, the argument fell on deaf ears. The Superfund was established, the EPA contended, to pay for emergency responses and take care of sites where no potentially responsible parties can be found. However, the **Superfund Amendments and Reauthorization Act** made it clear that Congress favors settlements. Use of the Superfund to pay for the orphan's share is permissable in situations where the agency believes settlement may result. This type of cleanup financing is called mixed funding.

The EPA recognizes three different types of mixed funding. In the first, the potentially responsible parties perform the work and are reimbursed for a portion of the costs. Such an arrangement must be worked out in advance of the work, but the EPA prefers this preauthorized method to other alternatives. The second type is a *cash-out*, in which the agency does the work and the potentially responsible parties contribute toward the costs but do not pay for the entire cleanup. In the third type of mixed funding, the agency and parties agree to do discrete parts of the cleanup. The agency then pursues the potentially responsible parties who are not willing to settle.

The agency sanctions saving the Superfund for sites where no viable parties exist, but it also has an interest in completing a cleanup. The EPA's guidance emphasizes the importance of obtaining substantial settlements from potentially responsible parties who are bargaining in good faith. The agency will not allow mixed funding to be used routinely to cover the orphan's share.

OZONE (O_3)   A form of oxygen composed of three molecules of oxygen instead of the more common combination of two. Ozone is important in two environmental situations: it is a pollutant at ground level; and it protects the earth from ultraviolet radiation in the stratosphere. Both types of ozone get special attention in the **Clean Air Act Amendments of 1990.**

Ozone at ground level is one of the five most common **air pollutant**s. It is highly poisonous gas that reduces the amount of oxygen inhaled and can cause severe respiratory problems. It is regulated by the **Environmental Protection Agency** through the **National Ambient Air Quality Standards,** which establish air quality criteria for common contaminants. Each state must have a plan designed to bring the state's air quality into compliance with the standards and then maintain the air quality. See **nitrogen oxides; nonattainment areas; state implementation plan.**

Ozone is not directly discharged, like many pollutants. Instead, it is created by chemical reactions involving other pollutants called *precursors*. The precursors for ozone are volatile organic compounds and **nitrogen oxides** released by motor vehicles and by some manufacturing processes, primarily during the use of internal combustion engines. Ozone formation is most rapid in the summer, and topography and winds play a role. If the area is in a depression, the gases tend to remain where they are, and chemical reactions can occur. However, winds tend to move the precursors away from their origins and cut down on the formation of the soup.

Stratospheric ozone is a buffer that has protected the earth from ultraviolet rays for millennia. However, the depletion of stratospheric ozone has been documented for years, caused by chemicals used for refrigeration, propellants, and fire suppression [see **chlorofluorocarbons**]. As a result of international concern and agreements, the chemicals responsible for ozone depletion are being phased out of production and use. The 1990 amendments to the Clean Air Act devote an entire title to stratospheric ozone. See also **Montreal Protocol.**

PARTICULATE A substance, either liquid or solid, that is small enough to be suspended in air. Particulates may be tiny enough to be invisible, or they may compare to soot in size. Those larger than 10 microns in diameter tend to be filtered out by the respiratory system when we breathe. Some are caught by the hairs within the nostrils; others get stopped before they get to the lungs. But the **Environmental Protection Agency** (EPA) has concluded that particulates 10 microns or less in diameter can be inhaled into the lungs. These particulates, called PM_{10}, are one of the air contaminants regulated by the **National Ambient Air Quality Standards.**

Most particulate matter in the air is the result of incomplete combustion of fossil fuels, primarily from automobiles and power plants. Power plants and automobiles reduce the amount of particulates in their emissions by using several different technologies. See **mobile sources; nonattainment areas.**

POLLUTION PREVENTION ACT (PPA) A statute enacted in 1990 that proclaimed a national policy of preventing and reducing pollution at the source. This policy was in sharp contrast to most environmental protection, which simply attempts to manage pollutants. The PPA highlights the need to prevent pollution and reduce the amount that must be managed.

Waste management has reached a critical stage. Landfills can no longer be used for many types of wastes, communities are up in arms about incinerators, and waste treatment has become a high-risk venture. Even recycling has its problems: most of the battery recyclers that existed in the 1970s are now out of business and bankrupt. As a result, Congress began edging toward a pollution prevention approach in the **Clean Air Act** and the **Clean Water Act,** which require ever-increasing regulation of new sources and their processes and encourage recycling through exemptions to the definition of **hazardous waste** in the **Resource Conservation and Recovery Act.**

The PPA spells out preferred methods for dealing with waste in order of priority: (1) avoid it or reduce it during production, (2) recycle it, (3) treat it, and (4) as a last resort, dispose of it in a responsible manner. The law targets the first method, prevention and reduction. Under the law, the EPA is required to gather and disseminate information about methods for reducing or preventing waste and to establish an award program and a Source Reduction Clearinghouse. Also, the EPA may give grants to the states to help them establish their own programs.

The statute puts pressure on companies by requiring them to supply information to the public. If a business is subject to the provision of the **Emergency Planning and Community Right-To-Know Act** that compels filing an annual report of toxic chemical releases, it must also report what it is doing to reduce the amount of toxic chemicals it generates. Reports must address a number of issues. The company must detail the quantity of toxic chemicals entering the waste stream and the percentage change over the last year. Discussions will also include the amount of chemical treated, the amount of recycling and percentage change, source reduction methods used, the amount of reduction expected over the next two years, production ratios, and techniques used to identify reduction methods. The EPA itself is required to make biennial reports to Congress on the progress businesses are making. If it has suggestions, it makes recommendations at the same time.

States, too, are instituting this type of regulation because of the lack of disposal options. California, for example, requires cities to come up with a plan to reduce the amount of waste they produce. Recycling is being encouraged throughout the United States.

The idea of pollution prevention is also gaining momentum in businesses that handle or produce **hazardous chemical**s or hazardous wastes. Hazardous wastes are expensive to manage, and many responsibilities fall on producers and users of **hazardous substances**. Companies are reducing their expenses by reducing the use and waste of such substances.

POTENTIALLY RESPONSIBLE PARTIES (PRPs)

Persons who fit into any of the categories Congress established in the **Comprehensive Environmental Response, Compensation, and Liability Act** to force cleanup of abandoned **hazardous waste** sites. A person includes any form of business, city, state and federal governmental agencies, individuals, and in some situations, officers, trustees, and other representatives of any of the above.

The law is designed to find as many solvent parties as possible with a connection to the disposal of hazardous waste at a particular site. The parties fall into these classes: (1) present owners and operators of the facility, (2) those who owned or operated the facility when the disposal occurred, (3) transporters, and (4) arrangers for disposal.

Defenses to liability include acts of God (such as a tornado, hurricane, or forest fire), acts of war, and acts of a third party totally unrelated to the potentially responsible party. The statute also exempts certain parties from being responsible for cleanup: transporters who did not select the waste disposal facility, generators of used oil, and governmental bodies that own the property because it was abandoned or seized to satisfy tax delinquency. Wrongdoing plays no role in the determination process. A relationship to the property or waste is sufficient to impose liability, regardless of whether the actions were legal when they were taken.

Successor and Officer/Director Liability

Businesses may take a number of forms: partnerships, corporations, or proprietorships. Corporations in particular are considered totally separate legal persons. If the corporation is run properly, only the corporation, not the officers and directors, is responsible for its actions. However, certain situations may trigger personal liability for officers and directors of a corporation. The general rule in law is that if the officers and directors ignore the corporation's existence by acting as if they are personally responsible for the company's debts, or if they are intending to defraud creditors, a court can "pierce the corporate veil" to reach the officers and directors for personal liability.

In environmental law, it is not uncommon for the EPA or other enforcing agency to try to hold the officers and directors responsible as owners or operators of an abandoned hazardous waste site, particularly if the corporation has no assets. Courts apply established principles when deciding whether to impose personal liability. If the officers or directors actively participated in waste management decisions, for example, it is likely that they will be personally liable. When a proprietorship (sole ownership) sells its assets or when the entire business is sold and then ceases to exist, the government will usually pursue the successor company, even if it did not exist at the time the waste disposal occurred.

Courts consider a number of factors when deciding what to do with successor companies. One is whether the business is simply a continuation of the earlier enterprise. Another is the agreement that outlined the terms of the sale. If the new company agreed to assume the debts and liabilities of the earlier business, it will be liable. If the new company continues the same waste disposal practices, again, it would probably be liable. Often, however, the issue of liability is murky. The courts look at the facts of each situation to determine the result.

Owners and Operators in General

One class of potentially responsible parties is current owners and operators of the site. The current owner or operator may not be disposing of hazardous waste on the property and may not even know that the hazardous waste is there. In some cases, the owner or operator may be able to prove that it is an **innocent purchaser** and should not be held responsible.

The theory behind including current owners and operators of the property is that the cleanup of the property will benefit them; therefore, they should pay. The distinction between owning and operating a facility is not as obvious as it seems. For example, an owner, for the purpose of the statute, may be a person who is leasing the property. An operator may be a trustee of a trust that has the facility as one of the assets. The key to determining the owner and operator is not only its legal status, but also its activities on the property. A landlord who allows a lessee to manufacture and dispose of hazardous waste on the property will still be the owner because of title to the land. But the factory owner will be both owner and operator of the facility for purposes of the cleanup, because the lease is broad enough to allow the manufacturer to act as if the property belongs to it as well as operate the enterprise there. Lenders may also wind up being owners or operators under the law. The statute exempts lenders that only hold title as an indication of their security interest, but if the lender exercises too much control over the operation or use of the property, it, too, may be considered an owner or operator [see **lender liability**].

Past owners and operators are also potentially responsible parties, but there is more of a logical connection with them. The persons who can be liable because of past ownership/operation of the facility owned or operated the site during the time disposal occurred. In a narrow sense, this definition excludes the person who owned the property between the time of the disposal and the current owner from the group of potentially responsible parties. Realistically, though, the government can also pursue the interim owner because the term disposal includes leaching, escaping, migrating, and so forth. So if the government could demonstrate that the waste was moving during the time the interim owner had the property, that person could also be a potentially responsible party.

Transporters and Arrangers for Disposal

Persons or businesses that hauled **hazardous substances** to the disposal site are also potentially responsible parties unless the transporter did not select the site. For example, a generator hired a transporter to carry the waste to a hazardous waste facility and did not specify which one. The transporter is an arranger for disposal if he chose the facility, and he is also liable as a transporter. The question of selection is a factual issue.

The biggest class of potential responsible parties, however, is the arranger category. It includes the generators (originators of the waste) and anyone else who may have been involved in getting it to the hazardous waste facility.

In some cases, it is easy to determine whether a party is an arranger. For example, a person who sends trichlorethane to a waste facility is arranging for its disposal. However, an intermediary may wind up being the arranger. A recycling facility may accept someone's batteries and crack them open, use the lead and dispose of the electrolyte. The recycler is an arranger for the electrolyte disposal. Occasionally, parties become arrangers when they are merely stepping in to clean up a property. For example, if a lender forecloses on a property and hires a company to take care of drums of solvent, it becomes an arranger of disposal. Also, if a person voluntarily cleaned up someone else's spill of a hazardous substance and sent the waste to a facility, that person became an arranger.

Consequences of Being a Potentially Responsible Party

The number of potentially responsible parties available to sue for the cost of cleaning up a hazardous waste facility varies greatly from site to site. The statute that creates the duty to pay for the remediation, the Comprehensive Environmental Response, Compensation, and Liability Act, provides that the potentially responsible parties are responsible, both separately and together, for the cost of cleaning up the mess.

Potentially responsible parties are encouraged to form groups to negotiate with the government. They may use allocation methods to decide what everyone is responsible for, or they may ask the government to assist them with the allocation [see **nonbinding allocation of responsibility**]. If they cannot demonstrate a basis for separating the harm caused by their waste from other waste, the government will maintain that they are all responsible for all of the costs. In some cases, the cooperating parties will do whatever is necessary to clean up the site, then sue other potentially responsible parties for contributions to the cost [see **contribution costs**].

Even parties who have contributed very little to a hazardous waste site, such as a box of poisoned cookies used as evidence in a criminal case, cannot rest easy. Unless they are able to work out an agreement for settlement with the government that protects them from contribution, they may find themselves contributing to the cleanup in vastly disproportionate amounts [see *de minimis/de micromis* **parties**].

PREMANUFACTURING NOTICE (PMN) The notice that must be filed with the **Environmental Protection Agency** (EPA) before a new chemical is manufactured or imported. The premanufacturing notice is required by the **Toxic Substances Control Act.**

If a person wants to begin manufacturing or importing a chemical, he or she must first determine whether it is on the Toxic Substances Control Act inventory. If it is not, the person checks the exemptions and exclusions. Finally, if the chemical is not exempt or excluded, a premanufacturing notice must be filed. A PMN may cover only one chemical or may cover two or more chemicals with similar molecular structure. Two or more companies may file a joint PMN, thereby increasing the resources available to get the notice through the process.

The PMN includes information about the chemical itself, such as identification, categories of use, by-products, and amounts to be manufactured or imported. The EPA also wants to know how many employees have been exposed to the chemical during research and testing and proper disposal methods. Test data and impacts on health and environment are naturally a part of the PMN.

Within ninety days of receipt, the EPA must review the notice. It may extend the period another ninety days, or it may limit the sale or manufacture of the product, place conditions on it, or ban it. The EPA may ask for additional information if the data is insufficient to determine the risk. If the EPA does nothing within the first ninety days, the manufacture or import may begin after a thirty day prior notice of intent is sent to the agency.

Exclusions from the premanufacturing notice requirements are chemicals regulated under another statute, such as the **Federal Insecticide, Fungicide, and Rodenticide Act** or the Food, Drug, and Cosmetic Act. Exempted chemicals either fit into one of the categories the EPA has created or fall under research and development. Some polymers and chemicals that are by-products of manufacturing are exempt, for example.

PRETREATMENT   Methods used to remove enough pollutants from industrial wastewater before it is sent to a municipal treatment plant so that the pollutants do not cause the plant to violate its permit. Pretreatment is also used to ensure that the wastewater is treated and not simply released because the treatment plant does not have the capacity to deal with it. The targets of pretreatment are toxic water pollutants and abnormally large amounts of conventional pollutants. See also **industrial user.**

PREVENTION OF SIGNIFICANT DETERIORATION (PSD) A program under the **Clean Air Act** designed to preserve the air quality of an area after it has met or exceeded the national standards for various pollutants. If an area is unclassifiable as either attainment or nonattainment, the PSD requirements also apply. Preconstruction review and permitting of new major sources and major modifications of existing sources are central to the PSD program. See **major source; National Ambient Air Quality Standards; New Source Review; nonattainment areas.**

The PSD requirements generally pertain to sources that are capable of discharging 250 tons per year of a regulated pollutant. However, if the facility fits into one of 28 categories listed by Congress, it is considered major if it can emit 100 tons per year. Pollutants regulated by the PSD provisions include the **criteria pollutant**s—lead, **ozone, sulfur dioxide**, nitrogen dioxide [see **nitrogen oxides**], and small **particulate**s—but also cover sulfuric acid mist, other oxides of nitrogen, other compounds containing sulfur, and larger particulates. Initially, the program focused on only sulfur dioxide and particulates. States must develop their own regulations to make certain the Clean Air Act requirements for Prevention of Significant Deterioration are followed.

If a source within an air quality area that has attained the national standards plans to make a modification that will significantly increase pollution, it must also go through preconstruction review. The EPA has issued regulations to specify what levels of increase it considers significant. For example, forty tons per year of sulfur dioxide or volatile organic compounds is a significant increase.

Classification

When an **air quality control region** has met the National Ambient Air Quality Standards for criteria **air pollutant**s, it is designated an attainment area. Attainment areas may be further described as Class I, Class II, or Class III areas. Of the classes, Class I has the tightest restrictions on degradation of air quality. Other than national monuments, parks, recreation areas, scenic or wilderness areas, Class I areas are rare. Class III areas are even more uncommon, since attainment areas are automatically classified as Class II. Moving an area to a different category involves affirmative steps by the state or federal government. The amount of deterioration allowed in a Class I area is only two percent, Class II areas may increase emissions by as much as twenty-five percent, and Class III areas are permitted to increase air pollutants by up to fifty percent. However, the increments may not be used to allow the air quality control region to fall below the national standards.

States establish baselines by measuring the air quality at the time the air district attains the standards. Each class is allowed a percentage increase from the baseline, as long as the increase will not cause the region to violate the National Ambient Air Quality Standards. The increase is called an increment. To determine what remains of the increment, all of the pollutants in the air quality district must be considered, not just the ones coming from major emitting facilities. For example, new small sources may emit a regulated pollutant like carbon monoxide. Although they do not have to go through preconstruction review and permitting, they do discharge pollutants that use up part of the allowable increment.

Features of Preconstruction Permitting

Before a major source of emissions begins construction, it must go through a lengthy review. The source will be required to perform air monitoring and modeling based on the proposed location, collecting data over a year in most situations. It will have to demonstrate that building the new facility or making the modification will not cause the area to exceed the allowable increment of deterioration. It must also prove that it will not cause a violation of the national standards in any air quality control region. That means the source must consider not only what will happen to its pollution within the same area, but also how the pollutants may travel and affect another area.

Finally, the new source or modification will have to use best available control technology (BACT) to control all pollutants it may emit in significant amounts. The state will be the final authority on whether the controls proposed for use in the facility will meet the requirements. To assist sources in deciding what is necessary, the EPA publishes information on various technologies.

PROMULGATION The process by which an **administrative agency** creates a rule that has the force of law. Promulgation is also referred to as rulemaking.

Administrative agencies that are regulatory agencies, such as the **Environmental Protection Agency** (EPA) or the **Occupational Safety and Health Administration,** have legislative power as well as enforcement authority. Often the statute spells out general goals and authorizes the agency to flesh out the details. The **Clean Water Act,** for example, states the basic principles and goals of the government and sets forth the framework of the law. It then designates the administrator of the EPA as the person who is to implement it. Specific duties are spelled out, such as the duty to list toxic pollutants and determine pretreatment requirements for industry. The EPA fills in the gaps in the law primarily through promulgation of regulations. The **Administrative Procedure Act** governs the promulgation process for all agencies unless the statute being implemented is more specific about procedure.

Rulemaking can take a significant amount of time. First, the agency must determine what the scope of the rule should be and what provisions it must contain to deal with the problem it faces. For example, before it can list a toxic pollutant, the EPA must gather information about toxicity and safe levels of exposure.

After the agency conducts its research, it proposes regulations. They are published in the *Federal Register,* a publication that contains all of the official agency records for federal agencies. Following the proposal, the public may comment and **hearings** may be held on the proposal. The agency must then consider the comments and revise the proposal if appropriate. It must respond to the comments it receives when it publishes the final regulation. Upon publication or at a later date specified by the agency, the final regulation becomes law. That action completes the promulgation process. See also **notice and comment.**

PUBLICLY OWNED TREATMENT WORKS (POTW)

The name for a wastewater treatment facility owned by a government agency and operated primarily for the benefit of the surrounding community. POTWs may handle only domestic wastes or they may also process both domestic and industrial wastes.

Wastes contributed by **industrial users** must be pretreated [see **pretreatment**] before they go through the POTW system. In some communities, the government may add special equipment so that the pretreatment can be done at the POTW. Otherwise, the industrial user is required to treat its wastes so that they are compatible with the capabilities of the POTW and do not simply pass through the system untreated. The POTW may enter into agreements with industrial users, fine them for not treating their wastes, or use other methods of control. Because the industrial user could easily cause the POTW to violate its permit, the **Environmental Protection Agency** (EPA) expects the governmental authority to do whatever is necessary to make its contributing industries comply with the law.

All discharges of pollutants to waters of the United States require a permit unless some other exemption applies. Publicly owned treatment works are not exempt. They must have a permit issued under the **National Pollutant Discharge Elimination System.** They are limited to specified types and quantities of pollutants, are required to keep records and report, and must meet the technology requirements the EPA establishes. See also **Clean Water Act.**

REAGAN, RONALD (1911–)

President of the United States from 1981 to 1989, Ronald Reagan appointed many people to environmental positions who were unsympathetic to the environmental movement. His agenda was clear: he wanted to cut down the amount of regulation impacting businesses and lessen federal involvement.

In the history of the environmental movement, Reagan's efforts are known as the Counter-Revolution. Although he was successful in slowing the regulatory flow, he did not stop the steady movement of environmental legislation. The public demonstrated through congressional elections that they considered environmental issues important. The environmental movement gained momentum during the Reagan presidency, and many attributed its growth to vigorous opposition to his policies.

During his first term, his appointees included James Watt [see **Watt, James**] as secretary of the Interior, Anne Gorsuch (later, Burford) [see **Burford, Anne Gorsuch**] as administrator of the **Environmental Protection Agency** (EPA), Robert Burford as head of the Bureau of Land Management, and John Crowell as assistant agriculture secretary, in charge of national forests. The appointees began systematic attacks on the agencies they headed, announcing programs that appeared directly opposed to the agencies' mandates.

James Watt, who treated his new position as a religious mission to get public lands into the hands of the private sector, announced that the outer continental shelf was ripe for development. He opened it for bidding, drilling, and exploration. He also intended to sell approximately thirty million acres of public land but was stopped by the real estate developers who worried about the effect of such sales on the market. Close to a religious fanatic, Watt expressed no concern for conserving resources. Instead, he believed it was his God-given right to exhaust them. He compared environmentalists to Bolsheviks and Nazis and implied that the environmental movement was anti-American. During his tenure, he added no land to the National Park Service reserves, even though such purchases were budgeted. Watt resigned from his position in 1983 after angering the public with numerous inflammatory statements.

Anne Gorsuch Burford, who had close ties with the regulated community, became embroiled in a scandal involving the use of the **Superfund** for **hazardous waste** cleanups. Under her leadership, environmental enforcement came to a standstill, and rumors circulated of special deals cut behind closed doors. Soon, Burford and Rita Lavelle [see **Lavelle, Rita**], another political appointee at the EPA, were the subject of a congressional inquiry into use of the fund. Later, Rita Lavelle was convicted of perjury, and Anne Burford was accused of obstruction of justice. She resigned in 1983, complaining bitterly about being a scapegoat.

Robert Burford, a rancher before he was hired by the Department of Interior, had benefitted from the use of public land for grazing. As head of the Bureau of Land Management, he favored privatization. He set fees for grazing far below the market rate, which encouraged overgrazing and angered ranchers who did not have access to public land. The man in charge of national forests in Reagan's Department of Agriculture, John Crowell, was the former general counsel and vice president of the company that was the biggest purchaser of public timber.

While the appointees were wreaking havoc on the agencies they represented, Reagan's main weapon operated within the Office of Management and Budget. David Stockman, head of that office, recommended slashing budgets for critical agencies. So at the end of Reagan's first term, the EPA's budget (adjusted for inflation) was the same as it had been ten years before.

In 1981, the first year of his presidency, Reagan had issued Executive Order 12291, which required a cost-benefit analysis for all proposed regulations. The order effectively transferred regulatory oversight to the Office of Management and Budget. Regulations were held up while they were scrutinized for economic impact analysis. Environmental and safety regulations were killed, sent back to the agency, or simply disappeared into the void. The staff of the Council on Environmental Quality was cut from 60 to 16. At the Department of Interior, money was available to develop roads, bridges, and buildings but not for preservation and acquisition of land. In the area of energy, money flowed to coal, oil, and nuclear producers; money for development of renewable energy sources virtually dried up.

Congress did not give up, however. The **Clean Water Act,** the **Comprehensive Environmental Response, Compensation, and Recovery Act,** and the **Resource Conservation and Recovery Act** were all strengthened during the Reagan presidency. The first of the reenactments, the Clean Water Act amendments, was passed over presidential veto. The message that environmental concerns were not a passing whim gradually became clear.

The primary effect of Reagan's incumbency was public mobilization. Large environmental groups like the **Sierra Club** and the **Natural Resources Defense Council** grew phenomenally in membership during Reagan's first term. In the 1984 elections, candidates often found their environmental stances under scrutiny. When it was over, no one doubted the importance of the environment to Americans.

RECEIVING WATERS   The stream, lake, river, or other surface water body to which a waste discharge is sent. Standards for the quality of the receiving waters are designated by the state where the water body is located. Using water quality maintenance as the basis of treatment, the state or federal government issues permits limiting the amount of waste that may be discharged. Permits for discharges of waste to surface waters are regulated by the **Clean Water Act** and the **National Pollutant Discharge Elimination System.**

RECLAMATION/RECYCLING   Processes used to recover usable materials from a waste stream. The need for resource conservation and waste reduction has grown sharply. Some communities have no more room for landfills. Raw products are being depleted, and cost of harvesting, developing, or mining natural resources rises as the availability of resources falls. Thus finding ways to recycle or reclaim materials instead of discarding them has become a national challenge.

Reclamation and recycling take many different forms, from merely separating waste into its components to using waste for energy. The benefits of recycling and reclamation are reduction in demand for both virgin resources and disposal facilities. Recycling of many materials, such as aluminum, paper, plastic, and glass, can be handled successfully on a local level. Some cities have made recycling mandatory, focusing on household waste, office waste, or a combination. Others find voluntary recycling sufficient to ease their waste problems.

Experience has shown that successful recycling programs must provide (1) easy entrance into the system, (2) facilities to do the recycling, and (3) a market for the recycled goods. Great strides have been made in all three areas: curbside collection of recyclable goods has been the most effective means of encouraging public participation; the number of recycling facilities has increased dramatically; and demand for recycled goods has grown so dramatically that many recycling facilities now have difficulty getting enough waste to recycle. In many places in the country, the initial market for recycled goods was government agencies, which were required to purchase recycled materials. But now the public, too, demands recycled products.

Two laws contain provisions that encourage recycling: the **Resource Conservation and Recovery Act** (RCRA) and the **Pollution Prevention Act of 1990**. RCRA, which governs primarily the management of **hazardous waste** and underground **storage tank**s, recognizes recycling and reclamation of hazardous wastes as legitimate national goals. To further those goals, Congress and the **Environmental Protection Agency** (EPA) have taken steps to reduce the regulation of hazardous wastes destined for recycling or reclamation.

Two different approaches to encouraging recycling apply to hazardous wastes. For some materials, such as used oil, management practices are specified in lieu of the entire regulatory scheme for hazardous waste handling and disposal. When these materials are delivered to the collection site or transported in large amounts, though, normal manifesting and notification requirements of the Resource Conservation and Recovery Act apply. Other wastes, such as scrap metals (gold, silver, platinum, paladium, irridium, osmium, rhodium, ruthenium, or any combination) must be tracked and a record must be kept about the amount recycled. Lead acid batteries that are sent to recyclers to recover the lead are not subject to the manifesting requirements for the generator or transporter, but the reclamation facility is regulated.

The Pollution Prevention Act of 1990 not only encourages resource recovery through recycling, but also emphasizes a new target: reducing the amount of waste produced from the beginning. This goal is called *source reduction*. Generators of hazardous waste are required to sign a statement documenting that they have a waste reduction program. Along with other forms filed to inform the community about the use and release of **hazardous substances**, some companies must file reports detailing the amount of waste disposed of in a year, amount recycled, reduction in waste amounts, and projections for the next two years. This information is publicly available.

The EPA is also part of the congressional scheme to emphasize recycling and reclamation. The Pollution Prevention Act mandates the establishment of a pollution clearinghouse, study of recycling methods, grants to states for programs, and reports to Congress. See also **Emergency Planning and Community Right-To-Know Act.**

RECORD OF DECISION (ROD)   The **Environmental Protection Agency's** (EPA) formal record of the selection of a remedy for a **hazardous waste** site on the **National Priority List** of sites targeted for federal cleanup. The ROD discusses why the site was listed, what types of pollutants are involved, the various methods that could be used to address the pollution, and the agency's selection of a remedy. It must also include the reasons the remedy was chosen and discuss why the EPA considers the remedy sufficient, cost-effective, and permanent. Responses to public comments are also included.

Preparation of a record of decision is required by the **Superfund** law, the **Comprehensive Environmental Response, Compensation, and Liability Act,** and by the regulations, the **National Contingency Plan.**

During the course of a cleanup of one site, more than one ROD may be completed; each will deal with at least one aspect of the cleanup. For example, if at a particular site barrels of hazardous waste are stacked in a building, drums of hazardous waste are buried, and the groundwater is contaminated, the EPA may either deal with all three problems in one document or may address them separately in successive records of decision. At a complicated site, breaking the remedial action into smaller units (called **operable units**) may speed up the work and make it easier to allocate responsibility for portions of the cleanup.

The ROD is completed after the **remedial investigation/feasibility study** is finished. The selected remedy and draft document must be publicly available for examination and comment. When the final version is issued, the next step is engineering and design, followed by implementation of the remedy. After the design phase begins, the EPA may make changes to the remedy based on engineering or scientific reality. In that case, it must prepare an amendment to the ROD or prepare an explanation in a separate document detailing the proposed changes and the reasons for them. If the changes are significant, public notice and an opportunity to comment are required. See also **applicable or relevant and appropriate regulations; notice and comment; remedial design/remedial action; Superfund; Superfund Amendments and Reauthorization Act.**

RECORDKEEPING   The requirement that regulated businesses and persons collect information and keep records has become a major component of environmental law. Permittees must monitor their own compliance, submit records to the agencies that granted their permits, and keep copies of all documentation.

Underground **storage tank**s, for example, are highly regulated. From the time they are installed, the owner or operator must maintain records such as permits, documentation on the installation of the tank, specific data on its construction, test results, and **financial responsibility** information. When a tank is taken out of service, records about the removal, site characterization, and cleanup must be kept.

Hazardous materials are also highly regulated. Records are required for receipt of **hazardous chemical**s in the workplace, shipping of hazardous materials, and disposal and transportation of **hazardous waste**. Not all pollutants are considered hazardous or toxic, but those pollutants, such as total suspended solids, can overload the **receiving waters** when they are discharged from treatment plants. Therefore, even though the discharge is not considered a toxic water pollutant, a limit will be placed on the amount of total suspended solids the plant may discharge, and it will have to monitor, report, and keep the records associated with the discharge.

Many environmental and health statutes require training for employees. When they do, government agencies expect some type of proof that the training has been completed. Generally, the employer can document the training by keeping a copy of the materials used along with a list of the persons who attended the training program.

Although recordkeeping may seem unimportant in the overall scheme of environmental protection, it is an important tool in enforcement. Business records can be used by the government to prove violations. If they are falsified, the person or business creating them can be criminally liable. Also, failure to keep the records may be a violation in itself.

REFUSE ACT One of the oldest statutes dealing with pollution of waterways. Passed in 1899, the Refuse Act's primary purpose was not environmental protection but preventing obstruction to navigation. However, the lack of a specific, comprehensive law to regulate water pollution led the government to rely on the Refuse Act.

The Water Quality Act of 1965 was the first attempt to regulate water pollution, but it left the work to the states. States were supposed to set water quality standards for the waters within their boundaries then issue discharge permits aimed at protecting water quality. However, no guidance existed for the permits, and no federal action could be taken unless the state approved it. Furthermore, violations were difficult to spot because the water quality standards were conceptually awkward.

In the late 1960s and early 1970s, the public became concerned with the oil spills, fish kills, and grossly contaminated water, along with air pollution problems. Congress was able to pass the **Clean Air Act** in 1970 but managed only a greatly scaled back Water Quality Improvement Act that year. Finally, in 1972, the **Clean Water Act** was passed over President Richard M. Nixon's veto.

Until then, the only law written broadly enough to cover water pollution and allow enforcement was the Refuse Act, which required a discharge permit from the **Corps of Engineers.** Though the Refuse Act was not an effective law for comprehensive water permitting, enterprising government attorneys used it as a weapon against water pollution. Though many criminal cases were brought under the Refuse Act, its deficiencies were apparent: the lack of regulations and standards to determine when a permit should or should not be issued, the lack of staff to support the permitting scheme, the fact that only criminal prosecution was authorized, and the need for a complicated environmental analysis for every permit decision.

REILLY, WILLIAM K. (1940–)   Administrator of the **Environmental Protection Agency** (EPA) during George Bush's [see **Bush, George Herbert Walker**] administration.

Reilly's appointment was lauded because he was well-known as an environmentalist. Reilly was head of the Conservation Foundation of the World Wildlife Fund when he was appointed to the EPA. Although he advocated a massive reorganization of the agency, that never materialized. His policies did accelerate the process of cleaning up **hazardous waste** sites, however, and one of his major goals was pollution prevention.

Bush's campaign had stressed his commitment to the environment, and Reilly's appointment was a symbol of that commitment. But Bush's approach to environmental regulation was not aggressive, despite his appointment of Reilly. Continuing the Reagan administration's [see **Reagan, Ronald**] distrust of regulations, Bush placed Dan Quayle at the head of the Council for Competitiveness, which oversaw and diluted environmental initiatives. Reilly was not as effective as either environmentalists or Reilly himself had hoped he would be, though he did uphold the reputation of the EPA.

RELEASE In environmental law, a release is an event in which pollutants are discharged or allowed to escape into the environment. After a release occurs, the person responsible for it may have duties associated with it.

For example, if a hazardous substance [see **hazardous substances**] is placed in a drum and buried, a release may occur after the drum deteriorates. Although the person who created the waste may not know it is now uncontained, he will be potentially responsible for reimbursing the government for its costs if a governmental agency becomes involved in cleaning up the site. This obligation originates in the **Comprehensive Environmental Response, Compensation, and Liability Act** and similar state laws.

Other types of releases, such as an unpermitted discharge of oil or **air pollutant**s, may trigger requirements to notify the government and to respond immediately to contain and clean up the release. The **Oil Pollution Act,** the **Emergency Planning and Community Right-To-Know Act,** the Comprehensive Environmental Response, Compensation, and Liability Act, the **Resource Conservation and Recovery Act,** and the **Clean Water Act** all contain notification and response provisions.

REMEDIAL DESIGN/REMEDIAL ACTION (RD/RA) In a cleanup of a **hazardous waste** site that has been listed as a priority for federal action, specific steps must be taken to determine the methods to be used. The **National Contingency Plan** describes them, along with the roles various people are to play. The remedial design/remedial action phase of the work occurs at the end of the lengthy procedure; it is the actual engineering, construction, and implementation of the cleanup.

Before the RD/RA is begun, the **Environmental Protection Agency** (EPA) issues a **record of decision,** which selects the remedy for either the whole site or for a discrete part of the cleanup. The decision is by no means a surprise; it follows a lengthy study of the site and the wastes that are there as well as detailed analysis of possible remedial methods. That work is done during the **remedial investigation/feasibility study.** All of the information compiled is available to the public, the **potentially responsible parties,** and the state in which the site is located. A proposal of the remedy is published and comments considered before the record of decision becomes final.

The selected remedy must be engineered and constructed before the cleanup can begin, so the RD/RA process sets the cleanup in motion. A work plan is developed with dates for completion of all of the work. Equipment is designed and engineering controls such as trenches and drains are created, along with systems for treatment. A health and safety plan is developed for workers who will be on the site. Then the construction is completed, and the remedial action is started. The RD/RA stage of a cleanup generally lasts about two years.

Work will continue at the site until the cleanup goals have been met. Construction activities, such as digging trenches, building treatment facilities or systems, excavating soil and drums, putting in liners and covers, and placing barriers to migration will be completed early. Some types of cleanup activities—**bioremediation,** pumping and treating groundwater, intercepting surface waters for treatment, removing seepage from collection devices—will continue over many years. During that time, the remediation systems must be maintained and operated. See also **Comprehensive Environmental Response, Compensation, and Liability Act; National Contingency Plan; National Priority List; remediation; Superfund; Superfund Amendments and Reauthorization Act.**

REMEDIAL INVESTIGATION/FEASIBILITY STUDY (RI/FS)

After an abandoned **hazardous waste** site has been listed on the **National Priority List** as a priority for federal cleanup, it moves through a procedure that leads to selection of the remedy. The phase of the process in which the site is thoroughly analyzed and alternatives are evaluated is called the remedial investigation/feasibility study, usually referred to by its acronym, RI/FS.

The RI/FS is a combination of an investigation and feasible alternatives evaluation, but the two overlap, with information from one looped to the other. For example, if data is needed about the type of waste at the site, it is obtained. Then that information is used to help select the methods of treatment, which may be tested in a pilot program. The pilot may result in additional knowledge about the characteristics of the site, which in turn may help fine-tune the remedial action.

These steps are required by the **Superfund** law (the **Comprehensive Environmental Response, Compensation, and Liability Act)** and the **National Contingency Plan,** the set of regulations that specifies how

hazardous substances are to be addressed. The RI/FS may be conducted by one or more of the **potentially responsible parties**—persons who have a legal responsibility to take care of the contamination—or it may be done by a governmental agency or its contractors. If someone other than the government conducts the RI/FS, the government will oversee the work. The only part of the RI/FS the government prefers to do itself is the baseline risk assessment.

The components of the RI/FS include scoping, data gathering, community and state involvement, evaluation of alternative methods of **remediation,** limited studies, and treatability studies. The aim is to determine which remedial techniques will work. The governmental agency, usually the **Environmental Protection Agency** or a state environmental agency, then selects the methods to be used and publishes the selection in an official document called the **record of decision,** or ROD.

Much information is needed to properly evaluate the site. The initial effort is scoping the project. During the scoping, the overall plans are established. For example, the project manager gathers all existing information, develops a concept of the problems posed at the site, determines what questions must be answered, meets with the community and forms a community relations plan, starts identifying the state and federal regulations that may apply to the cleanup, and decides what technologies might address the contamination at the site. A baseline risk assessment is also completed by another governmental group, the **Agency for Toxic Substances and Disease Registry,** so the agency can establish cleanup needs.

The cost and amount of work done at a given site during the RI/FS depends on its complexity, previously gathered data, and the effectiveness of tested technology. For a cleanup to be successful, all of the remedial activities must fit the conditions at the site. Thus, the RI/FS will result in a picture of the geology, topology, ownership, land use, waste volume and character, and anything else that is pertinent. The community will be consulted, interviewed, and informed about all proposed activities.

Alternatives for managing the site are identified early from among technologies. Technologies are broad categories of treatment, such as institutional controls, engineering, and treatment. Within each technology a number of variations may be screened, along with one alternative that must always be considered: the option of doing nothing. Screening of the alternatives identified takes place throughout the RI/FS. The specific type of remediation chosen is called a *process.*

Institutional controls include deed restrictions (to limit future use of the property) and erecting fences and signs (to limit access). Engineering includes installing drains to capture contaminated groundwater, placing an impermeable cap over a waste pile, and building a wall to cut the polluted area off from the rest of the site. Treatment includes digging up the waste and incinerating it, placing specialized microorganisms in the waste to accelerate decay, stabilizing it through a physical or chemical process, or aerating the ground to promote escape of gases.

If a technology is feasible, the RI/FS identifies it and its benefits and shortcomings for the site. Then representative processes are selected and screened. During the screening, studies may be done in a lab or at the site to determine how well the processes will work for the particular site being considered. Each process must be analyzed in detail. At the end of all the study and evaluation, a report is prepared that weighs all the options according to nine separate factors in three categories: threshold criteria, balancing criteria, and modifying criteria. After these criteria are considered, the processes are compared against each other and a proposed plan is recommended.

Unless they are waived, threshold criteria must be met by the processes being considered. Waivers are difficult to obtain, and it is easy to see why. The threshold criteria state that the remedy must provide overall protection of human health and the environment and meet all **applicable or relevant and appropriate requirements,** that is, any state and federal laws that apply. The next set of criteria is balancing criteria. They are short-term effectiveness; long-term effectiveness and permanence; reduction of toxicity, mobility, or volume of waste; implementability; and cost effectiveness. Balancing criteria actually weigh the projected success of the remedy. Finally, the modifying factors are a measure of acceptance of the proposed remedy. In addition to the lead agency's approval, the state must be comfortable with the remedy. Even more important, the community should have confidence in it. If the community or state does not agree with the proposed remedy, it may be modified provided it still meets the threshold criteria and some of the balancing criteria. The remedy has been modified at some sites where the residents are strongly opposed to incineration.

The entire RI/FS process will generally take two years. The final product is the report that will recommend and influence the decision of the agency. A summary of the report will be included in the **record of decision,** the agency document that selects the remedy. See also **bioremediation; cleanup technologies; Hazardous Ranking System; National Priority List; remedial design/remedial action.**

REMEDIATION Any action taken to repair damage to the environment. It may be as complex as a **hazardous waste** site cleanup or as simple as removal of a small quantity of chemicals that have been spilled.

Remediation of hazardous waste sites is typically broken into numerous actions. The source of the problem is isolated, treated, removed, or some combination of those methods. Waste that has migrated is then addressed, including contaminated soils, surface waters, and groundwater. Examples of remedial activites are oil removal from tanker spills, removal and destruction of buried waste, soil vacuuming, incineration, and groundwater pumping and treating.

In some situations, natural resources, such as animal or plant life or wetlands, have been impacted by pollutants. Part of the remediation required in those cases has been restoration. A person who has illegally filled a **wetland,** for example, may have to remove the fill and revegetate the wetland.

REPORTABLE QUANTITY (RQ) The amount of particular **hazardous substances** or **extremely hazardous substance**s that triggers the requirement to report a release to the environment. (Generally this means that the substance left private property.) Reporting requirements for nonhazardous substances depend on the circumstances and what media (air, surface water, groundwater, or earth) were affected.

Hazardous substance reporting is regulated by the **Emergency Planning and Community Right-To-Know Act** and the **Comprehensive Environmental Response, Compensation, and Liability Act.** Reportable quantities are set by the **Environmental Protection Agency.** Depending on the toxicity, corrosivity, flammability, or reactivity of the hazardous substance, the reportable quantity may be as little as a pound or as much as 10,000 pounds.

If the reportable quantity of a substance is released, the person who allowed the release must notify the National Response Center and the Local Area Planning Commission. Also, the person responsible must implement a response plan to contain and clean up the release as quickly as possible.

REQUESTS FOR INFORMATION One of the powers that environmental agencies have is to investigate whether a violation of a law has occurred. Under the **Comprehensive Environmental Response, Compensation, and Liability Act** (CERCLA), the **Environmental Protec-**

tion Agency (EPA) also has a right to find out who is involved in waste disposal at an abandoned **hazardous waste** site. Agencies gather much of their information from the reports required by permits and regulations, but they also send out requests for information. A person who receives such a request must answer it or face enforcement. Letters sent out for this purpose are called Section 104(e) letters, after the section of CERCLA that gives the EPA its authority. The EPA also has similar powers under the **Clean Air Act** (Section 114), the **Clean Water Act** (Section 308), and the **Resource Conservation and Recovery Act** (Section 3007).

RESOURCE CONSERVATION AND RECOVERY ACT (RCRA)
A statute enacted in 1976 to regulate solid and **hazardous waste** disposal. It significantly expanded the previous law, the Solid Waste Disposal Act, by adding a new subtitle that deals with hazardous waste.

The law established a system of tracking hazardous waste from its creation through its disposal. Due to the complexity of the law, the **Environmental Protection Agency** (EPA) acted very slowly to promulgate regulations. The law was amended in 1980, but the most far-reaching amendments were passed in 1984: the **Hazardous and Solid Waste Amendments.** These amendments took on a life of their own due to provisions that forced the EPA to act by a specific date or accept the requirements Congress set forth.

Because the primary programs under RCRA are the hazardous waste and underground **storage tank** provisions, this entry will focus on them. If waste is not hazardous, the federal role is insignificant compared to the state's role. If it is hazardous or if it relates to underground storage tanks, the states may administer the federal law by getting the federal government to delegate the responsibility to them. State regulations cannot be less stringent than federal regulations, but they may be more so.

Hazardous Waste Defined

To be considered hazardous waste, a substance must be (1) solid, (2) waste, and (3) either listed as a hazardous waste or have characteristics that make it hazardous. *Solid* goes well beyond the usual meaning to include liquids, semisolids, and contained gases, as well as solid substances. *Waste* is something discarded or abandoned. The waste's character must be determined by testing—unless the person creating the waste already knows its composition—or by referring to the EPA's lists of **hazardous substances**.

The EPA has listed numerous substances as hazardous wastes; these are called **listed wastes**. If the solid waste is not on the list but is ignitable, reactive, corrosive, or toxic, it is also hazardous waste and is called a **characteristic waste**. Listed waste may be delisted by the EPA on a case-by-case basis, if a **generator** files a petition with the agency and proves its particular waste is not hazardous. Some solid waste is exempted from being considered hazardous waste through regulatory provisions. Household waste, agricultural waste that is returned to the ground, mining overburden returned to the site, utility wastes from coal burning, and oil or gas exploration drilling waste are examples of exempted solid wastes.

Other materials are exempted from some, but not all, of the regulations. They include hazardous waste burned for energy recovery, precious metals, and spent lead acid batteries, providing they are recycled. A few categories are totally exempt, provided they fall within the specification. Examples are industrial ethyl alcohol, scrap metal, reclaimed oil, and used batteries returned to the battery manufacturer. The emphasis in these exclusions is on recovery of usable products, energy, and recycling.

Scope of the Hazardous Waste Regulations

The Resource Conservation and Recovery Act aims to control hazardous waste throughout its life. It is called a *cradle-to-grave* law, and that description is apt.

RCRA focuses on three classes of people: generators, transporters, and owners or operators of treatment/storage/disposal facilities [see **treatment/storage/disposal facility**]. Generators are the first link in the chain: whoever first causes the substance to become waste is a generator. Transporters move the waste from the generator or another transporter to another facility or another transporter. The treatment/storage/disposal facility usually treats or disposes of the waste, but it may simply store it.

If we begin with the idea that RCRA aims to control all handling and disposal of hazardous waste, the regulations are logical. Each class of handlers—generators, transporters, and owners/operators of treatment/storage/disposal facilities—must notify the EPA of its hazardous waste activities. (A small portion of generators who create only small amounts of waste do not have to comply with all of the RCRA provisions, although they must properly manage and dispose of the small amounts they have.) An identification number must be obtained by each of the facilities involved in hazardous waste handling.

Hazardous waste is tracked through the system by means of a document called a Uniform Hazardous Waste Manifest, which originates with the generator. At least four copies are required, but more may be necessary, depending on the number of hands the waste passes through and state requirements. The generator prepares the manifest and gives it to the transporter. Transporters of hazardous waste cannot accept hazardous waste without a manifest. The manifest is a critical document that includes identification of the waste, the amount, the generator's identification number and pertinent data, and the name and address of the designated recipient of the hazardous waste. The transporter must sign the manifest and leave a copy with the generator when accepting the waste for transport. The manifest is delivered to the next transporter or the treatment/storage/disposal facility in the same manner. Each party that handles the waste keeps a signed copy indicating the person to whom it was delivered. The final recipient, the treatment/storage/disposal facility, must send a signed and dated manifest back to the generator. Copies must be kept for at least three years. If the generator does not receive a copy of the manifest within 45 days, it must file a report with the EPA.

Transporters of hazardous waste must obtain EPA identification numbers, state licenses if required, and follow Department of Transportation regulations on transporting **hazardous materials**. They are responsible for emergency response and containment if a spill occurs during transportation, as well as notifying the appropriate agency concerning the event.

Treatment/storage/disposal facilities, a classification that includes not only the facilities where the hazardous wastes are stored but also recycling and reclamation facilities, are subject to technical, financial, and management requirements. For example, the generator of hazardous waste may have to comply with the requirements for treatment/storage/disposal facilities if it stores hazardous waste for a period greater than ninety days or reclaims the waste so it can be reused in its processes. Some generators dispose of their hazardous waste on their own property; if that is the case, their facilities are treatment/storage/disposal facilities.

RCRA regulations prescribe the controls necessary for treatment/storage/disposal facilities. In general, they must apply for and obtain a permit in order to operate. The only exception is the interim status facility, which must submit an application but may continue to operate while it is being processed. Permitted facilities and interim status facilities are responsible for managing the hazardous waste so it will not escape from where it is placed. They must provide for cleanup if previous disposals result in a release of hazardous wastes, and they must have closure plans for each unit where hazardous waste is treated, stored, or disposed of. In addition, owners and operators of these facilities must demonstrate that they have the financial ability to deal with releases, closure, and postclosure care.

Treatment facilities are those that use any method to change the chemical, physical, or biological character of the hazardous waste. The definition is broad enough to encompass virtually anything that can be done to hazardous waste to make it less hazardous, recover any part of the waste, reduce its volume, or neutralize it. A manufacturer that reuses spent solvents in its processes is a treatment facility if it must first treat those solvents. Storage facilities hold hazardous waste temporarily, then send the waste somewhere else for disposal. As noted above, most generators become storage facilities if they hold hazardous waste on site for more than ninety days. Disposal facilities keep the hazardous waste somewhere on site, even after the site ceases operation. Many kinds of disposal facilities exist: landfills, containment buildings, incinerators, surface impoundments, tanks, and chemical, physical, and biological treatment units. However, restrictions now prohibit untreated hazardous waste from being land disposed.

All of the parties involved in handling hazardous waste must maintain records of their activities. They have reporting requirements, training requirements, and are subject to inspections.

Enforcement of RCRA, Subtitle C

The hazardous waste provisions found in RCRA may be enforced in many different ways. The EPA may issue **administrative order**s, assess penalties, sue in federal court, bring criminal actions, obtain injunctions, and force the cleanup of hazardous waste units when appropriate. Civil penalties may be as high as $25,000 per day; criminal penalties involving a business may reach $1 million. For individuals, the maximum penalty is $250,000 for a criminal violation and imprisonment up to 15 years.

The Underground Storage Tank Provisions of RCRA

In 1984, Congress developed a new program in the Hazardous and Solid Waste Amendments to RCRA to deal with underground storage tanks. The new provisions, found in Subtitle I, quickly changed the practice of burying tanks without thought. They also imposed numerous requirements on the underground storage tanks that were already in place when the new program began.

Underground storage tanks are a common means of holding liquids. Many of them contain some type of petroleum, such as heating oil, gasoline, diesel fuel, or used oil. Most of those in the ground in 1984 were made of bare steel, which corrodes over time. The Environmental Protection Agency estimates that in 1988, two million underground storage tanks existed in the United States at approximately 700,000 different locations. The EPA believes at least 75 percent have leaked or will leak in the future. A 1992 estimate of costs associated with leaking tanks is $41 billion dollars.

RCRA regulates petroleum tanks as one object and hazardous substances as another. This entry covers the petroleum underground storage tank regulations, because they are the most defined.

Registration and Technical Specifications

The first mandate of the regulations is for registration. What happens after that depends on whether the tank already existed or was installed after the regulations took effect. Existing tanks must be upgraded; new tanks must meet the technical requirements when they are installed. Deadlines for upgrading vary according to the age of the tank, but the last deadline for upgrade is in 1998.

Typical criteria for underground storage tank upgrades include the addition of spill and overfill protection and cathodic protection to guide electrical energy away from the tank. Tanks must also be tested periodically to make sure they are still tight. Multiple tests to detect leaks are required, such as checking with a paste for water in the tank and inventory control monitoring.

New tanks avoid many of the maintenance problems of older tanks. Fiberglass, double-wall construction, built-in alarms, automatic shut-off devices to prevent overfilling, and other advances make new tanks less likely to release their contents. Installation is safer also, since installers are now required to be trained and certified by the regulating agency.

Upgrade and new tank specifications are not the only provisions of the underground storage tank regulations, however. The owner or operator of these tanks has a number of other duties: monitoring, recordkeeping, reporting, investigation of releases, and corrective action if a release occurs.

Reporting, Response, and Investigation

Suspected releases of petroleum from an underground storage tank must be reported within 24 hours under the federal law. Many states specify other time periods, ranging from "immediately" to the full 24 hours. The owner or operator need not be certain that a release has occurred before he or she is obligated to report a release. Petroleum odors, alarm activation, unexplained loss of fuel, or any unusual operating condition triggers the requirement to report.

An immediate response is required if the release can be contained, stopped, or cleaned up. Situations that require immediate response include overspills, threat of fire or explosion, or floating product visible on water. If the source of the release cannot be isolated, it may be necessary to drain the tank. Spills of 25 gallons or less need not be reported under federal law unless a sheen is visible on water, but they must be cleaned up.

After a suspected release is reported, the owner or operator must begin an investigation to either confirm or disprove the release. Federal law allows seven days for the investigation. Written notice must also be supplied to the environmental agency responsible for the underground storage tank program, usually a state or county agency.

Site Characterization and Remediation

Next, assuming a confirmed release, the owner or operator must characterize the site, which involves evaluating the amount of the release, the soil type, groundwater depth and impact as well as analysis of soils and water. These factors determine what type of corrective action plan is necessary. The owner/operator then prepares the corrective action plan and submits it along with the site characterization report to the environmental agency responsible for the site. Before remediation begins, the agency should approve the plan. The owner or operator then starts work on cleaning up the contamination. A closure report is prepared after the remediation is complete.

Corrective action at underground storage tank sites may be as simple as removing some soil and as complicated as putting in a groundwater pumping and treating system. Bioremediation (use of specialty organisms to break down the contamination) can be effective if the climate is right. For some soil contamination, wells can be put in and a vacuum applied to suck out hydrocarbons.

Owners and operators must clean up the damage caused by a release from their tanks. They must also address the problem that caused the release, which may require repair, upgrade, or a total replacement of the tank and piping.

Closure and Abandonment in Place

Tanks may be *closed*. A closure occurs when the tank is removed from the ground or pumped out and filled with sand, concrete, or other inert substance. The owner or operator of an underground storage tank scheduled for closure must notify the environmental agency in advance, often 30 days before the closure.

If the tank is pulled out of the ground, soil samples must taken from the walls and floor of the cavity where the tank was. Those samples must be tested to determine whether contamination exists or the hole is clean. If it is clean, the soil may be replaced in the cavity. If it exceeds the state contaminant levels, the owner or operator begins the the process of remediation. Often, small amounts of impacted soil can be removed and sent to a recycling facility. However, if contamination is extensive, the owner or operator must develop a corrective action plan and get agency approval for remedial work.

Most states restrict abandonment or in-place closure. Some require a notice on deeds if the property contains an abandoned tank. A situation that favors an in-place closure would be if the removal of the tank would threaten the integrity of a building or other structure.

Tank owners and operators who leave a tank in the ground still have to make sure it has not leaked. Groundwater monitoring wells are likely to be required, as well as soil sampling. Cleanup follows if contamination is discovered. The cost of abandonment is about the same as removal.

Financial Responsibility

Since investigation and cleanup can be costly, owners and operators of underground storage tanks must demonstrate their financial ability to take care of any harm caused by a release [see **financial responsibility**]. They may use a number of different methods, such as insurance, self-insurance, guarantee, trust fund, or state trust funds. The amount of financial capability necessary depends on the number of tanks and type of business the owner or operator is in.

Conclusion

RCRA resulted from growing public awareness. By 1984, when RCRA finally became a dynamic and effective statute, Americans knew they could not bury all their wastes and forget them. Hazardous waste sites are hard to handle once they start causing environmental and health problems. RCRA, therefore, aims to prevent future problems by regulating hazardous waste from the time it enters the waste stream until it is disposed of, recycled, or destroyed. See also **characteristic waste; corrective action; derived-from rule; mixture rule; solid waste management unit.**

RUCKELSHAUS, WILLIAM D. (1932–) The first administrator of the **Environmental Protection Agency** (EPA). He was appointed by President Richard M. Nixon and remained during part of President Gerald R. Ford's tenure. During Ronald Reagan's presidency [see **Reagan, Ronald**], Mr. Ruckelshaus returned as head of the EPA after the scandal involving Anne Burford [see **Burford, Anne Gorsuch**] became public knowledge. He restored the EPA's mission and silenced criticism of the way the agency was run.

SAFE DRINKING WATER ACT (SDWA)

SAFE DRINKING WATER ACT (SDWA) Passed in 1974, this law regulates water quality in public water supply (PWS) systems but does not cover some small systems and excludes private drinking water sources such as private wells. The goals of the SDWA are to ensure that water from the tap is safe to drink and protect groundwater from contamination. It is the only law that directly deals with groundwater quality, though two other laws, the **Resource Conservation and Recovery Act** and the **Comprehensive Environmental Response, Compensation, and Liability Act,** provide for cleanup of contaminated groundwater. Government officials rely on the SDWA's standards during a cleanup to determine the acceptable level of contaminants.

The public water supply systems covered by the SDWA are those serving at least 25 people having at least 15 service connections. When determining whether the system fits the definition, the key is whether an average of 25 individuals use the water daily at least 60 days a year. It does not matter how the water is used, as long as human consumption is anticipated. Thus, it includes water supplies used for bathing, cooking, dishwashing, and oral hygiene. It also includes water supplies for schools, factories, and offices.

National Primary Drinking Water Standards

Under the law, the **Environmental Protection Agency** (EPA) sets two types of drinking water standards, the National Primary Drinking Water Standards and the National Secondary Drinking Water Standards. The primary standards are enforceable because they relate to health; the secondary standards are not enforceable because they deal with aesthetics. The SDWA lists 83 contaminants for which the EPA was required to set drinking water standards. The EPA must also identify more contaminants for regulation every three years.

The primary standards establish **maximum contaminant levels** (MCLs). MCLs are usually numerical limits, stated in terms of milligrams of a designated pollutant per liter of water. If the maximum contaminant level

271

cannot be economically or technically determined for a particular contaminant, the EPA specifies treatment technology that will assure a dependable, safe water supply. Before setting the National Primary Drinking Water Standards, the EPA goes through an involved process to set maximum contaminant level goals (MCLGs). A goal is defined in the regulations and statute as the "maximum level of a contaminant in drinking water at which no known or anticipated adverse effect on the health of persons would occur, and which allows an adequate margin of safety." MCLGs are not enforceable; they are the ideals by which the MCL standards are measured.

For noncarcinogens, the goal for each contaminant is set by referring to a "reference dose," which is an estimate of the amount of a contaminant to which a person could be exposed everyday during a lifetime without an appreciable risk of having negative health effects. The EPA assumes that a person will drink two liters of water a day for seventy years.

If the contaminant is a carcinogen, the goal is determined differently. For chemicals that are strongly carcinogenic, the goal is automatically zero, because the EPA cannot decide a safe level of exposure. If the evidence about the contaminant's carcinogenic properties is limited, the EPA uses the reference dose described above, but adds an extra margin of safety to account for possible cancer effects.

After the maximum contaminant level goals are set, the EPA must establish the enforceable limits, the maximum containment levels. The Safe Drinking Water Act requires the EPA to set them as close as "feasible" to the MCLGs. The statute goes on to define what Congress meant by "feasible": "the term means feasible with the use of the best technology, treatment techniques, and other means . . . after examination for efficacy under field conditions and not solely under laboratory conditions, are available, taking cost into consideration." [SDWA, §1412(5)] Using the statute as a roadmap, the EPA considers the following factors while setting the MCLs: (1) technological removal efficiencies, compatibility with other water treatments, and availability; (2) degree to which a specified technology can remove the contaminant in a large water supply system with relatively clean raw water; (3) cost of technology use to large public water suppliers and the nation if the technology is the basis of the MCL; and (4) whether testing laboratories could accurately and consistently determine the contaminant level. The EPA also considers whether the MCL, if based on a particular technology, is protective of human health.

When the EPA sets the MCL for a contaminant, it is required to also publish the maximum contaminant level goal and specify the treatment technology used as the basis for the MCL. Public water suppliers need not use that specific technology if an MCL exists; they need only meet the numerical standard.

If the EPA decides it is economically or technologically unfeasible to determine an MCL for a specific contaminant, it can require the use of a particular technology. However, the aim is still to get the level of contaminants as close as possible to the maximum contaminant level goals. Selection of a technology would be done with the goal in mind, as opposed to an MCL.

The SDWA directs the EPA to establish two additional standards that apply to public water suppliers that draw their raw water from surface waters or groundwater that is closely influenced by surface water. Those standards govern filtration and disinfection. The EPA published the regulations in 1989. It requires states to analyze each public water supply within its borders and determine which systems are subject to the rules. The filtration and disinfection standards are the only two National Primary Drinking Water Standards that currently specify treatment technology in lieu of MCLs.

A public water supply can get a variance or exemption from the standards because of cost or availability of technology and quality of the raw water supply. Exemptions and variances are considered critical to the survival of some small public water supply systems. However, any variances or exemptions must require eventual compliance and cannot be granted if the water would pose an unreasonable risk to health. Hearings must be held before variances or exemptions can be allowed.

Most states have legal authority to enforce if a public water supply is out of compliance with the primary standards. Even in states with delegated programs, the EPA cannot enforce unless it first notifies the state about the violation and gives it thirty days to act. However, the EPA may act immediately if imminent or substantial danger to the public exists.

Public water supplies that are in violation of the standards are subject to penalties, but they must also notify their customers and the government. Notices of most violations must be published in the newspaper, with a follow-up in the mail. If an acute risk to the public may result, radio and television announcements are necessary.

Lead and Copper Elimination

The SDWA addresses a contaminant that plagues many public water supplies: lead. Lead has leached into water supplies from lead pipes or pipes repaired using lead. Particularly harmful to children, lead has been linked to severe damage to intelligence as well as acute poisoning. Effective 16 June 1986, repairs to public water supplies and new installations must be lead free. When a lead problem exists, those who manage public water supplies must inform their customers of the problem and its source, the adverse effects, ways to eliminate the lead, measures being taken to solve the problem, and whether an alternate water supply should be obtained.

In 1988, Congress amended the law to add another source of lead in water to its prohibitions: drinking water coolers. The EPA listed brands and models of water coolers that contained lead, and those listed could no longer be sold. The Consumer Product Safety Commission is responsible for determining how to repair them.

Copper may also leach into drinking water from pipes. It has not been as highly regulated as lead, but the EPA has added it to the regulations that deal with lead. Copper must be measured along with lead, and public water supplies must have a program that reduces corrosion in pipes. If the lead or copper in drinking water from taps is above the action level set by the EPA, treatment is required. The states work with the public water supplies to determine what type of corrosion control treatments must be used.

Underground Injection Control (UIC)

Concerned that injection wells would contaminate the groundwater, Congress established a permitting system for those that might endanger an underground source of drinking water as an important component of the SDWA [see **underground injection control**]. The permitting system, like the rest of the SDWA requirements, is primarily the responsibility of the states.

Underground injection wells include any structure, shaft, or hole deeper than it is wide in which fluids are placed. *Fluids* are any substance that moves. Before a new well is constructed, the person who wants to use it must apply for a permit. The regulating agency, either the EPA or the state, will consider the structural integrity of the well and emplacement of fluids. The regulating agency will also consider the topography and geological characteristics of the location. The requirements for underground injection wells depend on the nearness of the well to drinking water sources and the type of fluids to be injected.

Some well injections are not regulated by permit, either because the groundwater is already heavily contaminated or because the presence of the well would neither impact the public water supply's ability to meet the

National Primary Drinking Water Standards nor adversely affect human health. The permit program's emphasis is on preventing endangerment of drinking water. It protects only underground sources of drinking water, so the groundwater must actually be or reasonably be expected to become a source of drinking water.

Hazardous waste injection is governed by the **Resource Conservation and Recovery Act,** but a SDWA permit is also required. The SDWA permit system divides underground injection wells into five classes. Class I wells are those that inject fluids below the lowest level of a drinking water formation. Class II wells are used by the oil and gas industry, usually to inject water produced during extraction. Class III wells are used by mining industries for fluids used to aid in extraction of ore. Class IV wells are no longer allowed but were previously used for **hazardous waste** and radioactive material. Class V wells include all other underground injection wells, such as cesspools, septic systems, and wells associated with recovery of geothermal energy. They are authorized by rule instead of by a specific permit, but the owner must notify the government of their existence.

Miscellaneous Provisions

SDWA encourages development of wellhead protection programs to prevent contamination of wells that supply public water supplies, and grants are given to states that develop programs. So far slightly more than half of the states have some type of wellhead protection programs. The program must include the designation of agencies that will carry out the duties and state what the duties are; establish the area around wellheads that need protection; identify potential sources of contamination within the wellhead area; specify a plan to protect the area from the specified contaminants; and include a contingency plan to obtain alternate water supplies if contamination occurs.

Another provision of the SDWA establishes the EPA's authority to designate some aquifers as sole source aquifers. Once an aquifer is classified a sole source aquifer, no federal financial assistance can be given to any project that might damage it. The law also provided for grants to states that had designated sole source aquifers by 1988, but Congress never appropriated funds for the grants. The major reason for having a sole source aquifer is political: it reinforces public awareness of the value of the drinking water source.

SARA, TITLE III   The nickname for the **Emergency Response and Community Right-To-Know Act.** It was part of the **Superfund Amendments and Reauthorization Act** passed in 1986. The name comes from the acronym and the specific title that contains the provisions.

SCRUBBER   Air pollution technology that uses chemical reaction or absorption to remove pollutants from a polluted waste stream. A scrubber often uses a spray or mist and operates by causing the pollutant to precipitate so that it can be removed. Scrubbers are often used effectively for **sulfur dioxide**s generated through combustion of fossil fuels. See also **air pollution control technology; Clean Air Act; Clean Air Act Amendments of 1990.**

SECONDARY TREATMENT   Processes used by municipal wastewater treatment plants to reduce the amount of pollution released to surface waters. Primary treatment is simply removal of solids, done by flotation or settlement; secondary treatment usually involves the use of bacteria to break down the pollutants, followed by disinfection.

Now that the wastewater treatment plants are required to meet secondary treatment standards, a third level of treatment, tertiary treatment will be added. It involves further removal of suspended solids, nitrogen, and phosphorus. See also **Clean Water Act; National Pollutant Discharge Elimination System; publicly owned treatment works; water pollution control technologies.**

SIERRA CLUB   An organization founded in 1892 by John Muir. It is dedicated to environmental concerns and uses a number of methods to influence decisions: public education, lobbying, lawsuits, and involvement in administrative processes. The Sierra Club welcomes members.

The mission statement of the Sierra Club is broad: "To explore, enjoy, and protect the wild places of the earth; to practice and promote the responsible use of the earth's ecosystems and resources; to educate and enlist humanity to protect and restore the quality of natural and human environment; and to use all lawful means to carry out these objectives." The organization accomplishes these goals through political action committees, publication of books and a periodical, a legal defense fund, a foundation that sponsors a wide variety of activities, and an international group.

SIGNIFICANT NEW USE RULE (SNUR) Under the **Toxic Substances Control Act,** a person who wishes to manufacture or import a new chemical must register it with the **Environmental Protection Agency** (EPA) prior to beginning that activity if the chemical is not on the chemical inventory. Along with other required information, the intended use of the chemical must be specified. If it is different from the uses noted for it on the inventory, the EPA issues a significant new use rule.

After a SNUR is issued, persons who intend to import the chemical or use it in the new way must give ninety days prior notice to the EPA in a significant new use notice (SNUN). For the purpose of this procedure, the EPA considers significant to include much more than one might suppose. For example, a large production increase, change in location of manufacturing, or exposure of greater numbers of people to the chemical are all deemed to be significant new uses.

SOLID WASTE According to the **Resource Conservation and Recovery Act,** which governs **hazardous waste** and some solid waste, a wide variety of matter is included in the definition of solid waste: garbage, refuse, and sludge from a water treatment plant, water supply plant, or air pollution control facility in solid, semisolid, liquid, or contained gaseous form unless it is expressly excluded from the definition.

In order to be labeled solid waste, the material must also be discarded or abandoned, but that concept, too, is very broad. Intent is important here; if it is no longer being used by the owner, or if the owner does not intend to use it, it is considered discarded or abandoned, even if it actually remains on the owner's premises.

SOLID WASTE MANAGEMENT UNIT (SWMU) Any part of a **treatment/storage/disposal facility** that is used for solid waste placement, treatment, or storage. Each SWMU is considered a discrete part of the overall facility. These units are important when the business ceases operation entirely or stops using part of the facility for waste management, since they must be closed.

If, for example, a waste disposal facility has an incinerator that is later replaced by another incinerator, the first incinerator is considered a SWMU, so it must be properly *closed*. This may entail no more than cleaning the equipment to ensure that no **hazardous waste** residues remain, or it may require cleaning and dismantling the unit.

Landfills must also be closed when they reach capacity. For landfills, part of the closure will be putting in monitoring wells to make sure the groundwater does not become contaminated. Other safeguards include drainage for leachate, a special cover for the surface to retard the flow of rainwater into the unit, and a collection system for runoff.

The **Resource Conservation and Recovery Act** governs hazardous waste treatment/storage/and disposal facilities. All permitted facilities are obligated to clean up any solid waste management unit any time a release is discovered. This cleanup is called **corrective action,** and it is one of the provisions of every permit.

SPILL PREVENTION CONTROL AND COUNTERMEASURES (SPCC) PLAN A plan required by the **Clean Water Act** for some **storage tank**s that may release oil into surface water. An aboveground storage tank with a capacities of over 660 gallons, or two or more aboveground storage tanks with more than 1320 gallons capacity may be subject to the requirements. Underground tanks with a capacity of more than 40,000 gallons also fall into the volume class covered.

The other factor that determines whether an SPCC plan is required is the likelihood that water will be impacted if a release occurs. The owner or operator of the facility must consider the location of the tanks, topography, and other physical aspects of the facility. If a plan is required, it must address how the owner or operator will react to a release from the tank and how releases will be prevented. The plan must be certified by an engineer and kept on site. If the facility changes so that the plan is no longer valid, it must be amended.

The **Oil Pollution Act** of 1990 beefed up the requirements for SPCC plans. The Clean Water Act's SPCC provision has included onshore facilities for some time, but the Oil Pollution Act added SPCC provisions for tank vessels and offshore facilities. The new law has now been incorporated into the Clean Water Act.

SPCC plans must address response to a worst-case discharge. They must be consistent with the **National Contingency Plan,** which governs hazardous substance [see **hazardous substances**] release cleanups, even though petroleum is excluded from the definition of hazardous substance under the **Comprehensive Environmental Response, Compensation, and Liability Act.** All plans must specify a person at the facility who has authority to exercise the plan; require immediate notification to the appropriate agency; provide for training, unannounced drills, and equipment testing; and arrange for response personnel to be obtained. Reports must be made to the National Response Center in the event of a release.

Enforcement of the SPCC provisions is similar to that of other Clean Water Act sections. The government may assess administrative penalties up to $125,000 for violations. If the EPA sues, the authorized penalty is $25,000 per day or $1,000 per barrel of oil, and it may be tripled if gross negligence or misconduct is involved. Criminal penalties may range up to $250,000 for an individual and $1 million for an organization, plus imprisonment for up to 15 years.

STANDING A qualification for bringing a lawsuit. Before a person has the right to sue, it must have a protectable interest in the outcome. For example, the defendant in the case must have caused or threatened to cause an injury that will harm the plaintiff. It is not enough to have an intellectual or philosophical interest in the outcome; the plaintiff must be able to show that he or she is directly involved.

For environmental cases, the concept of standing was difficult at first. Public interest groups might value a natural resource that will be injured by proposed development, but that type of interest is too general to confer standing. On the other hand, if particular members of the group allege that they use the resource and their enjoyment will be directly harmed, the group may be able to bring the lawsuit on their behalf.

Early environmental cases spelled out a number of principles involved in standing. In *Sierra Club v. Morton,* decided in 1972, the Supreme Court denied standing to the **Sierra Club,** which was trying to stop development of Mineral King Valley. However, the complaint did not allege that Sierra Club members used the area or that they would be affected by the development. The court stated the person seeking review must be among the injured and there must be an injury in fact: "Mere interest in a problem by a representative of the public is not enough."

In 1973, an organization called Students Challenging Regulatory Agency Procedures (SCRAP) sued the Interstate Commerce Commission because it allowed an increase in rail rates for recyclable materials. SCRAP members, law students from the Washington, D.C., area, alleged that members would be harmed because natural resource use would increase and air pollution in the area would worsen. In *United States v. Students Challenging Regulatory Agency Procedures,* the Supreme Court found that the organization had standing.

A later case, *Duke Power Company v. Carolina Environmental Study Group*, was based on a challenge to a statute that allowed two nuclear power plants to be constructed. Individuals who lived in the area joined together and sued for future possible harm, present fear, and thermal pollution and radioactive emissions. The Supreme Court found standing on the issues of thermal pollution and radioactive emissions but was unconvinced on the other issues.

Lujan v. National Wildlife Federation, a 1990 decision, questioned the validity of the *United States v. Students Challenging Regulatory Agency Procedures* case. The National Wildlife Federation had sued the Department of Interior for its program to allow reclassification of lands so they can be used for mining. Although the members alleged that their recreational and aesthetic enjoyment of public lands would be injured by the reclassification, the Supreme Court held that the allegations were not specific enough. In the court's opinion, the challenge was premature and the plaintiffs had to wait until a particular piece of property was reclassified.

Attacks on agency actions and against persons who are alleged to be violating environmental laws may be authorized by statute. In those situations, usually based on **citizen suit** provisions of various environmental laws, the plaintiff must simply show that he or she is included in the group allowed to sue. The **Administrative Procedure Act** also gives standing to certain persons who are or may be injured by an **administrative agency**'s action.

STATE EMERGENCY RESPONSE COMMISSION (SERC) A commission, appointed by the governor of a state, responsible for coordinating and approving the emergency response plans required under the **Emergency Planning and Community Right-To-Know Act**. Because states have a larger role than the federal government in making the law work, the SERCs are critical.

STATE IMPLEMENTATION PLAN (SIP) A state plan for regulating air pollution required by the **Clean Air Act** to ensure that states meet the **National Ambient Air Quality Standards**. The **Environmental Protection Agency** (EPA) establishes limits for **air pollutants** that it determines must be controlled to protect human health and the environment. States are then required to prepare a state implementation plan outlining how the state will achieve the standards. State implementation plans must be at least as stringent as any part of the statute or any regulations the EPA has published. The state must have legislative authority to handle the administrative aspects of the air control program, and it must have the right to enforce its law.

Over the past twenty years or so, guidance has become more detailed on what must be included in the SIP. At first the guidance came primarily from the EPA, but Congress stepped in in 1990 when it amended the Clean Air Act, and requirements can be found both in regulations and the statute itself.

After the SIP is prepared, it must be submitted to the EPA, which will decide whether it meets the conditions for approval. The EPA may approve or disapprove the SIP; it may approve only part of the state plan, disapprove part, or request further revisions. Until it is approved by the EPA, it is state law only and can only be enforced by the state. After approval, it becomes federal law as well, and either the EPA or the state can enforce it. If the state involved does not submit an approvable plan within the time specified by the EPA or Congress, a federal implementation plan will be prepared by the EPA.

States may revise their SIPs as they wish, but any changes must be submitted to the EPA. The EPA has power to force amendments to the SIP if it decides that the plan is no longer adequate or does not include necessary changes reflecting federal law. This action by the EPA is labeled an SIP call. If the EPA issues regulations for a newly listed pollutant, the states must revise their state implementation plans to incorporate the new criteria. Congress may also specify—as it did in 1990—that amendments to the SIPs must be made to conform with the statute.

Even though a state cannot have a SIP that allows more air pollution than federal law does, it is permitted to include measures that will result in better control of air pollution. Most SIPs tend to follow federal law, though, sometimes by incorporating federal regulations almost verbatim. However, a state may choose to go beyond those standards.

STATIONARY SOURCE A facility with a fixed location that emits pollutants and is regulated by an environmental statute. The term is most widely used when discussing **Clean Air Act** requirements but could also be applied to facilities that discharge pollutants in other forms. A stationary source could be a manufacturing plant, production facility, office complex, treatment facility, or any other permanent or semi-permanent structure. Stationary sources can be expected to have cumulative affects on their surroundings, so if they discharge enough pollution, they will be subject to permitting and pollution control requirements.

The law distinguishes between stationary sources and **mobile sources** or temporary sources. Both mobile sources and temporary sources are controlled, but different legal provisions apply to them. See also **Clean Air Act Amendments of 1990.**

STORAGE TANK A container used to store liquid or gaseous material. Storage tanks are either aboveground storage tanks (ASTs) or underground storage tanks (USTs). An underground tank is one with 10 percent or more of its volume below ground. The definition does not include storage tanks in basements, however, if the tank rests on the floor and not in the ground.

Underground storage tanks are regulated under federal law unless they fall within an exception. The states also regulate underground storage tanks, and state laws are often more stringent than the federal requirements. The federal law that applies is the **Resource Conservation and Recovery Act.** Most underground storage tanks contain a petroleum product, such as gasoline, diesel, oil, or other fuel.

Underground storage tanks were targeted for regulation because a release can occur under the surface of the earth and be undetected for a long time, causing much damage. Older tanks (those installed before 1984) were often made of steel, and they tend to develop holes from corrosion. After the Resource Conservation and Recovery Act was amended by the **Hazardous and Solid Waste Amendments** in 1984, it required registration of underground storage tanks, reports of releases, upgrades of the tanks to make them safer, new standards for new tanks, closure procedures, and financial responsibility for cleanups. All existing underground storage tanks must be upgraded by 1998 or taken out of service.

Aboveground storage tanks have not been heavily regulated by the federal government. The federal law that applies to some aboveground tanks is the **Clean Water Act,** which may require the development of a **spill prevention control and countermeasures plan.** If they do not store **hazardous wastes,** they fall primarily under state and local jurisdictions. Some states regulate aboveground storage tanks similarly to underground storage tanks; others use fire codes to deal with them.

The reasons for a lessened standard for aboveground storage tanks are simple: a release is easier to see, and the tanks do not corrode as quickly if they are not buried. However, large aboveground storage tanks can cause significant environmental problems if a release occurs. As a result, states are becoming more particular about them, and an effort to regulate them under the Resource Conservation and Recovery Act has been pending in Congress for several terms.

To lessen the possibility of damage from underground and large aboveground storage tanks, the Clean Water Act and the **Oil Pollution Act** impose requirements on owners or operators of certain tanks. Facilities with tanks of specific sizes must have a spill prevention control and countermeasures plan if a release from them would cause damage to surface waters. These plans are largely preventive but also contain provisions for responding to a spill.

STORMWATER RUNOFF   The flow of precipitation over land until it reaches water. The **Clean Water Act** was originally designed to control *point source* discharges or those that came from a pipe or other conduit. Stormwater has not been controlled until recently.

In cities, stormwater picks up oil and grease from streets, then washes them into storm sewers. At an industrial complex, water could pick up chemicals and wastes, carrying them to a stream or a sewer. In either case, untreated water is discharged. So in 1987, Congress amended the Clean Water Act and established a permitting program for stormwater discharges. Large cities, most industrial facilities, and large construction projects (involving disturbance of five acres) are subject to stormwater permitting.

The essence of stormwater control is management of the runoff through various techniques, including channeling and water treatment. Also, storage areas may have to be redesigned so the water does not come in contact with pollutants.

STRICT LIABILITY   A standard used to determine whether a particular action or connection with an activity should be the primary basis for holding the actor responsible for damages caused by the activity. The concept does not require proof of fault.

Strict liability evolved as a theory in tort law, the branch of law that deals with private injuries, and has its roots in social issues. At first, it was imposed only in situations where the activity was ultrahazardous yet useful to society. For example, dynamiting an area to clear it may be justified, but it is hazardous, even when dynamiters are careful. Courts created a compromise of sorts so such activities could be carried out but innocent bystanders would be compensated for their injuries without having to prove **negligence.** The idea was an extension of a long-standing rule that if a person kept animals and they escaped and caused damage, the owner was responsible for any damage.

Historical Development

Strict liability in tort has its origins in an English case from 1866, *Rylands v. Fletcher,* which involved a water reservoir created by a mill owner on his own property. The mill owner's diversion of the water eventually resulted in its escape into an abandoned mine shaft. A neighbor was mining in an adjacent mine, and the water traveled into the active mine. When deciding the case, the court did not have a theory of liability to use that directly applied to the facts. There had been no negligence, and the court ruled out nuisance. However, a wrong had been done, so the court borrowed from the law about trespassing cattle. The law of the case formed the basis of strict liability.

Strict liability is not as onerous as many believe. To find strict liability for an activity on one's own property, the court must determine that it is either abnormal or unusual within the community and poses a great danger to others, even if it is done properly. For example, an oil well is not unusual in parts of Texas, but drilling in one's backyard in a residential community is an abnormal use of the land. Strict liability is not appropriate in the first situation but is in the second, if someone is injured.

Product Liability

Tort law reflects society's values. As a result, new theories evolve from time to time to address contemporary situations. When manufacturing and mass production began, courts had no explicit way of addressing injuries caused by those products. For example, in one case decided in 1842, *Winterbottom v. Wright,* a passenger injured in a coach that collapsed could not get damages because the passenger did not have a direct contract with the person who was supposed to repair the vehicle.

Quickly courts began to see a problem with that approach. *Privity of contract* had been a reliable way of limiting liability to the first sale of goods. Privity of contract is the relationship between the parties to a contract. Before the Industrial Revolution, it was often used as a bar to a lawsuit, because the plaintiff could only sue the person with whom he had dealt directly. As an example, if Tom bought an axle from a person who did not make it, he could not sue the person who made it if it was defective because Tom was not in privity of contract with the maker. But in an industrial society, products were usually sold to a distributor and then resold to the ultimate consumer. The injustice was apparent, since the person most likely to be harmed by a defective product is the person who takes it home.

Tort law changed to accommodate the societal changes. A new field of tort law, product liability, emerged, using established legal concepts as bases of liability: negligence, warranty, and strict liability. Courts determined that the manufacturer of goods could foresee that they would be passed on to an ultimate consumer. If the product was such that it could harm someone if not properly manufactured, the manufacturer was negligent if the consumer was injured by defective goods. This principle first appeared in the case of *MacPherson v. Buick Motor Co.* in 1916.

Product liability law added strict liability to its arsenal to cover inherently dangerous products that could cause severe injury if defective. In 1963, strict liability for products was adopted in *Greenman v. Yuba Power Products, Inc.*, a California case that dealt with an injury resulting from a defective multipurpose power tool. Since that time, the strict liability theory has been used for industrial equipment, motor vehicles, drugs, pharmaceutical products such as the Dalkon shield, disposal of **hazardous waste**, and escape of hazardous or toxic substances.

Toxic Torts

A new wave of problems accompanies today's lifestyles, so tort law is again expanding to encompass them. Chemical use and storage, waste disposal practices, and manufacturing by-products and emissions have all contributed to the growth of a new area of law called **toxic tort**s. It uses the familiar theories—**nuisance, trespass,** negligence and strict liability—but the name refers to an injury resulting from a toxic agent of some type.

A 1907 case involving a release of oil into the Potomac River that resulted in damage to boats was one of the first to apply a strict liability theory to environmental damage. The court in *Brennan Construction Co. v. Cumberland* determined that oil was a dangerous substance, certain to injure others if it escaped.

Toxic torts are often difficult to prove because the injured person must establish exposure, damage resulting from the exposure, and a connection between the exposure and the damage. Scientific testimony for toxic tort cases frequently conflicts. Also, toxic tort cases may involve hundreds of plaintiffs, as in asbestos cases, and managing the cases efficiently is a tedious and demanding job. Many courts now require plaintiffs to present enough evidence to show a scientific basis for their claim or they dismiss the cases. Also, in very large lawsuits the court may permit only a representative group of the plaintiffs to actually put on a case.

For toxic tort cases, the strict liability rule is similar to the *Rylands v. Fletcher* principle. Courts will look not only at the activity conducted, but also at the surrounding community. If the activity is abnormal, unusual, and dangerous for that location, strict liability is an option. For example, a hazardous waste disposal facility within a residential neighborhood is not a common enterprise. Neighbors injured by released hazardous waste should be able to convince a court to impose strict liability.

Statutes and Strict Liability

In environmental law, strict liability is used to establish violations of major statutes. The first primary law to embrace the concept was the **Clean Water Act.** The law simply prohibits a discharge of pollutants to waters of the United States without a permit or an exclusion. In a 1979 case, *United States v. Earth Sciences,* the defendant had discharged cyanide into a creek during its gold-leaching process. The defendant did not have a permit, and the court said the law did not require proof of intent. If the discharge occurred, strict liability applied.

Since the Clean Water Act, Congress has put strict liability provisions in the **Superfund** law, the **Comprehensive Environmental Response, Compensation, and Liability Act,** and the **Resource Conservation and Recovery Act.** The main impact of strict liability laws is reducing the amount of proof required for the government or interested citizens who sue the offender. It is not even necessary to show damage in many situations; the plaintiff need only prove that a prohibited act was committed.

Since many environmental laws require reporting of violations, the defendant will often have no defense to an enforcement action. However, it can—and often does—negotiate with the government on the remaining issue, the amount of the penalty. If negotiations do not occur, the court must consider a number of factors when setting the fine. The interesting effect of the penalty provisions is restoring negligence principles to the determination of the penalty amount. For example, both the court and the EPA must consider the seriousness of the violation, the duration, the past conduct of the violator, whether the violator gained an economic benefit, the cooperation of the violator, and ability to pay when they establish the penalty. In a sense, these components do figure in an analysis of the negligence and fault of the defendant. Thus, arguing about liability may not be as important as examining the defendant's conduct before and after the violation.

Conclusion

Strict liability has earned its place in tort law, but it has its limits. Because the theory ignores specific intent (and sometimes behavior) of the defendant, courts want to see a reason that the defendant should be held responsible for the results of the defendant's activity. Therefore, courts examine the type of activity, whether it is abnormal in the neighborhood, its inherent dangerousness, its utility to society, and whether it is a commercial activity. The basic question in tort law remains this: if a person is injured as a result of the defendant's actions, who should bear the cost?

Not only is strict liability used to address private injuries, but it is also the standard of liability for many environmental statutes. By using strict liability, the government has significantly reduced its burden of proof of the violation of a law. However, the courts can still take intent and behavior into consideration when they set the penalty for the violation.

SULFUR DIOXIDE (SO$_2$) A chemical compound made of sulfur and oxygen. A common **air pollutant,** sulfur dioxide is an irritant and a major cause of **acid rain.** Power plants emit the largest amount of sulfur dioxide, which results largely from combustion of fossil fuels, particularly lower grades of coal. Sulfur dioxide is one of the **criteria pollutant**s, so it is included in the **National Ambient Air Quality Standards** and regulated under the **Clean Air Act. The Clean Air Act Amendments of 1990** established a new program specifically geared to reduce sulfur dioxide and ease the problem of acid rain.

SUPERFUND The fund established by Congress in the **Comprehensive Environmental Response, Compensation, and Liability Act** to enable the **Environmental Protection Agency** (EPA) to clean up abandoned **hazardous waste** sites. The initial amount in the fund was $1.6 billion, and that was increased to $8.5 billion in the 1986 **Superfund**

Amendments and Reauthorization Act. Money to support the Superfund is obtained through taxes on receipt of hazardous waste at treatment/storage/disposal facilities [see **treatment/storage/disposal facility**], chemical feedstocks, and refined or crude oil.

Superfund is also a nickname for the statute itself (the Comprehensive Environmental Response, Compensation, and Liability Act). Sites listed as national priorities for cleanup are often called Superfund sites, because the EPA uses the Superfund to support most of the work done at those sites.

The use of the Superfund has shifted somewhat since it was first established. To preserve the money for cleanups at sites where no one can finance the cleanup, the EPA emphasizes enforcement and payment for work by the **potentially responsible parties** if they exist. The Superfund is used to address emergency removals and orphan sites. Persons who sent waste to, owned or operated a Superfund site, or arranged for disposal at a Superfund site are identified as early in the cleanup process as possible and are often assigned tasks. In situations where the Superfund must be used, the EPA tries to get the money back by bringing lawsuits. Although Superfund may be used for mixed funding (the fund pays for part of the Superfund site work), the EPA prefers to avoid that option.

SUPERFUND AMENDMENTS AND REAUTHORIZATION ACT (SARA) The 1986 amendments to the **Comprehensive Environmental Response, Compensation, and Liability Act.** SARA addresses many of the problems discovered when the **Environmental Protection Agency** (EPA) tried to administer the 1980 law. Reference to the Comprehensive Environmental Response, Compensation, and Liability Act includes the amendments, and that entry thoroughly discusses the statutory scheme. This entry will focus on how SARA changed the law.

Throughout SARA, Congress adopted the EPA's positions in the **National Contingency Plan,** the regulations that describe how the law must be implemented. For example, the revisions required using **applicable or relevant and appropriate regulations** to establish the cleanup levels. They also required health assessments, emphasized a preference for permanent solutions, and limited judicial review of the EPA's decisions until an enforcement action was taken.

A major shift, made to speed up the cleanups and preserve **Superfund** dollars, was to get **potentially responsible parties** into the process early and offer incentives for voluntary settlements. A grace period for negotiations prior to enforcement was specified. Early settlements with those who had contributed small amounts of **hazardous waste** [see *de minimis/de micromis* **parties**] were encouraged, reducing the number of people fighting over who should pay what. And for the first time, it was clear the Superfund could be used to help pay for the cleanup.

State and public involvement was also strengthened. The community could request up to $50,000 for technical assistance grants to help them understand and become knowledgeable about the site.

The **innocent purchaser** defense was clarified to some extent, so that a person who performed a reasonable investigation of the property and then acquired it without knowing that **hazardous substances** were present could escape liability. The other element of this defense is innocence of wrongdoing. The owner cannot have participated in disposal, storage, or release of hazardous substances after purchasing the property.

SARA stressed treatment rather than containment at Superfund sites, and onsite remediation was favored over shipping the waste elsewhere. Members of Congress were concerned that a cleanup could simply move the problem to a future Superfund site or that a solution would only be a stop-gap measure until it lost its effectiveness.

Overall, the amount of time required to get through the Superfund process was increased. That result was not desired but occurred because of additional public and state involvement and the hiatus on enforcement while negotiations were going on. Prior to SARA, the estimated time to complete a cleanup was about 58 months; that has now been lengthened to approximately 67 months.

SUPPLEMENTAL ENVIRONMENTAL PROJECT (SEP)

An environmental endeavor approved by the **Environmental Protection Agency** (EPA) and completed in lieu of part of a penalty payment for violations. To be considered by the EPA, the proposed project must be in addition to legal requirements. A defendant could not, for example, agree to put in new equipment to cut down on pollution as a supplemental environmental project if the equipment is necessary to comply with the law.

Because it looks better to the public for a company to do something for the community than to pay a fine, many companies like the idea of SEPs. The EPA is sensitive about the issue; it does not want a violator to benefit from being caught. For that reason, the project is not normally a comprehensive substitute for a penalty. The EPA generally requires significant amounts to be paid in exchange for a reduction. One regional office of EPA stated that approximately $2.5 million must be spent to reduce the fine by one dollar. However, in one case the EPA did allow a dollar-for-dollar credit for an SEP.

Examples of SEPs include educational projects, environmental enhancements (such as paving a gravel road to reduce dust), comprehensive audits, pollution prevention, and corrective action. The most common SEPs provide for pollution reduction, followed by pollution prevention. They are most often associated with violations of the **Emergency Planning and Community Right-To-Know Act,** the statute that deals with providing information to the community, and the **Toxic Substances Control Act,** which manages chemical substances.

In the beginning of the program, the EPA did not embrace SEPs, but now one in ten settlements with the agency involves them. The General Accounting Office has questioned the EPA's authority to enter into such agreements, and the criticism centers on the authority to divert penalties from the United States Treasury, where all environmental penalties are supposed to go. Another concern is the deductibility of some of the expenses of a SEP. Penalties are not deductible, but portions of a SEP may be. Despite the opinion of the General Accounting Office, the EPA now encourages the use of SEPs. It sees the policy as one that results in benefits to the environment not otherwise available.

TAKING   Physical entry onto private property or regulatory action by the government that significantly limits the property owner's rights associated with use of property. Under the Fifth Amendment to the Constitution, private property cannot be taken for public use without compensating the owner.

Although the taking issue is more pertinent to the law of conservation than to general environmental law, the concept is very important. Taking claims arise primarily in the context of land use, which is generally regulated through zoning restrictions. For example, quarries may be prohibited in residential areas because they are dangerous, and industrial concerns may also be excluded from a community for similar reasons. Zoning restrictions do not, for the most part, result in a taking. The constitutional question arises when a lawful economic use for the property exists at the time it is acquired and all viable economic use is later eliminated by the government.

Constitutional protection against taking is not limited to real estate but applies to any privately owned property. Most environmental cases focus on realty and its use, though the Supreme Court dealt with intellectual property in the case of *Ruckelshaus v. Monsanto,* a suit to prevent the **Environmental Protection Agency** (EPA) from using research belonging to Monsanto to support other applications for pesticide registration. That case involved the **Federal Insecticide, Fungicide, and Rodenticide Act,** and the statute authorizes such use but requires the applicant to compensate the owner of the data.

In *Monsanto,* a 1984 decision, the court was not faced with deciding whether a taking had occurred, but whether the government should be enjoined so it could not use the information. Nevertheless, the Supreme Court clearly recognized that a taking of intellectual property for public use was subject to the Fifth Amendment taking provision. But before it could show a taking had occurred, Monsanto had to prove it had a reasonable expectation the property would be kept secret.

A larger question loomed in the background, and that was whether the law itself (the Federal Insecticide, Fungicide, and Rodenticide Act) was unconstitutional. It is clear from this case and others that the fact that a statute may result in a taking is not enough to invalidate it. The Fifth Amendment does not prohibit the government from taking private property for public use; it simply requires payment for the property that is taken. The issue of whether a taking has occurred does not usually turn on the state's right to govern. State and federal agencies have great powers to protect the public, preserve the peace, and manage its resources. So a state may do what it wants to do in most situations, but it must pay if the action goes too far.

The *Monsanto* case attacked the government's right to use private property in such a way that other private parties would benefit. The Supreme Court upheld the government's right to act according to the statute but indicated that the end result could be a public—not a private—taking. It refused to issue an injunction, however, since injunctions are never favored if a remedy exists to compensate the party claiming injury.

In this situation, two possible remedies existed. The first was the provision within the statute itself that required the user of the data to compensate the owner and to submit to binding arbitration if the parties could not agree. The second, a special federal law called the Tucker Act, allows parties to sue the government when a federal statute or regulation has resulted in a taking of private property for public use.

Congress establishes or recognizes existing public values through statutes, such as protection of **wetland**s, coastal regions, and endangered species. The resulting governmental restrictions may interfere with the landowner's right to use the property as the owner sees fit. This is the heart of most environmental taking claims.

Early History of Taking Cases

Early cases allowed the government to use its police power very broadly without having to compensate the owner. The basis of analysis was public **nuisance** law. If the state declared an activity to be against the community's interest, it could then stop the activity because it was a public nuisance. Courts did not look far beyond the stated purpose of the law, and they did not consider the impact of the regulation upon the owner. Once they found that the state had a legitimate reason for the regulation, the analysis stopped.

Two types of taking cases exist: physical taking, which involves entry onto the property, and regulatory taking, where government action restricts the use of property. Most environmental takings are regulatory takings.

The case which established the right of a government to regulate "public nuisances," even though the regulation severely impacts a person's business in the United States, was *Mugler v. Kansas*, decided in 1887. In *Mugler*, the property owner was in the business of manufacturing beer. The state prohibited liquor, so the owner could no longer continue the business. The Supreme Court upheld the state's right to abate the nuisance; it accepted the legislature's findings that alcohol itself caused community problems and that the activity was a public nuisance. The state did not have to compensate the owner of the property.

The 1922 case of *Pennsylvania Coal Company v. Mahon* dealt with a regulatory taking. The Pennsylvania Coal Company was sued by a subsequent owner of property to force it to stop mining under its property. The property owner, Mahon, used a Pennsylvania law that prohibited coal mining under a dwelling due to potential for subsidence and damage to structures as the basis for the suit. Within the deed that transferred the land to the Mahons, the coal company had specifically reserved rights to mine beneath the surface. The law was enacted after the land was transferred, and essentially destroyed the coal company's previous rights.

The *Pennsylvania Coal Company* case is important because the court recognized that the stated purpose for limiting a use is not necessarily the end of the inquiry. In determining whether a taking had occurred, the court also had to consider the diminished value of the property after the government action. For the first time, the Supreme Court acknowledged that failure to consider impact on the landowner could destroy the meaning of the constitutional taking provision.

Later, in *Penn Central Transportation Co. v. New York City*, 1978, which prevented the landowner from building office space above an historic landmark, the court added another consideration: did the government activity interfere with investment-based expectations? This case advanced the balancing of factors involving the government's purpose and the economic impact on the landowner. However, in this case, the court did not find a taking.

Balancing Interests in Taking Claims

By 1980, courts were balancing interests to decide taking claims, but they usually sided with the government. In *Agins v. Tiburon*, a developer had bought five acres of land, intending to build a number of homes. After the purchase, the city rezoned the area with density restrictions, and the owner could only construct five single-family dwellings on the five acres. The

Supreme Court upheld Tiburon's police power. Furthermore, it believed the plaintiff still could profit in its use of the land, even though it could not sell as many homes. The test in the case was this: did the action substantially advance a legitimate state interest or did it deny the owner an economically viable use of the land?

Keystone Bituminous Coal Association v. DeBenedictis, decided in 1987, was another coal mining case. The state had prohibited removal of 50 percent of the coal beneath certain structures. The Supreme Court did not find a taking, because the owner still had access to part of the coal and the law was determined to be a valid exercise of police power.

Another case decided in the same year, *Nollan v. California Coastal Commission,* established a nexus requirement between the government action and the legitimate state interest. Courts began to look more closely at the underlying purpose of the law and the way it was pursued. In *Nollan,* the landowner bought a piece of beachfront property with the intention of tearing down a bungalow and building a two-story house. The California Coastal Commission would not allow it unless the owner dedicated a lateral public easement. The stated reason behind the requirement was visibility: building a two story house would interfere with the public's viewing the property. However, the Supreme Court could not find a relationship between allowing the public to go onto the property and their ability to view the ocean. It found that a taking had occurred.

Recent Taking Claims

Two cases decided by the U.S. Court of Claims in 1990 extended the analysis of taking claims to permit denials for wetland filling. In both *Florida Rock Industries, Inc. v. United States* and *Loveladies Harbor, Inc. v. United States,* the court decided that some permit denials resulted in taking and the owner had to be compensated.

About the time of those cases, President Bush [see **Bush, George Herbert Walker**] directed agencies to consider the effects of their decisions and budget for taking claims. Prior to the *Florida Rock* and *Loveladies Harbor* cases, the EPA and the **Corps of Engineers** believed that a permit denial could not result in a taking because permits are not rights that are removed by governmental action.

Timing is important in a taking claim. For example, if a speculator purchases real estate today, knowing it is in a wetlands, he would be hardpressed to prove a loss of a right if he is unable to get a permit to fill it. However, if a person bought property in 1971 with the intention of developing it, the court may agree that a permit denial is a taking, since at that time wetlands did not fall under federal regulation.

Two other cases have been decided by the Supreme Court since the *Loveladies Harbor* and *Florida Rock* judgments. One is *Lucas v. South Carolina Coastal Council*, a 1992 case; the other is *Dolan v. City of Tigard*, a 1994 decision. Both of the cases dealt with coastal management provisions.

In *Lucas*, in 1982 the landowner bought two lots on the coast, intending to build houses. In 1988, a new law was enacted that prohibited building permanent structures on the property. The stated purpose of the law was to protect a valuable public resource that was threatened. Lucas sued, claiming the new law deprived him of all economically viable use of the property. The state trial court agreed, but the state Supreme Court said no taking had occurred. Before the case was decided by the state Supreme Court, the law was amended to allow special permits. The state then argued in the U.S. Supreme Court that the case could not be decided yet because the landowner might get a permit.

The U.S. Supreme Court reversed the decision and sent the case back to the trial court, stating that even a temporary taking could justify compensation. It emphasized the need to look at the state's law concerning what rights accompanied land ownership. If a right exists at the time the property is acquired and the state later changes the law so that it eliminates economically viable use of the property, it must compensate the landowner. Thus, a state may have a legitimate interest in regulating for the public good, but if in doing so, it eliminates previously existing private rights, it must pay for taking property.

The *Dolan* case reinforced the nexus principle. The landowner had applied for a permit to build a new store on her property and to pave a parking lot. The city of Tigard refused to approve the owner's building application unless she agreed to dedicate a public greenway to minimize flooding and additional property to be used as a pedestrian and bicycle pathway to reduce traffic congestion.

Tigard's purposes were, the U.S. Supreme Court found, legitimate state interests. However, the owner was asked to dedicate 15 percent of her property to the government. The court believed a public greenway would be no more effective than a private one to prevent flooding. In dedicating the land to the public, the owner lost a significant right associated with land ownership: the right to exclude others from the premises. The court held that the city had taken the property and must compensate the owner. In its opinion, it found that the government's purpose did not bear a sufficient relationship to the action it took.

Analysis of Case Law

The recent cases involving taking claims emphasize private rights associated with property over the government's "legitimate state interest." Earlier cases often stretched to find the reason behind the action, and that ended the analysis. Today, the government may have authority to act as it does and still be liable for taking property if (1) it eliminates a previously existing right associated with the property, (2) it destroys all economically viable use of the property, and (3) there is no logical connection between the government's interest and the result.

Even with these principles, it is very difficult to predict the outcome of a taking claim. Supreme Court taking decisions are narrowly construed because they invariably apply only to the facts before them and do not attempt to establish bright-line rules. A successful taking claim does not invalidate governmental authority to act; it simply emphasizes the constitutional right to be compensated for property taken for the public's use.

THRESHOLD PLANNING QUANTITY (TPQ) The amount of extremely **hazardous substances** that triggers a reporting requirement under the **Emergency Planning and Community Right-To-Know Act.** The TPQ varies from one to ten thousand pounds, depending on the substance.

Companies that have the TPQ of a substance must report to the **state emergency response commission** and the local emergency planning commission within sixty days of becoming subject to the requirement. They must designate a facility representative and work with the agencies to develop emergency response plans. The main concern of the community is the ability to respond to all possible releases that may threaten the public. Without the information, it cannot plan properly.

TIMES BEACH A town in Missouri, located thirty miles southwest of St. Louis, that became one of the symbols of mismanagement of **hazardous waste**. In 1971, it was not uncommon to spray streets with oil to suppress dust. Unfortunately, at a number of sites throughout the country, the oil contained chemical residues. The oil used at Times Beach included dioxin, a toxic substance used in the production of Agent Orange and a number of pesticides. Thirty-three sites in Missouri were found to be contaminated with dioxin, one of the most dangerous chemicals known, according to the **Environmental Protection Agency** (EPA).

The contamination was not discovered until 1982, two years after the **Comprehensive Environmental Response, Compensation, and Liability Act** was passed. Unlike other contaminated hazardous waste sites, Times Beach did not go through the slow process created by the law to get the property characterized and remediated. Instead, in February 1983, the government spent $33 million dollars to buy the town and relocate the citizens. The money came from **Superfund,** a federal fund established to address abandoned hazardous waste sites and respond to imminent threats to health or the environment.

In 1988, the EPA determined what remedial action should be taken. Dioxin adheres to soil tightly, so it has not gotten into groundwater or been carried to surface water in harmful amounts. Contamination was found on roads, shoulders, and ditches.

Times Beach, where contamination was not as widespread as at many other sites, is being used as a collecting area for other dioxin wastes. The soil there is being incinerated and will remain on site. New soil is also being brought in. The state has placed restrictions on development in the area, but they may be unnecessary since Times Beach is subject to flooding and is not readily adaptable to building. However, flooding was rare when the houses and businesses were originally built in that town. Times Beach is unincorporated.

TORT   A civil, as opposed to a criminal, wrong that results in an injury to another party. Torts involve any harm to a protected interest, which is a right that society recognizes as important to individuals. Protected interests include the rights to personal integrity and noninterference with personal or real property, privacy, reputation, and earning capacity. Examples of torts include assault, battery, false imprisonment, **trespass, nuisance, negligence,** conversion, invasion of privacy, slander, libel, and interference with business.

Tort law, which originated in early English cases, was originally a way to keep the peace in communities. If an injury occurred, the injured party could sue and leave it up to the jury to decide whether the action of the defendant invaded a protected interest. In environmental law, many of the old tort theories are being used as a basis of liability for property damage and personal injuries from contamination. A new branch of tort law, called **toxic tort**s, includes issues involving pollution when some toxic or hazardous substance [see **hazardous substances**] may have caused the illness or contamination. See also **strict liability.**

TOXIC RELEASE INVENTORY (TRI)   A report of routine releases of toxic chemicals to the environment. It is prepared by the **Environmental Protection Agency**, based on information submitted due to the **Emergency Planning and Community Right-To-Know Act.**

Companies that manufacture or use chemicals listed under the statute must report every year if they (1) have ten or more full time employees, (2) fall within specified industrial classifications, and (3) manufacture or process 25,000 pounds per year or use 10,000 pounds per year. Information about releases must cover releases to air, water, land, and offsite locations.

The Toxic Release Inventory is available to the public. Compilation of the first inventory showed surprising results: the release of toxic chemicals to the environment was much greater than most people supposed. Prior to that, the government and public assumed exposure to many chemicals was confined to the workplace.

TOXIC SUBSTANCES CONTROL ACT (TSCA)   A statute enacted in 1976 to regulate commercial chemicals not regulated by other laws. Pesticides, drugs, cosmetics, and food additives were covered by existing laws, but toxic chemicals, mixtures, and compounds exist that do not fit into those categories. Congress intended to create a law that would allow for testing of new and existing chemicals. In fact, new chemical review is often thought to be the primary aim of TSCA, but the statute is much broader than that. The law gives the **Environmental Protection Agency** (EPA) power to remove chemical substances from the market, prohibit or limit their manufacture, or restrict their usages.

TSCA is divided into four main titles: Title I is the heart of the law, dealing with chemical substances in general; Title II covers **asbestos** in schools and is called the **Asbestos Hazard Emergency Response Act;** Title III addresses indoor radon abatement; and Title IV focuses on lead paint hazards.

Overview

TSCA governs persons who manufacture, import, process, and distribute chemical substances. It also controls some activities of those who use or dispose of them. Although the law has significant impact on the introduction of new chemicals (and new uses of existing chemicals), the agency may also require testing of existing chemicals.

The term chemical substances encompass both organic and inorganic substances that have a particular identity, including mixtures. Chemicals that do not exist in nature and are not the result of a single chemical reaction are subject to the law. Therefore, manmade bioorganisms are regulated under TSCA if they do not fall under a different statute, such as the **Federal Insecticide, Fungicide, and Rodenticide Act.**

Persons Regulated by TSCA

Manufacturers and importers of chemicals must test new chemicals (and existing ones, if required to do so) for health and environmental effects and supply the EPA with the test results. Even after the chemicals are on the inventory list, they must keep records, submit reports, allow inspections, and obey subpoenas. They must also maintain data concerning allegations of significant adverse reactions to most TSCA chemicals, unless they relate to a "known" human health effect.

Processors act as packagers of chemical substances after their manufacture. They must also keep records, obey orders, allow inspections and comply with subpoenas. They may have to provide data to the EPA or to users and cannot put the chemical to a new use without submitting information to the EPA.

Users of chemical substances must comply with the EPA's regulations, allow inspections and obey subpoenas. They may not use a substance that is banned or go beyond restrictions placed on a chemical. If they dispose of a substance regulated by TSCA, they must follow disposal restrictions.

Distributors are those who sell, introduce, hold for commercial distribution, or deliver chemical substances into commerce. They are subject to the same general categories as users, with the addition of recordkeeping. They cannot continue to distribute chemicals that have been recalled or banned.

TSCA's Scope

The statute regulates new chemical substances and existing chemicals that will be used in a significantly new manner by requiring that the EPA review information before manufacturing begins. It also allows the EPA to require testing of existing chemicals; regulate, restrict or ban chemicals found to pose a significant risk to human health or the environment; gather information on chemical substances through reporting and records; and declare an imminent hazard so that immediate action can be taken. The EPA's enforcement powers associated with TSCA are similar to those under other environmental laws.

TSCA Inventory

Before it could provide special procedures for new chemicals, the EPA had to determine what chemical substances already existed, so it created two inventory lists. One, the TSCA Inventory, covers all chemicals except those for which confidentiality was claimed; those will be listed only by generic name on the TSCA Inventory but listed in full on the other list, the EPA's master file. Only the EPA can search the master file, and it will do so if a person can demonstrate a bona fide intent to import or manufacture a substance not on the TSCA inventory. The inventory must be updated every four years.

Chemical substance manufacturing and research is highly competitive. Businesses regulated by TSCA may want to guard unique developments, and Congress recognized that concern. TSCA provides for the protection of confidential business information, including specific chemical formulas. To claim the confidentiality, the manufacturer must assert it from the beginning of the TSCA process and maintain it throughout. When the chemical is finally manufactured, EPA will list the chemical on the TSCA Inventory according to a generic name, but the actual data is contained on the Confidential Inventory.

Premanufacturing Process

Before a person may import or manufacture a chemical substance, he or she must check the TSCA Inventory. If the inventory contains a generic description that is protected under the confidential business information provisions, but the description is similar to the substance the person intends to introduce, the EPA will search the Master Inventory. But before it does the search, it must be convinced that the person making the inquiry is actually intending to manufacture or import it.

If the substance is not on the list, a notice called a **premanufacturing notice** (PMN) must be sent to the EPA. It must contain relevant information about the chemical, test data concerning health and environmental effects, its use, and amounts to be manufactured or imported. The EPA must review the information and act on it within ninety days or extend the review period. After that time, the manufacturer or importer may begin producing or importing the chemical as long as it files another paper called a notice of commencement of manufacture within thirty days.

Since TSCA is a gap-filler and regulates commercially marketed chemicals, some exceptions exist to the requirements of the law. For example, the Food, Drug, and Cosmetic Act, the Atomic Energy Act, and the Federal Insecticide, Fungicide, and Rodenticide Act have comprehensive requirements for the chemicals that fit their definitions. A pesticide is regulated under the Federal Insecticide, Fungicide, and Rodenticide Act, while drugs are regulated under the Food, Drug, and Cosmetic Act, even though they are both chemical substances by definition.

Substances used only for research and development are exempt from the requirements of the law, as are articles containing chemicals not exposed during normal operation and impurities created incidentally through another process. The EPA lists fifteen exemptions from the requirement to file a PMN. The underlying reasons for exemptions are (1) lack of significant human exposure, (2) encouragement of research, and (3) testing of chemicals that are likely to be commercially exploited. Other exemptions are not automatic and must be applied for, such as the limited volume exemption or the test-marketing exemption. The notice given to the EPA to request an exemption is not as extensive as the ordinary premanufacturing notice or significant new use notice, and the time period for review by the EPA is cut from 90 days to 21 days.

Significant New Uses

A person who wishes to manufacture, import, or process an existing chemical for a significant new use must submit to the EPA a notice similar to the premanufacturing notice. Before the action is subject to the significant new use provisions, the EPA must actually list a significant new use rule so the manufacturer or processor does not have to decide whether it must file a notice. A new use includes almost any change associated with the chemical substance, such as quantity being manufactured and location of manufacture, as well as any new method of using the substance.

Testing Rules

The EPA is responsible for evaluating data about chemical substances, not only new chemicals but also existing chemicals. The agency has the power to limit or ban the manufacture of new chemicals to allow it time to review the information. It can also request further testing if the information contained in the premanufacturing notice is not adequate for it to reach a conclusion about the risk posed by the chemical.

If the EPA determines that an existing chemical may present an unreasonable risk or that the number of people who will be exposed is high, and that additional data is necessary to evaluate it, the EPA can issue a rule requiring testing. A testing rule must include identification of the substance or mixture subject to the rule, standards to be used to develop test data, and the deadline for submitting standards to the agency.

After the rule is published, a manufacturer must file a notice of intent to test, a request for an exemption, or stop manufacturing the chemical. It is not necessary for every manufacturer to perform separate testing, however. One may design a testing program that will represent the rest of the manufacturers. However, anyone who relies on the tests must reimburse the company that does the testing.

Congress established an interagency committee, the Interagency Testing Committee, to recommend substances that should receive priority for testing under TSCA. It must consider the quantity of the chemical, extent and duration of human exposure, relation to other chemicals known to be toxic, available data on its effects, and whether additional information will help determine the risks of the substance. The EPA then establishes a priority list for testing. If the EPA decides not to list the recommended chemical substance, it must publish a public notice explaining its decision.

Regulating Hazardous Chemical Substances

The goal of TSCA is to prevent unreasonable risks to health or the environment. But like other environmental laws, TSCA requires a balancing of benefits and risks.

Section 6 of TSCA allows the EPA to restrict certain **hazardous chemicals** and even to ban manufacture or distribution in commerce. But before this authority can be exercised, the EPA must take into consideration (1) the effects of the substance on health and the magnitude of human exposure, (2) environmental effects and magnitude of environmental exposure, (3) the benefits of the substance and availability of substitutes, and (4) reasonably ascertainable economic consequences, including effect on national economy, small business, technological innovation, environment, and public health.

Assuming the EPA determines the chemical should be restricted, the remedy selected must be the least burdensome restraint that will protect against the risk involved. Examples of limitations include total prohibition or quantity ceilings on manufacturing, processing or distribution; restrictions on the use or concentration of chemical; worker protection and training; addition of clear instructions and warnings to labeling; testing and reporting; control of disposal and commercial use; and orders for public notice, replacement, or recall of the substance.

Few chemicals have been regulated by this provision of TSCA, but they are notable. Asbestos, polychlorinated biphenyls (PCBs), hexavalent chromium, metal working fluids, dioxins, and **chlorofluorocarbons** (CFCs) have been singled out. Of those, the prohibition on using CFCs as a propellant and the gradual phase-out of polychlorinated biphenyls (a chemical used primarily as a dielectric fluid in electrical equipment) have been most effective. Hexavalent chromium is no longer permitted in air conditioning cooling towers.

The EPA tried using TSCA to ban the use of asbestos in many products, but the rules were later struck down in court. The Fifth Circuit Court of Appeals found a number of problems with the asbestos restrictions: first, the public had insufficient opportunity to comment; second, the EPA did not rely on direct evidence but extrapolated to determine the harm caused by asbestos, assuming that each exposure resulted in an injury when that was not demonstrated; third, no suitable substitute appeared to be available; fourth, the EPA made no cost-benefit analysis; and finally, it failed to select the least burdensome method to address the harm. After the decision in *Corrosion Proof Fittings v. Environmental Protection Agency,* the only uses prohibited by the TSCA rule are new uses. Thus, the agency has announced it will probably not rely heavily on Section 6 of TSCA.

Recordkeeping and Reporting

In addition to reviewing data, the EPA must require manufacturers and processors to maintain records about chemical substances, including information about production, known environmental and health effects, worker exposure information, and disposal methods. They must also record allegations about unanticipated health effects and submit unpublished health and safety studies. If the manufacturer or processor has information that reasonably supports a conclusion that the substance or mixture poses a substantial risk to health or the environment, it must immediately report it to the EPA.

The EPA has issued two model rules listing chemicals for which information is required. The first is called the Preliminary Assessment Information Rule, and it was published in 1982. In 1988, the Comprehensive

Assessment Information Rule was promulgated. The latter rule may gradually take the place of the former. Nineteen substances are on the final list; five hundred were on the first.

If a chemical substance is recommended by the Interagency Testing Agency for priority listing and testing, it is also added to the Preliminary Assessment Information Rule list. That rule requires manufacturers or importers to file a two page report on the quantity of the substance produced and worker exposure data. The Comprehensive Assessment Information Rule requires manufacturers, importers, and processors to provide extensive information about the chemicals it covers: physical and chemical properties, treatment and disposal, environmental release and fate, and financial information.

Miscellaneous Agency Powers

If a substance presents an imminent danger, the EPA can apply for an injunction to stop manufacture immediately, cause it to be recalled, and require public notification about the risks. The EPA also can seize chemical substances using this authority. This power is not used widely; it is designed to apply only when health or environmental injuries are likely to occur and restricting the substance under Section 6 of TSCA would take too long.

Enforcement

The EPA has extensive subpoena rights under TSCA. If the recipient of a subpoena does not respond, a federal court can order compliance. The EPA also applies its subpoena powers under TSCA to gathering information for any alleged environmental violation, as long as a chemical is involved. Inspections are also authorized by the statute. Places which are subject to inspection range from transportation vehicles and storage premises to manufacturing plants.

In addition to issuing orders and subpoenas, inspecting, requiring testing and/or information, restricting or banning manufacture, the EPA has enforcement authority for violations of TSCA. Unlike the enforcement provisions of other major statutes, however, TSCA enforcement begins with an administrative procedure.

TSCA gives the EPA the right to file an administrative complaint. After providing the violator an opportunity for a **hearing**, the EPA may assess a civil penalty of up to $25,000 per day of violation. TSCA complaints go to an **administrative law judge,** and if a hearing is held, it is a formal proceeding. The EPA does not have the right to sue from the beginning, as it does when enforcing the **Clean Air Act** or **Clean Water Act.** If the agency prevails at the hearing and the respondent refuses or fails to pay, the case may then go to court.

Criminal cases, though, are taken directly to court, as any other criminal case must be. A criminal violation involves a knowing and willful violation of the law. The criminal fine is the same as the civil one, but the violator may also spend up to a year in jail.

Lead, Asbestos in Schools, and Radon

Congress has added separate statutes to TSCA to deal with lead, asbestos in schools, and radon. The asbestos in schools program, developed under the Asbestos Hazard Emergency Response Act, has been the most influential of the three laws. Many of its procedures and provisions are used in commercial settings as well as schools to determine how to take samples and establish the qualifications of inspectors.

Indoor radon problems are addressed in TSCA as well. Radon is a naturally occurring gas that results from decay of radioactive materials. When buildings are tightly constructed, they trap the gases inside, so indoor radon became an issue because of tightly sealed and insulated buildings. It tends to settle in the lower levels of a structure. The law requires the EPA to develop model construction standards for buildings and techniques for controlling radon levels. The agency is also directed to develop a study to find out the extent of radon contamination in school and federal buildings.

Finally, TSCA deals with another chemical that has caused health problems, particularly in children: lead. The EPA has issued a notice of proposed rulemaking for the use of lead and its compounds. It is also developing training and accreditation programs for lead abatement workers. Lead in drinking water systems is governed under the **Safe Drinking Water Act.** See also **criteria pollutant; National Ambient Air Quality Standards; National Emission Standards for Hazardous Air Pollutants; National Pollutant Discharge Elimination System.**

TOXIC TORT   A type of civil injury caused by exposure to toxic or **hazardous chemicals** or products. An evolving area of law, toxic torts have gained popularity as the public became aware of environmental and human impacts resulting from chemicals. Examples of toxic torts include defective or dangerous pharmaceutical products, illustrated by the Dalkon Shield cases; hazardous products, such as those containing asbestos; dangerous drugs, like diethylstilbestrol (DES); groundwater, surface water, and well water contamination; illnesses caused by chemical releases; and any other injury from toxins.

Theories used by plaintiffs in toxic tort cases fall within three major categories: **strict liability, negligence,** and **nuisance.** Often the cases are class action lawsuits involving numerous plaintiffs. In the case of hazardous products, the plaintiffs do not always know which manufacturer made the products they used, so they sometimes sue all manufacturers of the suspect product. If the cases establish liability, the amount of the judgment may be apportioned among the defendants based on market share at the time of the injuries or through some other method the court selects.

Often the plaintiff uses the reasoning behind product liability cases, trying to reach the manufacturer of the toxic agent. But if the injury occurred because of a release, the plaintiff may only be able to reach the person who allowed the release to occur. For example, if a hazardous substance [see **hazardous substances**] manufactured by Company A and stored by Company B escapes into groundwater, more often than not, Company A will not be liable, but Company B could be.

A number of state courts limit strict liability in tort to product liability. That means that the plaintiff must establish a direct connection between the manufacturer and the injury; otherwise, the plaintiff must rely on negligence or nuisance theories.

Because hazardous substances and **hazardous waste**s are intensely regulated, significant amounts of information are available to toxic tort plaintiffs. Statutes such as the **Emergency Planning and Community Right-To-Know Act,** the **Toxic Substances Control Act,** the **Resource Conservation and Recovery Act,** and the **Federal Insecticide, Fungicide, and Rodenticide Act** require recordkeeping and reporting. Material submitted to agencies is available to anyone who requests it under the Freedom of Information Act, with the exception of confidential business information. Federal agencies also publish the results of their own research regarding the effects of chemicals on the human body and the environment.

Evidence concerning release, disposal, storage, or production of hazardous substances aids the plaintiff in a toxic tort case, but it by no means establishes the defendant's liability. In addition to showing that an event occurred, the plaintiff must also demonstrate that he or she was exposed to the toxic agent. Traditional causation issues must also be addressed, such as whether the exposure is the cause of the disease, injury, or death. In short, the plaintiff must prove that the exposure is capable of causing the type of injury he or she suffered and that it did in fact cause it.

To demonstrate exposure in an environmental or occupational toxic tort lawsuit, evidence must be produced to show the toxic substance had a pathway to reach the plaintiff. Totally contained hazardous waste does not go anywhere, so there is no pathway. But if the container leaks and hazardous waste gets into the groundwater or rain carries it to a stream, a pathway exists. Field testing and computer modeling, along with expert testimony, are methods commonly used to prove that a pathway exists. Once that has been proven, the plaintiff must show that he or she was exposed to the contamination.

In addition, the plaintiff must prove that the concentration of the toxic agent was sufficient to cause his or her injury. Causation is the most difficult element in a toxic tort case. Agency information concerning safe levels of exposure is often too conservative to rely upon, since its purpose is to provide an ample margin of safety for the public. Tests done only on animals to prove toxicity are controversial because the correlation may not be valid. Since animal testing is typically done with extremely high doses of the substance, the plaintiff has to provide evidence that adjusts the dosage, accounts for different metabolisms, and shows the similarity of the animal tested to humans.

A lawsuit by veterans and their families involving Agent Orange, a defoliant used during the Vietnam War, ran into insurmountable problems involving causation. Although some of the parties did settle their claims in the 1984 case *In re Agent Orange Product Liability Litigation,* the others lost because they could not show a statistical link between the injuries they sustained and Agent Orange. Government studies were used, but they were not helpful.

Even if the plaintiff establishes that the substance is capable of causing harm, he or she must also show that his or her particular injury resulted from that exposure. Individuals vary greatly in response, metabolism, lifestyle, and general health. It is often difficult to find a medical expert who will testify that a particular exposure did cause the injury, and having found one, the plaintiff must then convince the court that the statement is true.

In some toxic tort cases, the plaintiffs are not yet injured. For example, a person may be exposed to a chemical and become afraid of developing cancer, a type of case called a "Fear of Cancer" case. Fear of cancer lawsuits are difficult to win, and prevailing plaintiffs generally only obtain medical monitoring.

Asbestos litigation has been at the forefront of toxic tort environmental cases. Many attorneys believe indoor air quality, possibly involving secondary cigarette smoke, will follow as the next wave of lawsuits.

TRAIN, RUSSELL (1920–) Administrator of the **Environmental Protection Agency** during 1974 and 1975, he was appointed by President Gerald R. Ford. Train has a long history of environmental involvement. He was president of the Conservation Foundation and founder of the World Wildlife Fund in the United States.

Before becoming administrator, Train served as under secretary of the Department of Interior and as the first chairman of the **Council on Environmental Quality** while Richard M. Nixon was in office. Mr. Train is widely respected as an effective and skillful leader in the environmental movement.

TREATMENT/STORAGE/DISPOSAL (T/S/D) FACILITY A regulated business that treats, stores, or disposes of **hazardous waste**. T/S/D facilities must either have a permit or be granted interim status to be able to operate legally. They are highly regulated to reduce the possibility they will threaten the environment in the future. The **Resource Conservation and Recovery Act** and the **Environmental Protection Agency**'s (EPA) regulations govern these facilities.

Contrary to what one might assume, the definition of these facilities does not include only places that intentionally handle hazardous waste. It also covers facilities that store hazardous waste before sending it to a disposal or treatment facility. For example, if a manufacturer uses a process that creates solvent wastes and keeps its wastes in drums on site for more than ninety days, it has become a storage facility and must have a permit.

Regulations for T/S/D facilities are comprehensive. The purpose of the regulations is to keep hazardous wastes from becoming a problem in the future because of inadequate treatment now. Therefore, the design, location, operation, and closure of T/S/D facilities are all regulated.

But some facilities are exempt from T/S/D rules. Primarily, the exemptions arise because a different environmental law governs them, such as wastewater treatment plants regulated by the **Clean Water Act,** facilities with permits for ocean dumping, and underground injection wells [see underground injection control] permitted under the **Safe Drinking Water Act.** Other exemptions are for short-term storage or emergency response actions.

General Requirements

All T/S/D facilities that are not exempt from the law must either be permitted or granted interim status. If the facility was built after 19 November 1980 or before the hazardous waste in question was first regulated, it is an **interim status facility**. That simply means the facility must submit Part A of the permit application (the shorter, simpler part), obey the technical requirements for interim status facilities, and continue operating. Interim status ends for a facility when a permit is issued or denied, or when the agency revokes the facility's interim status for some reason. Interim status was incorporated into the law because Congress knew it would take time to process all of the permit applications. In the meantime, it did not want to eliminate all of the existing facilities.

If a facility is not an interim status facility, it must have a permit before it begins operation. That will require submission of both Part A and Part B of the application. Interim status facilities must supply additional information beyond Part A if the EPA requests it. If it refuses, its status may be revoked or the permit denied.

Many of the requirements for T/S/D facilities are housekeeping details. In general, they apply to all T/S/D facilities, regardless of whether they are permitted or interim status. Each facility must have an EPA identification number and security system; analyze representative waste samples; train workers in handling the substance; develop handling precautions for reactive, ignitable, and incompatible wastes; be prepared to respond to releases; keep records and submit reports; demonstrate financial responsibility; and write closure and postclosure plans. All permits require the permittee to take **corrective action** for releases from any **solid waste management unit,** regardless of when the waste was first placed in the unit.

Specific Standards

In addition to general requirements are the standards for certain types of treatment units set by regulation. Standards have been established for containers, **storage tanks**, surface impoundments, waste piles, land treatment, landfills, incinerators, thermal treatment units, chemical physical and biological treatment units, underground injection wells, containment buildings, and miscellaneous units.

The rules address problems peculiar to the type of treatment unit. For example, an incinerator must have a 99.99 percent efficiency rate for destruction of organic compounds, along with emission controls. Containers and tanks must be compatible with the waste they will store, and they must be inspected and constructed according to the regulations. Regulations also limit the size of waste piles and specify liner requirements and control of leachate and stormwater flow. They may also be treated as landfills in certain situations.

TRESPASS A tort, or civil wrong, involving unauthorized entry onto real property in someone else's rightful possession. In early English law, a trespass could also involve personal property or a person. Over the years, however, the names for those torts have changed to terms more familiar to us: conversion, **negligence,** and battery.

Trespass on real property occurs if someone walks on property and does not have the right to be there. A person can also trespass by throwing an object onto property, allowing one's animals to stray onto someone's property, or operating any equipment on the property. The owner or rightful possessor of real property has the right to peaceful possession. He or she can sue trespassers, but the damages are generally limited to injury to the property.

Environmental lawyers use a number of tort theories for environmental harms in addition to the rights granted by statutes. Trespass is one of the theories used to deal with property damage. If, for example, a company disposes of **hazardous waste** in a lagoon and it eventually seeps into the groundwater and taints a neighboring well, a trespass has occurred. However, using the trespass theory does not address other types of injuries that may have occurred because of the contaminated well water. It is limited to the damage to the real property, so in some cases another theory, such as negligence, may be more useful.

To prove a trespass involving migrating contamination, the plaintiff must show that the person responsible knew that it would eventually move to another place. Some courts are willing to impute that knowledge to the defendant, though, since it is common knowledge that contamination does not stay in its burial place without assistance. See also **nuisance; strict liability; toxic tort.**

UNDERGROUND INJECTION CONTROL (UIC) The program established by the **Safe Drinking Water Act** to control the practice of disposing of wastes in a conduit, cave, well, or salt dome. Permits for such wells must be obtained from the **Environmental Protection Agency** (EPA) or the state, if the program has been delegated. The primary reason for requiring permits is to protect groundwater from pollution.

VALDEZ An Exxon oil tanker that hit Bligh Reef in Prince William Sound on 24 March 1989, spilling more than eleven million gallons of oil. The tanker, a single-hulled ship that was only three years old, was making a routine run from the town of Valdez, Alaska, to Long Beach, California.

The captain of the ship was Joseph Hazelwood, a veteran who had taken the *Valdez* on many trips to and from Long Beach, California. The 987-foot tanker had loaded oil in Valdez, where the Alaskan pipeline, operated by a consortium of six oil companies called Alyeska, terminates. The tanker was returning to Long Beach.

Glacial ice had moved into the area, and Hazelwood was allegedly drunk at the time the tanker hit the reef. He was not at the helm when the *Valdez* first ran aground, but he did appear and issue orders that aggravated the situation. According to records, Hazelwood had a history of alcohol abuse and had three drunk-driving convictions. At the time of the spill, Hazelwood did not have a valid driver's license because of those convictions.

Alyeska was the organization that had filed a contingency plan with Alaska, and under the plan, it was responsible for handling the spill. However, Exxon quickly acknowledged accountability for the wreck and took over the cleanup effort. Alyeska disappeared quietly while Exxon tried to develop and implement a plan.

But no one had anticipated a release of the quantity of oil that poured into the water. The situation worsened as untrained, unprepared people tried to gather equipment and get approval to contain and remove the oil. As word of the disaster spread, the media, the community, the government, and Exxon held numerous meetings but could not get organized.

Exxon spent millions of dollars trying to remedy the situation, but environmental damage was extensive. Oil destroyed aquatic life, birds, and shorelines. By the time it was over, Exxon had paid $3.5 billion in cleanup and civil and criminal fines; it also paid $9.7 million to Alaskan businesses. Exxon was also sued by numerous people, including governmental representatives, environmentalists, and fishermen. The case brought by fishermen resulted in a judgment against Exxon in the amount of $5 billion in punitive damages and $287 million to compensate for the loss.

The spill illustrated the need for the kind of emergency planning that could translate into an effective oil spill response. In 1990, Congress enacted the **Oil Pollution Act.** It requires double-hulled tankers, planning, training, drills, financial responsibility, and coordination.

VISIBILITY An air quality value relating to pollutants that affect the ability to see clearly. In 1977, Congress added a provision to the **Clean Air Act** to regulate manmade visibility problems for Class I areas, such as international parks, national wilderness areas, national parks, and national monuments.

Air pollution sources near Class I areas must use the best available retrofit technology if they interfere with visibility. New sources must obtain a permit, and the EPA is required to consider how the proposed activity will affect visibility. The federal land manager for the Class I area, either the National Park Service or the Forest Service, can participate in the permitting process, and they often insist on an offset of visibility-impacting pollutants to ensure that the new source will not cause a visibility problem.

WATER POLLUTION CONTROL TECHNOLOGY Tech-

niques used to restore wastewater after use. Both groundwater
and surface water are impacted by pollution.

Surface water is protected through the **National Pollutant Discharge
Elimination System,** the massive permit program established by the **Clean
Water Act.** Groundwater is protected indirectly. If groundwater is the water supply for a public system, it cannot exceed established levels of contamination. Injection of waste into the ground [see **underground injection
control**] is also regulated by the **Safe Drinking Water Act.** Disposal of waste
on land and safeguards to prevent underground **storage tank**s from leaking fall under the **Resource Conservation and Recovery Act.** When groundwater is contaminated by an abandoned **hazardous waste** site at which the
Environmental Protection Agency is ordering a cleanup, those activities
fall under the **Comprehensive Environmental Response, Compensation,
and Liability Act.**

Water, an essential ingredient of life, comes in limited quantities. It makes
the circuit through precipitation, percolation, runoff, and evaporation. Water
supply is impacted by all organisms, but humans have been far more in-
ventive about the use of water than other species. People pump groundwater and use streams and rivers for industry, drinking water, cooking,
sewage disposal, and generally end up with polluted water.

In this entry, wastewater refers to surface water that has been used in an
industrial process or for sewage before it is treated. Groundwater is water
that flows underground. The direction of the flow and its velocity depends
on the geological formations in the ground. Soil porosity, gradient of structural formations, fissures in formations, and water contamination all have
an influence on the flow of groundwater.

In the absence of treatment, the demand for and recycling of water causes
water quality to deteriorate rapidly. Water pollution treatment methods
are often old; human beings learned long ago that they had to have clean
water to survive. Treatment of water began with surface water, and only
some of the procedures have been adapted to groundwater treatment. This

entry examines the most common water treatment technologies and how they relate to environmental law.

Neither environmental statutes nor the regulations dictate specific techniques that must be used to treat wastewater. Instead, **publicly owned treatment works** and industrial treatment plants must obtain permits that set limits on the concentration of each pollutant discharged. The permit then becomes the standard the permittee must meet.

The reason results rather than technology are emphasized is simple: technology changes constantly, and the government wants to benefit from improvements. It can do that only if it allows permittees to choose whatever method works best. In most cases, treating wastewater requires more than one type of technology. Three general categories of wastewater treatment exist: mechanical, chemical, and biological. Some procedures combine more than one category in a single step.

Mechanical Water Treatment

Aeration—adding air to water—can be done by spraying water in the air and letting it fall back to the surface. This technique reduces odors and tastes. It also softens the water and eliminates some iron and manganese.

Sedimentation is used to separate solids from liquids. Large tanks hold the waste water, and floating wastes are skimmed off. Settled wastes are pumped out of the bottom for disposal.

Water may also be filtered to capture suspended materials. Filtration often follows sedimentation, coagulation, and microstraining (to remove algae and other particles). The water must have low turbidity during filtration. It seeps through sand to a layer of gravel. Suspended matter gets trapped, resulting in cleaner water.

Reverse osmosis is related to filtration, in that contaminants are captured by a membrane. Hydrostatic pressure is used to push a solution through a substance that will not allow pollutants through. They are caught on the membrane while the cleaned water continues to flow.

Chemical Treatment

A number of chemicals are used to restore wastewater. One of the processes is called coagulation or flocculation. Chemicals are added to wastewater, causing color, minerals, and other contaminants to clump together and settle. This is accomplished in two stages. The first involves rapid mixing and the second, extended slow mixing. The floc settles by gravity.

The process reduces the bacteria in the water but may cause hardness and corrosivity.

Water softening requires the removal of calcium and magnesium. Either chemical precipitation or ion exchange will achieve the removal. The most common method utilizes soda ash and lime or lime alone. If ion exchange is done, the water is sent through beds of ion-exchange resins. Water may have to be stabilized after softening.

Disinfection of wastewater can be done several ways. One is addition of chlorine, but **ozone** or ultraviolet radiation can also be used. Regardless of the method, disinfection is important. It not only destroys bacteria and inactivates viruses but also reduces faint odors and tastes. However, if chlorine is used for this treatment, it may combine with other organics and result in distasteful water.

Activated carbon is highly effective in removing contaminants from gases and wastewater. Activated carbon has a large surface area, and it attracts organic and toxic compounds as air or water is passed through it. When it no longer functions, it can be regenerated with high temperatures and put back in use.

Other chemicals used in treatment include hydroxide, used to precipitate metals and other inorganics, and copper sulfate, which controls algae. For wastewater treatment, chemicals have not been widely used until recently. Biological and physical methods were favored, primarily due to cost. However, as water pollution restrictions have strengthened, the relative cost of chemical treatment is no longer disproportionately high.

Biological Treatment

Microorganisms have been used to clean wastewater for more than a century. In a natural ecosystem with normal demands on water, normal processes gradually clean the water: solids will precipitate due to gravity, aeration will occur naturally, and bacteria will biodegrade organic materials. These naturally occurring processes are so important to water quality that three conditions in wastewater treatment systems are watched very closely: **biochemical oxygen demand,** dissolved oxygen, and total suspended solids. Fecal coliform and alkalinity/acidity are also monitored.

Biochemical oxygen demand is a measurement of how much dissolved oxygen wastewater will need to break down organic material. The higher the demand, the more polluted the water is. Dissolved oxygen is desirable; it enables aerobic activity to go forward. Total suspended solids are particles that float within water. They are not beneficial additions to water, because they will eventually interfere with oxygen intake, obstruct sunlight, and affect the taste, appearance, and odor of the water.

Metropolitan growth and industrialization have accelerated the demand for water and increased the load of contaminants entering the waste stream. As a result, wastewater treatment through unassisted natural processes is no longer effective. Assistance can be provided by bringing the bacteria in contact with the wastewater, ensuring that the bacteria remain healthy and active by providing nutrients, and allowing the bacteria the time it needs to work. Some microbes need oxygen to work; they are called aerobic microbes. Those that do not are designated anaerobic microbes. Either type of bacteria can be used for wastewater treatment, depending on the type of system.

Trickling filters are common components in wastewater treatment plants. They are not filters in the normal sense but are large shallow concrete tanks, filled with medium-sized stones that are covered with bacteria. Settled wastewater trickles through the stones, and the bacteria breaks down organic components in the wastewater.

Sludge may be activated by injecting compressed air into a tank containing wastes and circulating sludge to encourage biological activity. This method is used for raw sewage.

Digestion is a slight variation on activated sludge. The sludge is placed in a closed tank and heated, enhancing the speed and effectiveness of microbes.

Groundwater Treatment

The obvious problem with groundwater treatment is the location of the water. To deal with that issue, groundwater treatment systems generally pump the water to the surface, treat it, and return it to the source. Contamination in groundwater presents unique difficulties, though, because pollutants sink to the bottom, float on the top, or are suspended within the liquid. Suspended contaminants and those that float are considerably easier to remove than the "sinkers." In environmental parlance, sinkers are referred to as dense nonaqueous phase liquids or DNAPLs.

Before it is treated, groundwater must be analyzed to determine what the contaminants are. That is accomplished by drilling a well from which samples can be taken. Then pump and treat systems are designed for the particular sites where they operate. The designer will have to determine where to place extraction wells and how to create the correct hydraulic gradient so that the water flows in the direction of treatment. The object of the design phase is to get the contaminated water to the extraction wells in a short time with little dilution of the contaminants. A pilot system will actually test the accuracy of the design.

Treatment will vary, depending on the pollutants involved. Once the water is at the surface, many traditional types of wastewater treatment can be used on the groundwater.

Air stripping can be used to eliminate hydrocarbons from groundwater. The process is similar to aeration, but it involves building a tower, pumping the water up it, and then exposing it to air. Hydrocarbons are freed by this method, and they go into the air unless they are captured and destroyed.

Activated carbon is used in many pump and treat systems. It is combined with air stripping and other techniques of removing volatile organic compounds so that they do not escape. It can also be used to trap contaminants while they are still in liquid.

For removal of inorganic compounds, chemicals may be added to cause them to precipitate. Mechanical methods are then used to separate the particles from the treated water, and it may be necessary to restabilize the groundwater before returning it to the source.

Although groundwater is most commonly treated at the surface with pump and treat systems, biological methods may occasionally be used without removing the water from the source. Treatment procedures in which the contaminated groundwater remains in place are called *in situ* treatment. This technique can be used to destroy some volatile organic compounds. Nutrients and oxygen must be pumped into the aquifer to allow the bacteria to grow and break down the pollutants.

Selection of the type of technology to be used for groundwater cleanup follows extensive testing involving the water and subsurface conditions. The federal government will be involved in groundwater remediation when a federally listed abandoned hazardous waste site is determined to have groundwater contamination.

Federal water law does not protect groundwater in the same way that many state laws do. Surface waters fall under the Clean Water Act, but the definition of "waters of the United States" in that statute does not include groundwater. The indirect federal approach to preventing groundwater pollution stops some activities that could impact groundwater. States that depend heavily on their aquifers are more stringent with their regulations. See also **cleanup technologies; maximum contaminant levels; secondary treatment.**

🏛 **WATER QUALITY STANDARDS** Established by each state, water quality standards determine the existing uses of surface waters within their borders. For example, a stream may be used for wild-life, fishing, and recreation; a river may provide drinking water, recreation, fishing, and shellfish. The designated water quality may in fact be optimistic. Even though the water is not being used for a particular purpose at the time the standards are designated, the state can decide that it will meet those objectives in the future.

The concept of water quality standards is old, predating the current **Clean Water Act.** States were directed to establish the standards and issue permits that would maintain water quality. However, the system resulted in sporadic and ineffective control on water pollution. Issuing permits in terms of an end use of the receiving waters was too nebulous a concept, and the impact of one potential source on water quality is impossible to determine without considering all others that discharge contaminants into same water body. Furthermore, states felt economic pressure to attract new industry, but industry tended to go where the water pollution control was lenient. The federal government did not yet have any power to enforce state water regulations or permits, and federal law governing water discharges was insignificant.

Today, the federal permitting system for discharges, the **National Pollutant Discharge Elimination System,** has established its own criteria, mandated permits with numerical limits on pollutants, and requires states to certify that any permit it issues does not violate its water quality standards. When issuing a permit, a state must consider other dischargers, because they will be placing stress on the receiving water as well as the new one. If a source will be located in one state and the discharge will affect a downstream state, the downstream state must also be given the opportunity to review the permit and make its own certification or objection to the permit.

Water quality standards are still important in water pollution control; they are simply used differently than they were in the beginning. States must review their water quality standards at least once every three years and revise them when necessary. The goal, according to the Clean Water Act, is to restore the quality of all surface waters within the United States to fishable, swimmable water. If those objectives cannot be reached, the states are required to prevent any further deterioration of the water quality.

WATT, JAMES (1938–)   Secretary of Interior appointed by President Ronald Reagan [see **Reagan, Ronald**].

WETLAND   A locale distinguished by shallow water or saturated soil that supports aquatic plants, wildlife, and fish. Some wetlands contain saltwater; others are freshwater wetlands. Various names are used to describe them, and some indicate the wetland's characteristics. They include marshes, fens, swamps, bayous, bogs, tundra, mud flats, mangroves, and prairie potholes.

Wetlands tend to be near open waters, such as those found around lakes, rivers, streams, and coasts. Prairie potholes are usually nonadjacent wetlands, and they may be saturated with water only for short periods of time during the year. Wetlands support an abundance of life, including birds, plants, fish, and other wildlife. They serve as flood control systems, reduce erosion, purify water, and provide water supply. They are breeding grounds and nurseries for species that do not remain, as well as permanent habitats for many. Wetlands are home to a third of the species listed as endangered or threatened.

In the United States, wetlands were once thought to be useless land. The Fish and Wildlife Service estimates that approximately 100 million acres of wetlands have been eliminated through draining, filling, and damming. Construction projects requiring filling of wetlands were encouraged. Much of the filling was done for agriculture, fisheries, and construction.

Scientists then began to understand the significance of wetlands, and wetland protection began in earnest. The federal government has two major statutes to protect wetlands: the **Clean Water Act** and the **Coastal Zone Management Act.** States actually implement the Coastal Zone Management Act by developing their own statutes and establishing a coastal commission to protect those wetlands, so the federal government is only indirectly involved in coastal wetlands unless some other statute is involved. A state may also issue permits under the Clean Water Act if they become a "delegated state." State laws tend to be more stringent than the federal ones, however. States have much more to lose when an acre of wetland is filled than the federal government does.

Waters of the United States

Until the Clean Water Act was passed in 1972, the federal government did not assert jurisdiction over wetlands. The underlying authority for regulating waters of the United States is the Commerce Clause of the Constitution. When Congress passed the Clean Water Act, it demonstrated that it wanted the broadest possible protection for surface water.

The statute speaks in terms of regulating navigable waters—defined as waters of the United States, including interstate rivers and lakes, their tributaries (not normally considered navigable), and intrastate water. Under the Clean Water Act, the U.S. Army **Corps of Engineers** (COE) is responsible for issuing permits for dredge and fill operations in waters of the United States. At first, the COE used the traditional definition of navigability and did not regulate any waters that were not actually navigable.

In 1975, the COE was sued by the Natural Resources Defense Council for failure to protect covered waters. In *Natural Resources Defense Council v. Callaway,* the District Court of the District of Columbia agreed with the plaintiff. It ordered the Corps to amend its regulations to reflect Congressional intent. Congress, it held, meant to include national waters to the maximum extent necessary and did not limit the definition to traditional concepts of navigability. The revised definition of navigable waters included wetlands, along with open waters that cannot actually be navigated. To qualify as a water of the United States, the wetland had to be "inundated or saturated by surface or ground water at a frequency and duration sufficient to support vegetation adapted for life in saturated soil conditions."

Adjacent wetlands, those next to an open water body, were first recognized as waters of the United States. The connection was easy to see, because the interaction between open waters and adjacent wetlands is obvious. However, the Corps authority has been extended to isolated wetlands if migratory birds use them, because they affect interstate commerce. It also covers artificial or manmade wetlands.

In 1985, the Supreme Court considered the validity of the COE's definition in *United States v. Riverside Bayview Homes, Inc.* The Sixth Circuit Court of Appeals had found that the source of the wetlands in question was groundwater, as opposed to adjacent open water. It decided the COE could not regulate in such cases.

The Supreme Court disagreed with the appellate court. Looking at the history of the Clean Water Act and its revision in 1977, the Supreme Court found the COE's definition was supported by Congressional intent. After the *Riverside Bayview Homes* decision, it was clear the definition would stand unless Congress amended the statute. In fact, Congress knew about the COE's definition when it debated the reauthorization of the Clean Water Act in 1977, and it rejected attempts to narrow the definition.

Deciding Wetland Boundaries

One major problem with wetland regulation is called delineation. It is a process that precedes all permit requirements, because it determines whether a wetland exists, and if it does, where the boundaries are.

The Corps of Engineers, the **Environmental Protection Agency** (EPA), the Soil Conservation Service, and the Fish and Wildlife Service have all been responsible for wetlands delineation. Unfortunately, they have approached delineation from different perspectives, and the results have been confusing. Even within a single organization such as the COE, one office may be inclined to find wetlands, while another may not.

To make delineations more uniform, the four government entities developed a guide called the *Federal Manual for Identifying and Delineating Jurisdictional Wetlands* in 1989. The three criteria considered in the identification of a wetland are hydrology, vegetation, and soil. The COE makes most of the wetlands determinations for the federal government.

States may delineate their own delineations of wetlands. Since state regulation is more pervasive than federal, a person who wishes to know if property is a wetland must check with both the COE and the state involved.

Permitting

The Clean Water Act prohibits discharges of pollutants to navigable waters without a permit or a specified exception. If the discharge is wastewater or other refuse and a wetland is involved, the EPA or a delegated state will be the permitting authority. However, if the activity involves dredging and filling operations, the permitting authority for the federal government is the Corps of Engineers. The permit is generally referred to as a Section 404 permit, named after the Clean Water Act section that discusses that type of permit.

Section 404 permits may be general or individual. General permits cover many persons and go through the normal **notice and comment** review before they become effective. A general permit allows a particular activity to be done without requiring an individual to apply for his own permit. For example, up to one acre may be filled for a home.

Individual permit applications must be filed for any proposed activity in a wetland that will involve dredging and filling. The term filling is extremely broad. It includes putting in pilings to support a building, moving soil by means of a machine if the soil remains in the wetland, as well as bringing in dirt to build up the property.

The COE must involve the EPA in its permit process. As the ultimate guardian of waters of the U.S., the EPA has authority to veto a permit that the COE would otherwise grant. It has done so on several occasions, such as when the Two Forks Dam project in Colorado was vetoed and when the EPA barred the use of property in New England for a shopping mall. If the EPA and the COE cannot agree on the outcome, the facts go to the **Council on Environmental Quality** to see if the issue can be resolved. However, the EPA retains final say on the conclusion.

Enforcement may be done by either the EPA or the COE for unauthorized filling without a permit. The two agencies can bring administrative actions or file criminal or civil lawsuits through the Department of Justice. The agencies have developed a memorandum of understanding that discusses the roles each of them will play in enforcing and carrying out the law. The COE conducts the initial wetland delineation and usually investigates suspected violations. It is the primary enforcer of dredge and fill violations but can request the EPA's assistance or ask the EPA to take the lead. If the activity involves disposal of waste, the EPA is the primary regulator, even if it results in filling the wetland.

Regulation of wetlands is controversial, primarily because of the impact it has on landowners. A person may buy property hoping to develop it and then fail to get a permit for the development. If the denial of a Section 404 permit eliminates all economically viable use of the property, a court may decide the government has taken private property for public use. In those cases, the Fifth Amendment to the United States Constitution requires the government to pay just compensation for the property. See also **National Pollutant Discharge Elimination System; taking.**

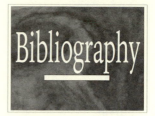

Bibliography

"Air Act Provisions on Trading, Flexibility Lack Certainty Public Needs, NRDC Lawyer Says." *Environment Reporter*, Vol. 22, No. 43 (Feb. 21, 1992), p. 2409.

American Society for Testing and Materials. "Standard Practice for Environmental Site Assessments: Site Assessment Process." E-1527-93.

―――. "Standard Practice for Environmental Site Assessments: Transaction Screen Process." E-1528-93.

American Trucking Association. *Handling Hazardous Materials.* Alexandria, VA: American Trucking Association (1993).

Anderson, David L. "EPA's Environmental Appeals Board Affords an Improved Opportunity for Review." *Environmental Law & Toxic Liability Report*, pp. 15–16. Arent Fox Kintner Plotkin & Kahn (Spring 1993).

Arbuckle, J. Gordon. "Liabilities and Enforcement." In *Environmental Law Handbook*, 12th ed., pp. 42–59. Rockville, MD: Government Institutes (1993).

―――. "Water Pollution Control." In *Environmental Law Handbook*, 12th ed., pp. 151–220. Rockville, MD: Government Institutes (1993).

Ayers, Kenneth W., and Willis Coroon. "Solid and Hazardous Waste Treatment and Disposal Technologies." In *Environmental Science and Technology Handbook*, pp. 177–208. Rockville, MD: Government Institutes (1994).

Azarmehr, Mehron. "Natural Resources Damages under CERCLA §107: How the Liability Rules Differ between Actions for Natural Resource Damages and Response Costs." *Environmental Law Reporter*, Vol. 22 (Oct. 1992), pp. 10655–10665.

Bayne, Katherine A. "*Lucas v. South Carolina Coastal Council*: Drawing a Line in the Sand." *Catholic University Law Review*, Vol. 42 (Summer 1993), pp. 1–93.

Bell, Griffin B. "$5 Billion Message to Congress in Exxon Valdez Case." *The Houston Chronicle*. Oct. 16, 1994, p. 1.

Bennett, Mark J., and Harriet L. Greenwood. "The Rise of the Environmental Transaction Screen." *Toxic Law Reporter*, Vol. 6, No. 24 (Nov. 13, 1991), pp. 735–740.

Brownell, F. William. "Clean Air Act." In *Environmental Law Handbook*, 12th ed., pp. 120–150. Rockville, MD: Government Institutes (1993).

Brownell, F. William, and Lee Zeugin. *Clean Air Handbook*. Rockville, MD: Government Institutes (1991).

Bumpers, William M. "Profitable Opportunities and Regulatory Hurdles under the 'Opt-In Provisions of the Acid Rain Title: How Non-Utility Sources of SO_2 May Profit from Participating in the Clean Air Act Allowance Trading Program." In *Environmental Reporter*, Vol. 23, No. 20 (Sept. 11, 1992), p. 1392.

Camp, Charles B. "Oil Spill Victims Subdued about $5 Billion Verdict." *The Dallas Morning News*. Sept. 19, 1994, p. 1A.

Carson, Rachel. *Silent Spring*. New York: Crest Books, Fawcett World Library (1962).

Case, David R. "Resource Conservation and Recovery Act." In *Environmental Law Handbook*, 12th ed., pp. 60–93. Rockville, MD: Government Institutes (1993).

Community Right-To-Know Manual. Salisbury, MD: Thompson Publishing Group (1990).

Conrad, James W., Jr. "CERCLA Does Not Invalidate Contractual Allocations of Liability." *Environmental Law Reporter*, Vol. 22. (Jan. 1992), pp. 10045–10051.

————. "Sliding Scale or Slippery Slope? The New ASTM's Standard Practices for Environmental Site Assessments." *Environmental Law Reporter*, Vol. 23 (Apr. 1993), pp. 10181–10184.

Cooke, Susan M., and Environmental Department of Goodwin, Proctor and Hoar. *The Law of Hazardous Waste*. Vols. I–III. New York: Matthew Bender & Co. (1994).

Corporate Counsel's Guide to Environmental Law. Vols. I–III. Edited by William A. Hancock. Chesterfield, OH: Business Laws, Inc. (1994).

Crump, Andy. *Dictionary of Environment and Development: People, Places, Ideas, and Organizations*. Cambridge: MIT Press (1993).

Davidson, Art. *In the Wake of the Exxon Valdez: The Devastating Impact of the Alaska Oil Spill*. San Francisco: Sierra Club Books (1990).

Environmental Law Library on CD. Search Master, version 4.20, release 5. New York: Matthew Bender & Co. (1994).

Environmental Law Reporter, *Superfund Deskbook*. Washington, DC: Environmental Law Institute (1992).

Environmental Protection Agency. "Asbestos, Manufacture, Importation, Processing and Distribution Prohibitions." 58 *Fed. Reg.* 58964 (Nov. 5, 1993).

————. "Changes to Regulations to Reflect the Role of the New Environmental Appeals Board in Agency Adjudications." 57 *Fed. Reg.* 5320 (Feb. 13, 1992).

————. "Corrective Action Management Units." 58 *Fed. Reg.* 8658 (Feb. 16, 1993).

————. "1987 Update to CWA Civil Penalty Analysis." Jan. 4, 1988.

————. "Emission Trading Policy Statement." Nov. 18, 1986.

————. "Guidance for Conducting Remedial Investigations and Feasibility Studies under CERCLA." OSWER Directive No. 93355.3-01. Interim Final. August 1988.

————. "Guidance on CERCLA Settlements with *De Micromis* Waste Contributors." July 30, 1993.

————. "Guidance on Implementation of the Superfund Accelerated Cleanup Model under CERCLA and the NCP." July 7, 1992.

————. "Guidance on Landowner Liability under Section 107(a)(1) of CERCLA, *De Minimis* Settlements under Section 122(g)(1)(B) of CERCLA, and Settlements with Prospective Purchasers of Contaminated Property." 54 *Fed. Reg.* 34235 (Aug. 18, 1989).

————. "Hazardous Waste Management System; Definition of Hazardous Waste; 'Mixture' and 'Derived-From' Rules." 57 *Fed. Reg.* 7628 (Mar. 3, 1992).

————. "Hazardous Waste Management System; Identification and Listing of Hazardous Waste." 57 *Fed. Reg.* 21450 (May 20, 1992).

————. "Integrated Risk Information System Background Paper." Feb. 1993.

————. "Interim Guidance on Settlements with *De Minimis* Waste Contributors under Section 122(g) of SARA." OSWER Directive No. 9834.7. June 19, 1987.

————. "Memorandum: Evaluating Mixed Funding Settlements under CERCLA." Oct. 20, 1987.

————. "Methodology for Early *De Minimis* Waste Contributor Settlements under CERCLA Section 122(g)(1)(A)." OSWER Directive No. 9834.7-1C. June 2, 1992.

————. "Microbial Pesticides; Experimental Permits and Notifications; Proposed Rule. In 59 *Fed. Reg.* 5878 (Jan. 22, 1993).

————. "Microbial Products of Biotechnology; Proposed Regulation under the Toxic Substances Control Act; Proposed Rule." In 59 *Fed. Reg.* 45526 (Sept. 1, 1994).

————. "Non-Binding Preliminary Allocation of Responsibility." 52 *Fed. Reg.* 19919 (May 28, 1987).

———. "Record of Decision; Love Canal." NYD000606947. May 6, 1985; Oct. 26, 1987; Sept. 26, 1988; May 15, 1991.

———. "Record of Decision; Times Beach, MO." MOD980685226. Sept. 29, 1988.

———. "Revised Policy on Discretionary Information Release under CERCLA." May 31, 1993.

———. "Streamlined Approach for Settlements with *De Minimis* Waste Contributors under CERCLA Section 122(g)(1)(A)." July 30, 1993.

———. "Subpart L—National Oil and Hazardous Substances Pollution Contingency Plan; Lender Liability under CERCLA." 57 *Fed. Reg.* 18344 (Apr. 29, 1992), codified at 40 C.F.R. 300.1100(c)(1).

———. "Superfund Enforcement Strategy and Implementation Plan." Sept. 26, 1989.

———. "Underground Storage Tanks: Lender Liability. Proposed Rule." In 59 *Fed. Reg.* 30448 (June 13, 1994).

"EPA Adopts CAMU Rule To Save Cleanup Costs." *Superfund Week,* Vol. 7, No. 3 (Jan. 22, 1993), pp. 6–7.

Findley, Roger W., and Daniel A. Farber. *Environmental Law in a Nutshell,* 3d ed. St. Paul: West Publishing Co. (1990).

Fisher, Perry W. "Air Pollution Control Technologies." In *Environmental Science and Technology Handbook,* pp. 155–175. Rockville, MD: Government Institutes (1994).

Fogarty, John P. C. "Principles of EPA Enforcement Against Lenders, Trustees and Fiduciaries under Superfund and RCRA Subtitle I" (1994).

Foreman, David. *Confessions of an Eco-Warrior.* New York: Crown Publishers, Inc., 1991.

Franck, Irene, and David Brownstone. *The Green Encyclopedia: An A-to-Z Sourcebook of Environmental Concerns—and Solutions.* New York: Prentice-Hall General Reference (1992).

Garrett, Theodore L., and Sonya D. Winner. "A Clean Air Act Primer." Parts I–III. *Environmental Law Reporter,* Vol. 22. Mar. 1992/Apr. 1992/May 1992: pp. 10161–10189; 10237–10262; 10303–10329.

Gellhorn, Ernest, and Ronald Levin. *Administrative Law and Process in a Nutshell,* 3d ed. St. Paul: West Publishing Co. (1990).

Gerry, Richard. "The Story Behind the Oil Spill Verdict." *San Diego Union-Tribune.* Oct. 14, 1994, p. B-5.

Gibson, Jeremy. "Clean Air Act: An Overview." *Environmental Insights* (July 1993).

———. "Clean Air Act: Do You Need a Permit?" *Environmental Insights* (Aug. 1993).

Halbleib, Wayne T. "Emergency Planning and Community Right-To-Know Act." In *Environmental Law Handbook*, 12th ed., pp. 454–481. Rockville, MD: Government Institutes (1993).

Harris, Tom. "The Asbestos Mess." *Garbage* (Dec./Jan. 1993), pp. 44–49.

Hathaway, Carolyne R., David J. Hayes, and William K. Rawson, "A Practitioner's Guide to the Toxic Substances Control Act: Parts I, II, and III." *Environmental Law Reporter*, Vol. 24 (May, June, July 1994), pp. 10207–10230, 10285–10304, 10357–10379.

Hayes, David J. "Beyond Cradle-to-Grave." *The Environmental Forum* (Sept./Oct. 1993), pp. 14–17.

Hodgson, Bryan. "Oil Spill Blots Science; Exxon Valdez Trials Hurt Credibility of Projects." *Cleveland Plain Dealer*, Nov. 15, 1994, p. 7E.

Jensen, Lawrence J. "Safe Drinking Water Act." In *Environmental Law Handbook*, 12th ed., pp. 256–266. Rockville, MD: Government Institutes (1993).

Jones, Gareth, Alan Robertson, Jean Forbes, and Graham Hollier. *The Harper Collins Dictionary: Environmental Science*. Edited by Eugene Ehrlich. New York: Harper Perennial (1992).

Jones, Richard D., and Myriam E. Hernandez. "The ASTM Standard Practices for Environmental Assessments: The Search for a Standard Ends." *Journal of Environmental Law & Practice*, Sept./Oct. 1993, pp. 18–29.

Kanner, Allan. "Continuity and Change in Toxic Tort Litigation." In *Hazardous Wastes, Superfund, and Toxic Substances*, pp. 509–590. Vol. II. Washington, DC: American Law Institute (1994).

Kenworthy, William E. *Occupational Safety and Health Law*. Chesterfield, OH: Business Laws, Inc. (1994).

Landfair, Stanley W. "Toxic Substances Control Act." In *Environmental Law Handbook*, 12th ed., pp. 348–401. Rockville, MD: Government Institutes (1993).

Lee, Robert T. "Comprehensive Environmental Response, Compensation, and Liability Act." In *Environmental Law Handbook*, 12th ed., pp. 267–320. Rockville, MD: Government Institutes (1993).

Lewis, Cynthia A. "Regulatory Requirements under the Toxic Substances Control Act 'TSCA'." In *Hazardous Wastes, Superfund, and Toxic Substances*, Vol. II, pp. 677–700. Washington, DC: American Law Institute (1994).

McClean, Donald C., and Andrew C. Cooper. "Asbestos in Buildings: Cause for Concern." In *Environmental Law & Toxic Liability Report* (Spring 1993). Washington DC: Arent Fox Kintner Plotkin & Kahn.

Manahan, Stanley E. *Fundamentals of Environmental Chemistry*. Chelsea, MI: Lewis Publishers (1981).

Matthew Bender & Co. *Treatise on Environmental Law*, Vols. I–II. New York: Matthew Bender & Co.

"Memorandum of Understanding between the Department of Transportation and the Environmental Protection Agency on Enforcement of Standards Applicable to Hazardous Waste Shippers and Transporters." 45 *Fed. Reg.* 51645 (Aug. 4, 1980).

Millan, Stan, and Andrew J. Harrison, Jr. "A Primer on Hazardous Materials Transportation Law of the 1990's: The Awakening." *Environmental Law Reporter*, Vol. 22 (Sept. 1992), pp. 10583–10596.

Miller, Marshall Lee. "Federal Regulation of Pesticides." In *Environmental Law Handbook*, 12th ed., pp. 412–453. Rockville, MD: Government Institutes (1993).

Moote, David Montgomery. "The Divisibility of Harm Defense to Joint and Several Liability under CERCLA." *Environmental Law Reporter*, Vol. 23 (Sept. 1993), pp. 10529–10535.

Moskowitz, Joel S. *Environmental Liability and Real Property Transactions: Law and Practice*, 2d ed. New York: John Wiley & Sons, Inc. (1995).

Nance, John J. *What Goes Up: The Global Assault on Our Atmosphere*. New York: William Morrow & Co. (1991).

Nardi, Karen. "Underground Storage Tanks." In *Environmental Law Handbook*, 12th ed., pp. 94–119. Rockville, MD: Government Institutes (1993).

Nixon, President Richard M. "Reorganization Plan No. 3 of 1970." July 9, 1970.

Nooney, Kathleen L., and Michele L. Niermann, "Complying with the Emergency Planning and Community Right-To-Know Act." *Environmental Insights* (Mar. 1993).

Ogle, Flint B. "The Ongoing Struggle between Private Property Rights and Wetlands Regulation: Recent Developments and Proposed Solutions." 64 *U. Colo. L. Rev.* 573 (Spring 1993), pp. 573–606.

Olney, Austin P. "Oil Pollution Act of 1990." In *Environmental Law Handbook*, 12th ed., pp. 221–249. Rockville, MD: Government Institutes (1993).

Parker, William P. *The Complete Guide to Environmental Law*. Vancouver, British Columbia: STP Specialty Technical Publishing Inc. (1993).

Parrish, Michael, and Stuart Silverstein. "Alaskans Go Fishing for Compensation." *The Guardian*, Sept. 22, 1994, p. 14.

Periconi, James J., and David Nelson. "The Precedent-Setting Use of a Pollution Prevention Project on an EPA Enforcement Settlement: The First Dollar-for-Dollar Penalty Offset." *Environment Reporter*, Vol. 24, No. 48. (Apr. 1994), p. 2049.

Pershkow, Barry L., and Robert F. Housman, "In the Wake of *Lucas v. South Carolina Coastal Council*: A Critical Look at Six Questions Practitioners Should Be Asking." In *Environmental Law Reporter*, Vol. 23, pp.10008–10014.

Pierce, Richard J., Jr., Sidney A. Shapiro, and Paul R. Verkul, *Administrative Law and Process*, 2d ed. Westbury, N.Y: Foundation Press, Inc. (1992).

Ponting, Clive. *A Green History of the World: The Environment and the Collapse of Great Civilizations*. New York: Penguin Books (1991).

"Proposed Guidance Would Allow Companies To Use Past Shutdowns To Offset New Emissions." *Environment Reporter*, Vol. 24, No. 2 (May 14, 1993), p. 30.

Prosser, William L. *Law of Torts*, 4th ed. St. Paul, MN: West Publishing.

Puszcz, Stanley G., and Michael V. Tumulty. "Groundwater Pollution Control Technologies." In *Environmental Science and Technology Handbook*, pp. 317–345. Rockville, MD: Government Institutes (1994).

Rarick, Phillip B. "The Superfund Due Diligence Problem: The Flaws in an ASTM Committee Proposal and an Alternative Approach." *Environmental Law Reporter*, Vol. 21 (Sept. 1991), pp. 10505–10510.

Rockwood, Linda L., and James L. Harrison. "The Alcan Decisions: Causation through the Back Door." *Environmental Law Reporter*, Vol. 23 (Sept. 1993), pp. 10542–10549.

Rosbe, William L., and Robert L. Gulley. "The Hazardous and Solid Waste Amendments of 1984: A Dramatic Overhaul of the Way America Manages Its Hazardous Wastes." *Environmental Law Reporter*, Vol. 14 (Dec. 1984), p. 10458.

Sale, Kirkpatrick. *The Green Revolution: The American Environmental Movement 1962–1992*. Edited by Eric Fover. New York: Hill and Wang (1993).

Sarvadi, David G. "Occupational Safety and Health Act. " In *Environmental Law Handbook*, 12th ed., pp. 482–530. Rockville, MD: Government Institutes (1993).

Schneider, Stephen. *Global Warming: Are We Entering the Greenhouse Century?* San Francisco: Sierra Club (1989).

Shabacoff, Philip. *A Fierce Green Fire: The American Environmental Movement*. New York: Hill and Wang (1993).

Siegler, Ellan. "Regulatory Negotiations: A Practical Perspective." *Environmental Law Reporter*, Vol. 22 (Oct. 1992), pp. 10647–10654.

Spensley, James W. "National Environmental Policy Act." In *Environmental Law Handbook*, 12th ed., pp. 321–347. Rockville, MD: Government Institutes (1993).

Stein, Edith C. *The Environmental Sourcebook*. Lyons & Burford (1992).

Stensvaag, John-Mar, and Craig N. Oren. *Clean Air Act: 1990 Amendments,* Vols. I and II. New York: Wiley Law Publications (1994).

Strand, Margaret N. "Federal Wetlands Law." Parts I, II, III. *Environmental Law Reporter,* Vol. 23 (Apr., May, and June 1993), pp. 10185–10214, 10284–10307, 10354–10377.

Sullivan, Thomas P. F. "Basics of Environmental Law." In *Environmental Law Handbook,* 12th ed., pp. 1–41. Rockville, MD: Government Institutes (1993).

"Title III: Emergency Planning & Community Right-To-Know." In *Executive Legal Summary.* Edited by W. A. Hancock. Chesterfield, OH: Business Laws, Inc. (1988).

Trager, James. *The People's Chronology.* New York: Henry Holt & Co. (1992).

"Updated Enforcement Policy Would Mean Wider Use of Supplement Projects, EPA Says." *Environment Reporter,* Vol. 25, No. 25 (Oct. 21, 1994), p. 1220.

"Use of Supplemental Environmental Projects by EPA, States Increasing as Familiarity Grows." *Environment Reporter,* Vol. 25, No. 6 (June 10, 1994), p. 282.

Warburg, Philip, and James M. McElfish, Jr. "Property Rights and Responsibilities: Nuisance, Land-Use Regulation, and Sustainable Use." *Environmental Law Reporter,* Vol. 24 (Sept. 1994), pp. 10520–10535.

World Resources Institute. *The 1993 Information Please: Environmental Almanac.* New York: Houghton-Mifflin Co. (1993).

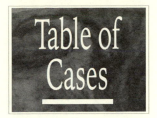

Table of Cases

Table of Statutes

Administrative Procedure Act (APA), 5 U.S.C. §562 *et seq.* (1946, as amended)

Asbestos School Hazard Abatement Act of 1984, Pub. L. No. 98-377, Title V; 98 Stat 1287, Title 20, Section 4011 *et seq.* (1984).

Coastal Zone Management Act (CZMA), 16 U.S.C. §§1451–1464 (1972)

Clean Air Act (CAA), 42 U.S.C. §7401 *et seq.* (1970, as amended)
Title I, Part A, 42 U.S.C. §§7401–7431, Sections 101–131 of CAA (Air Quality and Emission Limitations)
Title I, Part C, 42 U.S.C. §§7460–7469, Sections 160–169 of CAA (Prevention of Significant Deterioration of Air Quality)
Title I, Part D, 42 U.S.C. §§7471–7493, Sections 171–193 of CAA (Plan Requirements for Nonattainment Areas)
Title II, Part A, 42 U.S.C. §§7501–7519, Sections 201–219 of CAA (Motor Vehicle Emission and Fuel Standards)
Title II, Part C, 42 U.S.C. §§7541–7550, Sections 241–250 of CAA (Clean Fuel Vehicles)
Title III, 42 U.S.C. §§7601–7626, Sections 301–326 of CAA (General Provisions, Enforcement Authority, Citizen Suits, Emergency Powers and Definitions)
Title IV, 42 U.S.C. §§7627–7630, Sections 401–403 of CAA (Noise Pollution)
Title IV, 42 U.S.C. §§7651–7651(e); 7651(g)–7651(o), Sections 401–406; 408–416 of CAA (Acid Deposition Control)
Title V, 42 U.S.C. §§7661–7661(f), Sections 501–507 of CAA (Permits)
Title VI, 42 U.S.C. §§7671–7671(q), Sections 601–618 of CAA (Stratospheric Ozone Protection)

Clean Air Act Amendments of 1990 (CAAA), Pub. L. No. 101-549 (Nov. 1990).

335

Clean Water Act (CWA) (also called Federal Water Pollution Control Act),
33 U.S.C. §1251 *et seq.* (1972, as amended)
Title II, 33 U.S.C. §§1281–1299 (Grants for Construction of Treatment Works)
Title III, 33 U.S.C. §§1311–133 (Standards and Enforcement)
Title IV, 33 U.S.C. §§1341–134 (Permits and Licenses)
Title V, 33 U.S.C. §§1361–137 (General Provisions)

Comprehensive Environmental Response, Compensation, and Liability Act (CERCLA), 42 U.S.C. §9601 *et seq.* (1980, as amended)
Title I, 42 U.S.C. §§9601–9626, Sections 101–126 of CERCLA (Hazardous Substances Releases, Liability and Compensation)
Title III, 42 U.S.C. §§9651–9661, Sections 301–312 of CERCLA (Miscellaneous Provisions)

Departments of Veterans Affairs and Housing and Urban Development and Independent Agencies Appropriation Act, Pub. L. No. 102-389 (1993).

Emergency Planning and Community Right-To-Know Act (EPCRA) (SARA, Title III), 42 U.S.C. §11001 *et seq.* (1986, as amended)
Title III of the Superfund Amendments and Reauthorization Act of 1986, Pub. L. No. 99-499 (1986); Pub. L. No. 102-389 (1992)
Subtitle A, 42 U.S.C. §§11001–11005, Sections 301–305 of EPCRA (Emergency Planning and Notification)
Subtitle B, 42 U.S.C. §§11021–11023, Sections 311–313 of EPCRA (Reporting)
Subtitle C, 42 U.S.C. §§11041–11050, Sections 321–330 of EPCRA (General Provisions)

Federal Food, Drug, and Cosmetic Act (FFDCA), 21 U.S.C. §§301–392 (1938).

Federal Insecticide, Fungicide, and Rodenticide Act (FIFRA), 7 U.S.C. §136 *et seq.,* Sections 2–31 of FIFRA (1975, as amended)

Freedom of Information Act (FOIA), 5 U.S.C. §522 (1967)

Marine Protection, Research, and Sanctuaries Act (MPRSA), 16 U.S.C. §§1431 *et seq.* (1972, as amended)

National Environmental Policy Act (NEPA), 42 U.S.C. §4321 *et seq.*, Sections 2–209 of NEPA (1970, as amended)

Occupational Safety and Health Act (OSH Act), 29 U.S.C. §651 *et seq.*, Sections 2–33 of OSH Act (1970, as amended)

Oil Pollution Act, Sections 1001-9002, Pub. L. No. 101-380 (1990), amended by Pub. L. No. 102-389 (1992)

Pollution Prevention Act, Sections 6602–6620, Pub. L. No. 101-508 (1990), Omnibus Budget Reconciliation Act of 1990, amended by Pub. L. No. 102-389 (1992)

Refuse Act (Rivers and Harbors Act of 1899), 33 U.S.C. §407

Resource Conservation and Recovery Act (RCRA), 42 U.S.C. §6901 *et seq.*, Pub. L. No. 94-550, 90 Stat. 2796 (1976), as amended, Pub. L. No. 96-482, 94 Stat. 2334 (1980); Hazardous and Solid Waste Amendments of 1984, Pub. L. No. 98-616, 98 Stat. 3221 (1984).
Title II, Solid Waste Disposal
Subtitle A, 42 U.S.C. §§6901–6907, Sections 1002–1008 of RCRA (General Provisions)
Subtitle C, 42 U.S.C. §§6921–6925, Sections 3001–3005 of RCRA (Hazardous Waste Management)
Subtitle C, 42 U.S.C. §§6928–6979(a), Sections 3008–3023 of RCRA (Federal Enforcement, Monitoring, Mixed Waste)
Subtitle G, 42 U.S.C. §§6971–6979, Sections 7001–7010 of RCRA (Miscellaneous Provisions)
Subtitle I, 42 U.S.C. §§6991–6991i, Sections 9001–9006 of RCRA (Underground Storage Tanks)

Safe Drinking Water Act (SDWA), 42 U.S.C. §301f *et seq.* (1974, as amended)

Toxic Substances Control Act (TSCA), 15 U.S.C. §2601 *et seq.* (1976, as amended)
Title I, 15 U.S.C. §§2601–2630, Sections 2–31 of TSCA (Control of Toxic Substances)
Title II, 15 U.S.C. §§2641–2655, Sections 201–215 (Asbestos Hazard Emergency Response Act, also called Asbestos-in-Schools Act)

Table of
Regulations

Air Regulations

40 C.F.R. Part 50, National Primary and Secondary Ambient Air Quality Standards

40 C.F.R. Part 51, Requirements for State Implementation Plans

40 C.F.R. Part 52, Approval and Promulgation of State Implementation Plans

40 C.F.R. Part 60, New Source Performance Standards (NSPS)

40 C.F.R. Part 61, National Emission Standards for Hazardous Air Pollutants

40 C.F.R. Part 66, Assessment and Collection of Noncompliance Penalties by EPA

40 C.F.R. Part 73, Sulfur Dioxide Allowance System

40 C.F.R. Part 81, Designation of Areas for Air Quality Planning Purposes

40 C.F.R. Part 82, Protection of Stratospheric Ozone

40 C.F.R. Part 85, Motor Vehicles and Air Pollution Control

40 C.F.R. Part 86, Control of Air Pollution from New and In-Use Motor Vehicles

Consolidated Rules of Practices Governing the Administrative Assessment of Civil Penalties and Revocation or Suspension of Permits, 40 C.F.R. Part 22

Emergency Planning Regulations

40 C.F.R. Part 302, Designated Reportable Quantities and Notification

40 C.F.R. Part 355, Emergency Planning and Notification

40 C.F.R. Part 370, Hazardous Chemical Reporting

40 C.F.R. Part 372, Toxic Chemical Release Reports

Hazard Communication Standard, 29 C.F.R. §1910.1200

Hazardous Waste Regulations

40 C.F.R. Part 260, Hazardous Waste Management System

40 C.F.R. Part 261, Identification and Listing of Hazardous Waste

40 C.F.R. Part 262, Generators

40 C.F.R. Part 263, Transporters

40 C.F.R. Part 264, Owners and Operators of Treatment, Storage, and Disposal Facilities

40 C.F.R. Part 265, Interim Status Standards

40 C.F.R. Part 266, Standards for Specific Hazardous Waste and Types of Hazardous Waste Management Systems

40 C.F.R. Part 270, Hazardous Waste Permit Program

40 C.F.R. Part 280, Technical Standards and Corrective Action Requirements for Underground Storage Tanks

HAZWOPER, 29 C.F.R. §1910.120

National Contingency Plan, 40 C.F.R. Part 300

40 C.F.R. Part 300, App. A, Hazardous Ranking System

40 C.F.R. Part 300, App. B, National Priority List

40 C.F.R. Part 302.4, List of Hazardous Substances

Pesticide Regulations, 40 C.F.R. Parts 152–186

Solid Waste Regulations, 40 C.F.R. Parts 240–259

Toxic Substances Regulations

40 C.F.R. Parts 700–799, Toxic Substances Control and Regulation

40 C.F.R. Part 761, Polychlorinated Biphenyls

40 C.F.R. Part 762, Chlorofluorocarbons

40 C.F.R. Part 763, Asbestos

40 C.F.R. Part 766, Dioxins

Water Regulations

40 C.F.R. Part 110, Discharge of Oil

40 C.F.R. Part 112, Oil Pollution Prevention

40 C.F.R. Part 117, Reportable Quantities

40 C.F.R. Part 122, National Pollutant Discharge Elimination System

40 C.F.R. Part 125, Criteria and Standards for National Pollutant Discharge Elimination System

40 C.F.R. Part 129, Toxic Pollutant Effluent Standards

40 C.F.R. Part 130, Water Quality Planning

40 C.F.R. Part 131, Water Quality

40 C.F.R. Part 133, Secondary Treatment Requirements

40 C.F.R. Part 141, National Primary Drinking Water Regulations

40 C.F.R. Part 143, National Secondary Drinking Water Regulations

40 C.F.R. Part 144, Underground Injection Control Programs

40 C.F.R. Parts 220–233, Ocean Dumping

Index

Wisconsin Electric Power Co. v. Reilly, 69, 219
Worker protection, 145

World Wildlife Fund, 257, 308

Zoning, 21, 291

Vicki R. Patton-Hulce graduated from University of Dayton School of Law in 1980 and began her practice of law as an assistant prosecuting attorney. In 1984, she moved to Dallas, Texas, to work at Region 6 of the United States Environmental Protection Agency. She has been employed as an environmental attorney for a major corporation since 1989.

Ms. Patton-Hulce enjoys the field of environmental law because it is exciting and dynamic. The constantly changing nature of the field also opens the door for teaching and writing, and Ms. Patton-Hulce takes advantage of both.

She is married and has a step-daughter. She and her husband share a home with four cats. Her leisure time is spent playing the piano, reading, and working crossword puzzles.